Mastering Docker on Windows

Advanced containerization techniques for enterprise-grade Windows environments

Michael D. Smith

<packt>

Mastering Docker on Windows

Portfolio Director: Kartikey Pandey
Relationship Lead: Deepak Kumar
Project Manager: Sonam Pandey
Content Engineer: Sayali Pingale
Technical Editor: Simran Ali
Copy Editor: Safis Editing
Indexer: Manju Arasan
Production Designer: Vijay Kamble
Growth Lead: Shreyans Singh

First published: December 2025

Production reference: 1291225

Published by Packt Publishing Ltd.
Grosvenor House
11 St Paul's Square
Birmingham
B3 1RB, UK.

ISBN 978-1-83664-051-6

packtpub.com

If you've installed Docker correctly, this is where the fun starts. In your PowerShell window, type the following:

```
docker version
```

This shows whether the Docker CLI and Docker Engine are installed and talking to each other. You should see details for both the client and the server, including their version numbers.

If that all looks good, try the following:

```
docker info
```

This gives you a more detailed summary: number of containers, images, storage driver, system resources, and so on. It's not something you'll need every day, but it's useful when something feels off.

Pulling an image from Docker Hub

Docker Hub is the default image registry. Think of it like a package manager but for entire systems.

Let's pull something small:

```
docker pull alpine
```

This grabs the Alpine Linux image, which is a tiny, stripped-down version of Linux, perfect for testing.

If you want a specific version, add a tag:

```
docker pull alpine:3.18
```

Tags matter more than you might think. If you rely on the latest, you're trusting whatever the upstream decides is most current, which may not be what you want in production or testing.

Running a container

Now, let's put that image to use:

```
docker run alpine
```

That runs the image, but you'll notice it exits straight away. That's because Docker looks for a default command to run, executes it, then stops. If the image does not define anything interactive or long-running, it just exits.

Let's run it with a shell, interactively:

```
docker run -it alpine /bin/sh
```

You're now inside the container, running a shell. You can poke around:

```
ls
echo "Hello from Alpine"
```

When you're done, type `exit` to leave.

Again, it never hurts to revisit the basics. This is where Docker helps to understand the flow.

When you run `docker run`, Docker does the following:

1. Checks whether the image exists locally. If not, it pulls it.
2. Creates a new container from that image.
3. Allocates resources.
4. Runs the command you gave it (in this case, `/bin/sh`).
5. Cleans up (or not) depending on the flags you used.

By default, containers are ephemeral. If you don't name them or persist data, they disappear once they stop. That's not a problem, it's a feature, but it's something to be conscious of.

Quick one-liners

Knock knock!

Who's there?

Docker.

Docker who?

`docker: command not recognized.`

I'm sorry, really, I am. That joke has been in my head since 2016, and now it's in yours too.

But seriously, Docker is brilliant for running quick tasks without installing tools on your host system with single lines of commands.

For example, to check the version of Node.js, run the following:

```
docker run node node --version
```

This spins up a Node.js container, runs `node --version`, and exits.

No need to install anything locally. No impact on your dev environment.

Giving containers a name

By default, Docker gives your containers funny names such as `loving_borg` or `sleepy_dubois`. You can override that:

```
docker run -it --name scratch alpine /bin/sh
```

Now, the container is called `scratch`, and you can refer to it by name later. This is useful if you want to restart it, inspect it, or keep it running in the background.

Running containers in the background

Let's say you want a container running a service such as a web server. You don't need to keep your terminal tied up; you can detach it:

```
docker run -d nginx
```

This runs the container in detached mode, meaning it stays alive in the background.

Want to see what's running?

If you want to see what containers are currently running on your machine, just run this in PowerShell:

```
docker ps
```

It shows all active containers.

Accessing services on a specific port

Let's expose that NGINX server to your browser:

```
docker run -d -p 8080:80 nginx
```

Now, if you visit `http://localhost:8080`, you'll hit the containerized NGINX server.

What's happening here is **port forwarding**. You're telling Docker to map port `8080` on your machine to port `80` inside the container.

Clean runs with –rm

As I said, by default, containers stick around even after they stop. That is not always what you want. For one-off jobs, it is cleaner to remove them immediately after they exit:

```
docker run --rm alpine echo "Done and dusted"
```

This container starts, runs the echo command, and deletes itself as soon as it is finished. Perfect for short-lived tasks or utility runs.

There's a rhythm to using Docker once you get into it. You pull, you run, you pass in commands, you clean up. Everything starts with `docker run`, and with a handful of flags, you can control exactly how your container behaves. For now, it's worth playing around with the `run` command a bit. Try different flags. Pull different images. Break things and see how Docker reacts. It is hard to break anything permanently, and that is one of the best things about it.

Managing Docker images and containers

When I first started using Docker more regularly, I used to just run containers and walk away. I would get to the end of the week, list my containers or images, and be faced with a wall of forgotten projects, dangling volumes, half-built layers, and ridiculous container names I never gave a second thought to.

And while Docker makes it super easy to spin up new containers in a flash, it is just as important to understand how to manage what is already running or has been left behind.

So now, let's just touch on managing Docker containers and images once they are already part of your local environment. This includes listing what is running, stopping and removing containers cleanly, inspecting what each one is doing, and handling image cleanup so your system does not quietly fill up with chaff.

Listing running containers

Now, we know that running `docker ps` will give you a list of *running* containers, but what about *all* your containers, running or not? Well, for this, we'll need the following:

```
docker ps -a
```

This is especially useful when trying to understand why something exited unexpectedly or to clean up unused containers.

Inspecting container details

You can even deep dive into any container by inspecting it:

```
docker inspect <container-name-or-id>
```

This returns a detailed JSON output, including environment variables, network settings, volumes, restart policies, and more.

It's not something you will run every day, but it is incredibly helpful when you need to debug or understand what exactly is going on under the hood.

If you want something more focused, such as just the IP address, run the following:

```
docker inspect -f "{{ .NetworkSettings.IPAddress }}" <container-name-or-id>
```

This uses Go templating to extract specific fields.

Stopping and removing containers

If a container is running and you want to stop it, use this:

```
docker stop <container-name-or-id>
```

This sends a graceful shutdown signal.

If that does not work, and the container refuses to stop, you can force it:

```
docker kill <container-name-or-id>
```

To remove a stopped container, use this:

```
docker rm <container-name-or-id>
```

You can also combine flags. For example, stop and remove in one line with this command:

```
docker rm -f <container-name-or-id>
```

Note

Docker won't let you *remove* a container that is currently running unless you use `-f` (force).

For cleaning up many at once, my favorite command is the following:

```
docker container prune
```

It will prompt you before removing all stopped containers, because it's going to be a lot someday.

Working with images

To list all images on your system, run the following:

```
docker images
```

This shows a table of repository names, tags, image IDs, and sizes.

Over time, it is easy to build up unused images, especially if you are pulling tags such as `latest` or building local ones during testing.

To remove an image, run this:

```
docker rmi <image-id>
```

If an image is still used by a container (even if it is stopped), Docker will stop you from removing it unless you force the action:

```
docker rmi -f <image-id>
```

To remove unused images in bulk, don't forget about my friend Prune:

```
docker image prune
```

You can also do a full clean sweep:

```
docker system prune
```

That command removes unused containers, networks, images, and build cache. Use it with care, though, as it's super useful but can be a touch destructive if you're not careful.

Dangling images

Docker images without tags are called **dangling images**. I know, it sounds silly, but it is what it is. These often appear when you build an image multiple times and the `latest` tag moves. The older build stays behind, but without a tag.

You can spot these with the following:

```
docker images -f dangling=true
```

You can remove them with this:

```
docker image prune
```

Keeping on top of these is helpful, especially on smaller SSDs or when working with frequent builds.

Reusing containers

Sometimes you want to reuse a container that has already been created rather than starting from scratch.

You can restart a stopped container:

```
docker start <container-name-or-id>
```

Use the following to attach to it interactively:

```
docker attach <container-name-or-id>
```

If the container was originally run in interactive mode, you will drop straight back into the shell. This is useful for debugging or resuming a previous session in that container.

If the container was not started in interactive mode, you might just see raw logs, or it may immediately exit.

To avoid that, use `docker exec` instead:

```
docker exec -it <container-name-or-id> /bin/sh
```

This runs a shell inside a running container without restarting it or needing to attach to its main process.

Tagging and retagging images

Image tags help you keep things organized. If you have built an image and want to give it a meaningful tag, run the following:

```
docker tag <image-id> my-app:stable
```

You can then refer to it by name later:

```
docker run my-app:stable
```

This becomes essential when preparing images for sharing, deploying, or versioning over time.

You can also retag an image without changing its contents. This doesn't duplicate it; it just gives it another label.

Containers versus images

One of my early confusions with Docker is where the line is between a container and an image. Here is a simple way to think about it:

- An **image** is the blueprint
- A **container** is a running instance of that blueprint

Images do not change when you run them. Containers are temporary by default, but you can persist them if needed.

Keep your images lean, and treat your containers as throwaways unless you have a reason not to. Managing containers and images well is part of the discipline of using Docker effectively. It is easy to leave a trail of half-finished work behind you, especially when everything is so fast to spin up. But a bit of regular housekeeping keeps your environment clean, fast, and easy to reason about. And never forget about my friend Prune.

Dockerfile basics and image optimization

The first time I saw a Dockerfile, I was surprised by how simple it looked. Just a few capitalized keywords, a base image, and some commands. No loops, no conditionals, nothing complicated. And yet, it built a fully working container that ran a complete web app.

On Windows, your Dockerfile should sit in the root of your project folder, for example, `C:\Users\<you>\Projects\myapp\Dockerfile`, so that Docker can use the surrounding files when building the image.

That simplicity is part of Docker's power. But, like anything simple on the surface, the way you write and structure a Dockerfile makes all the difference, especially once your app starts growing.

In this section, we are going to write a basic Dockerfile from scratch, understand what each part does, and then look at how to optimize it so that our builds are faster, cleaner, and more reliable.

What is a Dockerfile?

Again, while it's easy to dismiss the basics of Dockerfiles, they are also super important to revisit every now and then. At its core, a Dockerfile is just a text file with a set of instructions. Each line tells Docker how to build a custom image by layering changes on top of a base image.

For example, here is a minimal Dockerfile for a Node.js app:

```
FROM node:18
WORKDIR /app
COPY package*.json ./
RUN npm install
COPY . .
CMD [ "node", "server.js" ]
```

Figure 1.8: A basic Dockerfile for a Node.js application

That is all it takes to create an image that can run your Node.js app. Each instruction becomes part of a layer that Docker caches and reuses when possible.

Okay, let's break it down and then explore how we can write our own from the ground up.

FROM – Picking your base image

Every Dockerfile starts with a `FROM` line. This defines your base image, the foundation on which everything else is built.

You can use official images from Docker Hub, such as the following:

- `FROM node:18`
- `FROM python:3.11`
- `FROM ubuntu:22.04`
- `FROM alpine`

Pick something that fits your needs, but don't just default to whatever is latest. Being explicit about the version helps you avoid surprises later.

Here are some general tips:

- Alpine is great for minimal builds
- Debian and Ubuntu are more forgiving and usually easier to debug...usually
- Language-specific images (such as `node` or `python`) are good for app containers

Choosing the right base image sets the tone for everything that follows.

> **Note**
>
> **A note on working with small images**: When you're building your own images, consider using slim or Alpine-based base images where possible. They're much smaller and faster to pull, which keeps your containers lean and efficient. Just make sure your app doesn't need libraries that are missing from these minimal builds.

WORKDIR – Setting your working directory

The `WORKDIR` instruction sets the working directory for all following commands. It is like saying "`cd` into this folder" and staying there:

```
WORKDIR /app
```

This avoids having to prefix every command with `cd` or messy relative paths. It also improves readability by clearly showing where your files will live inside the container.

COPY – Bringing in your application files

The `COPY` instruction moves files from your local machine into the container:

```
COPY package*.json ./
```

You can copy files or folders, and use wildcard matching. The `.` at the end means "copy into the current working directory," which you set earlier with `WORKDIR`.

It is really common to copy just your dependency files first, install dependencies, and then copy the rest of the code. This makes better use of Docker's layer caching (we will get into that later).

RUN – Executing setup commands

`RUN` lets you execute shell commands during the image build. This is often used to install packages or dependencies.

Here is an example:

```
RUN npm install
```

Here is an example for Linux packages:

```
RUN apt-get update && apt-get install -y curl
```

Use `&& to chain commands and clean up after yourself. Each` to chain commands and clean up after yourself. Each run creates a new layer, so try to combine related commands where it makes sense.

CMD – Defining the default command

The `CMD` instruction defines what happens when the container starts:

```
CMD [ "node", "server.js" ]
```

This is the default entry point. You can override it when running the container, but this is what Docker will fall back on if you don't specify anything.

`CMD` should always be the last instruction in your Dockerfile. Anything after it will be ignored.

> Note
>
> **Using a .dockerignore file**
>
> Before we get too deep into Dockerfiles, it is worth mentioning something that saves beginners a lot of pain on Windows. By default, Docker copies everything in your build context unless you *explicitly* tell it not to. That means folders such as `node_modules`, `.git`, `.vs`, `bin`, `obj`, and temporary build artifacts can accidentally end up inside your image, creating huge builds and slow context uploads.
>
> Create a `.dockerignore` file in the same folder as your Dockerfile. A simple, practical example looks like this:
>
> ```
> node_modules
> .git
> .vs
> bin
> ```

```
obj
*.log
*.tmp
Dockerfile
docker-compose.yml
```

This keeps your image lean and prevents Docker from sending gigabytes of unnecessary files into the build context.

A basic Dockerfile

Here is a simple but solid example for a Node.js application:

```
FROM node:18
WORKDIR /app
COPY package*.json ./
RUN npm install
COPY . .
CMD [ "node", "server.js" ]
```

You can build an image from this file using the following:

```
docker build -t my-node-app .
```

This tells Docker to build the image and tag it as `my-node-app` using the Dockerfile in the current directory.

> **Note**
>
> Make sure you run this command from the same directory that contains your Dockerfile. On Windows, it is easy to open PowerShell in the wrong folder and end up with a failed or empty build context.

Understanding Docker layers and caching

Each instruction in your Dockerfile becomes a **layer**. Docker caches these layers so that if you rebuild your image, unchanged steps can be reused.

This has a big impact on build time.

For example, let us say you wrote this:

```
COPY . .
RUN npm install
```

If you change one file in your app, `COPY . .` triggers a rebuild, which invalidates the layer cache for `RUN npm install`, meaning it runs again, even though your dependencies haven't changed.

Instead, it is better to do this:

```
COPY package*.json ./
RUN npm install
COPY . .
```

This way, Docker only reruns `npm install` if the package files change. Your actual app code can change all day long without slowing down the build unnecessarily.

That kind of structure pays dividends in CI pipelines where time and resources are at a premium.

Best practices for clean Dockerfiles

Here are a few things I've found that help keep Dockerfiles lean and maintainable:

- **Be explicit about versions**: Avoid using `latest` for base images. Pin a version so your builds are consistent.
- **Minimize layers**: Where it makes sense, combine commands in a single `RUN` command to avoid creating unnecessary layers.
- **Clean up after installing**: Run `apt-get clean` to remove the local package cache, remove temp files, and keep your image size down. Containers don't need a full operating system, just what the app needs.
- **Use .dockerignore**: Like `.gitignore`, this file tells Docker which files to ignore during `COPY`. It keeps your images smaller and avoids leaking credentials or unnecessary files.
- **Add comments**: Even though Dockerfiles are simple, a few well-placed comments make them much easier to maintain, especially when someone comes back to it six months later, maybe even you.

When to use multi-stage builds

If your build process involves compiling assets or binaries, you might not want to keep the build tools in the final image. This is where multi-stage builds come in.

You can use one base image for building, then copy only the compiled output into a smaller runtime image:

```
FROM node:18 AS builder
WORKDIR /app
COPY . .
RUN npm install && npm run build

FROM node:18-slim
WORKDIR /app
COPY --from=builder /app/dist ./dist
CMD [ "node", "dist/index.js" ]
```

This gives you a clean final image without all the dev tools, which is especially useful in production.

We will cover more advanced builds in later chapters, but it is worth knowing this is available.

Docker image workflow: From build to push

Let's bring it all together with a simple, practical example. This is the full Docker life cycle in action: you'll build an image, run it locally, tag it, and push it to a registry such as Docker Hub. Nothing fancy, just a quick way to prove everything's working and see what the flow looks like end to end. Plus, you can always refer to this part when you need to be in isolation, too:

1. Start by setting up a super basic Node.js app. Create a new folder somewhere, and inside it, drop in these two files:

   - `app.js`: This is your basic server code:

     ```
     const http = require('http');
     const server = http.createServer((req, res) => {
       res.end('Hello from Docker!');
     });
     server.listen(3000, () => {
       console.log('Server running on port 3000');
     });
     ```

   - `Dockerfile`: This tells Docker how to build your image:

     ```
     # Use the official Node.js image as a base
     FROM node:18
     ```

```
# Set the working directory
WORKDIR /app
# Copy your app code into the container
COPY . .
# Expose the port your app runs on
EXPOSE 3000
# Define the default command
CMD ["node", "app.js"]
```

2. In your terminal, run this from the same directory as your Dockerfile:

```
docker build -t my-node-app
```

   That tells Docker to build an image called `my-node-app` using the Dockerfile in the current folder.

3. Now, start a container from your image:

```
docker run -p 3000:3000 my-node-app
```

   That maps port `3000` on your machine to the container. Head to `http://localhost:3000` in your browser, and you should see the following:

```
Hello from Docker!
```

4. If you want to upload this image to Docker Hub (or any other registry, really), you'll need to tag it with your account name:

```
docker tag my-node-app yourusername/my-node-app:latest
```

   Swap out your username for your actual Docker Hub username. You can sign up on the Docker Hub website.

5. Assuming that you've run `docker login` and you're authenticated, push it like this:

```
docker push yourusername/my-node-app:latest
```

   That uploads your image so you can pull and run it from anywhere! Handy for sharing or deploying remotely.

And that's it: `build`, `run`, `tag`, and `push`. Four commands, one working app, and a Docker image that's ready to go wherever you need it. Smart!

Summary

So, a Dockerfile is not just a script; it's a bit of a contract for how your application should be built and run, and small improvements in structure or ordering can have a big impact.

This chapter gave you everything you need to get Docker up and running properly on Windows 11 and use it with intention, not guesswork.

We started by understanding what problem Docker solves and made sure your system was ready for it. Then, we installed Docker Desktop, dialed in some sensible settings, and got comfortable with the core commands you'll use every day.

Once you were up and running, we looked at how to manage containers and images without letting things spiral out of control. From listing and inspecting to stopping and cleaning up, you now know how to keep your environment tidy with my friend, Prune.

Finally, we built a Dockerfile from scratch and looked at how to structure it properly. You learned how layers work, how to keep builds fast, and how to avoid common pitfalls that slow teams down over time.

You're now well set up with a solid foundation, and you've got the tools and mindset to build custom containers that actually suit the way you work. Everything from here builds on this fundamental section.

Alright, now that we know what Docker is and what your machine needs to run it, let's actually get it installed. In the next chapter, we'll walk through downloading and setting up Docker Desktop on Windows 11.

Get This Book's PDF Version and Exclusive Extras

Scan the QR code (or go to `packtpub.com/unlock`). Search for this book by name, confirm the edition, and then follow the steps on the page.

UNLOCK NOW

Note: Keep your invoice handy. Purchases made directly from Packt don't require one.

2

Implementing Docker Networking on Windows 11

Networking in Docker is one of those things I assumed I'd never need to think too hard about. Containers would just talk, ports would just map, and `localhost` would just... ya know, work. Then one day it didn't. I remember running a container, mapping the port, hitting refresh in my browser, and staring at a blank page wondering what on earth had happened.

On Windows 11, Docker runs inside WSL 2, which means `localhost` does not always behave the same way as it does on native Linux. This chapter makes that clear and shows you how to test it.

This chapter is about pulling back the curtain on that moment. We'll look at how Docker actually wires things up on Windows, from the basics of bridge networks to the quirks of host mode and the more advanced overlay setups you'll use when scaling out. Along the way, we'll deal with the classic "why can't my containers see each other" puzzle, the oddities of WSL 2 port forwarding, and the small but mighty tricks that'll save you hours of frustration.

By the end of this chapter, you'll not just know how Docker networking works, but you'll have a go-to playbook for when it doesn't.

We'll be covering the following topics:

- Understanding Docker networking
- Creating bridge networks on Windows
- Configuring host networks for containers
- Secure networking with overlay networks
- Managing network security for containers

Let's begin!

Technical requirements

The code files referenced in this chapter are available at `https://github.com/PacktPublishing/Mastering-Docker-on-Windows`.

Understanding Docker networking

When you first dip your toes into Docker, networking feels like one of those background tricks you don't need to think too hard about. Containers just seem to talk to each other, ports get mapped, and suddenly your app appears on `localhost` like magic. At least, that's how it feels until the magic stops working.

As I said, I still remember the first time I confidently typed `docker run -p 8080:80` and sat there refreshing the browser, waiting for something that never showed up. Or the time I spun up two containers that were supposed to be best friends but couldn't even see each other across the void. That's the moment I realized Docker networking isn't just some hidden wiring; it's a whole system with rules worth understanding.

Note

Quick sanity check on Windows

Run this in PowerShell:

```
docker run --rm -p 8080:80 nginx
curl http://localhost:8080
```

Sometimes `http://localhost:<port>` will fail on Windows because Docker runs inside WSL 2. If that happens, get the WSL IP:

```
wsl.exe hostname -I
```

Then curl the WSL IP directly:

```
curl
```

This tells you immediately whether Docker's port mapping is working correctly inside WSL 2.

In this chapter, we'll unpack what's really going on under the hood. We'll look at how networks are created and assigned, the different types of networks you can use, and how containers communicate with each other and with the outside world. By the end, you'll not only have a clearer mental model of Docker networking, but you'll also know how to fix things when they don't "just work."

Why networking matters in containers

In a traditional setup, your app runs directly on your machine and talks to other processes via `localhost`, the loopback interface. But in Docker, every container is its own isolated environment. Even though they are running on the same host, they don't automatically share the same network context unless you explicitly connect them.

This isolation is intentional; it is part of what makes containers secure and predictable. But it means you need to be more deliberate about how they are connected. Take the following example:

- A web app might need to talk to a database container
- A backend service might need to talk to a cache or queue
- You might want to expose a single port to the host, but keep the rest private

Docker gives you control over all of that; you just need to know where to look. Before we start working with ports and networks, it helps to see how traffic actually moves between Windows, WSL 2, and your containers. This diagram shows the flow at a glance.

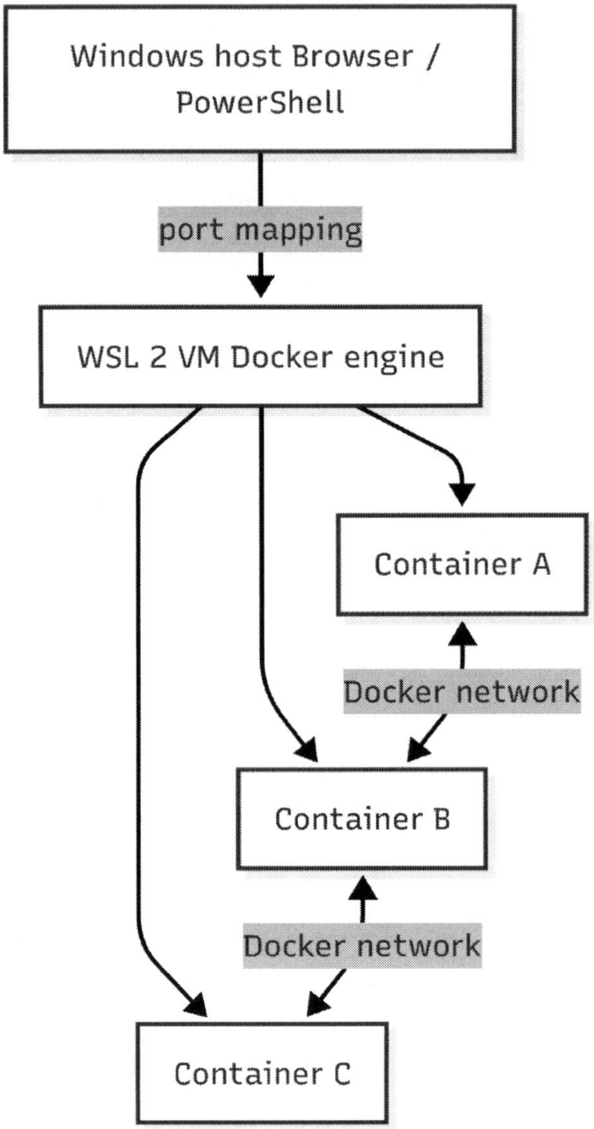

Figure 2.1: How networking flows on Windows

This diagram shows how a request from your Windows host travels through the WSL 2 Docker engine and then into your containers. Windows communicates with Docker through port mapping, Docker routes traffic inside its virtual network, and each container sits on that network as an isolated endpoint.

Now that you've seen how traffic actually moves on Windows, it makes sense to step back and look at the networks Docker gives us by default and how they behave.

The default networks in Docker

When you install Docker and start it up, it automatically creates a few default networks for you. You can see them by running the following:

```
docker network ls
```

You will usually see something like the following:

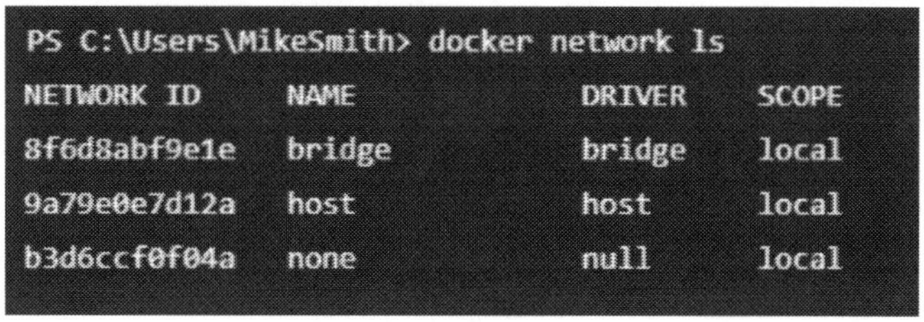

```
PS C:\Users\MikeSmith> docker network ls
NETWORK ID     NAME      DRIVER    SCOPE
8f6d8abf9e1e   bridge    bridge    local
9a79e0e7d12a   host      host      local
b3d6ccf0f04a   none      null      local
```

Figure 2.2: Listing Docker's default networks

Let's break these down:

- `bridge`: This is the default network Docker uses when you run a container without specifying a network. It creates a private internal network on your machine. Containers on this network can talk to each other by name, but they are isolated from the outside world unless you explicitly map ports.
- `host`: This effectively disables networking isolation. The container shares the host's network stack directly. This can be useful in very specific scenarios, but is generally not the default on Windows. We will cover it in more depth later.
- `none`: This is the nuclear option: no network access at all. The container gets started, but it has no network interface at all. It is good for ultra-secure or tightly scoped jobs.

You can inspect the network configuration of any running container with the following:

```
docker inspect <container-name-or-id>
```

This returns a lot of detail, but we will be looking for the `NetworkSettings` section.

```
PS C:\Users\MikeSmith> docker inspect my-app
[
    {
        "Id": "e1bfb2f4e9f26bd8a50b7f7c24c7a527b1fc2674e7d59d1fc4f1d9d90db9c6c1",
        "Created": "2024-04-14T13:15:52.7168465Z",
        "Path": "node",
        "Args": [
            "server.js"
        ],
        "State": {
            "Status": "running",
            "Running": true,
            "StartedAt": "2024-04-14T13:16:03.8213642Z",
            "FinishedAt": "0001-01-01T00:00:00Z"
        },
        "NetworkSettings": {
            "Bridge": "",
            "SandboxID": "c2c2b1e7d0c91ea8d4a8db9d7a8dc4b2",
            "HairpinMode": false,
            "IPAddress": "172.18.0.2",
            "IPPrefixLen": 16,
            "Gateway": "172.18.0.1",
            "Ports": {
                "8080/tcp": [
                    {
                        "HostIp": "0.0.0.0",
                        "HostPort": "8080"
                    }
                ]
            }
        }
    }
]
```

Figure 2.3: Inspecting a container's network settings

`NetworkSettings` will show the container's IP address, which network it is attached to, and how Docker has configured routing and DNS internally.

To pull out just the IP address, you can run the following:

```
docker inspect -f "{{ .NetworkSettings.IPAddress }}" <container-name>
```

Alternatively, to see which network a container is on, run the following:

```
docker inspect -f "{{ range .NetworkSettings.Networks }}{{ .NetworkID }}{{ end }}"
<container-name>
```

How Docker handles name resolution

One of Docker's best features is built-in DNS-based name resolution. If you start two containers on the same custom bridge network, they can talk to each other using their container names with no need to worry about IP addresses.

This only works on user-defined networks (which we'll set up in the next section). The default *bridge* network does not support automatic DNS-based name resolution between containers.

So, if you want containers to find each other by name, always create a user-defined network first.

More on that in a second, but right now, it is enough to understand that Docker manages an internal DNS system that allows containers to talk by name, as long as they are on the same network.

Viewing network interfaces from inside a container

If you want to see what is happening from the container's point of view, you can run the following:

```
docker run -it alpine /bin/sh
```

Then, run `ip a` inside the container:

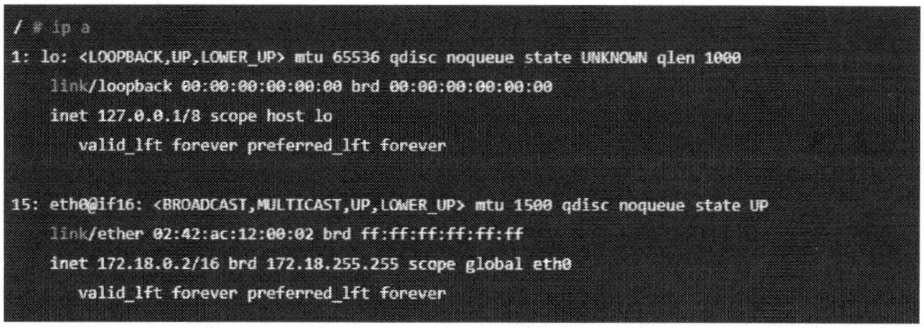

Figure 2.4: Viewing network interfaces inside a container

You'll see `eth0` assigned with a private IP, usually something such as `172.18.x.x`, as well as the loopback interface.

This shows that Docker is creating a virtual NIC inside each container and connecting it to an internal switch that Docker manages.

How Docker chooses subnets and addresses

When Docker creates a network, it automatically assigns a subnet and a gateway. These live entirely inside your host, so there is no risk of clashing with your main LAN, unless you explicitly overlap the ranges.

You can see the details of each network using the following:

```
docker network inspect <network-name>
```

```
PS C:\Users\MikeSmith> docker network inspect my-bridge-network
[
    {
        "Name": "my-bridge-network",
        "Id": "c2b4416e6e2f5d8cd24d9d6c395a12e9d3087bcb7f196f38e232aadcd947b3a6",
        "Created": "2024-04-14T14:27:15.8312345Z",
        "Scope": "local",
        "Driver": "bridge",
        "EnableIPv6": false,
        "IPAM": {
            "Driver": "default",
            "Options": {},
            "Config": [
                {
                    "Subnet": "172.18.0.0/16",
                    "Gateway": "172.18.0.1"
                }
            ]
        },
        "Containers": {
            "e1bfb2f4e9f2": {
                "Name": "my-app",
                "EndpointID": "3cc9a0f4f9f37f9d2e1a43d905a0a2c22170a5cd23d92f8df4c7b7de1
                "MacAddress": "02:42:ac:12:00:02",
                "IPv4Address": "172.18.0.2/16",
                "IPv6Address": ""
            }
        },
        "Options": {},
        "Labels": {}
    }
]
```

Figure 2.5: Inspecting a user-defined bridge network

This will show you the following:

- The subnet (e.g., `172.18.0.0/16`)

- The gateway IP
- Which containers are attached
- Which driver is being used

Docker chooses ranges such as `172.17.0.0/16` or `172.18.0.0/16` for bridge networks by default, but you can override this by specifying your own ranges when you create a network, which is useful for tighter control or avoiding overlaps in more complex setups.

Note

To pull only the subnet and gateway for a network without the full JSON output, use the following:

```
docker network inspect <network-name-or-id> \
  --format "Subnet: {{range .IPAM.Config}}{{.Subnet}}{{end}}, Gateway:
{{range .IPAM.Config}}{{.Gateway}}{{end}}"
```

This is the cleanest, most readable version of the output. It uses the `--format` option to extract the essential network data in a formatted way, being ideal for troubleshooting or report automation.

Each Docker network is backed by a network driver. These drivers define how connectivity is implemented.

Here are the main ones you will encounter:

- `bridge`: Default driver for isolated container-to-container networks on a single host
- `host`: Shares the host network directly
- `overlay`: For multi-host networking, usually used with Docker Swarm
- none: Disables networking entirely

We'll go deeper into each of these in the sections that follow. For now, just know that the driver defines the network's behavior and its scope.

Listing available drivers

To see which network drivers are available on your system, run the following:

```
docker network ls
```

Inspect each network using the following:

```
docker network inspect <name>
```

Alternatively, list available plugins with the following:

```
docker info
```

This includes which network drivers are supported on your platform, which is especially useful on Windows, where not all Linux drivers are supported natively.

> **Note**
>
> If you want to see only the network plugins without the full `docker info` output, run the following:
>
> ```
> docker info --format "{{json .Plugins.Network}}"
> ```

Understanding how Docker handles networking gives you far more control and confidence when working with containers. While Docker does a good job of wiring things up automatically, being able to reason about how containers are connected, or isolated, will save you time, especially when something stops working and you need to troubleshoot.

Creating bridge networks on Windows

So, the first time I realized I could wire up multiple containers to talk to each other on their own isolated network, I remember thinking, "*Ah, this is where Docker starts feeling like infrastructure.*" Not **virtual machines** (**VMs**), not some black box magic, but something I could actually reason about.

Bridge networks are where most of us start when we want containers to communicate, and for good reason. They're private by default, isolated from the rest of our system, and they just work for most internal setups.

What makes a bridge network useful?

A bridge network is a user-defined, container-to-container network. It behaves a bit like a mini switch inside your Docker engine; containers connected to the same bridge can talk to each other directly.

The key thing is isolation. Containers on a bridge network can't be seen by containers outside of it unless you explicitly allow that. This makes it ideal for running related services together, such as a backend and a database, without exposing everything to your entire system.

By default, Docker gives you a bridge network called, well, bridge. But this default network has some quirks. The biggest one is that containers on it don't get automatic DNS resolution, which means they can't find each other by using their container names. In practice, if you've got a web app container trying to reach a `db` container, `ping db` just won't work. You'd have to hardcode the container's IP address instead, which is brittle because those IPs can change every time a container restarts. That's why creating your own bridge network is the way to go when you want predictable, maintainable connectivity. Let's do a quick comparison to understand the difference between using the default and creating your own bridge:

Feature	Default bridge	User-defined bridge
DNS between containers	Not supported	Supported
Isolation	Basic	Stronger, clearly scoped
Typical use	Quick one-off containers	Any multi-container setup
Predictable container naming	No	Yes
Recommended for real projects	No	Yes

Table 2.1: Default bridge versus user-defined bridge

Since the default bridge only gets you so far, let's build a user-defined bridge network that behaves the way you actually need it to.

Creating a user-defined bridge network

Let's create a clean, isolated bridge network for our project:

```
docker network create my-network
```

That's it. Docker will use the bridge driver unless you specify otherwise. You can check that it was created using the following:

```
docker network ls
```

You should see something like this:

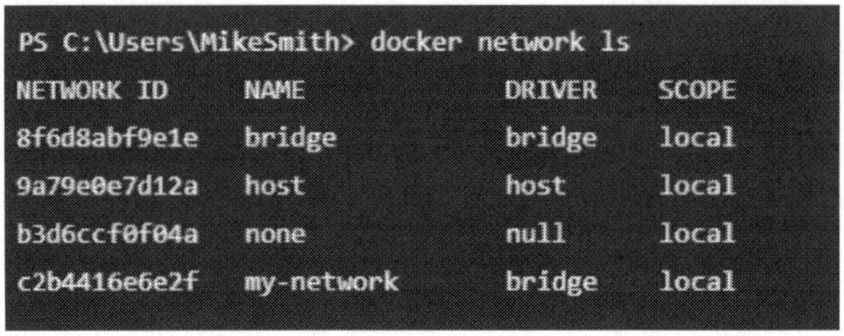

```
PS C:\Users\MikeSmith> docker network ls
NETWORK ID     NAME         DRIVER    SCOPE
8f6d8abf9e1e   bridge       bridge    local
9a79e0e7d12a   host         host      local
b3d6ccf0f04a   none         null      local
c2b4416e6e2f   my-network   bridge    local
```

Figure 2.6: Listing networks again, now showing the custom user-defined bridge network

If you want to see the full details of the network, run the following:

```
docker network inspect my-network
```

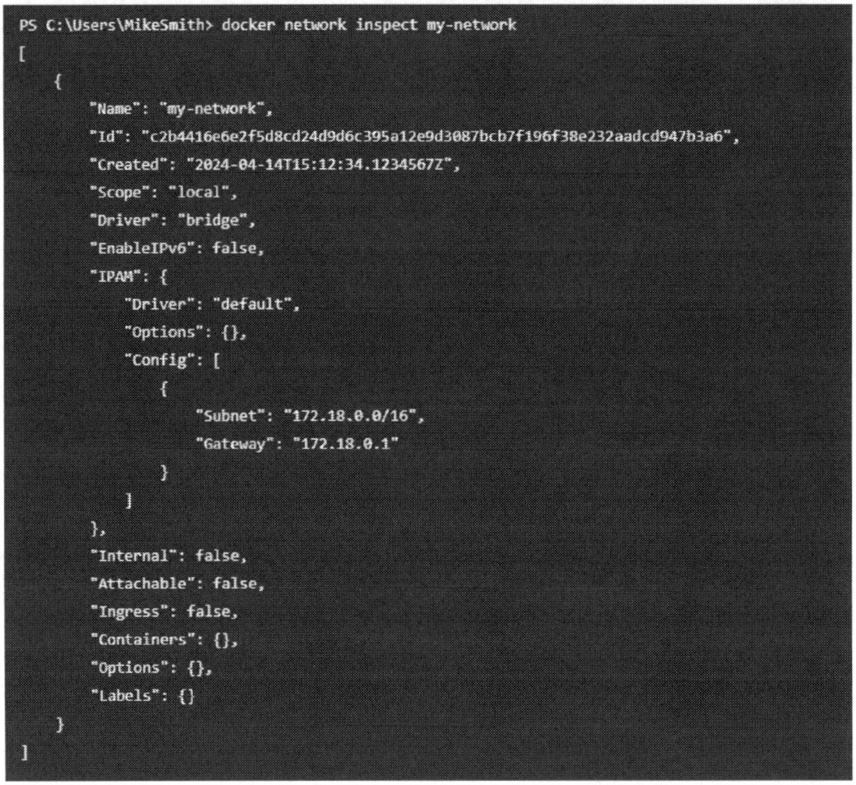

```
PS C:\Users\MikeSmith> docker network inspect my-network
[
    {
        "Name": "my-network",
        "Id": "c2b4416e6e2f5d8cd24d9d6c395a12e9d3087bcb7f196f38e232aadcd947b3a6",
        "Created": "2024-04-14T15:12:34.1234567Z",
        "Scope": "local",
        "Driver": "bridge",
        "EnableIPv6": false,
        "IPAM": {
            "Driver": "default",
            "Options": {},
            "Config": [
                {
                    "Subnet": "172.18.0.0/16",
                    "Gateway": "172.18.0.1"
                }
            ]
        },
        "Internal": false,
        "Attachable": false,
        "Ingress": false,
        "Containers": {},
        "Options": {},
        "Labels": {}
    }
]
```

Figure 2.7: Inspecting the custom bridge network

This will show you the subnet, gateway, and any containers currently attached, which at this point should be none.

Name resolution and DNS

One of the best parts of user-defined bridge networks is that containers can resolve each other by name automatically. This means no manual host file editing and no shared environment variables for Ips; just consistent, self-contained communication.

If something isn't resolving, make sure of the following:

- Both containers are on the same user-defined network
- The containers are still running
- You didn't mistype the container name (this happens more often than you'd think)

> **Tip**
>
> Container names are *case-sensitive* when used in `ping` or other shell commands. That'll trip you up more than once, trust me.

Attaching containers to your bridge network

Now let's spin up two containers and attach them to the network:

```
docker run -dit --name container-one --network my-network alpine /bin/sh
docker run -dit --name container-two --network my-network alpine /bin/sh
```

Both containers are now running in the same isolated network. Let's test that they can talk to each other.

We'll exec into one of them:

```
docker exec -it container-one /bin/sh
```

Then, inside the container, run the following:

```
ping container-two
```

```
PS C:\Users\MikeSmith> docker exec -it container-one /bin/sh
/ # ping container-two
PING container-two (172.18.0.3): 56 data bytes
64 bytes from 172.18.0.3: seq=0 ttl=64 time=0.094 ms
64 bytes from 172.18.0.3: seq=1 ttl=64 time=0.057 ms
64 bytes from 172.18.0.3: seq=2 ttl=64 time=0.056 ms
64 bytes from 172.18.0.3: seq=3 ttl=64 time=0.063 ms
```

Figure 2.8: Pinging container-two from container-one on the same user-defined network, confirming connectivity

If all goes well, you should see the replies. That's because Docker's internal DNS automatically resolves `container-two` by name, since they're on the same user-defined bridge network.

This is a powerful model. You don't need to hardcode IP addresses or configure anything manually; Docker handles the networking for you, as long as you structure it clearly.

You might be wondering, why not just run everything on the default bridge network? It's already there, after all.

Here's the rub: containers on the default bridge can't resolve each other by name. That means you'd need to work with hardcoded IP addresses, which is messy and brittle, especially as containers get recreated and those IPs shift.

User-defined bridge networks fix that. They give you predictable DNS, scoped isolation, and much clearer debugging when something goes wrong.

To check which containers are connected to your network, run the following:

```
docker network inspect my-network
```

```
PS C:\Users\MikeSmith> docker network inspect my-network
[
    {
        "Name": "my-network",
        "Id": "c2b4416e62f58dc24d9d6c395a12e9d387bcb7f196f38e232aadcd947b3a6",
        "Created": "2024-04-14T15:12:34.1234567Z",
        "Scope": "local",
        "Driver": "bridge",
        "EnableIPv6": false,
        "IPAM": {
            "Driver": "default",
            "Options": {},
            "Config": [
                {
                    "Subnet": "172.18.0.0/16",
                    "Gateway": "172.18.0.1"
                }
            ]
        },
        "Containers": {
            "e1bfb2f4e9f2": {
                "Name": "container-one",
                "EndpointID": "3cc9a0f4f9f37f9d2e1a43d905a0a2c22170a5cd23d92f8df4c7b7de12345",
                "MacAddress": "02:42:ac:12:00:02",
                "IPv4Address": "172.18.0.2/16",
                "IPv6Address": ""
            },
            "b3d6ccf0f04a": {
                "Name": "container-two",
                "EndpointID": "4bdc9f4baf9f37f9d2e1a43d905a0a2c22170a5cd23d92f8df4c7b7de67890",
                "MacAddress": "02:42:ac:12:00:03",
                "IPv4Address": "172.18.0.3/16",
                "IPv6Address": ""
            }
        },
        "Options": {},
        "Labels": {}
    }
]
```

Figure 2.9: Inspecting my-network to view connected containers

Look for the `Containers` section in the output. It'll show you each container's name, IP address, and MAC address.

To remove a container from a network, run the following:

```
docker network disconnect my-network container-one
```

To reattach it, run the following:

```
docker network connect my-network container-one
```

This is really useful when debugging, especially if you want to isolate a service temporarily or test what happens when something is disconnected.

Customizing your bridge network

By default, Docker assigns your network a subnet and gateway in the `172.x.x.x` range. But you can specify your own if you need tighter control or want to avoid conflicts.

Here is an example:

```
docker network create --subnet=192.168.100.0/24 --gateway=192.168.100.1 --
driver=bridge custom-bridge
```

This creates a bridge network with a predefined IP range. It's handy when integrating with other systems or when your containers need fixed addresses.

> **Note**
>
> Don't forget that on Windows, Docker runs inside a Linux VM (via WSL 2), so these subnets live within that context. You won't clash with your physical LAN unless you deliberately map ports or interfaces.

Cleaning up networks

When you're done with a network, you can remove it using the following:

```
docker network rm my-network
```

Oh, Docker won't let you remove a network that still has running containers attached. You'll need to stop or disconnect them first.

If you want to wipe all unused networks, use the following:

```
docker network prune
```

This removes any user-defined networks that have no containers attached. It's safe, but always read the prompt before confirming.

So, bridge networks give you the building blocks to connect containers in a predictable, private way. By creating your own user-defined bridge networks, you get access to automatic DNS resolution, better structure, and simpler debugging.

Configuring host networks for containers

At some point, we all reach for Docker's networking options to solve a real-world problem. Maybe you're running something that needs to expose a service directly on the host, or you've got a container that needs to blend into your existing network without any NAT or port mappings in the way. That's where the handy host network driver comes in.

On Windows, this concept behaves a little differently than on Linux, and it's worth being clear about what you can do, what you probably shouldn't do, and what to expect when you use it.

What does host networking actually do?

With most Docker networks, your containers live in a private virtual network managed by Docker, isolated by design. You access services running inside them by mapping ports from the host to the container, like this:

```
docker run -d -p 8080:80 nginx
```

That works fine, but the container still has its own network interface, its own IP address, and some level of indirection between the host and container traffic. Using the host driver removes that layer.

When you run a container with `--network host`, it skips all of Docker's network isolation and just runs with access to the host's network stack. There's no NAT, no virtual interface, and no port mapping. The container can bind directly to whatever interfaces the host has available.

But there's a catch: on Windows, the host driver is *not* implemented the same way it is on Linux.

Docker on Windows runs Linux containers inside a VM managed by WSL 2. This means that the container's "host" network is actually the network stack of that Linux VM, *not your real Windows host*.

So, when you run something such as `docker run --network host nginx`, you're telling Docker to bypass its usual container network and bind directly to the WSL 2 interface. It does not bind directly to your actual Windows network stack, meaning if you try to access the container from your browser on Windows at `localhost`, it probably won't show up.

There are workarounds for this, such as forwarding ports from WSL 2 to Windows using `netsh` or custom routing, but that adds complexity you probably don't want unless you have a very specific reason. This also extends way beyond the scope of this book, so if you need to venture into that territory, I would recommend using Google as your friend.

Despite the limitations on Windows, there are a few scenarios where host networking can still make sense:

- If you're building or testing network-level tools that need access to raw sockets or sniffing (e.g., `tcpdump` or WireGuard).
- If you're running inside WSL 2 and need a containerized tool to bind directly to an interface without Docker's port forwarding.
- If you're deploying into a Linux-based production environment and want to test how host networking behaves locally (just be aware that behavior on Windows won't always match Linux).

In most other cases, bridge networking with deliberate port mappings is simpler, more portable, and easier to reason about, especially if you're sharing your setup with others.

Running a container with host networking

If you want to try it, here's a simple example. Start a container using the host network driver:

```
docker run --rm -it --network host alpine /bin/sh
```

Then, install a basic tool and start a web server:

```
apk add --no-cache busybox-extras
httpd -f -p 8000 -h /tmp
```

That web server is now bound directly to port `8000` on the WSL 2 interface, but *not* on your Windows host interface. If you *curl* it from inside WSL or from another container using host networking, you'll see it respond. From Windows itself, you probably won't.

You can confirm that a container is running with the host network using the following:

```
docker inspect <container-name>
```

Look for the `"NetworkMode": "host"` section:

```
PS C:\Users\MikeSmith> docker inspect my-container
[
    {
        "HostConfig": {
            "NetworkMode": "host"
        },
        "NetworkSettings": {
            "Bridge": "",
            "SandboxID": "",
            "HairpinMode": false,
            "Ports": {},
            "IPAddress": "",
            "MacAddress": "",
            "Networks": {}
        }
    }
]
```

Figure 2.10: Inspecting a container running in host network mode

You won't see any IP addresses listed under `NetworkSettings`, because the container is no longer isolated from the network layer; it's sharing the stack with its parent context.

Cleaning up

If you've been testing host networking and want to go back to the usual way of running containers, do the following:

- Stop any containers using `--network host`
- Restart your containers with `-p` to explicitly forward only the ports you need

Here is an example:

```
docker run -d -p 8080:80 nginx
```

This ensures your container is still isolated by default, and it gives you full control over how your services are exposed, a better default in most cases.

When not to use host networking

Let's be honest, in a Windows environment, host networking is rarely the right default.

Unless you're doing low-level networking, building VPN-style apps, or replicating production behavior that depends on the host stack, it's safer and simpler to use bridge networks and just forward the ports you need.

It's also way easier to reason with, easier to explain to teammates, and less prone to strange platform-specific behaviors.

Because host networking removes isolation, it introduces some real security concerns:

- Containers can bind to any port or interface on the host
- There's no NAT or firewall separation by default
- If a process inside the container is compromised, it may have more direct access to host resources than usual

For this reason, host networking is generally discouraged for multi-tenant environments or anywhere you need strong boundary enforcement. Only use it when you explicitly need its behavior, and when you understand the trade-offs.

In general, host networking in Docker gives containers full access to the host's network interfaces, bypassing all of Docker's usual isolation. On Linux, that's powerful. On Windows, it's more complicated due to how WSL 2 handles networking under the hood.

Secure networking with overlay networks

When you're running containers locally, life is simple. Everything lives on your machine, networking stays internal, and it's easy to reason about who's talking to what.

But as soon as you start thinking about running containers across more than one machine, or even just wanting Docker to behave as it does in a production cluster, the rules change. This is where overlay networks come into play.

We're going to explore what overlay networks actually do, why they matter for secure container-to-container communication, and how you can set them up and use them on Windows using Docker Swarm.

Why overlay networks exist

When Docker is just running on one machine, it can manage everything internally: bridge networks, port mappings, and so on. But when containers need to communicate across different machines, those internal networks no longer cut it.

Overlay networks solve that problem by creating a virtual network that spans across multiple Docker hosts. Containers on different machines, or different WSL 2 instances, can talk to each other as if they were on the same LAN.

And the best bit? Docker handles all the messy bits for you (routing, encryption, and peer discovery) without needing to set up a VPN or open a dozen firewall ports.

Overlay networking is built into Docker Swarm, so that's what we'll be using here. While Swarm isn't as popular these days as Kubernetes, it's lightweight, fast to get started with, and perfect for learning how secure container communication works under the hood.

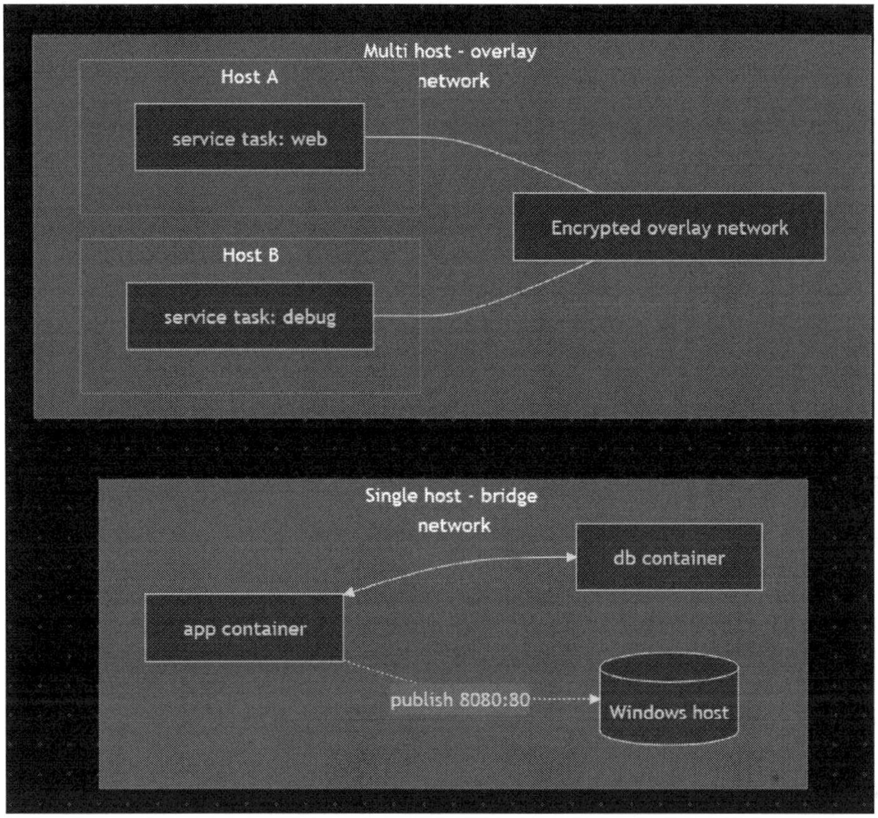

Figure 2.11: Bridge (single host) versus overlay (multi-host)

Docker's overlay networks use **mutual TLS (mTLS)** by default to encrypt all traffic between containers that talk across hosts. That means even if someone is sniffing the wire (eavesdropping on your communication online), they'll only see encrypted packets, not your app's actual data.

Each Swarm node gets its own cryptographic identity, and Docker manages the certificates automatically behind the scenes. You don't need to fiddle with OpenSSL or mess with trust stores. It just works.

Overlay networks also isolate container traffic from the host's own network, and from other overlay networks. So, if you're running multiple services across different teams or projects, you get strong boundaries out of the box.

Note

Setting up Docker Swarm on Windows

To use overlay networks, you need to enable Docker Swarm mode. Even if you're only running a single-node cluster (which is totally fine for local dev), Docker still uses the same overlay logic behind the scenes. To get started, run the following:

```
docker swarm init
```

This will initialize Swarm mode on your machine and make it the manager node. You can now create overlay networks.

In production, Swarm usually means more than one box. You'll have multiple manager nodes for quorum and one or more workers doing the graft. For learning on a laptop, though, a single-node Swarm is absolutely fine; it behaves the same way for the bits we care about here.

Creating a secure overlay network

Let's create one:

```
docker network create --driver overlay --opt encrypted my-secure-overlay
```

This command does two things:

- It tells Docker to use the overlay driver (so traffic can go across Swarm nodes)
- It enables encryption using the `--opt encrypted` flag

Even on a single-node Swarm, Docker still routes packets through the encrypted tunnel, so your setup stays secure and consistent. To verify it, run the following:

```
docker network inspect my-secure-overlay
```

Look for the `"Driver": "overlay"` and `"Options": { "encrypted": "true" }` fields.

```
PS C:\Users\MikeSmith> docker network inspect my-secure-overlay
[
    {
        "Name": "my-secure-overlay",
        "Id": "b7f637f4088d7b7323c302ae06b7ed223e04dfacac94cfcb18f1474204fbcdfa",
        "Created": "2024-04-14T17:43:01.6723195Z",
        "Scope": "swarm",
        "Driver": "overlay",
        "EnableIPv6": false,
        "IPAM": {
            "Driver": "default",
            "Options": {},
            "Config": [
                {
                    "Subnet": "10.0.0.0/24"
                }
            ]
        },
        "Internal": false,
        "Attachable": false,
        "Ingress": false,
        "ConfigFrom": {
            "Network": ""
        },
        "ConfigOnly": false,
        "Containers": {},
        "Options": {
            "encrypted": "true"
        },
        "Labels": {}
    }
]
```

Figure 2.12: Inspecting the secure overlay network, my-secure-overlay, showing subnet details and "encrypted": "true"

You'll also see here some other useful details in the output, such as the automatically assigned subnet (`10.0.0.0/24`, in this case), the scope of the network (`swarm`), and whether the network is internal or attachable. These settings confirm not just that the network exists but also how Docker has configured it under the hood.

To use this network, you'll want to deploy services instead of standalone containers. In Swarm mode, services are the way you define long-running container workloads. Here's a quick example using Nginx:

```
docker service create \
  --name web \
```

```
  --network my-secure-overlay \
  --publish 8080:80 \
  nginx
```

This tells Docker to create a service called `web`, attach it to the secure overlay network, and publish port `80` from the container to port `8080` on your host. You can then test it by hitting .

To inspect the service, do the following:

```
docker service inspect web
```

```
PS C:\Users\MikeSmith> docker service inspect web
[
    {
        "Spec": {
            "Name": "web",
            "TaskTemplate": {
                "ContainerSpec": {
                    "Image": "nginx:latest"
                }
            },
            "Mode": {
                "Replicated": {
                    "Replicas": 1
                }
            },
            "Networks": [
                {
                    "Aliases": [ "web" ]
                }
            ],
            "EndpointSpec": {
                "Ports": [
                    {
                        "Protocol": "tcp",
                        "TargetPort": 80,
                        "PublishedPort": 8080
                    }
                ]
            }
        }
    }
]
```

Figure 2.13: Inspecting the Swarm service web

You'll see that the task has been scheduled to your local Swarm node, and the container is running with access to the overlay network.

Running multiple services securely

Here's where it gets interesting. You can now deploy multiple services and have them talk to each other using container names, just like with bridge networks, except it works across nodes and with encrypted traffic.

Let's create a tiny Alpine container that pings Nginx:

```
docker service create \
  --name debug \
  --network my-secure-overlay \
  alpine sleep 10000
```

Then, exec into it:

```
docker exec -it $(docker ps -qf name=debug) sh
ping web
```

You'll see replies from the Nginx container, showing that DNS resolution and secure overlay routing are working as expected.

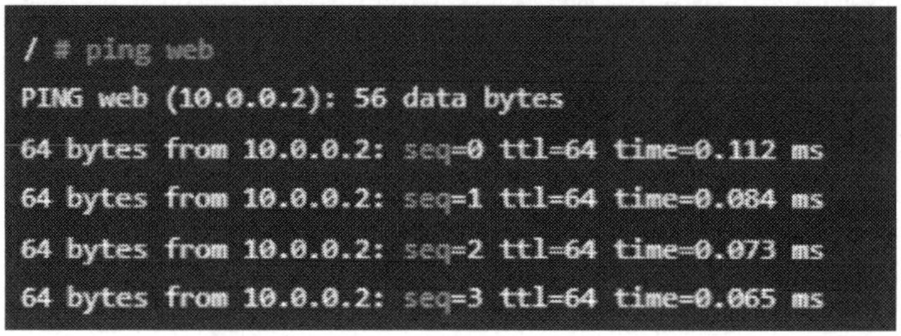

Figure 2.14: Pinging the web Swarm service from another container

Cleaning up

To remove a service, run the following:

```
docker service rm web
```

To remove the network, run the following:

```
docker network rm my-secure-overlay
```

Make sure no services are attached before trying to delete the network.

Understanding the security trade-offs

Overlay networks are secure by default, but there are still things to be aware of:

- All Swarm nodes must trust the manager that issued their certs. If someone joins a rogue node, they'll be trusted too.

- Encrypted overlay networks add a small amount of overhead, usually negligible, but it is worth knowing for high-throughput workloads.
- Only services can attach to overlay networks, not regular `docker run` containers. This keeps things cleaner, but might catch you off guard.

You should also consider firewall rules between Swarm nodes. Docker will open required ports on your local system, but in production, you'll need to allow TCP ports such as 2377 (Swarm management), 7946 (overlay gossip), and UDP 4789 (VXLAN traffic).

So, overlay networks give you a powerful, secure way to connect containers across machines. By using Docker Swarm and enabling encryption, you get mTLS, built-in DNS, and traffic isolation, all without extra tools or manual config.

Managing network security for containers

At some point, something breaks. Maybe a container suddenly can't reach another one. Maybe a service is unreachable despite being "running." Or maybe everything was working fine yesterday, and now you've got a black box that simply will not respond.

If you've been using Docker for a while, especially with custom networks or Swarm mode, you've likely hit one of these scenarios. The good news is that most Docker networking issues can be diagnosed with a fairly consistent playbook.

So, let's walk through how to troubleshoot common container networking problems and explore how to check, manage, and secure your Docker networks, especially on Windows 11, where WSL 2 and VM isolation add an extra layer of complexity.

Always ask, "Can I see it?"

Let's say you have two containers: `app` and `db`. They're running, they're attached to the same user-defined bridge network, and you're expecting them to talk.

The first question to ask is: can one container even see the other?

Step into one of the containers:

```
docker exec -it app /bin/sh
```

Try to ping the other one by name:

```
ping db
```

If you get replies, great, they can see each other. If you get `Name or service not known`, that's a DNS resolution failure.

Figure 2.15: Ping attempt showing a DNS resolution issue

If it hangs or says `Destination Host Unreachable`, that's a routing issue or firewall problem. If you're looking for specific fixes to these issues, then fear not, they are coming right up with DNS, routing, and firewall fixes.

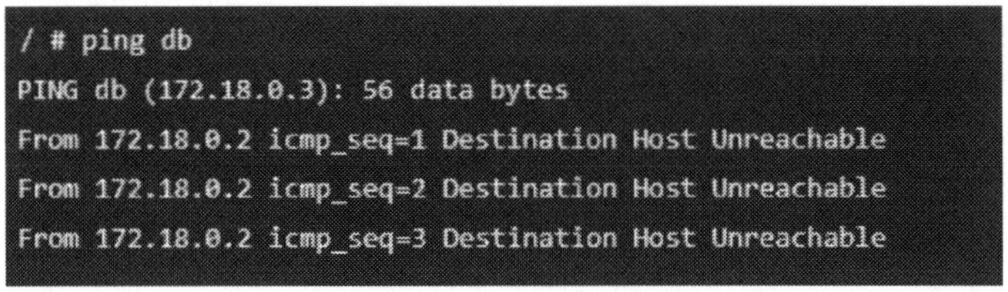

Figure 2.16: Ping attempt indicating a routing or firewall problem

Common DNS issues and how to fix them

In Docker, DNS is built into the network itself. When you create a user-defined network, Docker sets up an internal DNS server that resolves container names automatically.

But that only works in the following instances:

- Both containers are on the same user-defined bridge or overlay network
- The container name is correct and not misspelled
- The network driver supports DNS (host mode does not)

To check the networks, run the following:

```
docker inspect app
```

Look under `NetworkSettings` | `Networks` and confirm that the container is attached to the expected network.

```
"NetworkSettings": {
    "Bridge": "",
    "SandboxID": "2c587d9f39e14787dfd9cf78c29b8d1ef0d6b99c1352ff3e90b8f69b7a9a364b",
    "HairpinMode": false,
    "LinkLocalIPv6Address": "",
    "LinkLocalIPv6PrefixLen": 0,
    "Ports": {},
    "SandboxKey": "/var/run/docker/netns/2c587d9f39e1",
    "SecondaryIPAddresses": null,
    "SecondaryIPv6Addresses": null,
    "EndpointID": "0cbad0c1f3a2179462d06c81a568ba89ad310d2543ecfba21f8718e650c64fc1",
    "Gateway": "172.18.0.1",
    "GlobalIPv6Address": "",
    "GlobalIPv6PrefixLen": 0,
    "IPAddress": "172.18.0.2",
    "IPPrefixLen": 16,
    "IPv6Gateway": "",
    "MacAddress": "02:42:ac:12:00:02",
    "Networks": {
        "my-network-2": {
            "IPAMConfig": null,
            "Links": null,
            "Aliases": [
                "app",
                "3b28be8283d1"
            ],
            "NetworkID": "2e24a3b27865495a83c28db37d9e0cf91d30d3b8c0605e53ab3ceec78087f053",
            "EndpointID": "0cbad0c1f3a2179462d06c81a568ba89ad310d2543ecfba21f8718e650c64fc1",
            "Gateway": "172.18.0.1",
            "IPAddress": "172.18.0.2",
            "IPPrefixLen": 16,
            "IPv6Gateway": "",
            "GlobalIPv6Address": "",
            "GlobalIPv6PrefixLen": 0,
            "MacAddress": "02:42:ac:12:00:02",
            "DriverOpts": null
        }
    }
}
```

Figure 2.17: Inspecting container network settings

If you find the container is on the wrong network, disconnect and reattach it:

```
docker network disconnect my-network app
docker network connect my-network app
```

This often solves DNS issues straight away.

No DNS? Try IPs

If DNS fails, you can still test connectivity using IP addresses.

Get the IP of the target container:

```
docker inspect -f "{{ .NetworkSettings.Networks.my-network.IPAddress }}" db
```

Then, ping it directly from the other container:

```
ping 172.18.0.3
```

If that works, but pinging by name does not, you've got a DNS issue, not a networking issue.

Verifying port bindings

Let's say you're running a web service, and you're trying to reach it from outside Docker, say, your browser or `curl` from Windows. If it's unreachable, the first thing to check is whether the port is actually published:

```
docker ps
```

Look in the `PORTS` column. You should see something like the following:

```
0.0.0.0:8080->80/tcp
```

This means port `80` inside the container is mapped to port `8080` on your host.

If you don't see anything there, or you forgot to use `-p` when starting the container, then Docker hasn't exposed the service.

Here is a quick fix:

```
docker run -d -p 8080:80 nginx
```

Also, make sure you're not using `--network host` on Windows expecting it to behave like Linux. With WSL 2, host mode doesn't expose ports to your actual Windows interface.

Firewall and antivirus interference

Another common issue, especially on corporate laptops or in restrictive environments, is when Docker's traffic is blocked by the local firewall or antivirus software.

If pings fail or services are unreachable even with correct settings, try the following:

- Temporarily disabling your firewall to test connectivity, if you can.
- Checking whether Docker Desktop is allowed through Windows Defender Firewall.
- Ensuring that TCP and UDP ports such as 2377, 7946, and 4789 are not blocked (for Swarm mode).

On WSL 2, port forwarding between Linux and Windows can also break unexpectedly after Windows updates. If `localhost:8080` is not working, try curling the WSL IP directly.

Find the WSL IP:

```
wsl hostname -I
```

Figure 2.18: Finding the WSL 2 IP address

Then, test the service:

```
curl http://<WSL-IP>:8080
```

Figure 2.19: Testing localhost access with curl

This should work fine; however, you can sometimes get a `Connection Refused` error. You can set up a manual port proxy to forward traffic from Windows into WSL:

```
netsh interface portproxy add v4tov4 listenport=8080 listenaddress=127.0.0.1
connectport=8080 connectaddress=<WSL-IP>
```

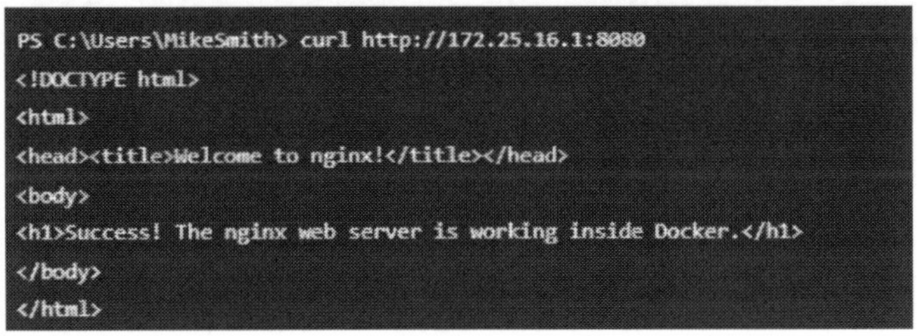

Figure 2.20: Accessing the containerised Nginx server via the WSL 2

Docker Swarm DNS oddities

When running services in Swarm mode, DNS works differently. You can ping a service name, such as `web`, from another service, but not from a regular container.

Only containers created as part of `docker service create` can resolve those internal names.

If your debug container can't ping a service name, check that it's actually a Swarm service and that the overlay network is configured correctly.

Use the following:

```
docker service ls
docker service inspect web
```

Misbehaving networks: Prune and rebuild

Sometimes Docker networks just act... weird. Maybe a container has a stale entry, or a network was partially removed.

If nothing else works, you can clean up unused networks using my favorite command:

```
docker network prune
```

Alternatively, you can explicitly remove and recreate the one you're using the following:

```
docker network rm my-network
docker network create my-network
```

Just make sure no running containers are attached before doing this; Docker won't let you delete in-use networks.

Best practices for securing Docker networks

Security is mostly about being deliberate. A few small choices here save a lot of pain later:

- **Expose only what you must**: Publish the minimum ports, and prefer mapping high host ports to low container ports. Avoid `-p 80:80` unless there's a real reason to use it.
- **Prefer user-defined networks**: Use your own bridge or overlay networks for clear boundaries and built-in DNS. Keep unrelated services on separate networks.
- **Avoid host mode unless you really need it**: Host networking removes isolation and makes firewalls trickier. Stick to bridge plus explicit `-p` mappings where possible.

- **Encrypt cross-node traffic**: On Swarm, create overlays with `--opt encrypted` so service-to-service chatter uses mTLS by default. Rotate join tokens and restrict who can add nodes.
- **Limit lateral movement**: Consider `--internal` networks for services that never need egress. Use network scoping to keep the blast radius small.
- **Name over numbers**: Don't rely on container IPs. Use container/service names and user-defined networks for predictable DNS.
- **Check the basics first**: Confirm published ports with `docker ps`, validate container network attachments with `docker inspect`, and test name resolution before diving deeper.
- **Monitor and log**: Track egress, DNS lookups, and published ports. Even lightweight flow logs or firewall events will surface surprises early.
- **Keep things tidy**: Prune unused networks and services to avoid stale records and weird routing artifacts.

Windows networking example

Before wrapping up, here is a short hands-on lab you can run right now. It walks through the core networking checks you'll use constantly on Windows and shows you how to spot the common failure points in seconds:

1. Create a user-defined network:

   ```
   docker network create my-network
   docker network ls
   ```

   You'll see `my-network` listed with the `bridge` driver and the `local` scope.

2. Run two containers and confirm DNS resolution. Start two Alpine containers on the network:

   ```
   docker run -dit --name c1 --network my-network alpine /bin/sh
   docker run -dit --name c2 --network my-network alpine /bin/sh
   ```

   Now drop into `c1`:

   ```
   docker exec -it c1 /bin/sh
   ping c2
   ```

   `ping` should resolve the name `c2` automatically and return replies.

3. Test port mapping from Windows and WSL. Run Nginx:

```
docker run -d --name web -p 8080:80 nginx
```

From PowerShell:

```
curl
```

If `localhost` fails, check the WSL IP:

```
wsl.exe hostname -I
curl http://<wsl-ip>:8080
```

You should get the default Nginx HTML page through either Windows `localhost` or the WSL IP.

4. Create a secure overlay network and verify Swarm traffic.
First, enable Swarm:

```
docker swarm init
```

Create an encrypted overlay:

```
docker network create --driver overlay --opt encrypted secure-net
```

Deploy Nginx on it:

```
docker service create --name web2 --network secure-net -p 9090:80 nginx
```

Check the service:

```
docker service ls
docker service ps web2
```

The service should show one running task. Visiting `http://localhost:9090` returns the Nginx page.

If all four steps worked, you've got a solid baseline for debugging almost any networking issue on Windows. If something didn't behave the way you expected, that's even better because now you can diagnose it using the same commands you just practiced.

Note

Windows networking quick checklist

Here is a fast set of commands to verify container networking on Windows:

- `docker network ls`
- `docker network inspect <name>`
- `docker ps --format "table {{.Names}}\t{{.Ports}}"`
- `wsl.exe hostname -I`
- `Get-NetTCPConnection -LocalPort <port>`
- `docker info` (for Swarm)

This gives you a quick read on network drivers, port mappings, WSL IP, active listeners, and Swarm state.

The Big Lab: Notes service

To make all this networking theory feel real, we're going to start building a small application that we'll keep coming back to throughout the book. You'll love it! This is the *Big Lab*. It's a simple Notes service made of two containers. Right now, it does almost nothing. That's fine. In later chapters, we'll gradually layer in storage, Compose, secrets, performance tweaks, an AI feature, and, eventually, a deployment pipeline. Running these commands will produce standard Docker output. Nothing special is required here; what matters is that the containers build and start and can see each other. All of the following commands should be run from the folder that contains your Dockerfile and `app.py`:

1. **Create the minimal Notes API**: This version returns a single message. Nothing clever yet.
   The Dockerfile file:

```
FROM python:3.12-slim
WORKDIR /app
COPY app.py .
CMD ["python", "app.py"]
```

The `app.py` file:

```
from flask import Flask
app = Flask(__name__)

@app.get("/")
def home():
    return {"message": "Notes API is running"}

if __name__ == "__main__":
app.run(host="0.0.0.0", port=5000)
```

Build the image:

```
docker build -t notes-api .
```

2. **Create an isolated network for the service**: Everything in this project will use this network, so we keep the traffic isolated and predictable:

```
docker network create notes-net
```

3. **Run the API and a backend container**: We'll swap this backend out later when the service becomes more serious. For now, it just gives the API something to talk to.

```
docker run -d --name notes-api --network notes-net -p 5000:5000 notes-api
docker run -d --name notes-backend --network notes-net alpine sleep 999999
```

4. **Check that the containers can see each other**: If this doesn't work, nothing else will either, so it's worth confirming early:

```
docker exec -it notes-backend ping notes-api
```

You should see replies using the container name. That tells you that DNS on the user-defined network is working the way it should.

5. **Check that the host can reach the API**: If you're on Windows and `localhost` refuses to behave, fall back to the WSL IP:

```
curl
```

If that fails:

```
wsl.exe hostname -I
curl
```

That's the first piece in place. In the next chapter, we will give the Notes service storage to make it useful.

Summary

Networking is one of those things that works great until it suddenly doesn't, and then it's the most frustrating thing in the world. In this chapter, we walked through the layers that Docker adds on top of your Windows setup and broke down how containers talk to each other and the outside world.

We looked at the basics of Docker networking, then stepped through bridge networks, host mode, and the more advanced overlay networks used in Swarm. We also dug into real-world troubleshooting, such as fixing DNS issues, dealing with port forwarding weirdness on WSL 2, and knowing when a firewall or network config is the culprit.

By now, you should feel pretty comfortable with setting up your own networks, diagnosing what's going wrong when containers can't connect, and keeping things secure whether you're working locally or scaling across machines. Let's move on, you've earned it.

Join us on Discord

For discussions around the book and to connect with your peers, join us on Discord at or scan the QR code below:

3

Managing Docker Volumes and Data Persistence

Data persistence is essential for applications that rely on stateful processes, and Docker volumes provide a powerful solution. This chapter explores advanced techniques for managing Docker volumes, including creating optimized workflows, implementing backup strategies, and resolving common issues. You'll also learn how to efficiently share volumes across containers for scalable application architectures.

Why is it important? Senior engineers need to handle complex data persistence requirements in enterprise environments. This chapter builds your skills in managing containerized storage effectively.

The following main topics are covered:

- Overview of persistent data management
- Implementing and optimizing volume usage in complex workflows
- Advanced backup and recovery solutions for Docker volumes
- Cross-container data sharing strategies for enterprise use
- Root cause analysis and fixes for volume management issues

Let's get started!

Technical requirements

The code files referenced in this chapter are available at `https://github.com/PacktPublishing/Mastering-Docker-on-Windows`.

Overview of persistent data management

Imagine this: You've deployed a robust web application using Docker, and everything works like a charm. Users are interacting with your app, and data is flowing in seamlessly. But then, the inevitable happens; you need to update your containers. Suddenly, the data your users have entered disappears, and their trust in your app vanishes with it. This scenario underscores the critical need for persistent data management in containerized environments.

For seasoned Docker engineers, managing data persistence is not just a technical necessity; it's a core skill that determines the reliability and usability of applications.

In this chapter, we're going to get hands-on with managing persistent data in Docker. We'll look at how volumes actually work and where they fit into your day-to-day container workflows. By the end, you'll have a clear idea of how to keep your data around when containers come and go, setting you up nicely for the deeper dive in the later chapters.

Understanding the basics

Containers, by design, are ephemeral. When a container stops or is removed, all data generated during its runtime is lost unless specifically stored elsewhere. While this stateless design is one of Docker's strengths, it also presents challenges for applications requiring data persistence, such as databases, content management systems, or data processing pipelines.

Docker solves this challenge with volumes, a mechanism to manage persistent data outside the life cycle of individual containers. Volumes are stored on the host filesystem and can be shared among containers, making them a versatile tool for managing data across distributed systems. On Windows, Docker Desktop stores named volumes inside the WSL 2 virtual filesystem, not on `C:`. You'll see paths such as `\\wsl.localhost\docker-desktop-data\data\docker\volumes`.

> **Note**
>
> Sometimes it helps to prove the basics before we get fancy. Here is a quick way to create a volume, write something into it, and then read it back:
>
> ```
> docker volume create demo-vol
>
> docker run --rm -v demo-vol:/data alpine \
>   sh -c "echo 'hello from volume' > /data/test.txt"
>
> docker run --rm -v demo-vol:/data alpine \
>   cat /data/test.txt
> ```

> You should see the text appear in the terminal. If that works, the volume is mounted correctly, and you know the data is actually being persisted. Nice one!

A lot of real-world systems fail here. A container gets rebuilt, its internal filesystem resets, and suddenly yesterday's data is gone. So before we look at the volume types themselves, let's anchor this in a simple workflow: imagine a service that needs to keep user uploads alive between deployments. That is the exact problem volumes are designed to solve.

I remember talking with a friend who worked for a logistics company that ran nightly batch jobs in containers that processed route data. The containers were disposable, but the job outputs were critical. Without volumes, every container rebuild wiped out the generated reports. Switching to named volumes meant the reports stuck around even after every deployment.

No single type of volume fits every workload. A CI pipeline, a local dev setup, and a production database all need persistence, but for completely different reasons. So, before choosing a volume type, it helps to picture the kinds of jobs these containers are actually doing.

Choosing the right volume type

Docker offers several options for managing persistent data, each suited for different use cases. Let's take a closer look:

- **Named volumes**: Named volumes are the go-to choice for most scenarios. They are easy to manage and provide a clear separation between application data and the container life cycle. Named volumes are particularly effective for multi-container setups where data needs to be accessed by multiple services simultaneously.
  This is the pattern you use when the container should be disposable, but the data absolutely is not. Anything that stores customer data, reports, or internal state benefits from a named volume. Think of it as the application having a protected storage locker that survives rebuilds. Think about a mid-sized bank using Windows Server that has strict audit requirements. Their transaction-processing container would write encrypted log bundles to a named volume so they could be collected by a compliance job outside the container life cycle. If the container died during reconciliation, the logs would still exist for auditors.

  Example: Running a WordPress site with a separate database container? A named volume is perfect for keeping your database data persistent between container rebuilds.

- **Bind mounts**: Bind mounts allow you to specify an exact directory on the host system for storage. While they offer more control, they come with increased complexity and potential security risks. These are best suited for scenarios where the host system's specific file structure needs to be leveraged. Bind mounts shine when the host machine itself is part of the workflow. For example, developers working on Windows often need the container to reflect edits saved in VS Code instantly. In that workflow, the container isn't the source of truth; the host filesystem is.

Think about a team building an internal pricing tool where analysts keep dropping spreadsheets onto a shared Windows network drive. The container needs live access to whatever the analysts save, so the host filesystem becomes the source of truth. With a bind mount, the container can read those files instantly, and nothing inside the container needs to be rebuilt when the analysts update their data.

Example: Say you're developing locally and want live updates in your container whenever a file changes on your machine, bind mounts are ideal for that.

> **Note**
>
> Bind mounts on Windows look different from Linux, and it is easy to get the syntax wrong, so here is a quick, real example to make it obvious:
>
> ```
> mkdir C:\docker-bind
> echo "from windows" > C:\docker-bind\msg.txt
>
> docker run --rm -v C:\docker-bind:/data alpine \
>   cat /data/msg.txt
> ```
>
> If the setup is right, the container prints the message that was created on your Windows host.

- **tmpfs volumes**: `tmpfs` volumes store data in memory rather than on the host filesystem. While this approach is not suitable for long-term persistence, it's ideal for temporary storage where high-speed access is critical.
  Example: Great for temporary caches or sensitive data you don't want written to disk, like session tokens during a test run.

> **Note**
>
> Windows does not support `tmpfs` volumes in Docker Desktop because the backing filesystem runs inside WSL 2. If you actually need in-memory storage on Windows, the common workaround is to create a RAM disk on the host (for example, with `ImDisk` or `OSFMount`) and bind mount that into the container. The container then treats the RAM-backed folder as a normal path, but reads and writes stay in memory.

The best practice would be to always choose the volume type that aligns with your application's performance and security requirements. For most enterprise-grade setups, named volumes strike the best balance between simplicity and functionality.

Integrating persistent data into complex workflows

Volumes shine in advanced workflows where multiple containers need access to shared data. Consider a typical microservices architecture where one service processes user uploads, another handles data analysis, and a third serves processed results to end users. Once an application breaks into multiple services, data isn't just something you keep around. It becomes something you *pass between* containers. A user upload might go from an uploader service to a processor to a frontend. This is where volumes stop being storage and start becoming glue.

A shared volume sits at the center of this workflow, giving each service access to the same dataset without duplicating files or passing them around manually.

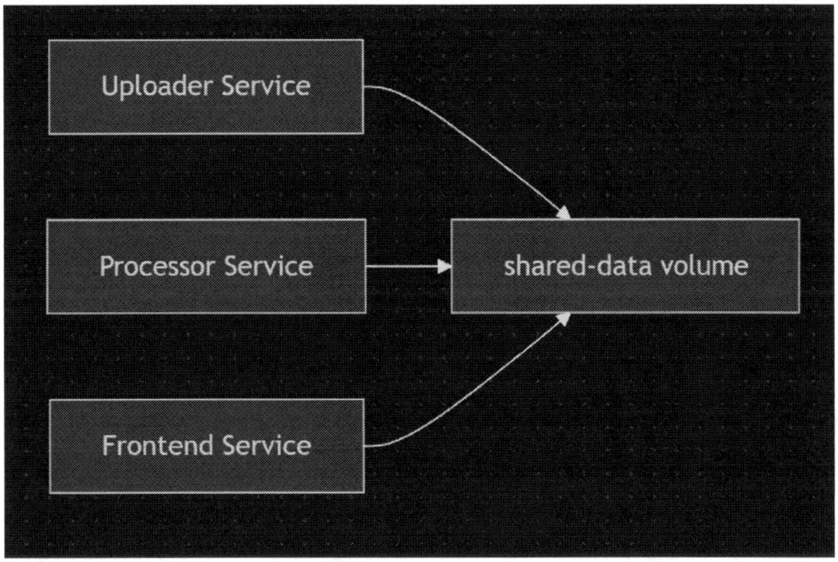

Figure 3.1: Three separate services writing to and reading from the same shared-data volume

Here is a stripped-down version of a pattern you see a lot in analytics and media workflows. One container writes data, another processes it, and another serves it. They all need the same folder, not three different copies. This Compose file shows exactly how that wiring looks in practice:

```
version: '3.8'
services:
```

```
  uploader:
    image: uploader-service:latest
    volumes:
      - shared-data:/data/uploads
  processor:
    image: processor-service:latest
    volumes:
      - shared-data:/data/uploads
  frontend:
    image: frontend-service:latest
    volumes:
      - shared-data:/data/uploads

volumes:
  shared-data:
```

For Windows bind mounts, you would instead write the following:

```
volumes:
  - 'C:\\data\\uploads:/data/uploads'
```

This example demonstrates how Docker Compose can manage data pipelines efficiently, ensuring that each service operates on the same dataset without redundancy.

Think about a media company with three simple services: an uploader that grabs raw images, a processor that compresses them, and a publisher that sends them to a CDN. Each service touches exactly the same files, so the safest place to keep them is a shared volume. It means the raw image only exists once, the processor always sees the latest version, and the publisher never ends up serving half-complete output.

Here is a small Compose file you can run right now to see two containers using the same volume. One writes a file. The other reads it. Nothing complicated, just a clean demonstration of real data flow:

```
version: '3.8'
services:
  writer:
    image: alpine
    command: sh -c "echo 'pipeline demo' &gt; /data/pipeline.txt; sleep 1000"
    volumes:
      - shared:/data
```

```
  reader:
    image: alpine
    command: sh -c "sleep 3 && cat /data/pipeline.txt; sleep 1000"
    volumes:
      - shared:/data

volumes:
  shared:
```

Run it with the following:

```
docker compose up
```

This looks at the reader's logs. You should see the text the writer put in the shared volume. That is the simplest possible proof that shared volumes work across containers.

Backup and recovery strategies

If a volume holds anything you can't regenerate quickly, you have to assume it will eventually need to be restored. A bad deployment, a corrupted container, or a faulty script can wipe out data instantly. So, this section focuses on the workflows that let you recover fast when things break.

Think about an insurance team running a claims engine in Docker. Every container rebuild should be trivial, but the claims data itself cannot disappear. A bad deployment could wipe a whole day's worth of processed claims because the data lived inside the container rather than on a volume. By adopting a simple `tar`-based backup workflow with a nightly backup of the volume, restoring the service can become a five-minute job instead of a post-mortem.

Persistent data is only as reliable as your backup strategy. In enterprise scenarios, ensuring data integrity and availability is critical. Here's how to establish robust backup and recovery workflows:

- **Volume snapshots**: Use tools such as `docker volume inspect` to identify volume paths on the host and leverage filesystem snapshot tools (e.g., LVM or ZFS) to create backups. Snapshots provide a point-in-time copy of data, ensuring minimal disruption to active services.
- **Automated backups**: Automate the backup process using scripts or orchestration tools. This is the simplest possible backup workflow. It is not sophisticated, but it

works everywhere, even on Windows. The idea is to mount the volume into a temporary container and pack it up into a single archive you can store anywhere:

```
# Backup script
docker run --rm \
  -v my-volume:/volume-data \
  -v C:\backup:/backup \
  alpine \
  tar czf /backup/my-volume-backup.tar.gz /volume-data
```

- **Disaster recovery testing**: Regularly test your recovery procedures to identify gaps in your strategy. Backup processes are only as good as their ability to restore data under real-world conditions.
  The fastest way to back up a named volume is to mount it into a temporary container and pack it into a tarball. Same idea for restoring it. Here's how you'd do that on Windows:
  - Backup:

    ```
    docker run --rm ^
      -v my-vol:/vol ^
      -v C:\backup:/backup ^
      alpine ^
      tar czf /backup/my-vol.tar.gz /vol
    ```

  - Restore:

    ```
    docker run --rm ^
      -v my-vol:/vol ^
      -v C:\backup:/backup ^
      alpine ^
      tar xzf /backup/my-vol.tar.gz -C /vol
    ```

If this completes without errors, the volume has been restored to the exact state of the backup.

Securing persistent data

Data security is a paramount concern in any production environment. Here's how to ensure that your persistent data remains protected:

- **Restrict access**: Use Docker's `--read-only` flag to limit write access to containers where it isn't necessary. Additionally, leverage Linux file permissions to restrict unauthorized access on the host system.
- **Encrypt sensitive data**: Encrypt volumes using tools such as `dm-crypt` or by running encrypted filesystems within your containers. This adds an extra layer of security, particularly for sensitive applications such as finance or healthcare.
- **Monitor and audit**: Use Docker monitoring tools to track volume usage and detect unauthorized changes. Tools such as **Docker Scout** can provide additional insights into security vulnerabilities.

Despite best practices, issues can arise. Here's how to tackle common problems:

- **Volume not mounting**: Check your `docker-compose.yml` files or CLI commands for typos or misconfigurations. Use `docker volume ls` to confirm the volume exists.
- **Data inconsistencies**: If data appears corrupted, verify the health of the host filesystem. Tools such as `fsck` or journaling filesystems can help identify and resolve underlying disk issues.
- **Performance bottlenecks**: If volumes are slowing down application performance, consider moving data to faster storage devices or optimizing volume size through pruning.

Persistent data management is important in advanced Docker workflows, ensuring that your applications retain critical information across container life cycles. By mastering volumes, implementing robust backup strategies, and securing your data, you can build reliable and scalable systems tailored to the demands of modern software development.

Implementing and optimizing volume usage in complex workflows

Picture this: a senior engineer at a major e-commerce company is managing a microservices-based platform. The platform is running smoothly until a containerized service hosting critical product images is updated. After the update, the engineering team notices that half of the product images are missing, leaving customers frustrated and the company scrambling to recover data. The culprit? An improperly configured volume that failed to persist data between container updates.

This scenario illustrates why effectively implementing and optimizing Docker volumes is critical in complex workflows. For experienced engineers, the challenge isn't just creating volumes but integrating them into multi-container architectures while maintaining scalability, performance, and reliability.

Volumes are the backbone of persistent storage in Docker. They allow data to exist independently of containers, enabling seamless updates, scaling, and inter-container communication. In complex workflows, volumes serve multiple purposes:

- **Data sharing**: Facilitate communication between services, such as sharing logs or passing intermediate data between processing pipelines.
- **Persistence**: Store critical data such as databases, user uploads, or configuration files across container life cycles.
- **Scalability**: Ensure that data remains consistent and accessible as the system scales horizontally or vertically.

For senior engineers, leveraging volumes effectively in these workflows involves balancing simplicity, security, and performance. Let's discuss a few advanced volume implementation techniques in the following sections.

Using named volumes for modular workflows

Named volumes are an excellent choice for organizing data in modular applications. Their separation from the host system makes them ideal for portable, repeatable environments.

Consider a containerized pipeline with three services: data ingestion, processing, and reporting. Each service interacts with the same dataset via a shared volume:

```
version: '3.8'
services:
  ingestion:
    image: ingestion-service:latest
    volumes:
      - shared-data:/data
  processing:
    image: processing-service:latest
    volumes:
      - shared-data:/data
  reporting:
    image: reporting-service:latest
    volumes:
      - shared-data:/data
```

```
volumes:
  shared-data:
```

This Compose file defines a shared volume called `shared-data`, which all three services mount to the same path (`/data`). When the ingestion service drops files into that folder, the processing service can pick them up straight away, and the same for reporting.

Not only does this avoid the mess of transferring data between containers, but it also makes debugging so much easier; you know exactly where to look if something breaks.

Combining bind mounts with named volumes

In some cases, using both named volumes and bind mounts can provide flexibility. Bind mounts are particularly useful when specific host directories need to be integrated into the container environment.

For example, consider a scenario where a development team uses local configuration files stored on the host, while other data persists in a named volume:

```
services:
  app:
    image: app-service:latest
    volumes:
      - named-volume:/data
      - ./config:/app/config
volumes:
  named-volume:
```

This approach allows teams to rapidly iterate on configurations during development without altering the main application data.

Optimizing volume mount points

An efficient mount point configuration can significantly impact container performance. Here are a few best practices:

- **Segregate volumes by purpose**: Avoid mixing different types of data (e.g., logs and user uploads) in the same volume. This practice simplifies monitoring and troubleshooting.

- **Minimize write overheads**: For high-write operations, use `tmpfs` volumes to store ephemeral data in memory, reducing disk I/O bottlenecks.
- **Align with application behavior**: Ensure that volume locations align with the application's data expectations. For instance, a database container's volume should match its configured data directory.

When your application grows, it often makes sense to run multiple instances of the same service to handle increased traffic or to improve reliability. But once you do that, keeping data consistent across all containers becomes more of a challenge, especially when they all need to read from the same dataset.

Shared volumes for read-heavy workloads

Let's say you're running a dashboard that pulls together analytics reports. This dashboard is mostly reading data that's been generated elsewhere and rarely writes to the disk. In that case, you can scale horizontally by spinning up multiple replicas of the analytics service, all of which mount the same volume, but in read-only mode. That way, you avoid accidental changes to your core dataset.

Here's a simple Docker Compose example:

```
services:
  analytics:
    image: analytics-service:latest
    deploy:
      replicas: 3
    volumes:
      - shared-data:/data:ro

volumes:
  shared-data:
```

This configuration runs three instances of the analytics service, all accessing the same shared volume at `/data` in read-only mode. You'd run this in a Swarm or Kubernetes context, where the `deploy.replicas` setting can actually take effect.

By keeping the volume read-only (the `:ro` bit of the Docker Compose file), you reduce the risk of write conflicts and protect your critical data. This setup works well for content delivery systems, documentation sites, or anything with high read demand and low write activity.

Replication strategies for write-heavy workloads

Write-heavy services such as databases or log processors need a bit more care. If multiple containers are trying to write to the same volume at the same time, things can go sideways fast. That's where replication strategies come in.

One common approach is a primary-replica setup:

- The primary handles all writes
- The replicas sync from the primary and serve read-only traffic

Here's a simple Docker Compose example using a PostgreSQL database with replication:

```
version: '3.8'
services:
  db-primary:
    image: postgres:latest
    environment:
      - POSTGRES_USER=admin
      - POSTGRES_PASSWORD=secret
    volumes:
      - db-data:/var/lib/postgresql/data
  db-replica:
    image: postgres:latest
    environment:
      - POSTGRES_USER=replica
      - POSTGRES_PASSWORD=secret
    - POSTGRES_REPLICATION_ROLE=replica
     - POSTGRES_PRIMARY_HOST=db-primary
    depends_on:
      - db-primary
volumes:
  db-data:
```

> **Note**
>
> This is a simplified setup. Real-world replication requires proper replication configs, user roles, and connection strings. This approach ensures that you avoid write conflicts and can scale your read operations across replicas, all while keeping your core dataset safe.

Volumes can be a huge help when you're building and testing containerized applications as part of your CI/CD pipeline. One of their most powerful use cases is caching, particularly when your builds are large or your dependencies take a while to install.

Caching build artifacts

Let's say you've got a service that needs to compile code, install packages, or generate assets. Rather than rebuilding these from scratch with every pipeline run, you can mount a volume to cache those outputs.

Here's how that might look in a Docker Compose setup:

```
services:
  builder:
    image: builder-image:latest
    volumes:
      - build-cache:/cache
      - ./source:/source

volumes:
  build-cache:
```

Let's break down this example:

- `build-cache` stores the compiled files or installed dependencies
- `./source` is your actual source code mounted into the container
- On subsequent builds, anything in `/cache` is already there, speeding up the process significantly

This kind of setup is really useful in local dev environments and in CI systems such as GitHub Actions, GitLab CI, or Jenkins when paired with a persistent workspace or volume management plugin.

Testing persistent data scenarios

Volumes also come in handy when you're testing how your application behaves with real-world data. Instead of running tests against an empty database or blank filesystem, you can preload a volume with sample or anonymized production data.

For example, in your testing step, you might mount a volume that already contains the following:

- A database dump with realistic user activity
- Log files your app expects to parse
- Cached config or data files

This ensures that your tests cover edge cases that only crop up with actual data in place.

You can even swap in different prepopulated volumes, depending on what you're testing: one for high-load scenarios, one for missing files, and so on.

> **Tip**
>
> You can create these test volumes ahead of time using `docker run` and `docker cp`, or use bind mounts pointing to a local `test-data` directory under version control.

Monitoring and optimizing volume usage

Once your containers are up and running in production, it's easy to forget about what's happening under the hood, especially with volumes. But over time, unused volumes and bloated data directories can quietly eat up disk space and slow things down. Here's how to keep things tidy and efficient.

Volume pruning

Docker doesn't automatically delete unused volumes when you remove containers. If you're running lots of short-lived containers as in CI pipelines, you'll quickly accumulate volumes you no longer need.

You can clean these up with the following terminal command:

```
docker volume prune
```

This is, without a doubt, my favorite command; it removes *only* volumes not currently used by any container. It's safe to run regularly as part of a maintenance script or manual check-in.

Here is the example output:

```
$ docker volume prune

WARNING! This will remove all local volumes not used by at least one container.
Are you sure you want to continue? [y/N] y

Deleted Volumes:
my_old_volume1
temp_data_volume
unused_cache

Total reclaimed space: 45.3MB
```

Figure 3.2: Cleaning up orphaned volumes with docker volume prune

Monitoring disk usage

To get a snapshot of how much space your volumes (and other Docker objects) are taking up, use the following terminal command:

```
docker system df
```

This command breaks down disk usage by images, containers, and volumes, helping you spot anything unusually large or unexpected. If one volume is significantly larger than the others, it might be time to dig in.

Here is the example output:

```
$ docker system df

TYPE            TOTAL     ACTIVE    SIZE       RECLAIMABLE
Images          5         2         1.73GB     1.10GB (3 unused)
Containers      4         1         305.3MB    250.1MB (3 stopped)
Local Volumes   6         3         912.7MB    420.4MB (3 unused)
Build Cache     8         0         1.02GB     1.02GB
```

Figure 3.3: Using docker system df to see how much space images, containers, volumes, and build cache are consuming

Profile volume performance

In high-performance systems, the speed of your volume I/O can make or break the app experience:

- Slow read/write speeds can delay file uploads or data processing jobs
- Overloaded disk I/O can bottleneck analytics dashboards or report generation

Use tools such as `iostat`, `iotop`, or even built-in Docker metrics (via monitoring platforms such as **Prometheus**, **Grafana**, or **cAdvisor**) to benchmark performance under realistic workloads.

On Windows, it's better to lean on native tooling rather than Linux-only commands. Tools such as **Resource Monitor**, **Performance Monitor**, and **Get-Process/Get-Counter** in PowerShell give you a clearer picture of disk activity when a volume is under load. You can still drop into WSL and use `iotop` or `iostat` if you want low-level Linux metrics, but your primary checks should be Windows-based.

Try simulating your most common operations, uploads, reads, and data processing, and observe how the volume handles it. If latency is high, consider switching volume drivers or offloading heavy workloads to another container.

Advanced backup and recovery solutions for Docker volumes

In 2022, a fintech start-up faced a near-catastrophic failure during a routine container upgrade. A misstep in their deployment script resulted in their primary application container being replaced without preserving its volume data. The customer database, holding months of transaction history, was wiped out. Fortunately, they had implemented a robust backup strategy the week prior. Within minutes, they restored their system, avoiding what could have been a devastating data loss incident.

For senior Docker engineers, scenarios like these highlight the importance of reliable backup and recovery strategies. Volumes are often home to the most critical data, and safeguarding them is not just best practice; it's a non-negotiable responsibility.

While containers themselves are ephemeral, the data they rely on often isn't. Persistent storage solutions such as Docker volumes are foundational to containerized applications, but they are not immune to risks such as hardware failures, human errors, or malicious attacks.

Backup and recovery strategies ensure the following:

- **Data integrity**: Safeguard against corruption or accidental deletion
- **Business continuity**: Minimize downtime and ensure seamless recovery during outages
- **Compliance**: Meet regulatory requirements for data protection and retention

In enterprise-grade systems, failing to implement robust volume backup practices can result in significant operational and reputational damage.

Understanding Docker volume backup options

Docker provides several methods to back up and restore volumes. Selecting the right method depends on the size, type, and criticality of your data.

Earlier in this chapter, the *Backup and recovery strategies* section walked through the complete workflow for backing up and restoring Docker volumes on Windows, including the `tar`-based approach, the restore flow, and the practical considerations for WSL 2. Rather than duplicate those commands again, treat that section as the authoritative reference for the hands-on steps. What follows here focuses only on the different backup options available, when to choose each one, and how they fit into real workflows:

- **Using volume snapshot tools**: Snapshots capture the state of a volume at a specific point in time, making them ideal for minimizing downtime during backups. Tools such as ZFS, LVM, or third-party solutions can integrate with Docker. Here's an example workflow with LVM snapshots:

    1. Identify the volume path on the host using `docker volume inspect`.
    2. Create an LVM snapshot of the `volume` directory.
    3. Back up the snapshot to external storage.

    ```
    lvcreate --size 1G --snapshot --name my-snapshot /dev/my-volume
    tar czf backup.tar.gz /dev/my-volume/my-snapshot
    ```

    Pros: Efficient for large-scale environments, as snapshots are nearly instantaneous.

    Cons: Requires integration with underlying host storage systems.

    > **Note**
    >
    > Windows Docker Desktop does not expose LVM, ZFS, or Linux block device paths. These snapshot workflows apply only when Docker runs on a native Linux host. On Windows, snapshotting volume data must be done via backup archives or host-level filesystem tools outside WSL.

- **Leveraging backup services in orchestration tools**: If you use container orchestration platforms like Kubernetes or Docker Swarm, built-in tools can streamline backups. Kubernetes, for example, integrates with tools like Velero for volume snapshots and restoration. Here's an example of using Velero with Kubernetes:

    1. Install **Velero** in your cluster.

2. Use Velero to create persistent volume backups:

```
velero backup create my-backup --include-
resources=persistentvolumeclaims
```

3. Store backups in a remote object storage service (e.g., **Amazon S3**).

Pros: Highly automated and scalable for dynamic environments.

Cons: Requires additional setup and orchestration platform integration.

Automating volume backups

Automating backups removes the need to remember them manually and reduces the risk of losing critical data due to human error. Here are two common approaches.

Scheduling backups with cron jobs

Use `cron` to schedule regular backups using the Docker CLI and a simple script:

```
#!/bin/bash
timestamp=$(date +%Y%m%d-%H%M%S)
docker run --rm \
  -v my-volume:/volume-data \
  -v /backup:/backup \
  alpine \
  tar czf /backup/my-volume-backup-$timestamp.tar.gz /volume-data
```

This script spins up a temporary container, mounts the target volume and a backup directory, and creates a timestamped archive of the volume.

Then, we can schedule it using `cron` (e.g., daily at 2 AM):

```
0 2 * * * /path/to/backup-script.sh
```

Pros: Simple, low-cost, and reliable for small setups.

Cons: Harder to manage as the number of volumes or backup schedules grows.

Using backup tools with Docker integration

For more robust setups, tools such as **Restic**, **Duplicati**, or **Bacula** offer encryption, deduplication, and incremental backups, ideal for production workloads.

Here is an example using Restic:

1. Initialize a backup repo using the following:

```
restic init -r /backup/restic-repo
```

2. Back up a volume:

```
restic backup -r /backup/restic-repo /var/lib/docker/volumes/my-volume
```

This assumes that you're backing up directly from the Docker volume path on the host. Restic will track changes and optimize storage through incremental backups.

Pros: Feature-rich, secure, and scalable.

Cons: Slightly more setup time and overhead.

Recovery strategies

Having backups is only part of the solution. Recovery workflows must be tested and optimized for quick turnaround times:

- **Restoring from a backup archive**: Restore using the compressed archive created earlier in the *Scheduling backups with cron jobs* section:

```
docker run --rm \
  -v my-volume:/volume-data \
  -v C:\backup:/backup \
  alpine \
  tar xzf /backup/my-volume-backup.tar.gz -C /volume-data
```

What happens here? A temporary Alpine container mounts the backup volume (`my-volume`) and a local directory (in this example, `C:\backup`) where the backup archive lives. It then extracts the `.tar.gz` file back into the volume, restoring its original contents.

- **Recovering snapshots**: For LVM or ZFS-based backups, activate the snapshot and copy its contents back to the volume path:

```
lvconvert --merge /dev/my-volume/my-snapshot
```

This command replaces the current state of the volume with the contents of the snapshot. You'll typically need to unmount the volume first, and in some cases, a system reboot might be required to complete the merge, especially if the volume is in active use.

- **Testing your recovery plan**: Regularly validate your recovery process in a staging environment. Simulate scenarios such as data corruption or accidental deletion to identify potential gaps in your strategy.

Before we end the section, let's look at a few best practices for volume backup and recovery:

- **Redundancy**: Store backups in multiple locations, including cloud storage, to protect against regional disasters.
- **Incremental backups**: Use tools that support incremental backups to minimize storage requirements and speed up the backup process.
- **Encryption**: Always encrypt sensitive data in transit and at rest to prevent unauthorized access.
- **Documentation**: Maintain clear documentation of your backup and recovery procedures so that all team members can follow them in case of emergencies.

By implementing these advanced backup and recovery solutions, you can safeguard critical Docker volume data and ensure seamless recovery in any situation.

Cross-container data sharing strategies for enterprise use

A logistics company running a global shipping network hit a snag: their containerized apps, each handling parts of the shipment tracking system, needed real-time access to the same data. At first, the team took the straightforward route and gave each container its own copy of the data. It worked, sort of, but it also led to sync issues, wasted storage, and inconsistent results.

The fix? A properly thought-out shared volume setup. It allowed containers to read from and write to the same dataset without duplication, streamlining performance and cutting down on complexity.

This kind of setup really shows how vital smart data-sharing strategies are, especially in enterprise systems where performance, reliability, and scale all matter. In this section, we'll look at how you can use Docker volumes and advanced sharing techniques to keep containers in sync and your architecture clean.

Understanding cross-container data sharing

At its core, cross-container data sharing involves enabling multiple containers to access and manipulate the same dataset.

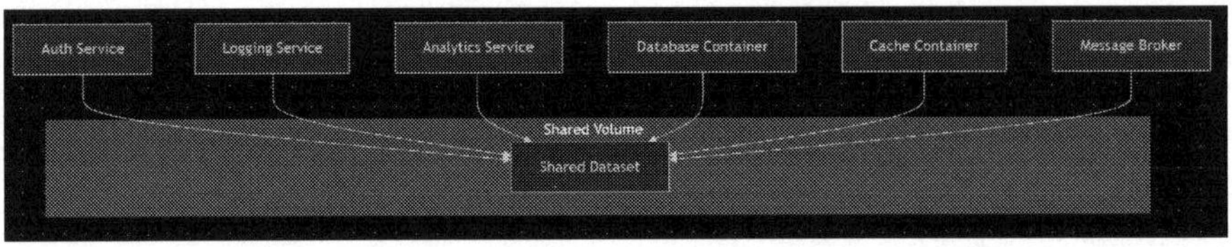

Figure 3.4: Multiple services consuming the same shared dataset through a shared volume

This is essential for many enterprise workflows, including the following:

- **Microservices communication**: Allowing services such as authentication, logging, and analytics to share data without redundancy.
- **Data pipelines**: Enabling sequential processing where one service generates data and another consumes it.
- **Stateful applications**: Providing shared storage for applications such as databases, caches, and message brokers.

The goal is to implement solutions that balance accessibility with performance, ensuring enterprise-grade reliability.

Let's look at a few options for sharing data to understand the concept better:

- **Named volumes for persistent and shared data**: Named volumes are the most straightforward approach to sharing data between containers. They are managed by Docker, abstracting the storage details while maintaining data persistence across container life cycles.
  Imagine an enterprise setup where multiple services generate logs. Instead of each service maintaining its own isolated logs, a shared volume can centralize them:

```
version: '3.8'
services:
  service_a:
    image: service-a:latest
    volumes:
      - shared-logs:/var/log/app
  service_b:
    image: service-b:latest
    volumes:
      - shared-logs:/var/log/app

volumes:
  shared-logs:
```

Advantages include the following:

  - Simplifies data management by centralizing storage
  - Maintains data consistency across services

Ensure proper permissions to avoid conflicts between containers writing to the same files.

> Note
>
> **Note for Windows**
>
> Inside a container, paths always use Linux syntax (e.g., `/app/data`). Only host-side paths follow Windows conventions.

- **Bind mounts for host-specific integrations**: For scenarios requiring direct interaction with the host system, bind mounts provide a powerful alternative. These mounts map a host directory to a container, enabling cross-container data sharing via the host filesystem.
  Consider a situation where multiple containers need access to dynamically updated configuration files stored on the host:

```
version: '3.8'
services:
  service_a:
    image: service-a:latest
    volumes:
      - /host/config:/app/config
  service_b:
    image: service-b:latest
    volumes:
      - /host/config:/app/config
```

  The main advantage is the flexibility to integrate host-level updates seamlessly.

  Note, though, that bind mounts are less portable and can introduce security risks if improperly managed.

- **tmpfs volumes for high-performance temporary storage**: `tmpfs` volumes store data in memory rather than on disk, making them ideal for temporary, high-speed data sharing between containers. These are especially useful in applications requiring fast read/write access without long-term persistence.

A caching service and a data processing service can share temporary datasets in memory using a `tmpfs` volume:

```
version: '3.8'
services:
  caching_service:
    image: caching-service:latest
    volumes:
      - type: tmpfs
        target: /cache
  processing_service:
    image: processing-service:latest
    volumes:
      - type: tmpfs
        target: /cache
```

The main advantage is its extremely fast data access. However, data is lost if the container stops or crashes.

Now that we've covered the fundamentals of sharing data across containers, let's look at how to apply those concepts in more complex, real-world setups.

Implementing advanced sharing scenarios

Whether you're dealing with things such as financial systems, content platforms, or anything in between, advanced sharing strategies can help keep your services aligned, efficient, and reliable. Let's look at a few options:

- **Managing shared data across multiple services**: In enterprise systems, it's common for several services to rely on a central dataset. Take a financial platform, for example, transaction processing, reporting, and compliance services might all need access to the same customer data.
  To implement this, define a shared volume in your `docker-compose.yml` file and mount it into each relevant container:

```
volumes:
  shared-data:

services:
  processor:
    volumes:
      - shared-data:/data
```

```
  reporter:
    volumes:
      - shared-data:/data:ro
```

- **Enabling data synchronization**: For real-time applications, data synchronization across containers is crucial. Implement file watchers or synchronization tools, such as **inotify**, to propagate changes instantly to all dependent services.
  You can enable this by running a lightweight file-watcher inside the container, for example, using an `inotify` loop that listens for changes in the mounted directory and triggers whatever update logic your service needs.

  An example is a content delivery system where uploaded media files are processed and served to end users. A shared volume ensures that processing and web-serving services operate on the same dataset without delays.

Optimizing performance in data sharing

When working with containerized applications at scale, poor data sharing strategies can quickly become a bottleneck. To maintain high performance and reliability, especially in enterprise environments, it's essential to make thoughtful decisions around storage and workload isolation. Here are two key strategies to consider:

- **Choosing the right storage backend**: In enterprise environments, the storage backend significantly impacts performance. For named volumes, options such as **NFS**, **Ceph**, or **GlusterFS** can provide scalable, high-availability solutions. Evaluate storage backends based on the following:
  - **I/O throughput requirements**: Assess the volume and frequency of data being read or written to ensure that the backend can handle peak loads without introducing latency or bottlenecks.
  - **Redundancy and fault tolerance**: Choose a backend that supports replication or high-availability configurations to minimize downtime and protect against data loss during hardware or network failures.
  - **Integration with existing infrastructure**: Evaluate how well the storage solution aligns with your current environment, including compatibility with on-premises systems, cloud services, and security or compliance requirements.
- **Isolating read-heavy and write-heavy operations**: Read-heavy and write-heavy workloads often have conflicting requirements. Isolate these operations into separate volumes or directories within a shared volume to prevent contention.

For example, you can store frequently accessed read-only data in a dedicated directory within a shared volume. Write-heavy operations can use a separate directory or another volume entirely.

Security and troubleshooting

When sharing data across containers, security must remain a top priority:

- **Restrict access**: Use container-specific user permissions and mount options (e.g., `:ro` for read-only) to control data access and prevent unintended modifications.
- **Encrypt sensitive data**: Encrypt volumes using tools such as **Linux Unified Key Setup** (**LUKS**) or integrate encrypted filesystems such as **eCryptfs** or **EncFS** within containers to safeguard sensitive information at rest.
- **Monitor activity**: Implement monitoring tools such as **Auditd** or **Falco** to detect unusual access patterns, permission changes, or potential breaches in real time.

Even with a well-designed data sharing strategy, issues can arise that disrupt container performance or cause data inconsistencies. Here are some of the most common problems and how to address them:

- **Volume access conflicts**: If containers experience conflicts accessing shared data, verify the following:
  - Permissions and ownership of the volume on the host system
  - Mount options (e.g., read-only vs. read-write)
- **Data synchronization delays**: For bind-mounted directories, ensure that host filesystem updates propagate correctly. Tools such as **lsyncd** can help synchronize files between the host and containers in real time.

By implementing these advanced cross-container data-sharing strategies, you can optimize enterprise workflows, enhance data consistency, and ensure scalable, reliable applications in production environments.

Root cause analysis and fixes for volume management issues

A senior engineer at a growing SaaS company received an urgent alert: application logs critical for debugging issues were missing. Everything seemed fine on the surface; the containers were running, the services were responsive, and no errors were reported. After hours of troubleshooting, the team discovered the issue: a misconfigured Docker volume. The logs were being written to a temporary directory inside the container rather than the intended persistent volume, causing them to disappear when the container restarted.

Stories like these highlight how volume mismanagement can lead to unexpected challenges, even for experienced engineers.

Volumes are indispensable for managing persistent data, but they are not without their challenges. Let's explore some common issues and their underlying causes:

- **Volumes not mounting correctly**: Containers fail to access the intended volume, often resulting in errors or data being written to an unintended location.
- **Data corruption**: Unexpected power failures, hardware issues, or race conditions during concurrent writes can lead to corrupted files in a volume.
- **Performance bottlenecks**: Poorly configured volumes can degrade application performance, particularly under heavy I/O workloads.
- **Volume orphaning**: Unused volumes accumulate over time, consuming disk space and complicating system management.
- **Access conflicts**: Multiple containers accessing the same volume without proper permissions or synchronization can lead to errors or inconsistent data.

Each of these issues requires a systematic approach to identify the root cause and apply an effective fix. In this section, we'll focus on identifying the root causes of common volume-related issues and implementing practical fixes to ensure robust volume management in complex Docker environments.

Root cause analysis techniques

Most persistent data issues come down to something small: a wrong path, a missing folder, or a container writing to a location you did not expect. This section shows a structured way to debug these problems instead of guessing. So, when containers fail to access shared volumes correctly, it's often due to subtle configuration issues. Performing a structured root cause analysis helps identify misconfigurations and prevent recurring problems. Start by reviewing how your volumes are defined and connected within your Docker environment:

- **Reviewing volume configuration**: The first step in resolving volume issues is to examine how the volume is configured in your Docker setup. Use the following tools and commands:
  - **Inspecting volume details**: The `docker volume inspect` command provides detailed information about a volume's configuration, including its mount point, driver, and usage:

    ```
    docker volume inspect my-volume
    ```

On Windows, the `Mountpoint` field will usually show a path inside the WSL 2 VM, such as `\\wsl.localhost\docker-desktop-data\data\docker\volumes\my-volume\_data`.

Look for mismatches between the expected configuration and the actual settings, such as incorrect mount paths or missing drivers.

  - **Validating docker-compose.yml files**: Misconfigurations in Docker Compose files can often lead to volumes not mounting as expected. For instance, check for typos or incorrectly specified relative paths:

    ```
    volumes:
      - ./data:/app/data
    ```

- **Monitoring file access patterns**: For issues such as performance bottlenecks or access conflicts, tools such as `iotop` or `lsof` can help identify which processes are accessing the volume and how.
  For example, if a volume is slowing down your application, run `iotop` on the host to monitor I/O operations and identify potential bottlenecks:

  ```
  iotop -o
  ```

  Check for high disk activity caused by competing container processes.

Once you know how to diagnose a broken volume, the next step is applying the correct fix. These are the repairs you will use constantly in production when things start behaving strangely.

Fixes for common volume issues

Volume-related problems can cause disruptions ranging from minor access errors to serious data corruption and performance degradation. This section outlines practical solutions for the most frequent volume issues encountered in containerized environments, covering everything from mount errors and data integrity to access conflicts and cleanup strategies:

- **Fixing volume mount errors**: Volume mount errors often stem from incorrect configuration or insufficient permissions. Here's how to resolve them:
  - **Verify directory permissions**: Ensure that the user running the container has the necessary permissions on the host directory. Use `chmod` to adjust permissions if needed:

    ```
    chmod -R 755 ./data
    ```

    The Windows equivalent would be the following:

    ```
    icacls C:\data /grant Everyone:(OI)(CI)F
    ```

  - **Ensure absolute paths for bind mounts**: Always use absolute paths in `docker-compose.yml` files to avoid relative path mismatches.

    This is incorrect:

    ```
    volumes:
      - data:/app/data
    ```

    This is correct:

    ```
    volumes:
      - /absolute/path/to/data:/app/data
    ```

    The Windows equivalent would be the following:

    ```
    C:\absolute\path\to\data:/app/data
    ```

- **Addressing data corruption**: Data corruption is one of the most critical issues in volume management. Here's how to mitigate and recover from it:
  - **Use journaling filesystems**: On the host system, opt for filesystems such as `ext4` or `XFS` with journaling features to reduce the risk of corruption during unexpected shutdowns.

  - **Enable application-level write buffers**: For databases or similar applications, enable **write-ahead logging (WAL)** to protect against partial writes.
  - **Backup and restore**: If corruption occurs, restore data from the most recent backup. For example, use a tarball to restore a volume:

```
docker run --rm \
  -v my-volume:/volume-data \
  -v C:\backup:/backup \
  alpine \
  tar xzf /backup/my-volume-backup.tar.gz -C /volume-data
```

- **Resolving performance bottlenecks**: Performance issues are often caused by high I/O demands or misaligned storage backends. Try these optimizations:
  - **Upgrade storage backends**: Switch to faster storage options such as SSDs or **network-attached storage (NAS)** solutions for high-demand applications.
  - **Optimize volume mount options**: Use `:delegated` or `:cached` options to improve performance for volumes where immediate consistency is not required:

```
volumes:
  - /data:/app/data:delegated
```

    On Windows, the `:delegated` and `:cached` mount options are not supported on Docker Desktop. These options apply only to macOS bind mounts.

  - **Separate workloads**: Isolate read-heavy and write-heavy operations into different volumes to minimize contention.
- **Managing orphaned volumes**: Unused volumes can accumulate over time, consuming valuable disk space. To address this, you can do the following:
  - **Prune unused volumes**: Regularly run `docker volume prune` to remove unused volumes. Short-lived containers tend to leave volumes behind. In a busy development environment, this adds up quickly. Cleaning these out is low effort and keeps disk usage predictable:

```
docker volume prune
```

Docker removes only volumes that are not attached to any container. It is safe, and it keeps things tidy.

- **Audit volume usage**: Use `docker system df` to identify volumes consuming significant space and evaluate their necessity:

```
docker system df -v
```

On Windows, the output will reflect WSL 2-managed volume paths rather than native `C:\` folders.

- **Handling access conflicts**: When multiple containers access the same volume, conflicts can arise if permissions or synchronization mechanisms are not properly configured. Address this by doing the following:
  - **Restrict write access**: Use read-only mounts for containers that only need to read data:

```
volumes:
  - /data:/app/data:ro
```

  - **Implement file locks**: Use application-level file locking to prevent race conditions during concurrent writes.
  - **Leverage NFS or shared storage solutions**: For distributed environments, configure shared storage solutions such as NFS with proper access controls.

Before you go chasing your tail, check whether Docker is even mounting the volume you think it is. These two commands tell you a lot:

```
docker volume ls
docker volume inspect my-vol
```

If you are on Windows, pay attention to the `Mountpoint` field. It will point into the WSL 2 filesystem, not `C:`. And if you suspect slow I/O, you can check disk activity through WSL:

```
wsl.exe iotop -o
```

If a container is thrashing the volume, you will see it instantly.

Proactive measures for volume management

Preventative measures can minimize the likelihood of encountering volume-related issues:

- **Standardize configuration practices**: Use templates or predefined configurations for Docker Compose files to ensure consistency across environments.
- **Monitor and alert**: Set up monitoring tools such as Prometheus or the ELK stack to track volume usage and trigger alerts for anomalies.
- **Test recovery scenarios**: Regularly simulate failure scenarios to validate the effectiveness of your fixes and recovery strategies.

By applying these root cause analysis techniques and fixes, you can ensure reliable and efficient volume management in your Docker environments while minimizing downtime and disruptions.

> **Note**
>
> On Docker Desktop for Windows, named volumes live inside WSL 2, and bind mounts always require fully qualified Windows paths such as `C:\data`.

The Big Lab: Adding persistence to the Notes service

Let's go back to the big lab. Now that the Notes service is up and running, it's time to make it actually remember things. At the moment, the API returns a fixed message and forgets everything the moment the container disappears. In this step, we give the service a place to store real data. Nothing fancy yet. Just a simple volume mounted into the API container so notes survive container rebuilds. This becomes the foundation for everything we do in the next few chapters:

1. **Create a folder on Windows for the data**: We want a clean place for the Notes service to persist its files.

   ```
   mkdir C:\notes-data
   ```

   This folder will become the `/data` directory inside the container.

2. **Update the API so it can read and write notes**: Replace your current `app.py` file with this version:

```
from flask import Flask, request, jsonify
import json, os


app = Flask(__name__)
DATA_FILE = "/data/notes.json"

@app.get("/notes")
def get_notes():
if not os.path.exists(DATA_FILE):
     return jsonify([])
with open(DATA_FILE, "r") as f:
     return jsonify(json.load(f))

@app.post("/notes")
def add_note():
    payload = request.json
    note = payload.get("note")
    notes = []
    if os.path.exists(DATA_FILE):
       with open(DATA_FILE, "r") as f:
           notes = json.load(f)
    notes.append(note)
    with open(DATA_FILE, "w") as f:
       json.dump(notes, f)
    return {"status": "ok", "count": len(notes)}

if name == "__main__":
    app.run(host="0.0.0.0", port=5000)
```

   This gives the service two endpoints: one to list notes and one to add them.

3. **Rebuild the image**:

```
docker build -t notes-api .
```

4. **Run the Notes service with a bind mount**: We attach the Windows folder to `/data` inside the container:

```
docker run -d ^
  --name notes-api ^
  -p 5001:5000 ^
  -v C:\notes-data:/data ^
  notes-api
```

If this starts cleanly, the container now has a persistent storage location.

5. **Add a test note**:

```
curl -X POST http://localhost:5001/notes ^
  -H "Content-Type: application/json" ^
  -d "{\"note\": \"first saved note\"}"
```

You should receive a small JSON response with the number of notes stored.

6. **Check that the note survived a container rebuild**:

    - Stop and remove the container:

    ```
    docker rm -f notes-api
    ```

    - Start it again:

    ```
    docker run -d ^
      --name notes-api ^
      -p 5001:5000 ^
      -v C:\notes-data:/data ^
      notes-api
    ```

    - Now, check the list of notes:

    ```
    curl http://localhost:5001/notes
    ```

You should see the note you added earlier. That confirms that the persistence is working as intended. The folder on Windows is now the permanent home for the Notes service data, no matter how many times the container is rebuilt or replaced.

Summary

At this point, you have everything you need to keep data stable, move it between containers, and recover it when things go wrong. We've covered a lot of ground in this chapter, digging into the practical side of managing persistent data in Docker. From picking the right storage backend to dealing with permissions, sharing data across containers, and recovering from the unexpected, we've focused on what actually helps in real environments, not just what sounds good on a whiteboard.

You've now got a solid toolkit to build workflows that are stable, secure, and scalable. We've looked at how to keep things running smoothly, how to fix common volume issues, and how to make sure your setup doesn't fall apart the moment you scale or something goes sideways.

Next up, we'll take things a step further by looking at how to orchestrate multi-container applications so you can start thinking in systems, not just services.

Get This Book's PDF Version and Exclusive Extras

Part 2

Advanced Docker Techniques on Windows

In this part, you will move beyond single containers and into setups that reflect real development and production environments. You'll define multi-container applications with Docker Compose, secure images and containers using Windows-focused best practices, and tune CPU, memory, and performance for Docker running on WSL 2. This part also introduces the Docker GenAI stack on Windows and shows how AI workloads fit into a Windows-based container workflow. By the end of this part, you'll be running more complex, secure, and performance-aware Docker stacks with confidence.

This part includes the following chapters:

- *Chapter 4, Orchestrating Multi-Container Applications with Docker Compose*
- *Chapter 5, Docker Security and Best Practices on Windows*
- *Chapter 6, Optimizing Docker for Performance on Windows*
- *Chapter 7, Docker GenAI Stack on Windows*

4

Orchestrating Multi-Container Applications with Docker Compose

Once you start building real-world applications with Docker, it doesn't take long before a single container just isn't enough. You've got a backend, a database, maybe a queue, a cache, and some workers, and suddenly you're trying to keep half a dozen services running in sync. This chapter is all about making that setup manageable. We'll start by introducing Docker Compose and how it simplifies running multi-container apps. Then, we'll define what a complete environment looks like, walk through running Compose apps smoothly on Windows, and explore how to handle dependencies cleanly. At the end, we'll wrap up with some best practices to help keep your setup tidy, flexible, and production-friendly.

The following main topics are covered:

- Understanding Docker Compose
- Defining multi-container environments
- Going beyond the default network
- Running Docker Compose applications on Windows
- Managing dependencies with Compose
- Best practices for multi-container orchestration

Let's begin!

Technical requirements

You'll need a Windows machine (Pro, Enterprise, or Home) with hardware virtualization enabled, at least 8 GB of RAM (16 GB is recommended for bigger stacks), a modern four-core CPU, and 10 GB or more of free SSD space. Install the latest version of Docker Desktop for Windows with the WSL 2 backend, along with a working WSL 2 setup running a supported Linux distribution such as Ubuntu 20.04 LTS or later.

Before we get into Compose, it's worth making sure your Windows setup is actually running the stack you think it is. Most of the weird behavior people hit comes from WSL 2 not being enabled properly or Docker Desktop falling back to the wrong engine. Run through this quick checklist now and you'll save yourself an hour of head-scratching later:

- Check that WSL is actually running in Version 2 mode by running `wsl --status` and confirming that it reports `Default Version: 2`.
- List your installed distros with `wsl -l -v` and make sure your Ubuntu environment is running Version 2, not Version 1.
- Open your BIOS or UEFI settings and confirm hardware virtualization (VT-x or AMD-V) is turned on, because Docker will not behave properly without it.
- In Docker Desktop, go to **Settings** | **Resources** and give Docker at least four CPUs and 8 GB RAM so your containers have enough room to run. You could do this at point of me writing but please bear in mind a future version of Docker Desktop might disable this but it's most likely somewhere else if I have a dig around.
- Still in Docker Desktop, open **Settings** | **General** and make sure the option to use the WSL 2-based engine is enabled.
- In PowerShell, run `docker --version` and `docker compose version` to confirm that Docker and Compose are installed correctly and responding.

If everything in that list checks out, the rest of this chapter will behave exactly the way it should. Now we can start working with Compose without fighting the environment.

The code files referenced in this chapter are available at `https://github.com/PacktPublishing/Mastering-Docker-on-Windows`.

Understanding Docker Compose

A few years back, I helped a team ship a training portal that started life as a single API in a container. Two weeks later, we had a frontend, a PostgreSQL database, Redis for sessions, a little auth service someone knocked together over coffee, and a background worker chewing through email jobs. Every morning began with a copy-paste ritual of `docker run` commands, and every morning, someone missed a flag. Cue half an hour of "why can't the worker see the database again?"

That's where Compose earned its keep.

In this chapter, we'll build a realistic "Bookings" stack and keep that example with us the whole way. We'll see how a single Compose file turns that pile of moving parts into one repeatable command on Windows, how to layer dev versus prod configs cleanly, how to scale services for concurrency, and how to tame networking, health, and startup timing so it feels deliberate rather than duct-taped.

Feel free to skip over the following sections if you're more than familiar with what Docker Compose actually is; I'll catch you up in the Bookings example we'll reuse throughout this chapter. However, as I've mentioned before, the basics are always worth a quick refresher.

> **Note**
>
> Before we start wiring services together, make sure Docker Compose is actually installed and responding on your machine. Run this in PowerShell:
>
> ```
> docker compose version
> ```
>
> If it prints the version number without errors, you're good. If it fails, Docker Desktop isn't set up correctly yet, and nothing in this chapter will behave the way it should.

What is Docker Compose?

Now, at its core, Docker Compose is a tool for defining and running multi-container Docker applications using a single YAML file.

Rather than writing out multiple `docker run` commands manually, you can declare all of your services in one place, including their networks, volumes, environment variables, build context, and dependencies, and run them all with one simple command on the terminal:

```
docker compose up
```

This takes care of everything for you, and that's the big win: simplicity and reproducibility. You'll start to see the containers being pulled down from the repository and whirring to life. If your setup includes more than one container, Compose is almost always a better way to manage it.

It's also great for local development. You can run a full stack with just a single file in version control; no setup scripts, no configuration drift.

Now that Compose V2 is fully integrated into Docker Desktop, you don't need to install anything extra; it's already there and ready to use.

The structure of a Compose file

Let's break down what a basic `docker-compose.yml` file looks like:

```
version: "3.9"
services:
  app:
    image: node:18
    volumes:
      - .:/app
    working_dir: /app
    command: ["npm", "start"]
    ports:
      - "3000:3000"
```

This file defines a single service called app using the official Node.js image. It mounts your local directory, sets the working directory inside the container, runs `npm start`, and maps port `3000` from the container to the host.

Let's walk through the parts:

- `version` tells Compose which format you're using. 3.9 is fine for most modern setups.
- `services` contains the list of containers you want to run.
- each service has its own config: `image`, `ports`, `volumes`, `environment`, and so on.

We'll go deeper into defining multiple services later. For now, let's just get something running:

1. Start by creating a new file called `docker-compose.yml` in your project directory. Paste the following into your editor of choice (VS Code, Notepad, etc.):

   ```
   version: "3.9"
   services:
   ```

```
app:
  image: nginx:latest
  ports:
    - "8080:80"
```

Save the file as `docker-compose.yaml` (or `.yml`, they do the same), then from the same directory, run the following:

```
docker compose up
```

This will do the following:

- Pull the `nginx` image if it's not already available
- Start a container called `app`
- Forward port `8080` on your machine to port `80` inside the container

2. Open a browser and go to `http://localhost:8080` you should see the Nginx welcome page.

Figure 4.1: Default Nginx welcome page

3. To stop the container, run the following:

```
docker compose down
```

Now, when you run `docker compose up`, Docker does the following:

1. Creates a default bridge network for your services (unless you specify otherwise).
2. Starts each service in the order defined in the file.
3. Names each container based on the project directory and service name (e.g., `myproject_app_1`).
4. Tracks everything so that `docker compose down` can clean it up later.

It's more than just a shortcut for `docker run`; Compose handles the orchestration, logging, networking, and teardown in a consistent, reproducible way.

We'll use this minimal `Bookings` base as our anchor, then grow it:

```yaml
version: "3.9"

services:
  api:
    build: ./api
    ports:
      - "3000:3000"
    environment:
      - DATABASE_URL=postgres://user:pass@db:5432/appdb
      - REDIS_URL=redis://cache:6379
      - QUEUE_URL=redis://queue:6379
    depends_on:
      - db
      - cache
      - queue

  frontend:
    build: ./frontend
    ports:
      - "8080:80"
    depends_on:
      - api
      - auth

  auth:
    build: ./auth
    environment:
      - DATABASE_URL=postgres://user:pass@db:5432/appdb
    depends_on:
      - db

  worker:
    build: ./worker
    depends_on:
      - queue
      - db

  db:
    image: postgres:15
    environment:
      POSTGRES_USER: user
      POSTGRES_PASSWORD: pass
      POSTGRES_DB: appdb
    volumes:
      - db_data:/var/lib/postgresql/data

  cache:
    image: redis:alpine

  queue:
    image: redis:alpine

volumes:
  db_data:
```

Figure 4.2: Snippet showing docker compose up with all seven services starting cleanly

Named projects and directories

By default, Docker Compose uses the folder name as the project name. So, if your code is in `C:\Users\yourname\my-app`, your containers will be named something like the following:

```
my-app_app_1
```

You can override this with the -p flag:

```
docker compose -p demo up
```

This gives you more control, especially if you're running multiple Compose stacks at once because they will have personalized names now instead of the dreaded `new folder` name we all usually end up with at least once.

Compose also supports environment variables, which can be passed in using a `.env` file or directly from your shell. Here's an example `docker-compose.yml` file:

```
version: "3.9"
services:
  web:
    image: nginx
    ports:
      - "${APP_PORT}:80"
```

The following is an example `.env` file in the same directory:

```
APP_PORT=8080
```

Now, when you run `docker compose up`, it will substitute the variable automatically.

> **Note**
>
> On Windows, treat `.env` as configuration, not as a vault for real secrets. Do not commit any passwords or API keys to Git. For development, keep secrets in a separate `.env` file that is ignored by Git and load it with `env_file`. For production-style setups, prefer mounting secrets as files into the container (for example, with Docker Compose secrets) instead of injecting them as plain environment variables.

Where Compose files belong

Your `docker-compose.yml` file should live at the root of your project directory. This makes it easy to version alongside your code and keep it portable.

A typical structure might look as follows:

```
my-project/
├── docker-compose.yml
```

```
├── .env
├── app/
│   └── index.js
└── README.md
```

If you ever want to use a different Compose filename, just pass it in with `-f`:

```
docker compose -f docker-compose.dev.yml up
```

You can also use multiple `-f` flags to override base configs with environment-specific overrides.

One Compose file will get you pretty far, but the moment you're juggling dev, test, and prod, things start to get a touch messy. That's why most teams I've worked with lean on a layered setup: you keep a clean base file, then stack overrides on top depending on where you're running.

The usual pattern looks like this:

- `docker-compose.yml`: Your base, environment-agnostic setup
- `docker-compose.override.yml`: Some tweaks for local dev (this one's auto-loaded)
- `docker-compose.prod.yml`: Production-style overrides

A base file might just define your services and sensible defaults like this:

```
# docker-compose.yml
services:
  api:
    build: ./api
    environment:
      - DATABASE_URL=postgres://user:pass@db:5432/appdb
  # plus the rest of the Bookings stack...
```

Figure 4.3: Base docker-compose.yml for the Bookings stack

Then, in development, you can loosen things up with hot reloads and file mounts:

```yaml
# docker-compose.override.yml
services:
  api:
    volumes:
      - ./api:/app
    command: ["npm","run","dev"]
  frontend:
    volumes:
      - ./frontend:/usr/share/nginx/html:ro"
```

Figure 4.4: A development override file (docker-compose.override.yml) mounting the local API and frontend code into the running containers

For a prod-like run, lock things down a bit more:

```yaml
# docker-compose.prod.yml
services:
  api:
    environment:
      - NODE_ENV=production
    command: ["node","server.js"]
  frontend:
    image: myorg/bookings-frontend:1.4.0
```

Figure 4.5: A production override file that enables NODE_ENV=production and uses a versioned frontend image for deployment

The nice thing is you don't need to memorize anything clever:

- Dev (override is picked up automatically): `docker compose up`
- Prod-ish, locally: `docker compose -f docker-compose.yml -f docker-compose.prod.yml up -d`

This way, you're not copy-pasting YAML between files every time you change environments; you just layer what you need on top of a stable base.

Useful Compose commands you'll actually use

Once you've started using Compose, you'll find a few commands keep coming up:

- `docker compose up`: Starts the application
- `docker compose down`: Stops and removes everything
- `docker compose ps`: Lists running services

- `docker compose logs`: Tails logs from your services
- `docker compose exec`: Runs a command inside a running container

For example, to get a shell in your app container, use the following:

```
docker compose exec app sh
```

You can run the following to see live logs from all services:

```
docker compose logs -f
```

To trace what Compose is doing behind the scenes (container startup, shutdown, health checks, or rebuilds), use the following:

```
docker compose events
```

This is great when a service keeps restarting and you need to see why.

To see which processes are running inside your containers right now, run the following:

```
docker compose top
```

This is much easier than exec-ing into each container one by one just to check what's alive and what's stuck.

These tools give you full visibility into what your services are doing, and they're much easier than juggling container IDs or names by hand.

Scaling services with Docker Compose

Sometimes one copy of a service just isn't enough. Maybe you've got a queue filling up with jobs and a single worker can't keep pace. That's where scaling comes in:

```
docker compose up -d --scale worker=5
```

With one flag, you've now got five workers (`worker_1` through `worker_5`) all happily chewing through the same queue. No code changes, no extra YAML; just more muscle on the same task.

There is one thing to watch for: you can't scale services that bind to a fixed host port. If you try to scale a frontend that's mapped to `8080:80`, every replica will fight over that port. The trick is to take those replicas off the host ports entirely and put them behind a small proxy.

```
services:
  proxy:
    image: nginx:alpine
    volumes:
      - ./ops/nginx.conf:/etc/nginx/nginx.conf:ro
    ports:
      - "8080:80"
    depends_on: [api]
    networks: [frontend_net, backend_net]

  api:
    build: ./api
    # no direct port mapping when scaling
    ports: []
    networks: [backend_net]

networks:
  frontend_net: {}
  backend_net: {}
```

Figure 4.6: Compose snippet showing an Nginx proxy in front of multiple API replicas

That way, your proxy takes care of traffic on port `8080`, and Compose can spin up as many `api` replicas as you like without anything clashing.

Before we end the section, let's quickly understand when to use Compose (and when not to):

- Compose is perfect for the following cases:
    - Local development
    - Small apps with multiple services
    - Prototyping stack configurations
    - Sharing a common setup with teammates
- It's not ideal for the following cases:
    - Running containers across multiple machines (use Swarm or Kubernetes)
    - Scenarios where container creation needs to be extremely dynamic (you may want a more granular scheduler)

That said, most teams benefit from using Compose as a local baseline, even if they eventually deploy using something else.

Docker Compose gives you a powerful, declarative way to manage multi-container applications with ease. You now know how to define services, run and update them, and understand what happens behind the scenes. You also know when to use Compose over the

CLI. Instead of memorizing complex `docker run` commands, you define your stack once and run it anywhere, which we'll explore next.

Defining multi-container environments

Remember, you'll only ever get so far with a single container.

I still remember a project where we started off with a single API container. Nice and simple. Then, someone added a database. A week later, we bolted on Redis for caching. Then came a worker to chew through background jobs. Before long, we weren't just spinning up "the app" anymore; we were juggling a whole stack of services, each with its own quirks. Every new dev that joined needed a mini training session just to get the thing running.

That's the tipping point where a proper multi-container setup stops being optional and starts saving your sanity.

Sure, for a small script or a single-purpose tool, one container will do the trick. But most real applications are built from parts: a backend API, a database, a queue, and maybe a frontend that calls into it all. Run those by hand and you'll drown in commands. Put them in Compose and you've got structure, repeatability, and something you can share with your team without a long `README` lecture.

In this section we'll look at how to write Compose files that tie these pieces together properly. We'll cover services, networks, volumes, and environment variables, and where everything fits in the bigger picture.

By the end, you'll have a Compose file that defines your whole stack in one place, and it'll feel like it was designed that way rather than glued together on a Friday afternoon.

Why multi-container definitions matter

It's very easy to let container sprawl creep in. One day you're spinning up a backend with `docker run`. Then you add a database. Then a cache. You start copying and pasting commands into your terminal or writing scripts to bring everything up.

But that approach breaks down fast!

You lose track of what's running. You forget to expose ports. You can't hand off the setup to someone else without explaining it over a video call. And if you ever want to start fresh, you're back to square one.

That is why multi-container definitions matter, not because you cannot wire things up manually, but because you shouldn't have to.

A multi-container environment typically includes the following:

- Two or more services (e.g., backend, database, and frontend)
- Shared or private networks so they can communicate
- Volumes for persistent storage
- Environment variables for configuration
- Health checks or dependencies to control startup order

Let's say you're building a typical web app. You'll probably have the following:

- A Node.js API
- A PostgreSQL database
- A Redis cache
- A frontend written in React or another JavaScript framework

Each one of those can run in its own container. But they need to talk to each other, reliably and in a predictable way. Compose gives you the structure to declare all of this.

Building a Compose file with multiple services

Let's build an example `docker-compose.yml` file step by step:

1. Start with version and services:

```
version: "3.9"
services:
  api:
    build: ./api
    ports:
      - "3000:3000"
```

2. Now, add a database:

```
  db:
    image: postgres:15
    environment:
      POSTGRES_USER: user
      POSTGRES_PASSWORD: pass
      POSTGRES_DB: appdb
    volumes:
      - db_data:/var/lib/postgresql/data
```

3. Then, add a Redis container:

```
cache:
   image: redis:alpine
```

4. Finally, add a frontend service:

```
frontend:
   build: ./frontend
   ports:
     - "8080:80"
```

5. Add the volume at the bottom of the file:

```
volumes:
  db_data:
```

That's it: four services, connected, with persistent storage for the database. The full structure is simple and easy to understand.

```yaml
version: "3.9"

services:
  api:
    build: ./api
    ports:
      - "3000:3000"
    environment:
      - NODE_ENV=development

  db:
    image: postgres:15
    environment:
      POSTGRES_USER: user
      POSTGRES_PASSWORD: pass
      POSTGRES_DB: appdb
    volumes:
      - db_data:/var/lib/postgresql/data

  cache:
    image: redis:alpine

  frontend:
    build: ./frontend
    ports:
      - "8080:80"

volumes:
  db_data:
```

Figure 4.7: Docker Compose file for a multi-service stack

This is where Compose really earns its keep. Instead of a messy set of `docker run` commands or Bash scripts, you've now got a single file that defines your stack in one place. Anyone on your team can run `docker compose up` and get the same environment without worrying about order, flags, or what needs to start first.

Let's talk through some of the key features:

- **Networks by default**: When you run `docker compose up`, Docker automatically creates a bridge network for your project and connects all services to it. This means that each container can reach the others using their service name.
  So, from inside the API container, you can connect to the database using `db:5432` or Redis using `cache:6379`. No extra configuration is needed.
- **Exposing only what you need**: Notice that we only exposed ports for the frontend and API. The database and Redis containers stay private; they're only accessible inside the Compose network.
  That's intentional and important. You want to minimize the attack surface. By default, Compose keeps services private unless you explicitly publish a port. So, if you accidentally deploy this file on a cloud machine, your database isn't exposed to the internet.
- **Sharing environment across containers**: You can also use a shared `.env` file to keep your configuration clean. For example, your `.env` file might contain the following:

```
POSTGRES_USER=user
POSTGRES_PASSWORD=pass
POSTGRES_DB=appdb
NODE_ENV=development
```

  Then, your Compose file can reference those:

```
db:
  image: postgres:15
  environment:
    POSTGRES_USER: ${POSTGRES_USER}
    POSTGRES_PASSWORD: ${POSTGRES_PASSWORD}
    POSTGRES_DB: ${POSTGRES_DB}
```

  This makes it easy to swap values between dev, test, and staging environments without rewriting the Compose file.

- **Using build contexts and local images**: If your services have custom code, for example, a Node API or a React frontend, you can define a build context instead of using a prebuilt image:

  ```
  api:
    build:
      context: ./api
      dockerfile: Dockerfile
  ```

  Docker will build the image locally using your Dockerfile. This is useful when developing or testing, especially when you want to bake source code into the container.

- **Managing volumes**: In our earlier example, we defined a volume for the database:

  ```
  volumes:
    db_data:
  ```

  This creates a persistent volume managed by Docker. If you restart your containers, your database data stays intact. You can inspect volumes with the following:

  ```
  docker volume ls
  ```

  You can clean up unused ones with the following:

  ```
  docker volume prune
  ```

  Just be careful; `prune` deletes anything not in use, so make sure nothing important is running before using it.

- **Keeping services independent but connected**: One of the strengths of Compose is that it encourages separation of concerns. Each service runs in isolation but is connected via the network and config. This makes it easier to do the following:

  - Swap out a service without affecting others
  - Scale services independently (e.g., more workers, fewer frontends)
  - Test or debug one part of your stack in isolation

  You get the flexibility of microservices with the ease of running everything locally.

Defining a multi-container environment is the next logical step once your app outgrows a single container. With Docker Compose, you can declare your entire application stack, containers, networks, volumes, and configuration, in one place and spin it up in seconds.

Going beyond the default network

By default, Docker Compose creates a single bridge network for your project and connects all services to it. That's fine for most setups, but real-world applications often need more control. Maybe you want to isolate some services or give a service more than one network connection.

When you move from single containers to multi-service stacks, the default network that Compose creates starts to matter in a very different way. This isn't about Docker's core networking fundamentals from earlier chapters; it's about how Compose wires services together and how you can take finer control when the stack grows. Once you need isolation, multiple networks, or clearer boundaries between services, Compose gives you a few small but powerful options that are worth understanding.

Named networks

A named network is one you explicitly define and control. This is useful if you want to share a network between multiple Compose projects or keep a consistent name in scripts and configs. Here's a simple example that shows what a named network actually looks like inside a Compose file and how two services share it.

```yaml
version: "3.9"

services:
  api:
    build: ./api
    networks:
      - backend

  database:
    image: postgres:15
    networks:
      - backend

networks:
  backend:
    name: my_backend_net
```

Figure 4.8: Docker Compose file setting up API and PostgreSQL services on a custom backend network

Here, both `api` and `database` join `my_backend_net`. You can inspect it with the following:

```
docker network inspect my_backend_net
```

Service aliasing

Sometimes you want a service to be reachable by more than one name, for example, both `db` and `postgres`, in case different apps expect different hostnames. You can do that with aliases:

```yaml
services:
  database:
    image: postgres:15
    networks:
      backend:
        aliases:
          - db
          - postgres

networks:
  backend:
```

Figure 4.9: Docker Compose file configuring a PostgreSQL service with multiple network aliases

Now, any service on `backend` can connect to the database using `db` or `postgres`.

Connecting a service to multiple networks

A service can also be on more than one network, allowing it to talk to different groups of services without exposing everything to everyone.

```yaml
services:
  proxy:
    image: nginx
    networks:
      - frontend
      - backend

  api:
    build: ./api
    networks:
      - backend

  web:
    build: ./frontend
    networks:
      - frontend

networks:
  frontend:
  backend:
```

Figure 4.10: Docker Compose file defining proxy, API, and web services connected through frontend and backend networks

Here, the proxy service can talk to both the `frontend` and `backend` networks, acting as a bridge between them. But `web` and `api` can't talk directly, improving isolation.

Here's a brief on when to use these patterns:

- Use **named networks** if you need consistency across multiple Compose projects or scripts.
- Use **aliases** to keep legacy configs working without renaming services.
- Use **multi-network setups** to isolate traffic between parts of your stack, reducing accidental cross-talk and potential security issues.

Here's how the Bookings example looks when we split things across two networks:

```yaml
networks:
  frontend_net:
  backend_net:

services:
  db:
    image: postgres:15
    networks:
      backend_net:
        aliases: [postgres, db]

  api:
    build: ./api
    networks: [backend_net]

  auth:
    build: ./auth
    networks: [backend_net]

  frontend:
    build: ./frontend
    networks: [frontend_net]

  proxy:
    image: nginx:alpine
    networks: [frontend_net, backend_net]  # bridge between the two
```

Figure 4.11: Example Bookings stack split across frontend and backend networks

Why bother with this setup? Well, a few reasons...

- **Isolation**: The frontend can't go poking around in the database. It has to talk through the API or auth service, which is exactly how we want it.
- **Aliases**: The database can be reached as `db` or `postgres`. This is handy if different tools or bits of legacy code expect different names.
- **Bridge**: The proxy is the only service that sits on both networks, so all external traffic comes through a single controlled entrypoint.

This keeps the stack predictable and stops services chatting to each other in ways they really shouldn't.

Running Docker Compose applications on Windows

The first time I ran Docker on Windows, it properly threw me. I was so used to Linux and living in the terminal that seeing a shiny GUI for containers felt... well, a bit alien. I was all thumbs in it.

But then I opened up a project folder, hit `docker compose up`, and suddenly had a database, API, cache, and frontend, all the usual jazz, wired together. It feels like it should be a simple step, going from a core Linux environment to Windows, but honestly, you'll stub your toes on more than one thing along the way. Trust me.

Aside from the last chapter in this book, this is the section that grew out of big red Post-it notes plastered around my monitors; a sort of "tech sunflower" of "don't forget" moments.

Let's walk through how to run Compose-based applications on Windows using WSL 2, what to expect during startup, how to monitor what is happening under the hood, and what to do when something is not working as expected.

Let us assume you have a `docker-compose.yml` file in your project folder with at least two services defined. From that folder, you can start the application stack using the following:

```
docker compose up
```

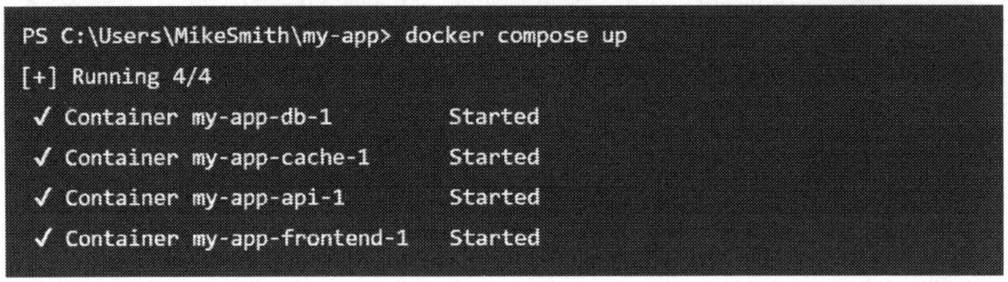

Figure 4.12: Docker Compose successfully started all four containers: db, cache, API, and frontend

By default, Compose runs in the foreground. You will see logs from all services streaming in real time. If that feels like too much noise, you can run it in detached mode:

```
docker compose up -d
```

Detached mode just means Compose starts your services in the background and frees up your terminal. You won't see live logs scroll past, but the containers are still running and you can inspect them at any time using `docker compose logs`, `docker compose ps`, and `docker compose exec` to interact with the stack.

Where Docker Compose runs on Windows

When using Docker Desktop on Windows with WSL 2, your containers are not running on Windows directly. They are running inside a Linux **virtual machine** (**VM**) that Docker manages behind the scenes. This has a few important implications:

- `localhost` means the Linux VM, not Windows

- File mounts come from your Windows filesystem, so paths such as `C:\Users` will be available inside the container at `/mnt/c/Users`
- Port bindings work, but sometimes have quirks around firewall rules or antivirus software

If you run `docker compose up` and cannot access a service via `http://localhost:3000`, try running this:

```
wsl hostname -I
```

Then use that IP address instead of `localhost`:

```
curl http://172.25.240.1:3000
```

Troubleshooting common issues

Let's look at some common errors you may encounter while running Compose on Windows, and how to resolve them.

Checking the logs

One of the most common Compose errors is when a service exits immediately after starting. This often happens with databases, misconfigured entrypoints, or containers expecting something that has not been initialized yet.

To investigate, run the following:

```
docker compose logs
```

Alternatively, follow logs for just one service:

```
docker compose logs -f db
```

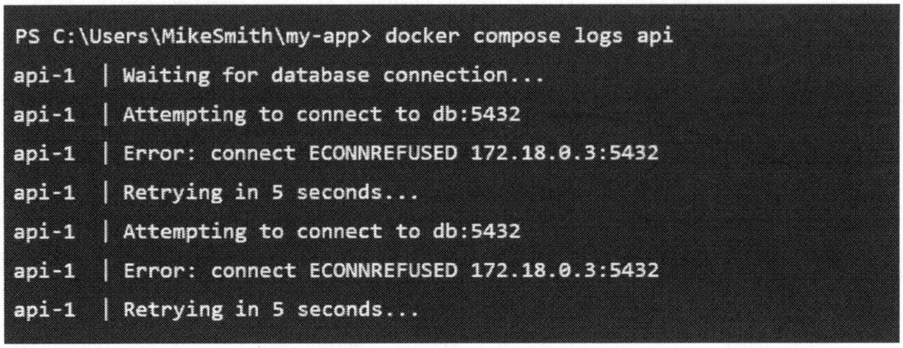

Figure 4.13: API container failing to connect to the database, showing repeated ECONNREFUSED errors on port 5432

This will usually reveal the issue. For example, a database might complain that it cannot write to its data directory, or an application might fail to connect to a dependency because it is not ready yet.

Listing running services and their ports

To see which services are currently running and what ports they are exposing, use the following:

```
docker compose ps
```

This will list each container, its status, and any ports mapped from the container to your host.

You can also inspect individual services using the following:

```
docker inspect <container-id>
```

Alternatively, you can run commands inside them:

```
docker compose exec api sh
```

This is extremely useful for debugging in real time, running migrations, or checking logs from inside the container.

Restarting and rebuilding services

If you make changes to your code, you may want to restart a service without restarting the entire stack:

```
docker compose restart api
```

If you change the Dockerfile or environment for a service, rebuild it like this:

```
docker compose up -d --build
```

This rebuilds any services that have changed and restarts them in detached mode.

You can also force a rebuild of just one service:

```
docker compose build frontend
```

Alternatively, clear out everything and start fresh:

```
docker compose down
docker compose up --build
```

These commands are safe and predictable. Compose tracks what has changed and rebuilds only what it needs.

When localhost fails

On rare occasions, Docker Desktop fails to forward ports correctly between the WSL 2 backend and your Windows host. If that happens, services inside Compose might be up and working, but not accessible via `localhost`.

In those cases, use the following:

```
wsl hostname -I
```

Figure 4.14: WSL host IP address returned: 172.25.240.1

Then forward the port manually with `netsh`:

```
netsh interface portproxy add v4tov4 listenaddress=127.0.0.1 listenport=3000
connectaddress=172.25.240.1 connectport=3000
```

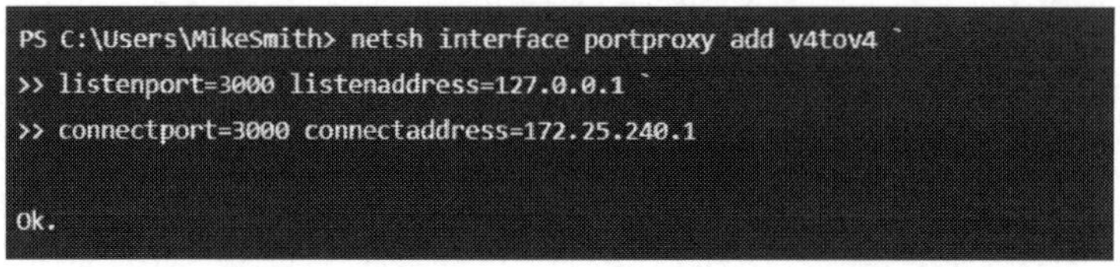

Figure 4.15: Using netsh portproxy in PowerShell to forward localhost:3000 to the WSL 2 IP address

To delete the proxy later, use the following:

```
netsh interface portproxy delete v4tov4 listenaddress=127.0.0.1 listenport=3000
```

This workaround is clunky but reliable. It is usually only needed for edge cases or after a Docker Desktop update. To confirm it's working, you can curl the forwarded port from Windows and check the response:

Figure 4.16: Verifying the port proxy by curling localhost:3000 and receiving the API response

Stopping and cleaning up

When you are finished working, you can stop everything with the following:

```
docker compose down
```

This shuts down all running services, removes their containers, and tears down the network Docker created.

If you want to remove volumes too, use the following:

```
docker compose down --volumes
```

This is useful when resetting your environment or starting fresh. Just be aware that any persistent data, such as database contents, will be deleted.

Checking network status and connectivity

To see the internal network created by Compose, use the following:

```
docker network ls
```

Look for a network named something such as `your-folder-name_default`. Then, inspect it:

```
docker network inspect myproject_default
```

You will see each service listed with its IP address. You can then exec into one container and ping another by name to test connectivity:

```
docker compose exec api sh
ping db
```

If this fails, your services may not be on the same network. Check the `docker-compose.yml` file and ensure all services are defined under the same network block or left to use the default.

Handling file permission issues

Sometimes services will fail to start due to file permission issues on bind mounts. This can happen when your Windows host shares a directory with a Linux container that expects Unix-style permissions.

For example, if your Dockerfile creates a directory with `chmod 700` and the host volume does not match, the container may not be able to access it.

To fix this, try using named volumes instead of host mounts, or add a startup command in the container to fix permissions:

```
command: sh -c "chown -R node:node /app && npm start"
```

This approach ensures that the container owns the files it is trying to use, even if they come from your Windows filesystem.

Performance and permission gotchas on Windows

Running Compose on Windows with WSL 2 is reliable once it's tuned, but there are a few quirks worth knowing about, especially if you start to notice sluggish performance or odd file access errors:

- **File I/O between Windows and WSL can be slow**: If your project files live on the Windows side (`C:\Users\...`) and you mount them into a container, file operations have to cross the Windows-Linux boundary. This can be noticeably slower for workloads with thousands of small files (for example, large `node_modules` folders).

> **Tip**
>
> Store your code inside your WSL home directory (e.g., /home/<lt;user>;/project) to avoid the translation overhead and get 2–3× faster file performance.

- **Antivirus and firewall scans**: Some security tools scan every file written to disk, including during `docker build`. On large builds, this can add minutes.

> **Tip**
>
> Exclude your Docker data directory and WSL virtual disk from real-time scanning. On most setups, Docker Desktop stores its Linux filesystem under `%USERPROFILE%\AppData\Local\Docker`.

- **Volume permission mismatches**: NTFS permissions don't map cleanly to Linux user permissions. Even if you've fixed basic `chmod` issues, you may still get `EACCES` errors when mounting Windows folders.

> **Tip**
>
> Use named volumes for persistent data. If you must mount from Windows, add a startup command to adjust ownership, as follows:
>
> ```
> command: sh -c "chown -R node:node /app && npm start"
> ```

- **Resource limits in Docker Desktop**: Docker Desktop can limit CPU and memory for the WSL 2 backend. If services are being killed unexpectedly or slowing down under load, you can also configure limits on memory, CPU, and swap size directly in a `.wslconfig` file in your Windows user profile directory, which gives you more precise control.
- **Path length limits**: Windows still has quirks with long file paths. Deep directory trees in build contexts can trigger errors.

> **Tip**
>
> Enable long paths in Windows settings, or simplify your directory structure.

These small adjustments can make a big difference when running larger or more complex Compose stacks on Windows.

Running Docker Compose applications on Windows with WSL 2 works brilliantly once you understand the path it takes behind the scenes. Services run inside a Linux VM, ports need to be correctly forwarded, and logs are your best friend when something goes quiet.

You should now know how to run and manage Compose applications on your machine without the confusion that sometimes comes with mixing Linux containers and the Windows host.

Practical tuning that actually helps

There are a few tweaks that can save you from slow builds, weird permissions, or containers just dragging their feet on Windows. These are the ones that I've found actually move the needle:

- **Keep your code in WSL for speed**: Stick your projects under /home/<lt;you>;/projects/bookings and mount from there. If you mount straight from `C:\...`, every file operation has to cross the Windows-Linux boundary, and big `node_modules` folders will crawl.
- **Fix file permissions with metadata**: Inside your distro, drop this into `/etc/wsl.conf`:

  ```
  [automount]
  options = "metadata,umask=22,fmask=11"
  ```

  Then, run `wsl --shutdown` in PowerShell and restart Docker Desktop. This makes Linux-style permissions behave properly on mounted drives.
- **Use named volumes for data**: Let Postgres (or anything else that stores state) live in a Docker-managed volume such as `db_data`. It sidesteps NTFS permission mismatches and makes backups easier.
- **Stop antivirus slowing you down**: Exclude `%USERPROFILE%\AppData\Local\Docker` and your WSL VHDX file from real-time scans. Otherwise, every build step gets poked by your AV software.
- **Give WSL 2 enough headroom**: Create `%UserProfile%\.wslconfig` and set some sensible limits:

  ```
  [wsl2]
  memory=8GB
  ```

```
processors=4
swap=2GB
```

Apply it with `wsl --shutdown`. This keeps your containers from being starved on busy laptops.

- **For heavy JavaScript projects**: If you're running into file watcher errors (classic Node/React issue), increase `inotify` watchers inside the distro:

```
echo "fs.inotify.max_user_watches=524288" | sudo tee -a /etc/sysctl.conf
sudo sysctl -p
```

These aren't just theory, either; they're the fixes that smooth out daily work (and have saved my bacon more than once) when you're running bigger Compose stacks on Windows.

Managing dependencies with Compose

Honestly, I've lost count of the number of times I've hit `docker compose up` and watched my API container start and then immediately die because Postgres wasn't ready yet. The logs fill with constant "connection refused" messages or retries, or just plain crash. A minute later, the database is happily running, but my app has already face-planted.

On a local dev machine, that's just irritating. In a shared environment or CI pipeline, it can bring the whole run to a halt.

Compose gives us a way to declare which services depend on which, but that doesn't automatically handle timing. A service can be *started* without being *ready*.

In this section, we'll look at how to stop this from tripping you up: dependencies, health checks, wait-for strategies, and a couple of practical tricks to make sure containers start in the right order and actually wait for each other on Windows.

Understanding service dependencies

Let us start with a basic example. You might have something like this:

```
version: "3.9"
services:
  app:
    build: ./app
    depends_on:
      - db
```

```
  db:
    image: postgres:15
```

The `depends_on` keyword tells Compose that the app service relies on the `db` service. That means Compose will start `db` first, and then start `app`.

But, and this is the important bit, `depends_on` only manages start order. It does not wait for `db` to be ready. If the database takes five seconds to initialize and the app starts in two seconds, the app will fail.

This is where most Compose setups fall short.

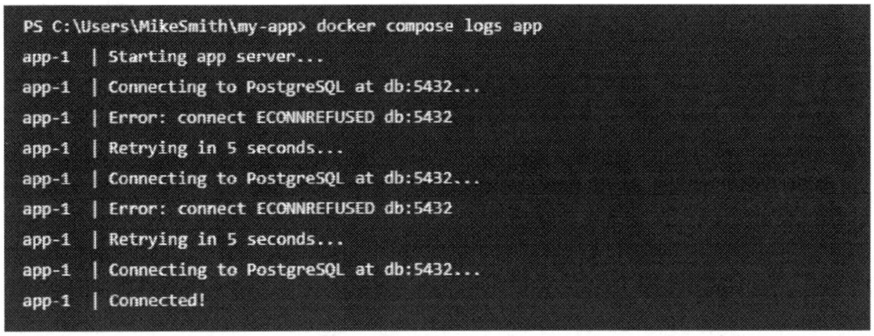

Figure 4.17: App container logs showing repeated connection failures until the database becomes ready

Sometimes just telling Compose "this service depends on that one" isn't enough. A container can be marked as started long before it's actually ready to accept connections, which is why apps often crash on first boot and only work on the second try. To deal with that, you need a way to make one service actively wait for another. Now, fair enough, this is pretty advanced, but that's why we're here, right?

There are a few common strategies for waiting:

- Use health checks
- Use a wait-for-it or wait-for script
- Use other third-party tools

Let's look at them.

Using health checks

You can define a health check for a service in Compose. This lets Docker track when the service is truly ready, not just running.

Here is an example with PostgreSQL:

```
version: "3.9"
services:
  db:
    image: postgres:15
    healthcheck:
      test: ["CMD", "pg_isready", "-U", "user"]
      interval: 5s
      timeout: 3s
      retries: 5
```

This tells Docker to run `pg_isready` every five seconds. Once it passes, the container is marked as healthy.

You can then use another tool to wait for that health status before starting the next service, or at least have your app check whether `db` is healthy before connecting.

Unfortunately, Compose doesn't natively delay starting one service until another is healthy. But you can inspect health status from within containers, or from your local machine:

```
docker inspect --format='{{json .State.Health.Status}}' <container-id>
```

This returns `healthy`, `starting`, or `unhealthy`.

Using wait-for scripts

The most practical solution is to use a wait-for script in your app's entrypoint. There are a few versions floating around, but the basic idea is as follows:

1. Ping the target service and port.
2. Retry until it is reachable.
3. Then, run your app command.

Here is an example `wait-for.sh` script:

```
#!/bin/sh
until nc -z db 5432; do
  echo "Waiting for db..."
  sleep 2
done
echo "Database is up. Starting app..."
exec "$@"
```

Then, in your `docker-compose.yml` file:

```
version: "3.9"
services:
  app:
    build: ./app
    depends_on:
      - db
    entrypoint: ["/wait-for.sh", "npm", "start"]
```

Now, make sure `wait-for.sh` is copied into your image as part of the Dockerfile.

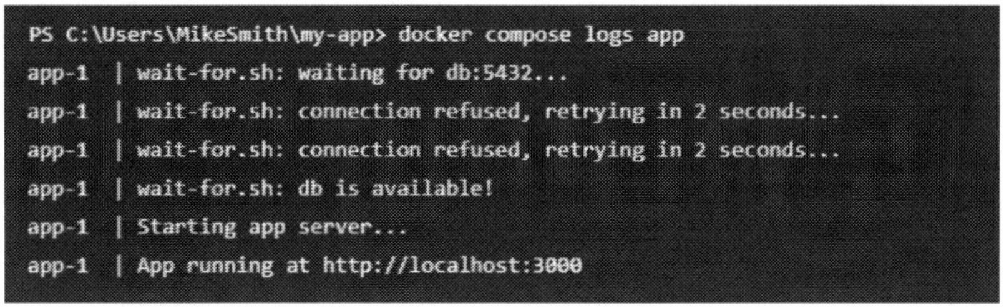

Figure 4.18: Logs showing wait-for-it holding the app until the database is ready, then starting successfully

This approach works consistently on Windows and Linux, and does not require anything extra from Docker or Compose.

Using third-party tools

There are also prebuilt solutions, such as the following:

- `wait-for-it` (Bash-based)
- `dockerize` (Go binary)

These offer similar functionality and are easy to drop into a container.

To use `wait-for-it`, do the following:

1. Download the script (`https://github.com/vishnubob/wait-for-it`). Don't forget, if you don't want to download it directly, you could make a similar one in Bash using this one as inspiration.
2. Copy it into your container in the Dockerfile.
3. Use it in your entrypoint.

Here's an example showcasing the steps:

```
COPY wait-for-it.sh /wait-for-it.sh
RUN chmod +x /wait-for-it.sh
ENTRYPOINT ["/wait-for-it.sh", "db:5432", "--", "npm", "start"]
```

You can also pass timeout flags or customize retries. This is useful when working with services that are slow to start or in CI environments where timing is unpredictable.

Managing inter-service timing on Windows

Even with health checks and wait-for scripts in place, things on Windows can still behave a little differently than you'd expect. That's because, under the hood, your containers aren't running directly on Windows; they're running inside the WSL 2 VM that Docker Desktop manages for you.

Now, because Compose services run inside WSL 2, they do not always behave the same as they would on a native Linux system.

The following are some things to watch out for:

- Disk mounts from Windows can slow startup
- Services may start in the right order but still fail to connect briefly due to port-forwarding lag
- Logging can appear out of sync, especially when using `tail -f`

Use health checks and retry logic to smooth these issues out. When timing fixes still aren't enough, the next thing to check is whether the containers can actually see each other. Most failures at this point come down to name resolution, networking, or simple reachability, so let's walk through the quick checks that surface those problems fast.

Debugging stubborn dependencies

If a service still refuses to connect, and it happens, try the following:

1. Exec into the container and ping the other service.
2. Check that the service name (not the container name) matches.
3. Use `curl` or `nc` to test the port.
4. Confirm that both services are on the same network.

Here is an example:

```
docker compose exec app sh
/ # ping db
/ # nc -z db 5432 && echo "Port is open"
```

If you get a `name or service not known` message, the container is probably on the wrong network.

To confirm, run the following:

```
docker inspect app
```

Look under `NetworkSettings` and confirm that the container is connected to the correct network.

```
PS C:\Users\MikeSmith\my-app> docker inspect app

[
    {
        "Id": "8a7c8e3f8b27...",
        "Name": "/my-app_app_1",
        "NetworkSettings": {
            "Networks": {
                "my-app_default": {
                    "IPAMConfig": null,
                    "Links": null,
                    "Aliases": [
                        "app",
                        "8a7c8e3f8b27"
                    ],
                    "NetworkID": "e1f8a5d4c73b...",
                    "EndpointID": "3cd9bfe37b2c...",
                    "Gateway": "172.25.0.1",
                    "IPAddress": "172.25.0.2",
                    "IPPrefixLen": 16,
                    "IPv6Gateway": "",
                    "GlobalIPv6Address": "",
                    "MacAddress": "02:42:ac:19:00:02"
                }
            }
        }
    }
]
```

Figure 4.19: Partial docker inspect output showing the app container attached to the my-app_default network

Building in retries and graceful failure

Even with wait-for logic, some applications still fail the first time and recover on the second or third try. This is especially true for apps that connect to databases on boot and do not retry automatically.

To work around this, do the following:

1. Add retry logic inside the app.
2. Use a wrapper script to restart the app if it fails.
3. Run a small delay before launching your app.

Take the following example:

```
sleep 5 && npm start
```

It is not elegant, but it works, especially in dev setups where you just want to get things up and running reliably.

So, managing dependencies between containers in Docker Compose is all about timing. Services may be technically started but not ready, and Compose does not wait for readiness by default.

Getting timing right is one piece of the puzzle, but once your stack grows beyond a couple of containers, there are broader habits worth adopting. That's where best practices for multi-container orchestration come in.

Best practices for multi-container orchestration

I once inherited a project a few years ago where the Compose file had basically grown like an untended garden. Services were named `app1`, `app2`, and `testthing`. Ports were scattered all over the place, some commented, but most not. Nobody dared run `docker compose down --volumes` because we weren't sure what data would vanish. It technically worked, but it was painful to maintain and even harder to share with the rest of the team.

That's the moment when you realize: once Docker stops being something you spin up for a quick demo and becomes part of your daily workflow, that structure really does matter.

So, in this section, we'll talk about practical best practices for orchestrating multi-container applications with Docker Compose on Windows. This is about more than just writing functional YAML. It's about making Compose files clear, scalable, and predictable; especially in environments where WSL 2, file mounts, and mixed tooling can throw curveballs.

Use explicit service names

The default behavior of Docker Compose is helpful, but not always readable. If you leave your service names vague or skip explicit port mappings, your stack will quickly become hard to reason about. Always name your services clearly.

Here is a bad example:

```
version: "3.9"
services:
  app:
    build: .
  db:
    image: postgres
```

Here is a better example:

```
version: "3.9"
services:
  api:
    build: ./api
  database:
    image: postgres:15
```

Similarly, avoid relying on implicit ports. Always map them deliberately and comment them, if needed:

```
ports:
  - "3000:3000"  # API server
  - "8080:80"    # Frontend
```

This makes it easier for someone new to the project, or yourself in six months, to know what is running and where to find it.

```yaml
version: "3.9"

services:
  api:
    build: ./api
    ports:
      - "3000:3000"  # API service port

  frontend:
    build: ./frontend
    ports:
      - "8080:80"    # Frontend served on HTTP

  database:
    image: postgres:15
    environment:
      POSTGRES_USER: admin
      POSTGRES_PASSWORD: secret
    volumes:
      - db_data:/var/lib/postgresql/data

  redis:
    image: redis:alpine

```

Figure 4.20: Compose file with clear service names and explicit port mappings

Avoid using latest tags in production-like stacks

While `latest` is convenient for quick tests, it introduces unpredictability. If you are using an image such as `postgres:latest` or `node:latest`, your builds may break silently the next time you run them, due to changes upstream. Instead, use versioned tags:

```
image: postgres:15
```

You still get updates, but only when you choose to update the version. This makes your Compose setup far more stable and reproducible, especially when shared across machines or teams.

Use named volumes

When you need persistent data, especially for things such as databases, use named Docker volumes rather than mapping folders from your host machine.

Here is a bad example:

```
volumes:
  - ./data:/var/lib/postgresql/data
```

Here is a better example:

```
volumes:
  - db_data:/var/lib/postgresql/data
```

Named volumes are easier to back up, easier to inspect, and not tied to your host file structure. They also avoid permission issues that can happen when your Windows filesystem interacts with Linux-based containers.

If you need to inspect what is inside a named volume, spin up a quick container:

```
docker run --rm -it -v myproject_db_data:/data alpine sh
/ # ls /data
```

Keep environment variables in a separate .env file

Docker Compose supports `.env` files by default. You can keep all your config in one place and load it automatically.

Create a file called `.env`:

```
POSTGRES_USER=admin
POSTGRES_PASSWORD=secret
API_PORT=3000
```

Then, reference those in your Compose file:

```
environment:
  POSTGRES_USER: ${POSTGRES_USER}
  POSTGRES_PASSWORD: ${POSTGRES_PASSWORD}
```

This keeps your Compose file clean and makes it easy to manage different environments without duplicating the whole stack.

Structure your Compose files clearly

Group related services together and use consistent indentation and spacing. Comment anything that is not obvious. If your stack grows large, consider splitting it into multiple files:

- `docker-compose.yml`: Base stack
- `docker-compose.override.yml`: Development overrides
- `docker-compose.prod.yml`: Production-ready config

You can then combine them as needed:

```
docker compose -f docker-compose.yml -f docker-compose.prod.yml up
```

Keep your services lean

Each service should do one thing well. Do not run your API, frontend, and cron tasks in the same container. This keeps logs clean, scaling simple, and debugging less of a mess.

If you have a task runner or worker queue, give it its own service:

```
version: "3.9"
services:
  worker:
    build: ./worker
    depends_on:
      - api
      - queue
```

This also makes it easier to scale only the parts that need it.

Use health checks

Health checks are not just for show; they can dramatically improve how your stack behaves. Add them for services that may take time to become usable, such as databases or queues:

```
healthcheck:
  test: ["CMD", "pg_isready", "-U", "user"]
  interval: 5s
  retries: 5
```

Use a retry loop or wait-for script in services that depend on others. It will make your Compose up runs much more predictable and reduce the chance of silent failures.

Keep cleanup simple

At some point, you're going to want to reset your environment. Maybe something's gone sideways, or maybe you just want to start fresh. Either way, `docker compose down` (and its louder cousin `docker compose down --volumes`) are the tools for the job. Just make sure you know what they're about to nuke before you hit *Enter*.

I always recommend testing this regularly, especially once you start introducing bind mounts or external volumes. Document what gets destroyed and what sticks around so there are no surprises later.

A couple of handy checks you can use are the following:

```
# List all volumes
docker volume ls
```

This gives you something like the following:

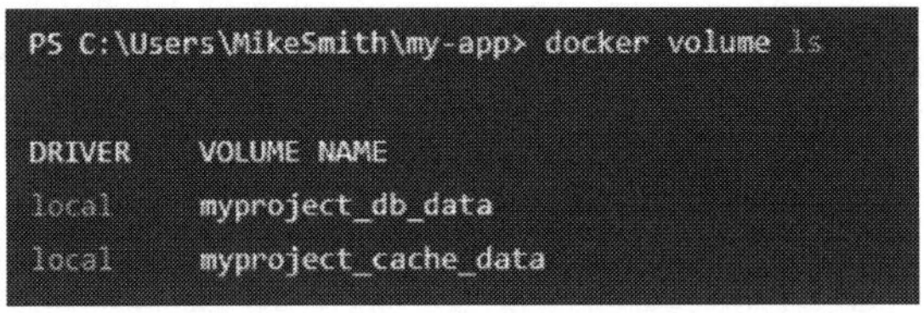

Figure 4.21: Output of docker volume ls, listing the project's database and cache volumes

If you want to peek inside a specific one, use the following:

```
docker volume inspect myproject_db_data
```

Here's a bit of the output you'd see from this:

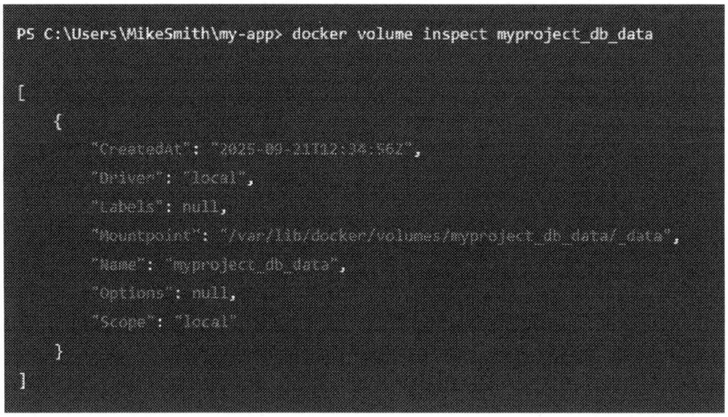

Figure 4.22: Output of docker volume inspect myproject_db_data

That way, you've got eyes on what's actually living in Docker's volume space, rather than finding out the hard way that you've just blown away your database.

Check network behavior regularly

If services are not talking to each other, inspect the default network:

```
docker network inspect myproject_default
```

Make sure all services are listed under `Containers`, and that each has a valid IP address and hostname.

From within a container, ping another service:

```
docker compose exec api sh
/ # ping database
```

If you see connection refused, double-check your network config and service names.

Document the stack for other developers

If your stack is going to be used by other developers, document the following:

- Prerequisites (Docker Desktop, WSL 2, and version)
- Common commands (up, down, and restart)
- Known issues (port conflicts and slow start times)
- What services are exposed and how to access them

Trust me when I say that a simple `README` at the root of your project goes a long way.

The best Compose setups are not just the ones that work; they are the ones that stay easy to maintain, debug, and hand off. In this section, we have covered practical habits that help you write clearer Compose files, manage dependencies reliably, and avoid common pitfalls when running multi-container applications on Windows.

A more realistic multi-service stack

Our earlier `api`, `db`, and `cache` setup is a solid teaching baseline, but let's make it a bit more like a real-world microservices application. In practice, you might have the following:

- **frontend**: Serves the web interface to users
- **api**: Handles business logic and data processing
- **auth**: A dedicated authentication service
- **queue**: Message broker to handle background tasks
- **worker**: Processes jobs from the queue
- **database**: Stores persistent application data
- **cache**: Speeds up repeated queries or session storage

Here's what that could look like in Compose:

```yaml
version: "3.9"

services:
  frontend:
    build: ./frontend
    ports:
      - "8080:80"
    depends_on:
      - api
      - auth

  api:
    build: ./api
    environment:
      DATABASE_URL: postgres://user:pass@database:5432/appdb
      CACHE_HOST: cache
    depends_on:
      - database
      - cache
      - queue

  auth:
    build: ./auth
    environment:
      DATABASE_URL: postgres://user:pass@database:5432/authdb
    depends_on:
      - database

  queue:
    image: redis:alpine

  worker:
    build: ./worker
    environment:
      QUEUE_HOST: queue
      DATABASE_URL: postgres://user:pass@database:5432/appdb
    depends_on:
      - queue
      - database

  database:
    image: postgres:15
    environment:
      POSTGRES_USER: user
      POSTGRES_PASSWORD: pass
      POSTGRES_DB: appdb
    volumes:
      - db_data:/var/lib/postgresql/data

  cache:
    image: redis:alpine

volumes:
  db_data:
```

Figure 4.23: A complete multi-service Compose stack wired together with dependencies and shared services

Here's why this example works:

- **Clear separation of concerns**: Each service does one job well, which makes it easy to test, replace, or scale individually.

- **Realistic interdependencies**: The API depends on the database, cache, and queue; the worker depends on the queue and database; the frontend depends on the API and auth service.
- **Extensible**: You could add more workers with `--scale worker=5` or swap Redis for RabbitMQ without touching the other services.
- **Close to production**: While still manageable locally, it reflects patterns used in distributed systems.

All of that together is why this example holds up: each piece does its own job cleanly, the wiring stays predictable, and you can evolve the stack without everything collapsing under its own weight.

The Big Lab: Turning the Notes service into a real multi-container stack

By this point, the Notes service is doing something useful. It can run, it can talk to the outside world, and it can remember things. That's all great, but it's still just one container tied together with manual commands. Real applications aren't built that way. They live as stacks, not single processes. So, in this part of lab, we're going to take the Notes service and turn it into a proper multi-container setup using Docker Compose.

Compose is where the Notes app stops feeling like a toy and starts behaving like something you could actually develop against. One file. One command. One predictable environment every time. Let's build that:

1. **Start with a clean project structure**: Create a folder for the full application. Remember this structure as we're going to come back to it a few times in this lab:

```
notes-app/
  compose.yaml
  compose.override.yaml   (we'll fill this in later)
  api/
    Dockerfile
    app.py
  frontend/
    Dockerfile
    index.html
  data/
```

   You already have the `api` folder from the previous chapters. Now we're adding a small frontend just to demonstrate how Compose wires services together.

2. **Create a simple frontend service**: Inside `frontend/`, add a tiny static site. Nothing complex, just enough to show the API connection.
   Create `frontend/index.html`:

```
<!DOCTYPE html>
<html>
  <body>
    <h1>Notes App</h1>
    <p id="notes"></p>

    <script>
      fetch("http://localhost:5001/notes")
        .then(r => r.json())
        .then(n =>
        document.getElementById("notes").innerText =
        JSON.stringify(n));
    </script>
  </body>
</html>
```

   Create `frontend/Dockerfile`:

```
FROM nginx:alpine
COPY . /usr/share/nginx/html
```

   This gives us a frontend that can call the API and show whatever notes exist.

3. **Write the main Compose file**: Now, create the central `compose.yaml` file:

```
services:
  api:
    build: ./api
    ports:
      - "5001:5000"
    volumes:
      - C:\notes-data:/data
    networks:
      - app-net

  frontend:
    build: ./frontend
```

```
    ports:
      - "8080:80"
    networks:
      - app-net

networks:
  app-net:
```

Here's what this does:

- The API exposes port `5001` on Windows
- The frontend exposes port `8080`
- Both services run on the same network (`app-net`) so they can talk cleanly
- The API still mounts the Windows folder so notes survive rebuilds

  This is already enough for a real stack.

4. **Use an override file for clean development workflows**: We don't want to rebuild images every time we change a line of code in development. Enter the override file, `compose.override.yaml`, in the same location as your `compose.yaml`:

```
services:
  api:
    volumes:
      - ./api:/app
    command: ["python", "app.py"]

  frontend:
    volumes:
      - ./frontend:/usr/share/nginx/html:ro
```

This tells Compose the following:

- In dev, mount the live code so changes refresh instantly
- Run `python app.py` directly so you don't fight caching layers
- Serve the frontend straight from your local folder

Compose merges this automatically.

5. **Bring the whole thing up**: Now, open PowerShell inside the `notes-app` directory and run the following:

```
docker compose up --build
```

You should see both services start, attach to the shared network, and come online. Now, test both endpoints:

```
curl http://localhost:5001/notes
curl http://localhost:8080
```

The browser should show an empty notes array, fetched through the API.

6. **Seed some data**: Let's make sure persistence is still working under Compose. Run this in PowerShell:

```
echo "[\"Welcome to the Notes App\"]" > C:\notes-data\notes.json
```

Reload the frontend:

```
http://localhost:8080
```

You should now see the seeded note appear instantly, pulled from the volume-mounted JSON file.

7. **Explore logs and debugging using Compose**: This part is about Compose, so here are the commands you'll actually use:

    - See live logs from everything at once:

    ```
    docker compose logs -f
    ```

    - See running processes inside each service:

    ```
    docker compose top
    ```

   - Trace what's happening under the hood (startup, shutdown, and health events):

     ```
     docker compose events
     ```

   - Get a shell inside the API container:

     ```
     docker compose exec api sh
     ```

   Compose becomes your single source of truth for visibility. Everything you need is one command away.

8. **Add a simple production override**: We're not going deep into deployment here, just enough to show how environments switch cleanly.
   Create `compose.prod.yaml` in the same place as your `compose.yaml`:

   ```
   services:
     api:
       environment:
         - ENV=production

     frontend:
       image: myorg/notes-frontend:1.0.0
   ```

   The idea is simple:

   - **In dev**: Mount files, run loose, hot-reloading commands
   - **In prod**: Ship a versioned image and lock configuration down

   Switching modes:

   ```
   docker compose -f compose.yaml -f compose.prod.yaml up --build
   ```

One command, and the stack behaves differently. With Compose in place, the Notes service goes from a single container to a predictable, repeatable multi-service stack that behaves the same every time you run it. This is exactly how real applications evolve: a few services at first, then better wiring, then clean separation between dev and prod. The best part is that Compose handles the heavy lifting, so you don't have to. In the next Big Lab, we will tighten the screws a smidge and treat the stack like something that might see real users.

Summary

This chapter was about building containers that work together properly. We looked at how to use Docker Compose not just to get things running but to define and manage full multi-container environments that behave reliably. We walked through writing Compose files, running them on Windows with WSL 2, handling service dependencies cleanly, and setting up patterns that scale as your stack grows. If you've followed along, you should now have a solid foundation for using Compose in a way that feels deliberate, repeatable, and dependable, not just convenient. As your container setups become more and more capable, it is just as important to make sure that they are also secure, well isolated, and built with the right safeguards in place, and that's exactly what we will look at next.

Join us on Discord

For discussions around the book and to connect with your peers, join us on Discord at or scan the QR code below:

5

Docker Security and Best Practices on Windows

Once you start relying on containers to run meaningful parts of your workflow, it becomes less about just getting things running and more about keeping them secure, stable, and intentional. Whether you're building your own images or running ones from elsewhere, understanding what those containers can do, what they have access to, and how they're isolated from the host becomes essential. Let's explore how Docker handles security by default, what parts you need to take control of yourself, and how to build up confidence that your containers are behaving exactly as you expect, and nothing more.

We'll cover the following topics:

- Understanding Docker security
- Managing user access and permissions
- Securing Docker images and containers
- Implementing isolation with namespaces
- Monitoring security and auditing containers

Before we start tightening anything, we need a clear picture of what Docker actually does to protect you by default. The next section lays out the security model you're building on top of, so the rest of the chapter makes sense.

Technical requirements

The code files referenced in this chapter are available at `https://github.com/PacktPublishing/Mastering-Docker-on-Windows`.

Understanding Docker security

There's a moment early on when using Docker when it feels like everything is just working. Containers run exactly what you tell them, they start up fast, they keep your environment isolated, and you think, *This is brilliant.*

But then, something catches your attention. Maybe it's a CVE alert. Maybe it's a conversation about supply chain risk. Or maybe it's just a weird feeling when you realize that your container is running as root and has access to things you weren't expecting. That's when the penny drops.

Security in Docker isn't just about setting a password or using a firewall. It's about understanding the container model, how isolation works, what containers can access by default, and where the trust boundaries really are.

This section is all about that moment, the one where you start thinking a bit more carefully about how secure your containers and images actually are. We'll talk about how Docker approaches security, why it's different from traditional virtual machines, and how to think about containers not just as convenient units of code, but as real parts of your infrastructure that need the same attention and safeguards as anything else. Once you understand the general security mindset, the next step is to look at the actual mechanics. This section walks through the defaults that Docker gives you, what they isolate, and where the boundaries really are.

Docker's security model

One of Docker's biggest strengths is also its biggest challenge from a security point of view; containers share the host kernel.

> **Note**
>
> A virtual machine gets its own fully isolated OS and kernel, which means even if something escapes the guest, it still has to break through a second boundary before reaching the host. A container doesn't have that extra layer. It shares the host kernel, so a misconfiguration or exploit has a more direct path to the underlying system. The trade-off is speed and efficiency versus a tighter blast radius if something goes wrong.

Unlike a virtual machine, which emulates hardware and runs a completely separate OS, a Docker container runs as an isolated process on the same kernel as the host. This makes it lightweight and fast, but it also means that there's a closer relationship between the container and the host than most people realize.

If a container escapes its boundaries, or if it's misconfigured in a way that allows unintended access, the impact can be more serious than it would be in a fully virtualized environment.

This is not to say Docker is inherently insecure; it's not. But it does mean that you need to be clear on what the defaults are and what steps you can take to reduce risk.

Container security is not just about locking down the host. It's also about the following:

- The base image you start from
- The software you install
- The way your Dockerfile is written
- The runtime configuration of the container
- The way containers talk to each other and to the outside world

Each of these layers introduces choices, and each choice has security implications:

- Are you using the latest tag without knowing what it points to?
- Are you running the container as root when it does not need that level of access?
- Have you opened ports you did not mean to expose?
- Is your image pulling in vulnerable libraries through dependencies?

You can get away with this in small setups, but as things scale, or as you start sharing your images more widely, these choices matter.

Now, before we get too deep into the risks, it's worth acknowledging what Docker already does out of the box.

When you run a container, Docker does the following:

- Isolates the process from the host using namespaces
- Restricts access to devices and kernel features using `cgroups` and `seccomp`
- Provides a virtual network with controlled routing
- Supports read-only filesystems and non-root users
- Uses a copy-on-write layer for image changes, so your base image stays intact
- Validates the image checksum when pulling from Docker Hub

On Windows, Docker Desktop adds further abstraction by running Linux containers inside a WSL 2 virtual machine. This means that even if a container escapes its Linux isolation, it still hits the boundary of WSL before reaching your Windows host.

That is a useful safeguard, but it's not something to rely on as a primary defense. It's still better to secure containers properly rather than depend on the environment to protect you. Now that we've covered what Docker does well, it's time to look at the parts that trip people up. These are the risks that show up in real workloads and the ones developers hit long before anything exotic or advanced.

> **Note**
>
> WSL 2 provides an extra boundary, but it is not a security boundary in the way Microsoft defines one. It was designed for convenience and compatibility, not isolation. Microsoft's own hardening guidance recommends treating WSL as part of the host and not relying on it to contain a compromised container. In other words, secure the container properly rather than assuming WSL will save you (`https://learn.microsoft.com/en-us/windows/wsl/enterprise`).

Where things start to get risky

Let's step through the three common places security breaks down, starting with the base image itself. If the foundation is weak, everything you build on it inherits the same problems:

- Images that contain vulnerabilities
- Containers that run with too much privilege
- Misconfigured networks or volumes that expose too much

Let's look at each one briefly:

- **Images that contain vulnerabilities**: This is one of the most overlooked issues. If you base your image on something like `ubuntu:latest` or `node:alpine`, you are inheriting all the packages and libraries inside that image and all of their potential vulnerabilities. Unless you're scanning your images regularly, you might never know whether something in your image is out of date or insecure. It's like installing an app that comes bundled with a stack of old dependencies and assuming it is safe because it still runs. We'll cover image scanning and hardening later, but the main point here is this: if you're not checking the contents of your image, you're accepting a lot of risk by default.
- **Containers that run with too much privilege**: By default, containers run as root inside the container, even though they are not root on the host. That can be confusing because it means you can do things inside the container that feel powerful, such as install software, modify config files, and access system paths, but you do not necessarily realize how far those permissions extend. In some cases, if you mount a host volume into the container, you can read or write to places you were not meant to. If you run with `--privileged` or `bind /var/run/docker.sock`, you can escalate to host-level control.

Running containers as root is fine for development, but it is a poor practice in shared or production environments. It increases the blast radius of any compromise.

- **Misconfigured networks or volumes**: It's so easy to expose a port without realizing it, as in this example:

```
ports:
  - "80:80"
```

This exposes your *container's* port `80` to your *host* machine's port `80` – which is fine locally, but potentially dangerous if the host is reachable from the network.

Likewise, mounting sensitive directories can cause issues. Mapping your SSH folder or environment files into a container might seem like a shortcut, but it can expose secrets without any logging or warning.

These are the kinds of things that slip through unnoticed, especially when `compose` files get copied and reused across teams.

A good rule of thumb is this: give your containers the least access they need to do their job, and nothing more.

Area	Bad practice	Better practice	Compose/CLI example
Ports	Expose all ports, default to `0.0.0.0:80`	Only expose required ports, restrict IP binding	Compose: `ports: ["127.0.0.1:5000:5000"]` CLI: `-p 127.0.0.1:5000:5000`
Volumes	Mount sensitive host paths directly	Use named volumes, restrict mount paths	Compose: `volumes: ["app-data:/data"]` CLI: `-v app-data:/data`

Area	Bad practice	Better practice	Compose/CLI example
User access	Run containers as root	Define a non-root user in the Dockerfile	Compose: `user: "1000:1000"` CLI: `--user 1000:1000`
Capabilities	Run with default Linux capabilities	Drop all (`--cap-drop=ALL`), add back minimal	Compose: `cap_drop: ["ALL"]` CLI: `--cap-drop=ALL`
Docker socket	Mount `/var/run/docker.sock` by default	Avoid socket mounts; use API proxies if needed	Compose: (avoid) CLI: (do not mount sock unless required)

Table 5.1: Common container security pitfalls

Most of this is achievable with minimal effort once you start thinking in these terms. The key is to make it a habit.

In production, I've seen containers left running as root for months simply because nobody wanted to refactor the Dockerfile. It only took one compromised service to remind the team that defaults are not safe defaults.

Containers do not equal security by default

There's a common assumption that "because it's running in a container, it's secure." That is not always the case. Containers give you process isolation and immutability, both of which are helpful, but they are not a silver bullet.

A container is only as safe as the way it's built and the limits you put around it. Misconfigurations, over-privileged users, unscanned base images, or wide-open network settings can undo every bit of protection that Docker provides out of the box. In practice, a poorly configured container can be just as dangerous as a poorly configured virtual machine or server, sometimes more so, because containers are so easy to spin up and forget about.

On Windows, Docker adds some default separation via WSL 2, but that does not remove the need to understand what your containers are doing, what they are connected to, and what they are allowed to access.

So, how do you take back control of that security story? It starts with the basics: knowing who your containers are running as, what they can touch, and how to stop them from having more power than they need. Let's dig into that next by looking at user access and permissions. With the high-level risks covered, the next step is focusing on who a container actually runs as and what that user can touch. User access is where a lot of hidden problems start.

Managing user access and permissions

When you first start using Docker, it's easy to assume that the container runtime takes care of everything: process isolation, security boundaries, and even user access. But under the surface, the way users are handled inside containers, and how permissions interact with the host system, is something that deserves a proper look.

If you've ever seen a container running as root and thought, *Well, that's probably fine for now*, you're not alone. Most of us start there. But in real environments, the defaults are rarely enough, especially when containers are sharing volumes, running on shared infrastructure, or holding sensitive data.

Let's take a look at how user access works in Docker, how permissions are handled inside containers, and what you can do to take control of that access. Let's also look at the interaction between container users and host users, the risks of running as root, and how to reduce privilege without breaking your setup. Before we fix anything, it's worth understanding why container users matter at all. The user ID inside a container isn't just a technical detail; it defines what the process can and can't do.

Why user access matters

Every container starts with a user. By default, that user is `root`, not the root of your host system, but the root user inside the container itself.

This is a useful default. It means containers can install packages, modify files, and run processes without hitting permission errors. But it's also risky, especially when you start mounting volumes from the host.

For example, if a container running as `root` writes to a volume mounted from your Windows system, it can change file ownership in ways that are hard to reverse. It can also create files with permissions that block access later, or in some cases, overwrite things it shouldn't touch.

The bigger concern is privilege escalation. If someone compromises a container that's running as `root`, they've got a lot more room to move, particularly if you've mounted sensitive paths or granted additional privileges.

So, while running as `root` is common, it's not ideal. And the good news is, there are better ways to manage it. Once you know why user access is important, the next step is controlling it. The Dockerfile is where you make those choices permanent.

Defining users in Dockerfiles

Inside every container, there's a Linux-style user model, even on Windows with WSL 2. When you run a container, Docker gives it a **user ID** (**UID**) and **group ID** (**GID**). If you do nothing, that's UID `0`, the root user.

You can check this by running the following command in PowerShell or your VS Code terminal:

```
docker run --rm alpine id
```

Here's the expected output:

```
PS C:\Users\MikeSmith> docker run --rm alpine id
uid=0(root) gid=0(root) groups=0(root)
```

Figure 5.1: The default root user (UID 0) inside an Alpine container

To specify a different user, you can use the `--user` flag:

```
docker run --rm --user 1001:1001 alpine id
```

Now, the container is running as a non-root user with UID `1001`.

This becomes really useful when you're running containers that should not have full access to everything inside. It also helps when matching container users to host users for volume access.

The more sustainable approach is to define the user in your Dockerfile:

```
FROM node:18

RUN useradd --create-home appuser
USER appuser

WORKDIR /home/appuser
COPY . .
```

```
CMD ["node", "server.js"]
```

This sets up a new user and switches to it before running your application.

Now, your container starts with reduced privileges by default, and you don't need to remember to pass extra flags when running it.

If you're using a multi-stage build, you can build as `root`, then switch to a non-root user in the final stage. That way, you still get flexibility during image creation, without sacrificing safety at runtime.

> **Note**
>
> Here are the Compose equivalents (`user`, `read_only`, and `cap_drop`):
>
> ```
> services:
>   app:
>     image: myapp:latest
>     user: "1001:1001" # same as --user 1001:1001
>     read_only: true # same as --read-only
>     cap_drop:
>       - ALL # same as --cap-drop=ALL
> ```
>
> When mounting Windows folders into containers, match the container user to an expected host UID/GID (for example, `1000:1000`) to avoid root-owned files appearing inside the mounted directory under WSL.

Now, let's tackle two of the riskiest flags in Docker. Both look harmless at first glance, but they effectively remove the boundaries that containers rely on.

Avoiding --privileged and the Docker socket

Two of the most dangerous patterns in Docker are as follows:

- Running containers with `--privileged`
- Mounting the Docker socket (e.g., `/var/run/docker.sock`)

Both of these effectively give the container full access to the host. If a container can access the Docker socket, it can start containers, stop them, or even mount the host filesystem.

This is occasionally needed for things such as CI pipelines or Docker-in-Docker setups, but it should never be the default.

Safer alternatives to mounting the Docker socket

If your container really needs to interact with the Docker engine, avoid mounting the raw socket. Use a scoped proxy such as `docker-socket-proxy`, which exposes only the API endpoints you choose, or issue least-privilege API tokens for per-job automation instead of giving containers full host access.

Here's an example of running Docker commands safely via `docker-socket-proxy`:

```
services:
  docker-proxy:
    image: tecnativa/docker-socket-proxy
    volumes:
      - /var/run/docker.sock:/var/run/docker.sock
    environment:
      CONTAINERS: 1 # expose only the specific API you need
      IMAGES: 0
      NETWORKS: 0
  job-runner:
    image: my-ci-runner
    environment: DOCKER_HOST: tcp://docker-proxy:2375
```

This pattern gives the container only the permissions required for the task, instead of full control of the host's Docker daemon.

If you need access to host resources, look at narrowing the scope instead; maybe mount only the paths you need, or use a read-only mount. Avoid giving containers access to the socket unless there's no alternative. Permissions get even more interesting once containers start touching host files. This is where Windows users hit confusing behavior unless they understand how WSL handles ownership.

Managing file permissions

One of the trickiest parts of user access is file ownership when using mounted volumes.

If your host creates a file with one UID, but your container runs as a different user, you'll hit permission errors.

This happens often when using bind mounts like this:

```
volumes:
  - .:/app
```

To avoid this, you can do one of three things:

- Run the container with a matching UID
- Use a startup script to chown the files before running the app
- Use named volumes managed by Docker, which do not inherit host permissions

For example, your entry point script might include the following:

```
chown -R appuser:appuser /app
exec "$@"
```

On Windows, WSL 2 handles much of the permissions layer internally, but you'll still see this issue if your container expects Unix-style ownership on volumes coming from the host.

Another useful technique is to limit what the container can modify. You can run containers with a read-only root filesystem like this:

```
docker run --rm --read-only nginx
```

This blocks any writes to the filesystem, unless you explicitly mount writable volumes.

You can also drop Linux capabilities – features that control what processes can do – using the `--cap-drop` flag, as in this example:

```
docker run --rm --cap-drop=ALL --cap-add=NET_BIND_SERVICE nginx
```

This drops all capabilities, then adds back just what's needed to bind to ports below `1024`.

This is a strong way to limit what a container can do, even if it's compromised.

A super common trap I've run into in Windows environments specifically is mounting a host folder that really shouldn't be writable. One team I worked alongside had a containerized job that needed access to a shared configuration folder on their Windows host. They mounted it directly:

```
volumes:
  - C:\CompanyConfig:/config
```

The container was running as `root`, which was the default, and it started writing files into that folder. Everything worked until users on the host side noticed they couldn't open or delete some of those files. See, inside WSL 2, the files had `root` ownership, but from Windows Explorer, they looked locked and inaccessible.

The diagnosis came from a quick check with `ls -l /config` inside the container; the culprit was pretty obvious. The fix was to stop running the container as `root`. They rebuilt the image with a non-root user, switched the service over, and just like that, the host permissions lined up again. The broader point here is that if you mount Windows paths into containers, always think twice about which user is writing to them. In a container, `root` can leave you with some very confusing permission issues on the Windows side.

Alright, so let's actually try this out on Windows. Open PowerShell and run an NGINX container the usual way:

```
docker run --rm nginx whoami
```

Here is the output:

```
root
```

That's the default, and it shows that you're running with full privileges inside the container.

Now, run the same container but specify a user ID:

```
docker run --rm --user 1001 nginx whoami
```

Here is the output:

```
1001
```

Straight away, you can see that the container is no longer running as `root`. In practice, this means if the container writes files to a Windows-mounted folder, they won't be locked to `root` ownership in the same way.

For something more permanent, add this to your Dockerfile:

```
FROM nginx:1.25
RUN adduser --disabled-password --gecos '' appuser
USER appuser
```

That way, every build defaults to a non-root user, and you don't need to remember the `--user` flag.

Here's a quick troubleshooting guide for Windows bind-mount permission issues:

Symptom (error)	Likely cause	Fix
`EACCES` or `EPERM` when writing to a bind mount	Container user UID/GID does not match host metadata (NTFS via WSL2)	Run with `--user 1000:1000` or define matching UID in Dockerfile
Files created by the container appear "locked" or unreadable in Windows Explorer	Root-owned files created inside the WSL 2 volume mounted from Windows	Use `chown` on startup, or avoid `root` by defining a non-root user
Container cannot modify the mounted folder, but commands run fine inside the image	Mount path inherits NTFS permissions not understood by container	Switch to named volumes (Docker-managed) instead of bind mounts
Sudden permission failures after a Windows ownership change	NTFS metadata no longer matches expected Linux UIDs	Recreate the bind mount or reset permissions in WSL (`wsl.conf` adjustments)

Table 5.2: Troubleshooting guide for Windows

Checking who a container is running as

To confirm which user a container is using, run the following:

```
docker exec <container-name> whoami
```

Or, for full detail, run this:

```
docker exec <container-name> id
```

If you see `uid=0(root)`, that container has full access inside its environment.

You can also inspect the container:

```
docker inspect <container-name>
```

Look under `Config.User`. If it's blank, that means `root`.

So, as we can see, managing user access and permissions is one of the most effective ways to limit risk in Docker. While containers offer isolation, they still inherit a lot of assumptions from the host, especially when it comes to file access and privileges.

So, once you've got a handle on who your containers are running as and what they can access, the next step is to look at what they're built from. Even the most carefully configured container can still inherit risks if the image underneath isn't secure. With user access and privileges under control, the next logical layer is the image itself. This is where most security debt hides, usually without anyone noticing.

Securing Docker images and containers

At some point, the image you use to run your container becomes just as important as the code that runs inside it. Whether you are using a public image from Docker Hub or building your own, every layer in that image has a footprint. And that footprint is either helping to secure your container or creating risks you might not even see.

Let's really focus on how to think about image and container security from the very start. Let's look at how to choose safer base images, how to strip out unnecessary components, and how to reduce the attack surface by keeping containers small, focused, and predictable. Everything you ship starts with the base image. If that layer is bloated or unpatched, the rest of your container inherits the same weaknesses.

Why your base image matters

A container image is essentially a stack of layers. Each layer adds files, binaries, libraries, or configuration to the one below. If your base image starts with hundreds of packages you do not need, then you are building on top of unnecessary risk.

The safest base images are usually minimal. Options such as Alpine or distroless contain only what is absolutely needed to run your application. That means fewer dependencies, less attack surface, and fewer packages that need patching.

If you need a full OS environment, use a slim variant. For example, `node:18-slim` is lighter than `node:18` and has fewer moving parts.

You can also build your own base image, but if you do, make sure you document what goes into it and how it is maintained. Base images are the foundation for everything else, and if they are not kept up to date, vulnerabilities can linger for a long time.

Here's a bit of a real-world example from the Windows side. I've seen more than one team standardize on the official Microsoft .NET Framework base images, something like this:

```
FROM mcr.microsoft.com/dotnet/framework/runtime:4.8
```

Figure 5.2: Example of a .NET Framework 4.8 base image from Microsoft's container registry

Sure, it *feels* safe because it's straight from Microsoft, but in one case, the image hadn't been updated in months and still contained a CVE affecting Windows libraries. Developers were happily building on top of it and pushing to production, none the wiser.

The fix was straightforward once they knew: pin to a patched version (4.8-20230509 instead of just 4.8), and bake image scanning into the CI/CD pipeline. That way, every new build surfaced vulnerabilities immediately rather than months down the line.

The lesson here is that even first-party images can lag. If you don't scan, you don't see.

In my experience, base images are the number one blind spot. Teams trust "official" too much. I've had to step in more than once and explain that official doesn't mean immune to CVEs.

Docker Scout also provides built-in CVE visibility directly inside Docker Desktop, which complements local scanners such as Trivy by showing vulnerability summaries, affected packages, and fixed versions as part of the image details pane.

If you want to try this yourself on Windows, which I really hope you do, given the book title, you can install Trivy locally. Using Chocolatey, it's just his simple command:

```
choco install trivy
```

Once installed, scan a base image like this:

```
trivy image mcr.microsoft.com/dotnet/framework/runtime:4.8
```

The output will list known CVEs and their severities. Here's a shortened example:

```
2025-09-30T12:34:56Z INFO Vulnerability scanning...
dotnet-framework/runtime:4.8 (windows/amd64)

┌─────────┬────────────────┬──────────┬─────────────┐
│ LIBRARY │ VULNERABILITY  │ SEVERITY │ FIX VERSION │
├─────────┼────────────────┼──────────┼─────────────┤
│ openssl │ CVE-2023-5678  │ HIGH     │ 1.1.1w      │
│ zlib    │ CVE-2022-37434 │ MEDIUM   │ 1.2.13      │
└─────────┴────────────────┴──────────┴─────────────┘
```

Figure 5.3: Example Trivy scan output in PowerShell showing vulnerabilities in a Windows base image

That tells you straight away whether your supposedly "safe" base image is actually lagging behind. For enterprises, wiring this into a CI job means every new image gets checked automatically before it's pushed.

If you've not come across it before, Chocolatey is a Windows package manager. Think of it like `apt` on Linux or `brew` on macOS, but for Windows. It lets you install tools from the command line without hunting down installers and clicking through wizards.

However, with a command such as `choco`, I often slip up and call it *chocobo* (after the Final Fantasy series), but that's just me.

To set it up, open PowerShell as administrator and run the following:

```
Set-ExecutionPolicy Bypass -Scope Process -Force; `
[System.Net.ServicePointManager]::SecurityProtocol = `
[System.Net.ServicePointManager]::SecurityProtocol -bor 3072; `
iex ((New-Object System.Net.WebClient).DownloadString('https://
community.chocolatey.org/install.ps1'))
```

Once that finishes, close and reopen PowerShell. You'll now have the `choco` command available, so you can do things such as this:

```
choco install trivy
```

That's it, Chocolatey takes care of downloading and setting up the tool for you. Once your base image is clean, the next step is tightening the way you actually build your containers. The Dockerfile is usually where problems creep in unnoticed. Even with a clean base image, the Dockerfile can reintroduce risks if you're not deliberate about how you build the final container.

Hardening and scanning containers

Now, before we move on, let's talk about the Dockerfile itself, the blueprint of your container. Even with a good base image, the way you build your image can either harden or weaken its security. Every instruction you add leaves a little footprint: a new layer, more dependencies, and potentially, more vulnerabilities.

I've seen so many production Dockerfiles that start out neat and quickly turn into a patchwork of copied lines, ad-hoc installs, and leftover cache files. The problem isn't just cleanliness; it's that every forgotten package or unnecessary layer increases the attack surface.

So, cleaning up your Dockerfile isn't busywork; it's one of the simplest ways to harden your images and make them predictable. It's part of what I'd call **build-time security**, securing the container before it even runs.

Here are a few practical best practices to follow:

- Combine `RUN` statements to reduce layers and avoid leaving behind caches.
- Use `COPY` instead of `ADD` unless you need `ADD`'s extra features.
- Avoid installing build tools unless you need them at runtime.
- Remove package manager caches (`apt-get clean`, etc.) at the end of `RUN` chains.

Here's an example Dockerfile:

```
FROM node:18-alpine
WORKDIR /app
COPY package*.json ./
RUN npm install --production && npm cache clean --force
COPY . .
CMD ["node", "index.js"]
```

This creates a lightweight image with just your dependencies and application code. If you need to compile or build assets, consider using multi-stage builds. Here's what a clean, minimal Node.js Dockerfile looks like when you put those best practices into action:

```
# Use a minimal Node.js base image
FROM node:18-alpine

# Set working directory inside the container
WORKDIR /app

# Copy only the dependency definition files
COPY package*.json ./

# Install only production dependencies and clean up cache
RUN npm install --production && npm cache clean --force

# Copy the rest of the application code
COPY . .

# Start the application
CMD ["node", "index.js"]

```

Figure 5.4: Example of a clean, minimal Node.js Dockerfile following best practices for lightweight, secure image builds

When you combine this kind of image hygiene with the principles in *Build Once, Run Safely Anywhere*, you get the best of both worlds – smaller, more portable containers that are easier to trust and maintain. Clean builds aren't just faster; they're safer, too.

Now, even if your Dockerfile is clean, you are still relying on upstream images. That means inherited packages, inherited bugs, and inherited vulnerabilities.

Docker Desktop includes built-in image scanning through Docker Scout. You can also use tools such as Trivy or Snyk to scan images locally or in CI. Here's an example with Trivy:

```
trivy image node:18-alpine
```

This should list known **Common Vulnerabilities and Exposures** (**CVE**) in the image and show which packages are affected:

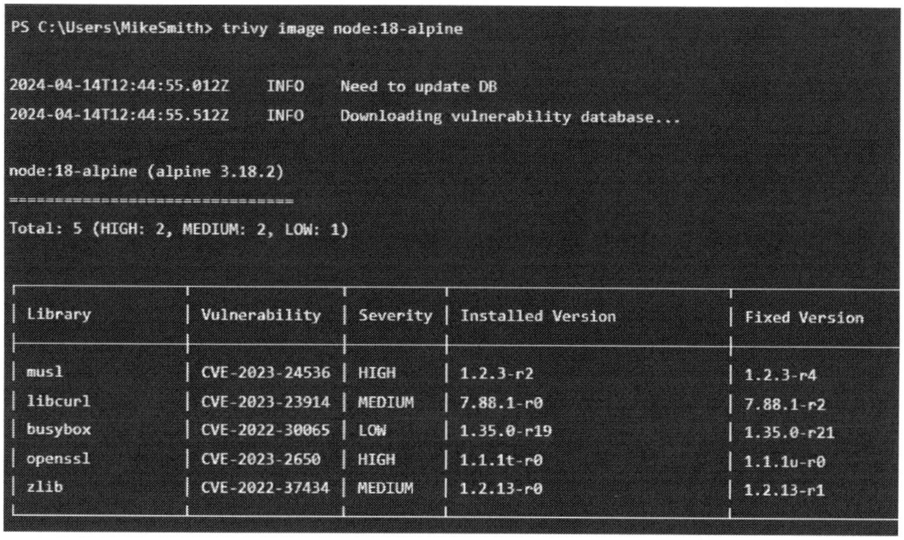

Figure 5.5: Example Trivy scan output in PowerShell showing detected vulnerabilities

It is worth doing this as part of your build process. Even a small app can bring in dozens of libraries, and a vulnerability in a transitive dependency can cause trouble if left unchecked.

If you're using Docker Desktop on Windows, you can also try this visually through the Docker Scout interface:

1. Open Docker Desktop and go to the **Images** tab.
2. Find the image you want to check, for example, `node:18-alpine` or your latest build.
3. Click the image name to open its details.
4. Switch to the **Security** tab to see the vulnerability summary.

Docker Scout automatically pulls data from its CVE database and lists known issues by severity: *Critical*, *High*, *Medium*, or *Low*. You'll see something like this:

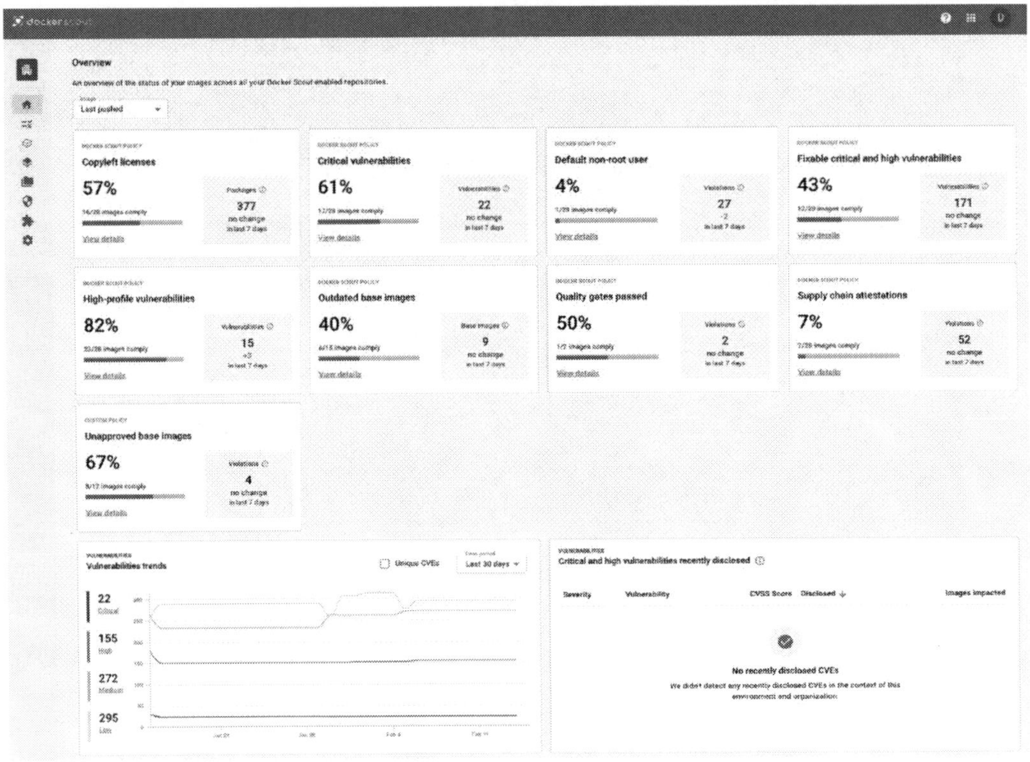

Figure 5.6: Overview of image security posture

Each vulnerability entry links to the affected package, the CVE ID, and (if available) a fixed version. It's a really quick way to catch problems before pushing your image anywhere near production.

I've found this super useful when I'm doing a sanity check before committing a change to a CI/CD pipeline; it's a fast, visual confirmation that the image is safe.

Something else that's more than a little bit useful is keeping your containers small and specific, remember that a container should do one single thing very well, whatever that one single thing is (hosting NGINX, a database, etc.), which means no combining unrelated services, no extra utilities "just in case," and no bundling in debugging tools you do not plan to use.

Smaller images are easier to reason about, faster to pull, and safer to run. They reduce the time window for attacks and the complexity of patching.

If you need debugging tools, create a debug variant of your image, or use `docker exec` to temporarily install them while troubleshooting.

Limiting what a container can do

Even a perfect image can become a risk if the container runs with too much privilege. There are a few quick ways to reduce that risk:

- Run as a non-root user (set in Dockerfile or with `--user`)
- Use `--read-only` to prevent filesystem writes
- Use `--cap-drop` to remove kernel capabilities
- Use `seccomp profiles` to limit syscalls

Here is an example:

```
docker run --rm --user 1000 --read-only --cap-drop ALL nginx
```

This tells Docker to run NGINX with reduced access, blocking writes to the container filesystem and stripping away extra privileges.

In one Windows shop I worked with, they ran multiple line-of-business apps in containers that all logged to the same shared volume. Without anything like `--read-only`, one misconfigured app wiped part of another's logs. But switching to read-only containers with explicit writable mounts fixed the issue almost immediately.

Build once, run safely anywhere

One of the benefits of containerizing your application is portability. But if you rely too heavily on what the host provides, that portability breaks down. Try to keep your containers self-contained, as follows:

- No assumptions about the host OS
- No reliance on mounted volumes for config unless documented
- No reading or writing outside of intended paths

The less your container depends on the host, the easier it is to run securely in different environments.

Securing images and containers starts with the small choices: what base image you choose, how you build your Dockerfile, and what you include by default. But those choices add up quickly.

Once your images are lean, secure, and self-contained, the next challenge is keeping them isolated when they actually run. Building safely is half the story; running safely is the other. That's where Docker's isolation model comes in, and why understanding namespaces matters.

Implementing isolation with namespaces

Most of the time, when we talk about containers, we talk about them like they're their own little virtual machines. They feel separate. You can exec into one and move around like it's its own box. And when it's running properly, it behaves that way too.

But containers are not virtual machines. They don't emulate hardware. They don't run a full guest OS. What they do instead is a lot smarter and a lot leaner, and the reason that works is because of namespaces.

If you've ever wondered how Docker manages to keep one container's processes, filesystems, and network interfaces invisible to another, or why you can run a dozen containers on your laptop without melting it, namespaces are why.

Let's really focus on how container isolation actually works, and about how Linux namespaces give containers their illusion of independence, even when you're running Docker on Windows. Under the hood, Docker Desktop uses a lightweight Linux kernel inside WSL 2, so the same namespace model still applies. We'll look at which namespaces Docker uses by default, and how those boundaries can be tightened when needed.

Understanding Docker namespaces

At the most basic level, a namespace in Linux is essentially a way to provide an isolated view of a system resource to a process. That could be one of the following:

- The list of running processes
- The network interfaces
- The mounted filesystems
- The hostname and domain name
- User and group ID mappings
- IPC resources, such as shared memory and semaphores

Each of these has its own namespace. When a container starts, Docker creates new namespaces for each of these types and assigns them to the container process. That process, and any children it spawns, sees only what's inside those namespaces.

It's like running the same OS multiple times, but with each version only seeing its own set of files, users, and devices.

On Docker's side, this isolation is handled under the hood using the same kernel primitives you'd use if you were creating a container manually. But let's not go there; let's stay focused on what matters when you're working with containers on Windows.

To see this in action, here's what a container sees when you list processes from inside it. Notice how it only shows its own environment, not the host:

Figure 5.7: Output from PowerShell showing a container listing only its own process

Docker uses several types of namespaces to isolate containers:

- **PID (Process ID)**: Each container gets its own process table. It can only see and interact with processes running inside it.
- **NET (Network)**: Each container gets its own network stack: interfaces, IP addresses, routing tables, and so on.
- **MNT (Mount)**: Each container sees only its own filesystem mounts. It cannot access host filesystems unless they're explicitly mounted.
- **UTS (UNIX Timesharing System)**: This includes hostname and domain name information. Containers can set their own hostnames.
- **IPC (Inter-Process Communication)**: Containers don't share semaphores or shared memory with the host or other containers.
- **USER**: Maps user and group IDs in the container to different IDs on the host. This one is not enabled by default in Docker on most systems, but it's available if you configure it.

Each of these namespaces can be isolated, shared, or dropped altogether, depending on how you run the container.

Now, this might sound like some deep plumbing, but here's why it matters.

- Let's say you're running two containers: one for your app and one for a temporary tool such as a database migrator. If you don't isolate their `PID` and `IPC` namespaces, they could see or interact with each other's processes. That's not what you want.
- Or imagine a container with access to the host's `UTS` namespace. It might be able to spoof DNS or tamper with hostname-based logic.

  Even more critically, if user namespaces are not used, the `root` user inside the container is also `UID 0` on the host, which is why running as non-root is such a big deal. It reduces the impact of that shared namespace.

Another scenario I've come across in enterprise settings is with networking. A finance company had a containerized reporting tool that they ran with the following:

```
docker run --network host reporting-app
```

They did this because it simplified access to an internal SQL server running on the host. What they didn't realize was that `--network host` effectively bridged the container directly onto the corporate LAN. The app was now broadcasting itself with no isolation at all.

The giveaway came when their security team noticed unusual SQL connection attempts showing up in Defender logs. The fix was to move the container back to Docker's default bridged network, then create an explicit internal network just for the reporting tool and its database dependency.

The result was tighter control; the containers could talk to what they needed, but nothing else. That one flag had turned out to be a serious oops, and it's something you'd only really run into if you accidentally set that up without thinking about it, a common mistake.

What I've seen in real environments is that people reach for `--network host` as a quick fix during testing, then forget to remove it. Weeks later, it's quietly running in production with no isolation at all.

Now that we've looked at what namespaces are conceptually, let's switch gears and see how they behave when you use them explicitly.

Using namespace flags in practice

If you want to adjust namespace behavior, Docker provides a few flags to do it. For example, to run a container with the host's network stack (i.e., not isolated), run this:

```
docker run --rm --network host nginx
```

That skips the `NET` namespace and gives the container direct access to the host network interfaces.

Similarly, to share the `PID` namespace with the host, use this:

```
docker run --rm --pid host alpine ps aux
```

This shows all host processes from inside the container, which is rarely something you want in production.

You can also run with IPC or UTS sharing, though it's uncommon:

```
docker run --rm --uts host alpine hostname
```

Here's the expected output:

```
PS C:\Users\MikeSmith> docker run --rm --pid host alpine ps aux
PID   USER     TIME  COMMAND
    1 root      0:03 /init
    7 root      0:00 /usr/bin/dockerd
   14 root      0:00 containerd
   22 root      0:00 docker-proxy
   27 root      0:00 nginx: master process nginx
   34 root      0:00 nginx: worker process
   45 root      0:00 alpine
   46 root      0:00 ps aux
```

Figure 5.8: Output from PowerShell showing a container sharing the host's PID namespace

Now that we've looked at what namespaces actually do under the hood, let's see how you can enable one of the most powerful types, the `user` namespace, to give your containers even stronger isolation on Windows.

Using user namespaces for stronger isolation

User namespaces are one of the more advanced tools in the Docker security toolbox.

They let you map container users to non-root users on the host. So, even if a container is running as `root` inside, it's actually mapped to a low-privilege user outside.

To enable `user` namespaces on Docker Desktop, follow these steps:

1. Go to **Docker Desktop** → **Settings** → **Features in development**.
2. Enable **User namespace support**.
3. Apply and restart Docker.

Then, in `daemon.json` (usually in `~/.docker` or `C:\ProgramData\Docker\config`), add the following:

```
{
  "userns-remap": "default"
}
```

Figure 5.9: Example of enabling user namespace remapping in the Docker daemon configuration

This tells Docker to remap container UIDs to a predefined non-root user on the host. It's not magic, and it can break some images that assume full root access, but it's a strong way to reduce the blast radius of any compromise.

Docker will then create a default user and group on your system and map container UIDs accordingly.

If you want to inspect whether `user` namespaces are active, run this:

```
docker info | Select-String "userns"
```

You should see output like this:

```
userns: enabled
```

> **Note**
>
> User namespace remapping works in Docker Desktop, but some images assume full root access and may fail when the UID/GID is remapped behind the scenes. This is most noticeable when images write to mounted volumes or expect to manage system paths inside the container.
>
> If your system doesn't already have `daemon.json`, you can create one with only the remapping setting, and Docker will supply sensible defaults (`daemon.json` is usually located in `C:\ProgramData\Docker\config`. Edit it using VS Code or Notepad.):
>
> ```
> {
>   "userns-remap": "default"
> }
> ```
>
> Images that rely on system-level tooling or privileged operations may break under remapping, so test critical workloads before enabling this globally.

Limiting host access with namespace isolation

So, here are a few rules of thumb when thinking about namespaces and security:

- Don't share the host's `PID`, `NET`, or `IPC` namespace unless absolutely necessary
- Use the default isolated namespaces for each container
- Enable `user` namespaces for an extra layer of UID/GID protection
- Run each container as a dedicated user with the least privilege necessary

These boundaries are what prevent containers from seeing each other's processes, memory, or filesystem structure. They're what keep isolation real.

It's worth saying here that namespaces are not a firewall. They don't encrypt data, they don't audit traffic, and they don't prevent someone from abusing access if they're already inside the container.

They're more like walls between rooms in the same house. They make sure people stay in their own spaces, but you still need to lock the front door and check what people are bringing in.

That's why namespaces are just one part of the container security model. They work best when combined with other features such as permissions, seccomp, and AppArmor, even though these aren't directly configurable in Docker Desktop on Windows.

So, you can see that namespaces are what make containers feel like their own isolated worlds. They control what a process sees, what it can interact with, and what boundaries exist between containers and the host. Once your containers are built and running safely, the next challenge is keeping them that way. That's where monitoring and auditing come in.

Monitoring security and auditing containers

Once your containers are up and running, the question shifts from "Is this secure?" to "How will I know if it stops being secure?"

It's dead easy to assume that once a container is built, scanned, and launched with the right flags, your job is done. But in practice, security is not a one-off event. It's ongoing. And it's often the quiet things (a container misbehaving, a suspicious outbound request, or a config that silently changed) that matter the most.

Let's talk about that next level of visibility. Let's look at how to keep an eye on your containers, spot unexpected behavior, and respond to issues before they become something worse. Whether you're running on your local dev machine or looking ahead to production, it's worth building the habit of monitoring early. Because the sooner you notice something odd, the easier it is to fix, and the less likely it is to cause real damage.

Why visibility matters

Containers are meant to be ephemeral. You build them, run them, maybe restart them, and throw them away when you're done. That makes them great for deployment, but also easy to lose track of.

If a container gets compromised, modified, or starts doing something unexpected, such as reaching out to a strange IP or spiking CPU usage, you won't know unless you're watching.

The same goes for subtle mistakes: an image built with the wrong config, an old base layer with a known CVE, or a container that was meant to be running as a non-root user but quietly isn't.

These things don't crash your app. They don't break builds. They just sit there. And that's why having a way to monitor what's running and how it behaves is just as important as setting things up correctly in the first place.

A good starting point for visibility is seeing what Docker already gives you out of the box. These tools catch most problems before you need anything more advanced.

Auditing with Docker's built-in tools

For quick checks, some commands we've already covered but are worth mentioning. The built-in Docker CLI gives you a few useful ways to spot trouble. Start with the following:

```
docker ps
```

This shows what's currently running, how long it's been up, and which ports are exposed.

To dig deeper, use this:

```
docker stats
```

This shows live CPU, memory, and network usage for each container:

```
PS C:\Users\MikeSmith> docker stats

CONTAINER ID   NAME                CPU %    MEM USAGE / LIMIT    MEM %     NET I/O
a1b2c3d4e5f6   web-app             2.33%    78.5MiB / 2GiB        3.84%     1.2MB / 973kB
b2c3d4e5f6a7   db                  1.12%    250.4MiB / 2GiB       12.25%    8.1MB / 3.4MB
c3d4e5f6a7b8   background-worker   89.76%   1.5GiB / 2GiB         75.00%    15.4MB / 14.9MB
```

Figure 5.10: Output from PowerShell showing live container statistics using docker stats

If a container starts eating resources unexpectedly, you'll spot it here.

For logs, use the following:

```
docker logs <container-name>
```

That gives you `stdout` and `stderr` from the container, which is often where runtime errors, warnings, or unexpected behavior show up.

If something looks off, run this:

```
docker inspect <container-name>
```

That shows everything about the container, including its environment, user, volumes, and what image it was built from.

Docker also provides an event stream, a live feed of what's happening at the engine level:

```
docker events
```

You'll start seeing real-time messages for `container start`, `stop`, `create`, `destroy`, and more.

This is incredibly useful for auditing activity. For example, if a container is being restarted constantly or if something is creating containers in the background, `docker events` will show it.

You can also filter by container or time range:

```
docker events --since 10m --filter container=my-container
```

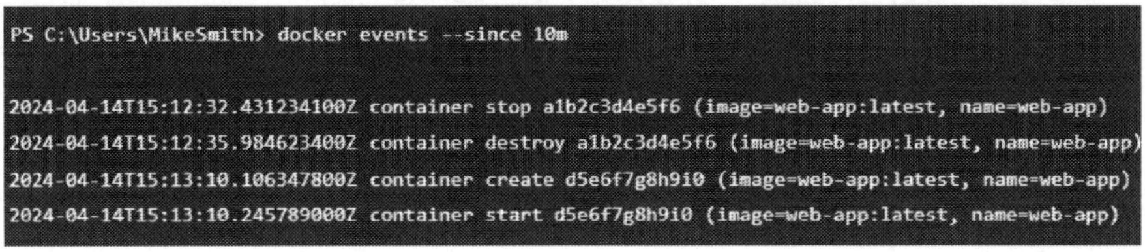

Figure 5.11: Output from PowerShell showing recent Docker events, including container stop, destroy, create, and start actions

For local development, this is great for catching unexpected behavior. For production, it forms the basis of audit logging and forensic analysis if something goes wrong.

Note

If you need deeper insight or want to detect subtle issues, there are specialized third-party scanners that go much further than Docker's built-in options, but they do sit outside the scope of this book, though we do touch on them lightly. If you want to explore that ecosystem, two solid starting points are the OWASP Container Security Verification Standard (`https://github.com/OWASP/Container-Security-Verification-Standard`) and Aqua Security's Trivy documentation (`https://trivy.dev/`).

Advanced security and scanning tools

Even after you've scanned an image once, vulnerabilities can be found later. That's why it's worth setting up regular scans, especially in CI, but even locally if your images live a while.

Trivy is fast and lightweight. To scan all your local images, run the following:

```
trivy image --quiet --severity HIGH,CRITICAL
```

This flags any known CVE in the images you've pulled or built. You can also scan your Dockerfile to catch risky instructions before they become part of the image:

```
trivy config .
```

That checks for hardcoded secrets, unsafe patterns, and other misconfigurations.

Here's a quick example of a Trivy scan in action, showing detected vulnerabilities within the `node:18-alpine` image and their recommended fixed versions:

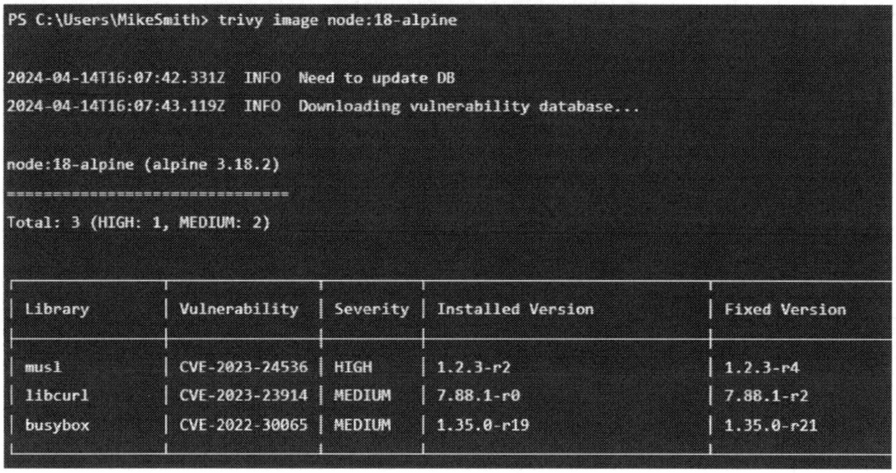

Figure 5.12: Example Trivy scan output showing detected vulnerabilities in the node:18-alpine image

If you're serious about container auditing, you'll want to track changes to files, permissions, and active processes inside containers. There are a few tools that can help:

- **Advanced Intrusion Detection Environment** (**AIDE**)
- Falco (from Sysdig)
- osquery (from Meta, now open source)

These tools can watch container filesystems for unexpected changes, alert on system call anomalies, and give you visibility into what's actually happening inside your containers, not just at the Docker layer.

Falco, for example, runs as a sidecar and can be configured to flag things such as the following:

- A container spawning a shell
- Writing to sensitive files such as `/etc/passwd`
- Unexpected outbound network activity

To get started with Falco on Docker Desktop, follow these steps:

1. Pull the image:

```
docker pull falcosecurity/falco
```

2. Run it with access to your host:

```
docker run --rm -it \
  --privileged \
  -v /var/run/docker.sock:/host/var/run/docker.sock \
  -v /proc:/host/proc:ro \
  -v /boot:/host/boot:ro \
  falcosecurity/falco
```

Now, you're watching live for policy violations and suspicious behavior. Here is the example output:

```
22:04:17.456123819: Warning Container started shell (user=root user_loginuid=-1
command=sh parent= container_id=7d7e3218c3a5 image=alpine:latest)
```

You don't need to use these tools daily, but knowing they exist and testing them once or twice gives you a serious edge if something ever goes wrong. Running Docker on Windows adds another layer of signals you can watch. The Windows host and WSL both give you clues when something isn't right.

Monitoring in Windows environments

If you're running containers using WSL 2 on Windows, you can still use all the preceding tools; they just run inside the Linux VM Docker sets up. But you can also add extra layers of visibility from the Windows side, as in these examples:

- Use Windows Defender or endpoint protection to monitor Docker's files and processes.

- Check your WSL distribution's resource usage with `wsl --status` and task manager.
- Use Windows Event Viewer to spot service-level errors from Docker Desktop.

These give you a dual view: one from inside the Linux container world, and one from the Windows host. If you're managing containers as part of a larger Windows-based environment, this matters.

One thing I've learned the hard way is that problems rarely announce themselves with big errors. More often, it's a tiny anomaly, a container restarting too often, or a log line you'd usually ignore that ends up being the real signal. When something feels off, having a simple, repeatable checklist removes guesswork and stops you from jumping between tools randomly.

Now, here's the secret sauce – this is my incident checklist that works well when something seems off. I've used it for years now, and I rarely get to the bottom of the list without finding the problem:

1. Use `docker ps` and `docker stats` to spot the problem.
2. Run `docker logs` to look for container-level errors.
3. Inspect the container with `docker inspect` to check for configuration drift.
4. Use `docker events` to see whether the container is being restarted or recreated.
5. Use Trivy or Scout to rescan the image for newly discovered vulnerabilities.
6. If needed, stop and remove the container and rebuild from a known good image.
7. Document what happened. This part is easy to skip, but incredibly valuable.

So, here's a case where monitoring made a huge difference. In a past job, we had a containerized HR system in a large Windows shop, and it started making outbound requests to an IP address in Eastern Europe. The requests were small, infrequent, and would have gone totally unnoticed if not for Windows Defender flagging unusual outbound traffic from the WSL 2 VM. You know, one of those annoying little popups in the bottom corner of your Windows screen you usually ignore.

The lead developer dug into it with `docker logs` and found nothing obvious. A rescan with Trivy, however, revealed the real problem: a compromised `npm` dependency baked into the container image. Rolling back to a previous, signed image immediately stopped the traffic.

What saved them wasn't just having Defender on the host but combining it with container-level tools. `docker logs` told them what the app thought it was doing, Trivy told them what was inside the image causing it, and Defender gave visibility at the Windows layer. Without all three, they might have missed it completely.

The faster you respond, the less time an attacker or buggy container has to do damage, and the more confident you'll feel when containers are doing something unexpected. What I've learned is that the biggest risks aren't the exotic zero-days. It's the small missteps, mounting the wrong folder, forgetting to scan an image, and leaving a port open. Containers magnify little mistakes fast.

The Big Lab: Hardening the Notes service

By now, the Notes service is running as a small but real multi-container application. It has a frontend, an API, a shared network, and persistent storage on Windows. The next step is making it behave like something that could survive in the real world. Security is a huge topic, but for this lab, we're keeping things deliberately tight and achievable. The goal is dead simple: harden the stack with practical safeguards that matter for everyday container work.

We're going to isolate the API onto its own private network, lock down the frontend so it can't mutate anything, mount secrets safely, and enforce the idea that only the right traffic should ever reach the internal service:

1. **Add a private internal network for the API**: Right now, both the API and the frontend sit on the same `app-net`. That's fine for early chapters, but it's too open. We want a world where the frontend can talk to the API, but nothing else can. To do this, update `compose.yaml` to add another network:

    ```
    networks:
      app-net:
      api-private:
    ```

    Then, update the API service:

    ```
    services:
      api:
        build: ./api
        ports:
          - "5001:5000"
        volumes:
          - 'C:\\notes-data:/data'
        networks:
          - api-private
          - app-net
    ```

The order doesn't matter, but the intent does. The API now lives on a dedicated internal network that only the services we approve can join.

2. **Lock the frontend into the public-facing network**: The frontend should never join the `api-private` network. It should only have access to `app-net`, which acts as the public interface for the whole stack. Update the `frontend` service:

```
frontend:
  build: ./frontend
  ports:
    - "8080:80"
  networks:
    - app-net
  read_only: true
```

The `read_only: true` flag means the container's filesystem can't be modified at runtime. This is a simple but really meaningful hardening step. A compromised frontend container cannot easily write malware, drop files, or change its own state.

3. **Move secrets into a file on Windows**: We're not storing production secrets here, just demonstrating the pattern. Create a file called `api.secrets` in the project root:

```
API_KEY=supersecretkey123
```

Add it to `.gitignore`:

```
api.secrets
```

Then, wire it into `compose.yaml`:

```
services:
  api:
    env_file:
      - api.secrets
```

Inside the API, update `app.py` to read it:

```
import os
API_KEY = os.getenv("API_KEY")
```

This gives us a clean pattern:

- `.env` contains non-sensitive config
- `api.secrets` stores secrets
- Git ignores real secrets
- Compose loads them automatically

4. **Add a simple API key check**: We're not adding OAuth or JWTs or anything heavy. This is a minimal guard, so you can see that the secret is actually being used. Modify the `POST /notes` endpoint:

```
from flask import abort

@app.post("/notes")
def add_note():
    if request.headers.get("X-API-Key") != API_KEY:
        abort(401)
    ...
```

Now, the frontend can still read notes, but anything that wants to write them must present a key.

Let's test it manually:

```
curl -X POST http://localhost:5001/notes ^
  -H "Content-Type: application/json" ^
  -H "X-API-Key: supersecretkey123" ^
  -d "{\"note\":\"secured note\"}"
```

Try it again without the header. You should get a `401` error. This demonstrates the point that small guards can go a long way.

5. **Inspect the network and container security**: A big part of security is simply verifying that the configuration matches what you think it is, so check the container's networks:

```
docker inspect notes-app-api
```

Look under `Networks`, and you should see the following:

- `app-net`
- `api-private`

These will have the correct IP ranges. This is going to be different for everyone reading this, so I'll not list them here. You understand.

Check that the frontend is *not* attached to the private network:

```
docker inspect notes-app-frontend
```

Check the mount mode and permissions:

```
docker inspect notes-app-frontend --format
"{{json .HostConfig.ReadonlyRootfs}}"
```

It should return `true`.

This is the bit most people skip: actually confirming what the system is doing, not what they *believe* it is doing.

6. **Test the isolation**: Now, prove to yourself that the frontend cannot talk to the API through the private interface. Exec into the frontend:

```
docker compose exec frontend sh
```

Inside the container, use the following:

```
ping api
wget http://api:5000
```

Both should fail or hang. Only the public address should work:

```
wget http://api:5000 --header="X-API-Key: supersecretkey123"
```

The difference is intentional. We now have a proper public network and a private one.

That's enough security for this stage of the Notes service. The app is still simple, but now it behaves like something that could survive a messy development environment or accidental exposure. We've isolated the API, locked down the frontend, moved secrets into a safer layout, and added a minimal guardrail at the application layer. Secure foundations are in place.

In the next chapter, we'll make it fast.

Summary

Contrary to some beliefs, security is not something you set and forget, especially with containers. They change, update, rebuild, and restart constantly. And that means monitoring and auditing are not optional extras; they're part of doing containers properly.

This chapter focused on building containers that are not just functional, but safe and intentional. We looked at how Docker handles security by default, how to reduce unnecessary access and privilege (always remember the principle of least privilege), and how to isolate and monitor what your containers are doing. From the images you build to the way you run and observe them, each decision shapes the trust you can place in what you deploy. With that foundation in place, we can now start focusing on performance: how to keep things fast, efficient, and responsive, especially when running Docker on Windows.

Get This Book's PDF Version and Exclusive Extras

6

Optimizing Docker for Performance on Windows

I've lost count of the number of times I've seen a container slow down for reasons that had nothing to do with the actual app itself. Sometimes it's the way Docker Desktop's tuned, sometimes it's WSL quietly eating more memory than it should, sometimes it's the phase of the planet Venus (that one's a joke...mostly). Performance tuning on Windows isn't glamorous, but it is the difference between a container that flies and one that drags its feet. It is key to efficient containerized workflows.

This chapter covers advanced performance optimization strategies, from analyzing metrics to fine-tuning resource allocation and leveraging benchmarking tools. As senior engineers, we must ensure our Docker environments are both efficient and scalable. By the end, you will have the skills to optimize resource utilization and improve system performance.

We'll be covering the following main topics:

- Resource allocation for Docker on Windows
- Optimizing container startup and execution
- Managing CPU and memory limits
- Scaling Docker environments
- Monitoring and fine-tuning performance

Let's get started!

Technical requirements

The code files referenced in this chapter are available at `https://github.com/PacktPublishing/Mastering-Docker-on-Windows`.

Resource allocation for Docker on Windows

There's a moment every developer hits when the machine they trust starts pushing back. Maybe it's the fan spinning a bit louder than it should, or that slight delay in your IDE that wasn't there yesterday. You know the one. You open **Task Manager**, and sure enough, Docker's sitting there, arms folded, helping itself to more memory and CPU than you expected. And the truth is, it's doing exactly what you let it do.

By default, Docker Desktop can be a bit of a resource hog. It assumes you're happy to share generously with the backend VM, and unless you step in and tell it otherwise, it won't think twice about using most of what your system can offer. But on Windows, with Docker running under WSL 2, you've actually got a lot of say in what gets shared and how much.

In my previous job, I was mentoring a pair of university students through their final-year project, which involved running AI models inside containers on Windows. Every afternoon, their laptops would grind to a halt, fans blasting, even when the models weren't actually running. Task Manager showed Vmmem ballooning past 10 GB of RAM. The root cause wasn't their code at all; WSL 2 had no limits, so Docker just kept expanding to fill all available memory. Once we added a simple `.wslconfig` cap (4 GB RAM, 2 CPUs), everything stabilized instantly, and their containers became more predictable. It looked like a performance bug, but it was really just WSL's defaults doing what they're allowed to do.

In this section, we'll look at how Docker on Windows allocates resources, how to configure it properly using Docker Desktop and WSL, and how to make smarter decisions when tuning it for your daily work. We won't go deep into performance tuning or container execution speed here; that's covered in just a little bit. This is about the foundational resource setup that makes the rest of Docker behave.

How Docker uses system resources on Windows

Before we touch any settings, it's important to know what's happening under the hood.

When you install Docker Desktop on Windows and choose the WSL 2 backend (which is the default), you're not just running containers on Windows directly. You're spinning up a lightweight Linux virtual machine managed by WSL 2. This VM is what actually hosts your containers. From a system resource perspective, Docker's not using Windows memory and CPU directly; it's using what the WSL 2 VM has access to.

That's why things feel a bit murky when Docker starts using more memory than you expected. Windows Task Manager doesn't show individual containers, but you might see a process called Vmmem chewing through your RAM. That's the WSL 2 VM in action, taking what it needs for Docker and anything else running inside WSL.

By default, WSL 2 doesn't impose any hard limits. If Docker needs more memory, it'll take it. If it needs more CPU, it'll grab that too. This might be fine for some people. But if you're running Docker alongside a heavy-duty IDE, a browser with 20 tabs, or anything else that eats resources, things can get sluggish fast.

So, let's look at how to take the wheel.

Controlling and limiting resources

If you've used Docker Desktop in the past, you might remember a set of sliders that let you manually allocate memory, CPUs, and swap space directly in the **Resources** tab. That layout has since changed, especially for users running the WSL 2 backend.

Now, instead of adjusting resources directly in Docker Desktop, you'll see a simplified **Resource Saver** interface. This setting reduces Docker's footprint when no containers are running, automatically scaling down CPU and memory use until activity resumes.

You'll find it by opening **Docker Desktop**, heading to **Settings**, and clicking **Resources** > **Advanced**.

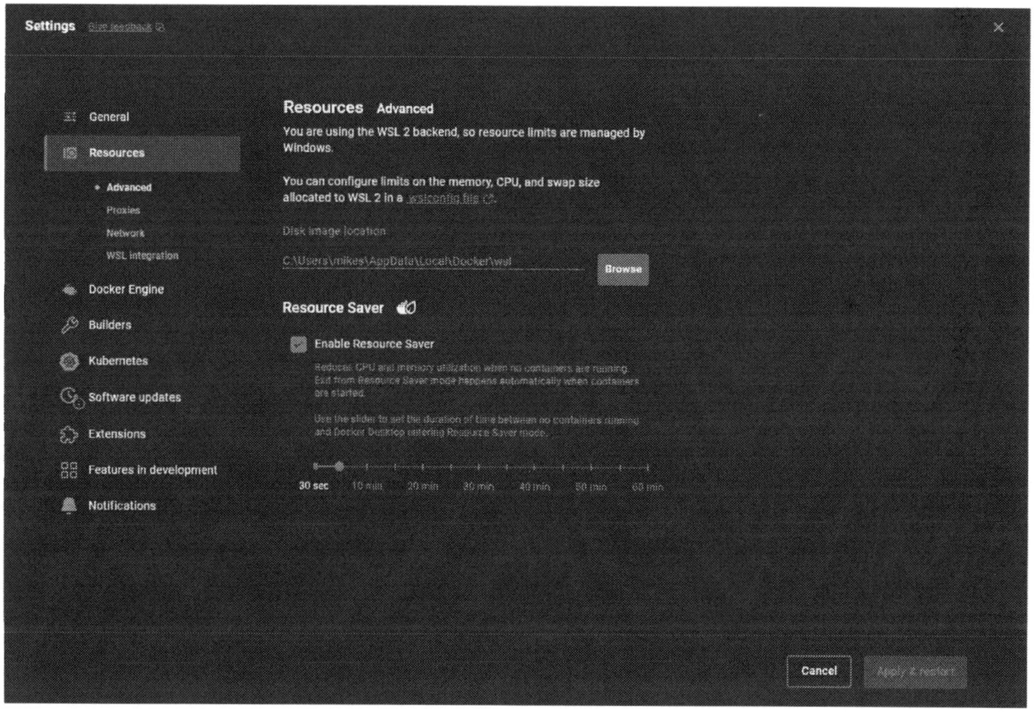

Figure 6.1: Resource Saver settings in Docker Desktop for Windows

Checking **Enable Resource Saver** tells Docker to go into a low-usage state once your containers have been idle for a set period of time. You can configure the delay using the slider, anything from 30 seconds up to 60 minutes. As soon as a container starts again, Docker exits **Resource Saver** mode automatically.

This is a helpful default for most users. It keeps the WSL 2 VM from using unnecessary resources while Docker's idle, without requiring any manual tweaking. That said, if you're running into persistent performance issues or want stricter limits, you'll need to fall back on WSL-level settings.

If you want more control over how WSL behaves generally – not just for Docker, you can define global resource limits using a `.wslconfig` file.

This file lives in your Windows user directory (typically `C:\Users\YourName`) and controls how all WSL 2 distributions, including Docker's backend, allocate resources. If you've never created one before, open Notepad, save a file named `.wslconfig` in your home directory, and add something like this:

Figure 6.2: Example .wslconfig file defining memory, CPU, and swap limits for WSL 2

Save the file, then restart your system (not just Docker) for the changes to take effect. These settings will apply to all WSL 2 instances, not just Docker's virtual machine.

Here's what's actually happening behind the scenes: When Docker starts, it reads all those values and constrains the virtual machine that WSL uses to host the containers. So, if you've capped memory at 4 GB, every container inside that VM now competes within that same pool of RAM. That's why builds start to fail when limits are too tight – you're not starving Docker; you're starving Linux itself. Knowing that helps you tune limits deliberately rather than by guesswork.

For accessibility, here's a table of safe defaults for WSL 2 resource limits:

Machine Type	Recommended Memory Limit	Recommended CPU Limit	Swap Guidance
Everyday laptop (8–16 GB RAM)	3–6 GB	2–4 cores	Keep 1–2 GB swap (never set `swap=0`)
Developer workstation (16–32 GB RAM)	6–12 GB	4–8 cores	2–4 GB swap for large builds
CI agent / heavy build machine	8–16 GB	6–12 cores	4 GB+ swap for parallel builds
Low-resource or battery-sensitive device	2–4 GB	2 cores	1 GB swap to avoid disk churn

Table 6.1: Recommended WSL 2 memory, CPU, and swap "safe defaults"

Let's look at common `.wslconfig` mistakes, symptoms, and quick fixes:

Mistake	Symptom	Quick Remedy
Setting `swap=0`	Containers die with exit `137`, long builds fail halfway	Set `swap=2GB` (or higher for heavy builds) and run `wsl --shutdown`
Memory limit set too low (e.g., 2–3 GB)	WSL freeze, sluggish Windows apps, random Docker failures	Increase to 4–6 GB, depending on machine RAM
Over-allocating memory (e.g., 12–14 GB on a 16 GB laptop)	Vmmem consumes almost all RAM; Windows UI becomes laggy	Reduce the memory cap to 6–8 GB and restart WSL
Giving WSL all CPU cores	Windows UI stutters, high fan usage, background lag	Limit WSL to half your logical cores (e.g., `processors=4` on an 8-core CPU)

Mistake	Symptom	Quick Remedy
Forgetting to restart WSL	No changes apply; config seems "ignored"	Run `wsl --shutdown`, then reopen Docker Desktop

Table 6.2: Quick troubleshooting guide for common .wslconfig misconfigurations

> Note
>
> **Quick rule of thumb**: If you see exit 137, WSL freezing, or Vmmem ballooning, your `.wslconfig` is almost certainly too aggressive.

These aren't hard rules, just safe starting points. The goal is to prevent WSL 2 from starving Windows under load while still giving Docker enough room to breathe.

Best practices for resource allocation

Now that we've covered the "how", let's talk a bit about the "why."

There's no one-size-fits-all setting here. Allocating 4 GB of memory and 2 CPUs might be perfect for a lightweight Node.js app and a Postgres container. But it might not hold up for a full microservices stack with 10 containers and a heavy frontend build.

Your goal here isn't to restrict Docker for the sake of it; it's to strike the right balance between giving Docker what it needs and preserving your machine's performance for everything else you use.

Here are some guidelines I often recommend:

- Start small. Give Docker just enough to run your core stack, then scale up only if you need to.
- Avoid maxing out memory or CPU unless you're sure your machine can take it.
- Leave headroom for the host OS, your editor, browser, and whatever else is running.
- Never be afraid to tweak. You'll likely change these settings several times as your projects evolve.

Once you've made some adjustments, it's worth checking what impact they've had. Here are a few ways to inspect Docker's resource usage:

- In Docker Desktop, the **Dashboard** gives you a basic view of running containers, their logs, and health.
- Open **Task Manager** and check for the Vmmem process. Its memory usage reflects what the WSL backend, including Docker, is currently using.

- From your WSL terminal, you can run `free -m` or `top` to see memory usage inside the Linux VM.
- The `docker stats` command is handy for watching live resource usage per container.

```
docker stats
```

This shows you real-time metrics, including CPU, memory, and network usage per running container – great for spotting which services are being greedy.

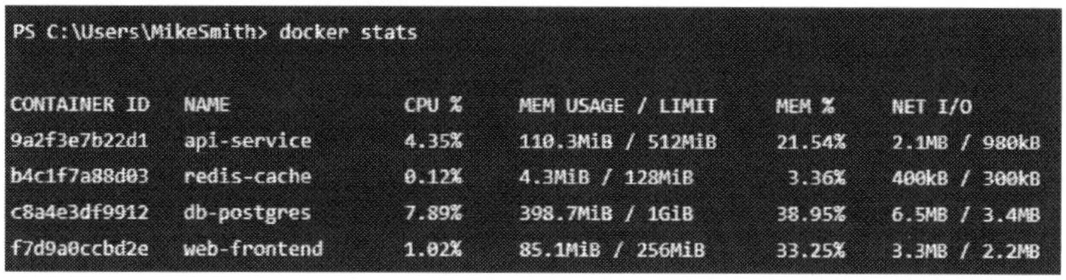

Figure 6.3: Monitoring live container CPU and memory usage with docker stats

If you notice one container spiking repeatedly, that's your cue to check for runaway processes, memory leaks, or misconfigured services.

If you're still seeing high usage even after applying limits, there are a few habits that help keep Docker lean on Windows:

- Shut down containers you're not actively using. They still consume memory, even if idle.
- Avoid mounting volumes directly from the Windows filesystem where possible; this is slower and more memory-intensive than named volumes.
- Clean up unused images, volumes, and networks with our old friend, `docker system prune`.
- Restart Docker every so often to clear up hidden usage and stale processes. It's not glamorous, but it works.

These aren't hard rules, but they're easy wins for smoother local development.

So, sometimes performance problems come down to more than just the code inside your container. Often, it's the setup around it, the number of cores Docker can use, the amount of memory it's been handed, or the swap buffer when things go wrong. Getting this right helps you avoid sluggishness, protects your system from overload, and gives your containers a stable foundation to run. If you've ever felt Docker slowly taking over your machine, now you know why, and more importantly, how to stop it.

That brings us neatly to the next challenge: even with your resources tuned correctly, you still need containers that start fast and behave predictably.

Optimizing container startup and execution

When you're working in containers day in and day out, there's a point where you stop being impressed by the magic of `docker run` and start getting a little impatient with the wait. It's not that Docker is slow; it's that now you know what to expect, and that split-second delay between starting a container and actually being able to use it starts to matter more. Especially when you're spinning things up a dozen times a day or trying to tighten your CI pipeline.

In this part, we're going to look at how to make those containers start faster and behave more predictably from the moment you hit go. It's not about squeezing out theoretical milliseconds; it's about removing avoidable friction. We'll cover how to reduce the container image size, how to build smarter and cache better, and what sort of choices slow containers down without adding much value. These are the small changes that, once baked into your workflow, speed things up for everyone using your stack. So, let's get stuck in, eh?

On one project, our CI pipeline kept slipping by four to six minutes per run, and nobody could explain why. The app itself was fast, the tests were fine, but every build waited for a container that took nearly 30 seconds just to become "ready." Multiplied across 20–30 stages, it added proper friction. After profiling the startup sequence, we found the culprit: a bloated image spending its first few seconds doing unnecessary boot-time work such as running database migrations, regenerating config files, warming caches, and spawning helper scripts before the actual app process even started. Once we moved that preparation into the build phase and switched to a leaner base image, startup dropped to five seconds, and the CI delays vanished overnight.

Why startup speed matters

Startup time isn't just about how long it takes to launch a container. It's about all the moments that slow you down when you're trying to get something done: when you're working locally, and every container rebuild takes longer than expected; when you're running tests and half the time is spent waiting for services to boot; when your production deployment pipeline gets held up because some background worker insists on rebuilding an entire image with every commit.

None of these are blockers on their own. But they add up. And once you're in the habit of tuning things to be fast and reliable, they start to stand out more.

It also matters for operational reliability. The longer a container takes to start, the more likely it is to fail health checks, miss service registration windows, or be slow to scale in response to load.

Building lean images

Most containers take too long to start because of the way their images are built. Sometimes the app itself is fast, it's just buried under layers of unnecessary setup.

The Dockerfile is the place to begin. Here's an example of a clean, efficient image:

```
FROM node:18-alpine

WORKDIR /app

COPY package*.json ./
RUN npm install --production && npm cache clean --force

COPY . .

CMD ["node", "index.js"]
```

Figure 6.4: A clean and efficient Dockerfile

What makes this clean? It installs dependencies early, it clears the cache, and it uses a small base image, which we talked about previously, but it's always a good thing to remember. It also does not try to do too much at runtime – more on that shortly.

Now compare that to this:

```
FROM node:18

RUN apt-get update && apt-get install -y git curl vim

COPY . /app

WORKDIR /app

RUN npm install
```

Figure 6.5: A bloated and inefficient Dockerfile

Here, we're installing unnecessary tools, copying everything up front (which breaks caching), and not cleaning anything. This is the kind of image that gets bigger and slower over time.

Try to keep these points in mind:

- Use the *smallest* base image that gets the job done. Alpine variants are a great place to start.

- Copy your dependency files first, run `npm install` or `pip install`, then copy the rest of your code. This lets Docker reuse the cached install step when only your app code changes.
- Clean up package caches, temp files, or build artifacts before your image finishes.
- Avoid installing interactive tools such as editors or shells in production images; they're just dead weight.

If you need to build your app – for example, translate TypeScript, compile Go binaries, or bundle frontend assets – then consider using a multi-stage build. Here's a typical example for a Node app:

```
# Stage 1: Build everything
FROM node:18-alpine as builder
WORKDIR /app
COPY . .
RUN npm install && npm run build

# Stage 2: Only copy built code
FROM node:18-alpine
WORKDIR /app
COPY --from=builder /app/dist .
CMD ["node", "index.js"]


```

Figure 6.6: A multi-stage Dockerfile

In this case, the final image has none of the source code or build tools – just the compiled app and a minimal Node runtime. This makes images smaller and startup faster. It also reduces the attack surface, avoids redundant dependencies, and keeps your containers tidy in environments where size matters, such as CI runners or edge devices.

If you've got something such as Webpack or Babel in the mix, get it out of the final image. Let it do its job in the build phase and then leave it behind.

Here's a quick comparison of bloated versus optimized images:

Image Type	Approx Build Time	Final Image Size	Average Startup Time (WSL2)	Notes
Bloated image (multiple tools installed, large base image, no cache cleanup)	45–90 seconds	800–1200 MB	2.5–4 seconds	Extra layers and tools slow caching and runtime initialization
Optimized image (lean base, multi-stage build, caches trimmed)	15–30 seconds	150–300 MB	0.5–1.2 seconds	Smaller layers load faster; fewer dependencies at boot

Table 6.3: Comparing typical build times, image sizes, and startup performance

These numbers vary by language and framework, but the pattern is always the same: smaller images build faster and start faster, especially on Windows, where WSL2 has extra disk I/O overhead.

Trim and measure what runs at startup

A lot of apps spend the first few seconds of container life doing things they probably shouldn't. That might be, but is not exclusively, the following:

- Waiting for a database to become available
- Running a migration or seed script
- Generating config from environment variables
- Spawning a child process and backgrounding it
- Starting a bash wrapper before running the app

All of these things can introduce a delay between when the container is considered started and when it's actually ready to do its job.

If your app needs to wait for another service, consider putting that in a health check or external wait script, not in the entry point. If your app depends on some config being present, bake that into the image ahead of time or make it a separate prep step.

Try to avoid startup wrappers such as the following:

```
CMD ["sh", "-c", "node index.js"]
```

Prefer something like this:

```
CMD ["node", "index.js"]
```

That way, Docker can track the process properly and respond to signals such as `SIGINT` or `SIGTERM` without delay.

Note

Under WSL 2, shell wrappers such as `sh -c` introduce extra overhead and can interfere with signal forwarding. When you use a wrapper, `SIGINT` and `SIGTERM` are sent to the shell, not your app, which can delay shutdown or prevent Docker from stopping the container cleanly. Using the direct form (`CMD ["node", "index.js"]`) avoids this problem on Windows and ensures Docker can manage the process correctly.

However, startup time isn't just affected by what's in your Dockerfile. It's also about what your app is loading on boot. Large dependency trees, especially in interpreted languages, can increase the time it takes your app to become ready. That's not always obvious, because you don't always see the cost. Take a moment to run a tool such as `npm audit` or `pipdeptree` and see what's hiding in your install process.

Now, if you're only using about 10 percent of a library, consider replacing it or trimming it down. If you're using a tool such as `express-generator`, it may have pulled in dev dependencies you no longer need. A quick way to slim down your image is to install only what your app actually needs to run in production. Development dependencies, such as testing frameworks or build tools, add bulk but serve no purpose once the container's deployed. By installing just the production dependencies, you keep the image smaller and faster to start:

To use the production tag, try this:

```
npm install -production
```

Or, better still, set `NODE_ENV=production` and rebuild your image.

In Python, you can use separate `requirements.txt` files for dev and prod. It's also worth reviewing what gets copied into your container. If your `.dockerignore` file is empty, you might be copying logs, node modules, or other clutter by mistake.

Before and after you make changes, it's good practice to measure the actual startup time. Here's a really basic timing trick:

```
time docker run --rm my-image
```

You can also look for the first log line that indicates your app is ready, and compare timestamps from container start to that point. For example, if your app logs "Server listening on port `3000`" when it's ready, and it takes five seconds to get there, you've got room to improve.

Don't forget to use `docker logs` or `docker events` to trace when the container is actually considered "up." To get a quick, measurable sense of how long your container actually takes to start, you can time the `run` command directly:

```
$ time docker run --rm my-image
Starting application...
Application running on port 3000

real    0m1.327s
user    0m0.056s
sys     0m0.048s
```

Figure 6.7: Measuring container startup time using the time command

On Windows, especially with WSL 2, container startup is slightly different from native Linux. There's a bit of overhead when containers spin up, especially the first time after boot.

That said, all the preceding principles still apply. Smaller images start faster, fewer dependencies mean quicker boots, and cleaning up your layers keeps WSL from dragging over time.

Note

If your container starts instantly on Linux but feels sluggish on Windows, especially when running code directly from your project folder, the culprit is usually slow Windows bind mounts. WSL 2 bridges NTFS into the Linux VM, and heavy file activity across this boundary can drag performance down. A quick test is to copy your project into the WSL filesystem (`\\wsl$\Ubuntu\home\yourname\project`) and run the same container again. If startup becomes dramatically faster, the bottleneck is the bind

> mount. The fix is simple: develop inside the WSL filesystem or use Docker named volumes instead of Windows-path mounts for performance-critical workloads.

If you're working on a project that uses a mix of Linux and Windows containers, make sure you're not relying on tricks that only work in one context. Keep your Compose file structure modular, so you can test and iterate quickly.

Fast containers aren't just nice to have; they're part of a healthy developer workflow. They make testing snappier, make local feedback loops shorter, and make scaling feel less brittle. Most of the changes we covered here are low-effort but high-value, and once you build them into your project structure, they're just how things work. If your containers are still slow after this, it's probably not the container; it's what's inside it. Time to start trimming.

Of course, even the fastest containers will struggle if the host itself is running out of headroom. Once startup time is under control, the next step is making sure Docker plays nicely with your system's CPU and memory limits.

Managing CPU and memory limits

It's one thing to get a container running smoothly on your machine. It's another to make sure it behaves nicely, both with the other containers you're running and with everything else your system needs to do. That's where managing CPU and memory comes in. Whether you're working on a local development stack, prepping a production image, or trying to troubleshoot a flaky service, setting resource boundaries can save you a lot of time and frustration.

This section is all about how to manage CPU, memory, and swap settings effectively when you're running Docker on Windows. That includes container-level limits, WSL configuration, and Docker Desktop resource controls. We'll look at how to prevent runaway containers, how to keep your system from overheating or hanging, and how to create a more predictable, stable experience for everyone using the same stack.

Let's start by understanding what Docker is actually allowed to use.

Resource usage in WSL2

If you're running Docker Desktop on Windows, and you're using the default setup, then Docker is running your containers inside a WSL 2 virtual machine. That VM behaves like a mini Linux host, and it dynamically shares resources with Windows, but not always perfectly.

By default, WSL 2 will try to grab whatever memory and CPU it thinks it needs. That can work fine for simple workloads. But the moment you're running more than a couple of containers, or doing anything heavy, such as database work or build tooling, it's easy to run into problems:

- Docker consumes too much RAM and starves the rest of the system
- CPU spikes cause your laptop fans to go into orbit
- Background containers slow down your foreground apps
- Performance starts to feel inconsistent, even between rebuilds

The solution is to stop letting Docker take everything by default and instead set deliberate limits. You can do this through Docker Desktop's resource settings or by editing the `.wslconfig` file directly, which gives you full control over WSL's allocation.

If you want a bit more control or just prefer working from the terminal, you can also configure resource limits via a `.wslconfig` file. This lets you define memory, processor, and swap limits globally for WSL and, by extension, for Docker's virtual machine.

To start, create a new text file in your user directory (for example, `C:\Users\YourUsername`) and name it `.wslconfig`. Make sure there's no `.txt` extension or anything at the end. Then add something like this to the file:

```
[wsl2]
memory=6GB
processors=4
swap=2GB
localhostForwarding=true
```

Figure 6.8: Example .wslconfig file setting memory, CPU, swap, and localhost forwarding options for WSL 2

This tells WSL to use no more than 6 GB of RAM, 4 processor cores, and 2 GB of swap space. Once this file is saved, run the following:

```
wsl --shutdown
```

Then restart Docker Desktop, and the new limits will be in effect.

This setup is great for consistency because it gives you the same resource profile every time Docker starts, which helps when debugging or running repeatable tests.

In one of my test environments a lifetime ago, a teammate set `swap=0` in `.wslconfig`, thinking it would free up memory. Instead, large Docker builds began failing midway with `exit 137` errors, and Windows became sluggish because WSL 2 had no buffer to spill memory into. Once we reinstated a modest swap (2 GB) and limited the VM to 6 GB RAM, build times dropped from 18 minutes to 11, and the IDE stopped freezing.

So, what's the takeaway from this? Well, an aggressive `.wslconfig` can look efficient on paper, but it can starve WSL's virtualized kernel under load.

Setting limits on individual containers

Beyond limiting Docker globally, you can also control how much CPU and memory each container is allowed to use. This is helpful when you're running multiple services, or if you want to prevent a "noisy neighbor" scenario where one container hogs everything. Here's a basic example using the CLI:

```
docker run --name limited-app --memory="512m" --cpus="1.0" my-image
```

This restricts the container to 512 MB of RAM and 1 CPU core. But you can also limit swap like this:

```
docker run --memory="1g" --memory-swap="1.5g" my-image
```

That gives the container 1 GB of RAM and allows it to use an extra 500 MB of swap. Think of swap as additional resources in case the "core resources" run out.

There's also a soft memory reservation flag:

```
docker run --memory="1g" --memory-reservation="512m" my-image
```

That tells Docker to try to keep memory usage under 512 MB when possible, but allow up to 1 GB if needed.

These settings are enforced at runtime, so if a container tries to use more memory than allowed, it will be killed. You'll see `exit code 137` if that happens.

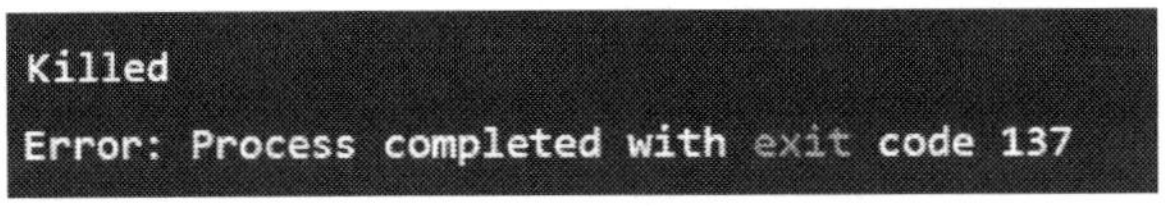

Figure 6.9: Container terminated due to exceeding memory limits (exit code 137)

This is why testing with realistic data and traffic patterns is important – so you know whether your limits are too tight.

Use the following table as a quick reference for diagnosing OOM kills in containers:

Symptom	Likely Cause	Fix
Container exits with code `137`	Memory limit too low; process was OOM-killed by the kernel	Increase memory limit in Compose or `.wslconfig`; reduce app memory use
Container restarts repeatedly under load	Memory spikes exceed the container's limit	Add headroom; profile memory hotspots; reduce concurrency
App becomes slow before crash	Container is swapping heavily (WSL2 or Linux)	Increase RAM allocation; reduce image bloat; optimize dependencies
Everything works locally but fails in CI	CI runner has stricter memory ceilings than dev	Align your compose/limits with CI; simulate load with real data
OOM only happens on Windows	WSL2 VM defaults are too tight or auto-expanding uncontrollably	Set explicit WSL2 ceilings in `.wslconfig` (memory, swap, processors)

Table 6.4: Common OOM symptoms, their causes, and practical fixes when running Docker on Windows.

Most OOM crashes under Docker on Windows come down to either tight WSL2 limits or unexpected memory spikes in the application.

Using limits in Docker Compose

If you're working with Docker Compose, and let's be honest, you probably are, then you can set limits in your Compose file too. Here's an example:

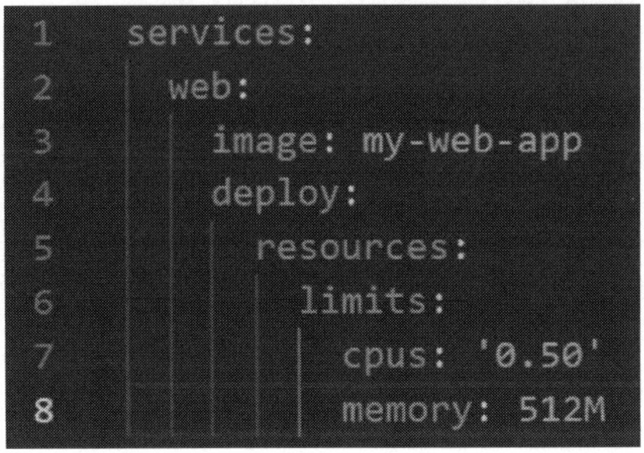

Figure 6.10: Example Docker Compose service with CPU and memory limits defined

This caps the container at half a CPU and 512 MB of RAM.

> **Note**
>
> These deploy and resource settings only work with Docker Swarm or similar orchestrators. If you're using Compose locally, they'll be ignored. For local Compose use, you'll need to pass resource flags via the command or use separate scripts to launch containers with limits.

Alternatively, you can set limits directly in the Dockerfile's entry point or run script, but that's less portable and harder to maintain across environments.

Okay, let's say you've got a local dev stack with three services: a web frontend, a backend API, and a Postgres database. You want to do the following:

- Keep Postgres stable even under heavy queries
- Avoid the frontend slowing down the rest of the system
- Let the backend burst when needed, but not hog memory

To kick things off, your Compose file might look like this:

```yaml
services:
  frontend:
    image: my-frontend
    deploy:
      resources:
        limits:
          cpus: '0.25'
          memory: 256M

  backend:
    image: my-backend
    deploy:
      resources:
        limits:
          cpus: '1.0'
          memory: 512M

  db:
    image: postgres
    deploy:
      resources:
        limits:
          cpus: '0.75'
          memory: 768M
```

Figure 6.11: Example Docker Compose file defining CPU and memory limits for multiple services

If you were running this locally, you'd want to set global limits in `.wslconfig` to something such as 3 CPUs and 2 GB RAM, so the whole system stays stable.

When you're tuning CPU and memory limits, the quickest way to see what's actually happening at runtime is to use `docker stats`. It gives you a live view of container CPU and memory usage, and it's usually the first place to look if something feels off or a container is using more than you expect. Here's what that looks like in practice:

```
CONTAINER ID   NAME           CPU %    MEM USAGE / LIMIT     MEM %    NET I/O
f3b9e7c2e5b1   web-frontend   1.23%    85.4MiB / 256MiB      33.36%   1.3MB / 1.0MB
8c1e19e4715f   api-service    4.87%    144.6MiB / 512MiB     28.24%   3.1MB / 1.5MB
6db24a11bc92   redis-cache    0.09%    3.8MiB / 128MiB        2.97%   512kB / 432kB
9f5c79b8142a   db-postgres    7.44%    416.2MiB / 1GiB       40.65%   6.5MB / 2.7MB
```

Figure 6.12: Real-time container resource usage displayed using docker stats

You could also run the following and look for fields such as `HostConfig.Memory` or `HostConfig.CpuShares` to confirm what limits are applied:

```
docker inspect my-container
```

You can also extract just the values you care about using Go templates, which keeps the output short and easy to scan:

```
docker inspect --format='Memory={{.HostConfig.Memory}}
CpuShares={{.HostConfig.CpuShares}}'
```

This will print only the memory and CPU share limits that Docker actually applied.

```
"HostConfig": {
    "CpuShares": 512,
    "Memory": 536870912,
    "MemorySwap": 1073741824,
    "NanoCpus": 1000000000
},
"Config": {
    "Image": "my-web-app:latest",
    "Hostname": "my-container",
    "Cmd": [
        "node",
        "server.js"
    ]
}
```

Figure 6.13: Checking container CPU and memory limits using docker inspect

Giving your containers too many resources can starve your system. Giving them too few can cause performance issues and crashes. This section gave you the tools to find that nice balance, both at the Docker Desktop level and inside individual containers, so you can keep your environment predictable and responsive. Whether you're just running a couple of services or juggling half a dozen, managing CPU and memory is a key step towards stability. With the basics of resource control in place, the next challenge is what happens when your stack grows, and those limits start to interact at scale.

Scaling Docker environments

When I was working at a regulatory systems development house (I'm trying to be quite careful with clues to the business here), we started with just a few Dockerized services that shared data and context with some of our core systems. It was tidy and manageable, until it wasn't. Within just a few sprints, those few containers had become dozens. Services were spinning up faster than we could keep track of them and test them, and what once ran fine on a single machine quickly became unwieldy. Builds slowed, local resources were pushed to the edge, and even simple tasks such as running integration tests became awkward. That was the moment scaling stopped being a nice-to-have and became absolutely essential. Let's explore how to scale your Docker setup effectively, why it matters, and how Windows fits into that process.

Why scaling matters

So, at its core, scaling addresses variability, be it traffic spikes, parallel testing, or CPU-heavy workloads. On Windows, it also helps keep containers isolated from each other and your host, making sure one runaway service doesn't choke the rest. Scaling isn't just adding more containers; it's about managing replicas, networking, and ensuring service continuity. Scaling gives you the following:

- **Resilience**: Run multiple instances in case one crashes
- **Load distribution**: Balance across services, especially under load
- **Better resource usage**: Only use what you need, when you need it

Scaling comes up a lot in conversations, and a lot of people will talk about horizontal versus vertical scaling. Well, what does that actually mean?

- **Horizontal scaling** means adding more containers, perfect for stateless services such as web servers
- **Vertical scaling** means beefing up CPU or memory for a container, useful for databases or heavy compute workloads

So, here's a quick example of how that plays out in practice.

Let's say you're running something such as a Postgres container on a Windows host that's starting to struggle with query loads. You could do either of the following:

- **Go vertical**: So, tweak the container limits directly, for example:

```
docker run --name db --cpus="4" --memory="6g" postgres:15
```

  This gives Postgres more breathing room, useful if you're CPU-bound but not maxed out on overall containers.

- **Go horizontal**: You spin up replicas and add a lightweight load balancer in front, say with HAProxy or something similar:

```
services:
  db:
    image: postgres:15
    deploy:
      replicas: 3
      resources:
        limits:
          cpus: "2"
          memory: 3G
  proxy:
    image: haproxy:alpine
    ports:
      - "5432:5432"
```

Figure 6.14: Scaling a database service horizontally using Docker Compose replicas

  Each instance handles part of the read load.

But, the million-dollar (pound?) question is: how do you decide which way to scale? Well, let's look at a few things...

- Check what's running out first: CPU, memory, or concurrency
- If it's CPU, try adding replicas (horizontal) so each instance actually does less
- If it's memory or disk I/O on a single service, go vertical first to stabilize it
- Once stable, introduce replicas for fault tolerance

This reasoning mirrors how most enterprise systems evolve: start vertical to survive, then grow horizontal to scale sustainably.

It all depends on what you need and want, really. I've seen vertical scaling cut query latency by up to 25% sometimes, but horizontal scaling I've seen boost throughput by maybe double that under concurrent users. The best option depends on whether you're chasing speed for a single job or stability under load.

So, with that in mind, let's focus on horizontal scaling, where Docker really shines, but remember that vertical scaling is still your friend for the heavier services.

Scaling containers

Even without orchestration, Docker makes it easy to run multiple instances locally. Here's how to do it from your terminal:

```
docker run --name web1 -d my-web
docker run --name web2 -d my-web
docker run --name web3 -d my-web
```

You now have three instances of that service running in parallel. This is simple and effective for local stress tests or load balancing using something such as HAProxy. Just don't forget to publish different ports on the containers; otherwise, all that traffic will come through the same ports.

For serious multi-container scaling, Swarm is a built-in option. Start by enabling swarm mode:

```
docker swarm init
```

Then deploy your service:

```
docker service create --name web --replicas 3 -p 8080:80 my-web
```

This creates three identical instances, automatically load-balanced. You can check their status:

```
docker service ps web
```

Now, once your service is deployed, you can verify that each replica is running and distributed across nodes by listing the service tasks:

```
ID              NAME      IMAGE        NODE           DESIRED STATE
a1bcdefghijk    web.1     my-web:1.0   docker-node1   Running
b2cdefghijkl    web.2     my-web:1.0   docker-node2   Running
c3defghijklm    web.3     my-web:1.0   docker-node3   Running
```

Figure 6.15: Output from docker service ps web showing three running replicas

To scale up or down, you can use the following command:

```
docker service scale web=5
```

Five replicas will now be running. Swarm immediately reschedules new tasks to nodes with capacity. Even outside Swarm, you can scale in Compose:

```
services:
  web:
    image: my-web
    ports:
      - "8080:80"
    deploy:
      replicas: 4

```

Figure 6.16: Docker Compose file example defining a web service with port mapping and four replicas

Then run something like this:

```
docker stack deploy -c docker-compose.yml mystack
```

This uses Swarm under the covers, but keeps the Compose format you're familiar with. It's a quick way to replicate workloads locally.

Why Swarm on Windows?

Well, it's pretty simple, really. It provides native clustering, built-in load-balancing, and declarative scaling, all without installing extra orchestration software or leaving the comfort of the Docker CLI. For many teams, that means fewer moving parts, simpler onboarding, and a smoother transition from local development to distributed environments.

At a previous company that specialized in finance for sub-prime customers, we had a set of overnight middleware jobs that absolutely couldn't fail. They were running on a couple of ageing Windows servers, held together with batch scripts and hope. We needed something a little more predictable, but without introducing a full orchestration platform the team didn't have the skills for.

We ended up joining three Windows Server hosts into a Swarm cluster using the same Docker tooling we were already using on our laptops. They developed it, and I assisted with the infrastructure testing side of things. Each overnight job was packaged as a .NET container and deployed as a Swarm service with multiple replicas spread across the hosts. If one machine went down, the jobs continued running elsewhere. Scaling was trivial:

```
docker service scale jobs=6
```

Rolling updates were pretty automatically and health checks ensured bad builds never made it into the nightly run. For that environment, Windows-heavy, risk-sensitive, and resource-constrained, Swarm gave us clustering, resilience, and hands-off deployments without redesigning the whole estate.

When you update an image, Swarm handles rolling updates really gracefully using something like this:

```
docker service update --image my-web:2.0 --update-parallelism 2 --update-delay 10s
web
```

This updates *two containers* at a time, with a 10-second delay between batches. That means minimal downtime. On Windows, this ensures container updates happen smoothly without disrupting users or developers.

Now, some things to remember and be aware of when scaling containers on Windows.

- **Host resource limits**: Watch for WSL2 memory and CPU caps. Scaling past those limits can cause throttling or failures.
- **Local development versus production**: Use Compose for testing services together, but plan jobs or Swarm for production-level scaling.
- **Persistent storage**: Stateless services scale easily, but stateful ones (databases, caches) need careful volume design. Shared volumes or cloud storage may be needed.

Swarm doesn't provide built-in autoscaling. But you can add it with tools such as Prometheus, and a simple script to do the following:

1. Monitor containers/service metrics.
2. Trigger scale commands based on thresholds (for example, if >80% CPU usage for >10 minutes, increase swarm size).

You could also run Prometheus on Windows. It's lightweight, customizable, and works well for services with predictable load patterns. I've always found it to be one of my favorite monitoring tools.

A few years back, I worked very briefly with a logistics client that ran around 80 containers across 3 Windows Server 2019 VMs using Docker Swarm. Each host ran Docker Desktop in WSL 2 mode, capped at 8 cores and 12 GB of RAM through `.wslconfig`. Swarm handled roughly 3,000 requests per second for a .NET 6 API (quite admirable), sitting behind an Nginx reverse proxy. CPU plateaued at around seventyish percent, and latency stayed roughly under 90 milliseconds during load tests. The trick wasn't fancy automation; it was consistent resource reservations in Compose and letting Swarm spread workloads sensibly.

So, what's the takeaway? Well, scaling on Windows can be perfectly stable when host limits, Compose constraints, and Swarm replicas are tuned to work together.

Tips for forget-free scaling

Forget-free scaling is absolutely not an official term in Docker, but as someone who has had too many "Oh, I forgot to do that" moments, it's a phrase I find myself using a lot.

It's about putting sensible constraints and defaults in place so that scaling just works – even when you're not watching it like a hawk. Think of it as the difference between winging it and baking in reliability from the start. So, with that in mind...

- Label your nodes (e.g., `--constraint node.role==worker`) to control the deployment location.
- Use `--reserve` in service YML to earmark CPU/memory for each replica.
- Combine replicas with read-only volumes for cache-heavy services.
- Keep an eye on logging and monitoring – logs from dozens of containers can become a flood.

At this point, you have a solid toolkit: manual replicas for quick tests, Swarm for declarative scaling and rolling updates, and scripts or external tools for autoscaling in production. Scaling isn't about just adding more containers; it's about growing responsibly, efficiently, and predictably.

Scaling isn't magic, but it can feel like it when you get it right. It's a practice that begins at build and carries through to deployment and monitoring. In our Windows environments, it's a balancing act between container orchestration and host resource limits, but executed well, it delivers reliability and performance at scale.

Once your environment is scaling reliably, the next step is making sure it stays that way. That means keeping a close eye on how containers behave under real workloads and knowing what to tune when they don't.

Monitoring and fine-tuning performance

There was a week back in a previous role, where every time we ran a test build, it felt like flipping a coin. Sometimes it flew, and sometimes the container just sat there, sluggish and awkward. And it wasn't always clear why. Same base image, same hardware, same Compose file. What was missing was proper visibility. That's really what this section is about, making sure you've got eyes on the right parts of your setup, and knowing what knobs to turn when things aren't moving as quickly or cleanly as they should.

So, let's dig into the how and why of monitoring Docker performance on Windows. We'll walk through some of the built-in tools, third-party options, and little tweaks that can make a big difference over time. We're aiming to help you spot problems early, fine-tune for some smoother workloads, and build habits that keep your containers lean, healthy, and fast.

Using Docker's built-in tools

When things slow down, it's tempting to immediately start fiddling with settings. But without data, you're just guessing. Docker might be slow because your container is memory-bound, or maybe it's an I/O bottleneck, or maybe you've just got a massive log file running away in the background.

On Windows, where Docker typically runs inside a WSL 2 virtual machine, you've got one more layer to consider too. CPU and memory allocation isn't just about containers; it's about the relationship between your host, WSL, and the containers themselves. So, the first principle here is: measure before you optimize.

One of the simplest starting points is the `docker stats` command. It shows live CPU, memory, and network usage for each running container:

```
docker stats
```

You'll see something like this:

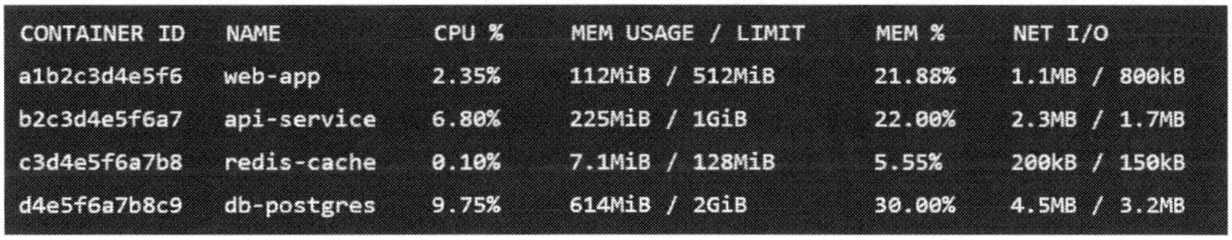

CONTAINER ID	NAME	CPU %	MEM USAGE / LIMIT	MEM %	NET I/O
a1b2c3d4e5f6	web-app	2.35%	112MiB / 512MiB	21.88%	1.1MB / 800kB
b2c3d4e5f6a7	api-service	6.80%	225MiB / 1GiB	22.00%	2.3MB / 1.7MB
c3d4e5f6a7b8	redis-cache	0.10%	7.1MiB / 128MiB	5.55%	200kB / 150kB
d4e5f6a7b8c9	db-postgres	9.75%	614MiB / 2GiB	30.00%	4.5MB / 3.2MB

Figure 6.17: Example output from docker stats showing real-time CPU, memory, and network usage for running containers

This gives you a solid real-time sense of how each container is behaving. If one container consistently spikes or runs hot, that's a red flag worth investigating.

Here's how I normally use it in practice. Let's say I see one service's CPU usage hovering around 180% That's my cue to open its logs and check whether background jobs are looping or mis-scheduled. If everything looks normal, I'll run `docker inspect` to confirm the CPU limit. If none's set, I'll add one and rerun stats to confirm the reduction.

It's a super small diagnostic loop: measure – check limits – adjust – re-measure.

> **Tip**
>
> If you want to narrow this down to a single container, just use the following:
>
> ```
> docker stats <container-name>
> ```

But sometimes, performance issues come from those unexpected restarts, stops, or random resource changes. The `docker events` command lets you watch what's happening across the system as it happens:

```
docker events
```

This will stream a log of actions such as `start`, `stop`, `die`, `oom` (out-of-memory), and more. It's a bit noisy, but in the middle of debugging something weird, it can be incredibly helpful.

```
2025-06-12T10:14:21.123456Z container stop a1b2c3d4e5f6 (image=web-app:latest, name=web-app)
2025-06-12T10:14:23.654321Z container destroy a1b2c3d4e5f6 (image=web-app:latest, name=web-app)
2025-06-12T10:15:10.789012Z container create d5e6f7g8h9i0 (image=web-app:latest, name=web-app)
2025-06-12T10:15:12.345678Z container start d5e6f7g8h9i0 (image=web-app:latest, name=web-app)
```

Figure 6.18: Output from docker events showing container lifecycle actions such as stop, destroy, create, and start

If you pair this with a timestamped issue (such as an alert from your CI/CD), you can often catch problems in the act.

If you've been generous with your resource allocation, some containers will happily eat everything you've got. But Docker can also throttle them or kill them if they exceed the configured limits. You'll often see containers exit with code 137 when memory limits are breached:

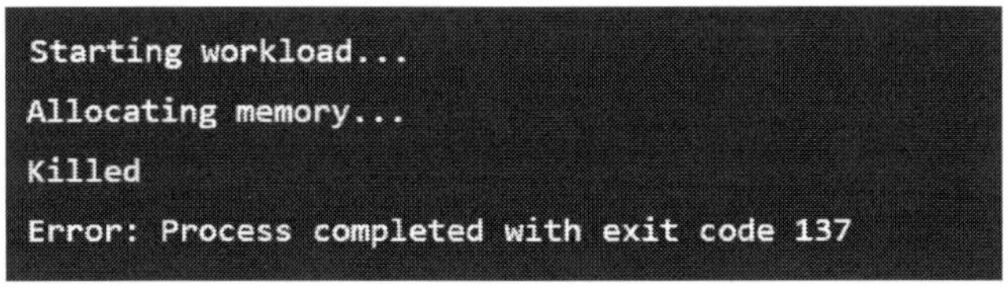

Figure 6.19: Example container log shows termination due to memory overuse (exit code 137)

This usually means the container was using too much memory, and the kernel (within WSL) terminated it. If you see this, it's time to revisit your `--memory` or `--memory-swap` settings in your `docker run` or Compose file.

Advanced monitoring and scanning

Performance is not just about CPU and memory. I/O, especially with volume mounts from Windows into Linux containers, can become a bottleneck. If your container is writing large log files or reading lots of small files in a tight loop, it's worth measuring disk access. Try these steps:

1. Run with a local Linux-only volume instead of mounting from Windows:

   ```
   volumes:
     - /data/logs:/app/logs
   ```

   This avoids WSL's performance hit from syncing across file systems.

2. Use `iotop` or `perf` inside the container (for Linux containers):

   ```
   apt-get install -y iotop && iotop
   ```

   These tools show which processes are eating up disk activity. You might be surprised how chatty a single misconfigured log line can be.

Image-level issues can also degrade performance. Bloated images, packages with known CVEs, or outdated base layers can slow down start times and runtime execution.

Tools such as Trivy or Docker Scout help here. If you do not have Trivy installed, Docker makes it easy to run it as a containerized scanner without even installing anything locally. You can simply pull and run the Trivy image directly:

```
docker run --rm aquasec/trivy image node:18-alpine
```

That will pull the latest Trivy scanner image, run the vulnerability scan against your local Docker image, and clean up when it's finished. You get the full scan output without needing to set up anything extra on your host machine.

This is actually one of the nice things about these container-native tools: you can pull them in when you need them, do the thing, and move on – perfect for occasional checks or when you're working on someone else's machine.

Fine-tuning based on real-world usage

So, you've got metrics. What next? Here are a few practical strategies based on what your monitoring might reveal:

- If memory usage hovers near the cap: increase `--memory` slightly or optimize the app's memory handling
- If CPU sits too high: consider splitting the workload or throttling with `--cpus`
- If I/O is spiky: investigate logging patterns or try moving volumes to `tmpfs` for speed
- If containers restart often: check for exit codes and investigate via `docker inspect`

The goal here isn't perfection, it's responsiveness. Adjust things a bit, observe the change, and repeat.

It's one thing to guess at a container's health. It's another to know with confidence that your containers are behaving well, using resources wisely, and not dragging your system down. Windows adds a bit of complexity to the mix, but also gives you the power to dial things in at the host level, WSL level, and container level.

Pair `docker stats` with logs, use Trivy to keep your images as honest as they can be, and keep an eye on events when things feel off. Once these habits are in place, performance tuning becomes part of your everyday flow, not a fire drill.

The Big Lab: Making the Notes service observable

By now, the Notes service behaves like a real stack: it stores data, it runs as multiple services under Compose, and it's been hardened enough to survive normal development mistakes. But right now, you're still flying a bit blind. If the API slows down, if containers start to misbehave, or if something silently consumes memory inside WSL2, you don't have any visibility into what's actually happening.

This part of the Big Lab fixes that. We're going to add practical, lightweight monitoring to the Notes stack so you can diagnose slowdowns, spot resource spikes, and understand how your containers behave on Windows. Nothing heavy, nothing enterprise. Just the essentials that make troubleshooting predictable.

1. **Add a monitoring container to the stack**: We'll use cAdvisor, a simple container monitoring tool maintained by Google. It runs anywhere, including Windows with WSL2, and gives you live CPU, memory, filesystem, and network metrics for every container. Update your main `compose.yaml` and add this service:

```
services:
  # ... existing services (api, frontend)

  monitoring:
    image: gcr.io/cadvisor/cadvisor:latest
    container_name: notes-monitor
    ports:
      - "8081:8080"
    volumes:
      - /:/rootfs:ro
      - /var/run:/var/run:ro
      - /sys:/sys:ro
      - /var/lib/docker/:/var/lib/docker:ro
    networks:
      - app-net
```

   Bring the stack up:

```
docker compose up -d
```

   Now open `http://localhost:8081`. You should see live graphs for CPU, memory, I/O, and container-specific stats. What does this actually give you? A clean, browser-based dashboard that updates in real time and attaches automatically to every container in the Notes stack.

2. **Check Notes service volume health from the monitoring container**: We don't need full file-level inspection, but it's useful to see if your Notes API's data directory is accessible and behaving normally. To do this, exec into cAdvisor:

```
docker compose exec monitoring sh
```

Check whether the Notes volume is visible:

```
ls -lah /var/lib/docker/volumes
```

This confirms that cAdvisor can report disk I/O and space usage for containers backed by your persistent data. Then exit with `exit`.

3. **Use docker stats to understand live container behavior**: You saw `docker stats` earlier in the chapter. Now you'll use it with your full stack running.

```
docker stats
```

Watch out for the following:

   - API CPU usage when hitting `/notes`
   - Frontend spikes on refresh
   - Monitoring container load when the UI is open
   - WSL2 memory behavior (**Task Manager** | **Vmmem**)

Trigger a bit of traffic:

```
curl http://localhost:5001/notes
```

Refresh the frontend a few times. You should see clear, distinct usage patterns between the services.

4. **Use docker system df to understand disk and image usage**: The Notes stack grows as you add layers, networks, and volumes. This command shows what's consuming space:

```
docker system df
```

Look at the following:

   - Total image size
   - Space used by volumes
   - Container layer usage

This is often the first clue when Docker starts to feel "slow" on Windows due to disk bloat.

5. **Use docker events to observe container lifecycle behavior**: This gives you a live stream of everything happening inside the Docker daemon.

```
docker events
```

While it's running, restart the API:

```
docker compose restart api
```

You'll see the following:

    - Container start
    - Health events (if configured)
    - Kill and stop signals
    - Network attaches and detaches

This should clarify what Docker actually does under the hood for you. Stop the event stream with *Ctrl* + *C*.

6. **Use Windows tools to cross-check container performance**: Remember, Docker ≠ the whole machine. On Windows, WSL2, Vmmem, disks, and networking all play a part. You need to check system-wide behavior:
Open **Task Manager** | **Performance** | **Resource Monitor** (`resmon.exe`) | **Performance Monitor** (`perfmon.exe`).

While the API is under load, observe the following:

    - CPU consumption under Vmmem
    - Disk I/O attributed to WSL
    - Network spikes from API/monitoring traffic
    - Frontend static serving behavior

These tools show what Docker stats can't: the impact on Windows itself.

7. **Validate the monitoring setup end-to-end**: With everything running, test the whole pipeline:
Hit the API:

```
curl http://localhost:5001/notes
```

Refresh the frontend:

```
http://localhost:8080
```

a. Watch cAdvisor dashboards change

b. Watch `docker stats` update live

c. Check WSL2 loads in Task Manager

d. Look for any warning or kill events in `docker events`

If everything is wired correctly, you now have full visibility across the following:

- Container performance
- Network behavior
- Disk usage
- Startup/shutdown lifecycle
- Windows-side resource patterns

This is the beginning of actual observability.

Before you move on, there's one more point worth calling out. You've already seen CPU and memory allocation earlier in the book, and we aren't repeating that here because optimization isn't the job of this section. What matters right now is that you can see the behavior clearly enough to make good decisions later. Once you can measure load, you can decide whether the fix is a higher memory limit, a smaller image, fewer replicas, or simply better code. Monitoring comes first. Optimization only works when you understand the bottleneck.

If you want a quick sanity check while you're here, run the following:

```
docker inspect api --format '{{json .HostConfig.Resources}}' | jq
```

You'll see the current CPU and memory settings that the API is actually running with. That's enough for now. You'll tune these properly when you scale the stack in the next chapter.

Alright, you've now added enough monitoring to treat the Notes service like a *real* application rather than a black box. You can see where resources go, what the containers are doing, and when the system starts to strain under load. Most importantly, you now have the tools to understand why something feels slow, rather than guessing.

Well done, the stack is now observable. Next chapter, let's scale it.

Summary

When it comes to Docker performance on Windows, the devil's in the details. We've looked at how resource allocation, startup optimization, CPU and memory limits, scaling, and proper monitoring all work together to build stable, efficient container environments. From managing WSL resource usage to trimming Dockerfiles and keeping dependencies honest, small adjustments add up quickly. Performance tuning isn't about chasing perfect numbers; it's about reducing friction, preventing surprises, and giving your containers room to breathe without starving your machine. With these techniques in place, you're no longer flying blind.

You've got the tools, the metrics, and the control to keep your Docker workloads fast, responsive, and ready for whatever you throw at them next.

Coming up, we're going to shift gears a bit and dive into the Docker GenAI Stack on Windows. This is where things get a bit more experimental and a bit more complicated to boot. We're going to be running AI models inside containers, managing data pipelines, and pushing Docker beyond traditional workloads. It's the same principles you've learned about here, just applied to a much bigger (and slightly smarter) playground.

Join us on Discord

For discussions around the book and to connect with your peers, join us on Discord at or scan the QR code below:

7

Docker GenAI Stack on Windows

There was a point recently when I was experimenting with a handful of GenAI models locally. I had a summarizer in one container, an embedding model in another, and a tiny vector store in yet another. Now, it sounds like chaos, but initially, it all felt streamlined and elegant. But as soon as I hooked in a chatbot frontend and scaled a second summarizer container, things began to fall apart. Containers were talking past one another, performance fluctuated, and data consistency became a nightmare. So, I did what most senior engineers would do in that situation: I went for a walk to clear my head. After a while, I realized that deploying GenAI locally isn't just about spinning up a single model; it's about managing a stack. I was thinking about it as a shiny new toy to play with instead of a stack of software like I'd deployed hundreds of times before. And that's precisely what we'll tackle in this part of the book: understanding the architecture, orchestration, and design decisions that make Docker not just useful but essential for GenAI on Windows.

So, let's gain a practical overview of a "typical" GenAI stack running on Windows with Docker. We'll cover why each piece is important and how they fit together. We'll walk through model inference containers, data processing helpers, orchestration layers, and how to keep everything working smoothly and in unison. By the end, you'll have a clear mental model of how the GenAI stack is structured.

We'll be covering the following main topics:

- Introduction to the GenAI stack
- Deploying AI models with Docker on Windows
- Managing data for AI workflows
- Best practices for AI deployments with Docker

Let's get started!

Technical requirements

The code files referenced in this chapter are available at

`https://github.com/PacktPublishing/Mastering-Docker-on-Windows.`

Introduction to the GenAI stack

Okay, before we start pulling containers together, let's take a second to unpack what a *GenAI stack* actually is. Think of it as the plumbing that keeps your AI workflows running smoothly, a collection of containers and services that handle everything from data prep and model serving to orchestration and APIs. In other words, it's the practical foundation that turns clever models into working apps.

First things first, a mature GenAI stack usually includes the following:

- **Model serving**: One or more containers running the actual AI models; think Hugging Face, ONNX Runtime, and so on.
- **Data pipelines**: Containers responsible for fetching, cleaning, or transforming input data before it hits the models.
- **Storage/vector databases**: Lightweight self-hosted stores such as Redis or SQLite, or more specialized vector databases managed in containers.
- **Orchestration and API layer**: A coordinator (could be another container) that routes client requests through authentication, caching, and model calls.
- **Frontend or consumer service**: It doesn't matter if it's a UI, CLI, or another consumer, this container integrates with the GenAI pipeline.

This separation allows you to iterate on one component, such as upgrading a model container, without ripping the rest of the stack apart to do it.

For example, imagine an analytics team in a large bank running a Windows-based GenAI workflow. One container serves a summarization model for regulatory reports, another generates embeddings for search, and a third handles classification for customer communications. Each model evolves at a different pace, but because they're isolated behind the same Docker network on Windows, the team can upgrade or replace one container without disrupting the others. The stack behaves as a single system while still letting each component move independently.

We'll explore these roles in more detail in later sections, but for now, it's important to have a bit of a mental picture of how everything hangs together.

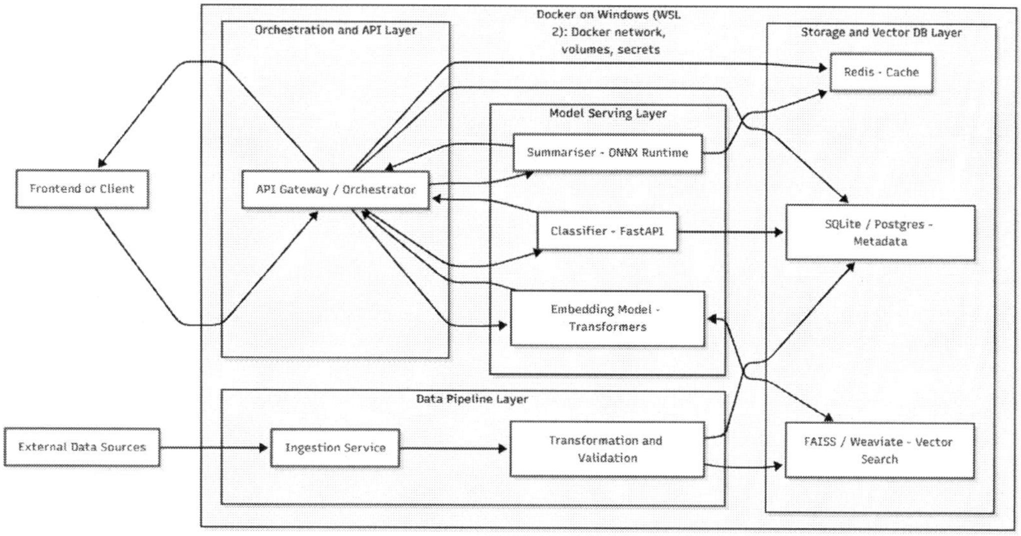

Figure 7.1: High-level GenAI stack architecture on Windows

This diagram shows how the main components of a GenAI stack interact when deployed on Windows with Docker. Data flows from external sources through ingestion and transformation containers into model-serving layers, while orchestration and storage layers manage routing, scaling, and persistence across the stack.

But when you start running GenAI workloads, you realize super quickly that these models come with complex dependencies and heavy resource demands. Docker gives you the isolation, flexibility, and control you need to manage them cleanly, even on Windows.

- **Isolation and independence**: Models vary; some rely on Python with TensorFlow, others need Rust-based runtimes. Docker lets each model container run in its own clean environment without version clashes.
- **Reproducibility**: With containerized environments, you can pretty much guarantee that a GenAI pipeline tested last week behaves the same today, on any Windows machine; no "it worked on my machine" surprises.
- **Scalability and testing**: You might start with a single model instance, but soon you may want two or three replicas for parallel inference. Docker Swarm or Compose lets you scale containers without rewriting your app.
- **Resource management**: GenAI demands memory, CPU, and potentially GPU (with future Windows GPU support; fingers crossed for those of us with powerful gaming graphics cards!). Docker lets you control how much each container can use, keeping your workload balanced.

The following diagram illustrates how the main components of a local GenAI stack connect and communicate within a shared Docker network on Windows.

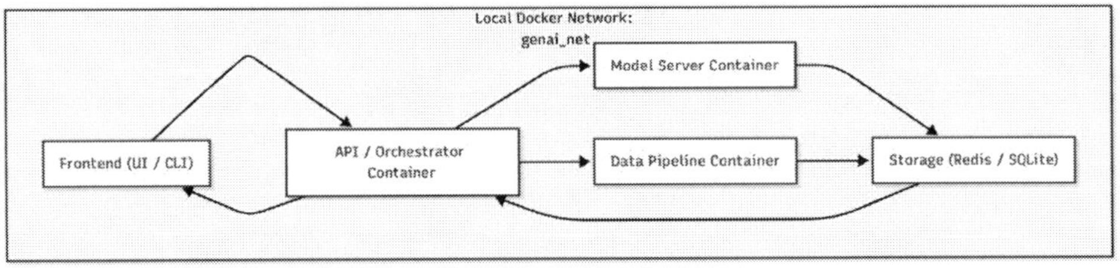

Figure 7.2: Local GenAI stack on Windows showing interconnected containers

Here, containers communicate over an isolated network. You may use `.env` files or a shared Compose network so each service can resolve others by name. As we move through the chapter, you'll construct this stack piece by piece, gradually adding monitoring, scaling, and security layers.

Platforms, frameworks, and models

Let's talk about the typical pieces you are likely to pull into your GenAI stack. Each one comes with its own quirks and strengths, but Docker helps keep them isolated and working together:

- **Hugging Face Transformers**: This is one of the most popular model libraries and, honestly, the first one I learned GenAI using. It is often deployed inside containers running Python with `uvicorn` or FastAPI to serve requests via REST APIs. Hugging Face models are great for a wide variety of NLP tasks, such as summarization, translation, question-answering, and text generation.
- **ONNX Runtime**: This is a portable format optimized for inference speed, especially when you want to deploy models trained in one framework but served in another. ONNX can run across platforms, and under WSL 2 on Windows, it often delivers solid performance thanks to reduced dependency complexities.
- **LLaMA-based FB models**: These **large language models** (**LLMs**) are increasingly finding their way into private GenAI deployments. Now, they're very memory-hungry, often requiring careful resource planning and high RAM allocations. That does, however, make them ideal for stress-testing your Docker resource limits and figuring out how your stack handles more demanding inference workloads.
- **FastAPI or Flask API wrappers**: Most GenAI models don't expose APIs natively, so you will often wrap them inside lightweight Python frameworks such as FastAPI or Flask

(my personal favorite). These give you HTTP endpoints that other services in your stack can call, and they fit very naturally inside Docker containers.

- **Redis or SQLite**: Let's be honest: as your models ingest or generate more and more, you will often need fast, temporary storage for these vectors. Redis is great for caching and quick lookups, while SQLite works well for lightweight persistence without requiring full-blown database infrastructure.

The nice part is, all of these pieces happily run together under Docker on Windows using WSL 2. Each service lives inside its own container, fully isolated, but they can discover each other through Docker networking. Updating a model version becomes as simple as pulling a new container and restarting the service, without disrupting the rest of the stack.

Once you've got these core components running in their own containers, the next step is making sure they can actually talk to each other. That's where Docker's networking and service discovery come in.

One of the things that'll quietly save you hours of frustration when building a GenAI stack is how Docker handles networking. You do not need to mess around with IP addresses, `localhost` files, or weird port forwarding tricks just to get containers talking to each other.

When you are running things locally with Docker Compose or Swarm, each container gets its own internal hostname that other containers can reference directly. So, if your model container is named `model`, your API container can simply call `http://model:8000` to reach it. The same goes for `ingester`, `frontend`, `db`, or whatever you happen to call your services. The networking just works.

This is especially helpful in GenAI stacks where multiple components are constantly calling each other behind the scenes. Your data ingestion pipeline needs to send data to the model, the model needs to fetch context from the vector database, the API needs to stitch it all together, and your frontend needs to stay blissfully unaware of how complicated it is under the hood.

Security considerations

Even if you are only running your GenAI stack locally, you are still dealing with potentially sensitive data. Model inputs might contain private customer information, embeddings can leak patterns from your training data, and even logs may accidentally capture something you don't want lying around. So, it pays to build good security habits into your stack from the very beginning, rather than trying to bolt them on later.

Here are a few simple (but super important) principles to follow as you build:

- **Least-privilege principles**: Each container should only have access to what it *absolutely needs*. If your model container does not need to touch the database, just don't give it access. If your data ingester only reads from an S3 bucket, it should not have write permissions elsewhere. Reducing privileges limits how much damage any single container can do if something goes wrong.

- **Internal-only networks**: Your model containers should not be directly accessible from the outside world. Expose your public endpoints through your API layer or frontend only. This keeps the core logic protected and reduces the attack surface, even in dev environments.
- **Secrets management**: Use `.env` files or Docker secrets to store API keys, credentials, tokens, and so on. Never hardcode these into your Docker files or Compose files. It's easy to do but hard to come back from later. This way, you avoid leaking sensitive information if someone accidentally shares a config file or uploads a repo.
- **Volume isolation**: Keep logs, model weights, and persistent data in well-defined, isolated Docker volumes. This helps you avoid accidental cross-contamination between services, makes backups easier, and ensures you know exactly where your data lives inside the stack.

> **Note**
>
> On Windows, one of the most common mistakes is storing secrets or model data inside folders that are automatically synced or scanned, such as `Documents`, `Desktop`, or anything under `C:\Users` if OneDrive or corporate antivirus is active. These tools can silently copy, quarantine, or lock files mid-runtime, which leaves containers unable to read model weights or configuration files. Keeping sensitive data inside WSL's Linux filesystem prevents these background processes from interfering and avoids accidental exposure through sync services.

Now, we've covered Docker security in a few places in the book already, such as *Chapter 4*, where we covered securing Docker Desktop, managing user accounts, and limiting privileges. We'll go into some more details in *Chapter 8*, where we'll talk about securing data in hybrid cloud workflows, but the key takeaway is simple: start secure, stay secure. Even on your local machine, it's good practice to assume your stack deserves the same care you would give in production.

Data considerations

Running Docker on Windows works brilliantly almost all of the time, but there are a few little quirks, especially once you start stacking up GenAI workloads that lean heavily on models, files, and system resources. None of these are showstoppers, but it's better to be aware of them early than to run head-first into them halfway through your build:

- **File I/O performance**: This one sneaks up on people. When your containers are reading or writing files, particularly large model weights or logs, things can feel sluggish if you are mounting Windows folders directly (such as `C:\Users\Whatever`). That's because Docker has to constantly translate between the Windows filesystem and the WSL 2 Linux filesystem. That translation adds overhead, especially when you have lots of small files or frequent reads and writes. The simple fix is: wherever possible, keep your Docker data inside native Linux volumes. The access speeds are much better because everything stays inside the WSL VM, and Docker does not have to do extra work.
- **Networking quirks**: Now, by default, Docker maps container ports onto `localhost`, and 90 percent of the time, this works just fine. But as soon as you bring in VSCode Docker extensions, browser-based frontends, or any tooling that tries to connect in from Windows directly, you can run into some confusing scenarios. You might be exposing `localhost:5000`, but some tools expect `127.0.0.1`, and others might not like WSL's network bridge. Most of this comes down to understanding how your Docker network is being exposed and being explicit about your port mappings when needed. It isn't difficult, but it's one of those things that feels very Windows-y when you hit it.
- **Resource contention**: This is the one you'll notice the quickest if you're running larger models. GenAI workloads *love* RAM, and Docker's happy to take as much as you give it. If you have not set memory or CPU limits, you can very quickly find your machine grinding to a halt. This is where your `.wslconfig` file and sensible resource caps come in. Limit Docker's share of your system so your editor, browser, and everything else you need for your day aren't getting starved every time you load a new model.

We'll run into each of these again as we build up the stack throughout this part of the book. The point isn't to avoid them completely (they're just part of the game when you're using Docker on Windows), but to spot them early and put good habits in place before they turn into painful debugging sessions.

Getting into the components

Alright, now that we've mapped out the shape of the stack, we're going to start breaking it down into the actual building blocks. This is where we move from high-level theory into the practical side of getting your GenAI stack up and running properly inside Docker on Windows. And crucially, we're not just going to spin containers up blindly; we're going to wire everything together in a way that'll actually hold up as you scale, test, and iterate. Imagine an enterprise team deploying an internal LLM inference endpoint for analysts. The model sits inside a container, exposed through a lightweight API, and CI pipelines rebuild the image whenever the model or preprocessing logic changes. Each component of the stack needs to stay isolated so that updating the model doesn't break ingestion, caching, or downstream services. This is exactly the type of workflow we're about to break down:

1. **Deploying AI models with Docker on Windows**: First up, we'll get our models into containers. This is where we take real inference code, wrap it in lightweight API servers, and get everything exposed and callable. You'll see how to containerize models cleanly, manage dependencies properly, and start tuning for performance right from the start. No more "it works on my machine but not in Docker" headaches.
2. **Managing data for AI workflows**: Then, we get into the data side, because honestly, the model's only half the story. You've got data coming in, you're probably generating embeddings, and you need somewhere to store all that. We'll cover ingestion, caching, and local storage options that won't trip you up on Windows, as well as how to wire these data services into the pipeline smoothly.
3. **Optimizing AI container performance**: Once your models and data layers are in place, we start tightening things up. This is where we shrink image sizes, sort out caching layers, apply CPU and memory tuning, and get hands-on with some Windows-specific optimizations so WSL 2 doesn't quietly eat your machine alive while you're training or serving models.
4. **Best practices for AI deployments with Docker**: Finally, we'll deal with the long-term side of running AI workloads properly. That means sensible security defaults, keeping your models versioned, managing secrets safely, logging in a way that doesn't flood your system, and generally setting yourself up so you're not fighting fires two months down the road.

Each one of these layers builds on the foundation we're laying right now. You don't need to solve everything up front, but as we work through these, you'll avoid a lot of the usual "ah, I should've handled that earlier" moments that hit when you try to scale things up after the fact.

The GenAI stack isn't just about running a model and calling it a day. It's a full pipeline, with moving parts talking to each other, handling data, and coordinating responses. If you don't get the foundations right early on, you'll feel the pain later when things start getting messy. That's why we're not just jumping straight into spinning up GPT-style endpoints in isolation. Instead, we're building out the stack properly, container by container, with each piece doing its job cleanly. So, when it comes time to scale up or lock things down, you're not trying to untangle a ball of string; you're adding pieces to a system that was designed to grow from the start.

Deploying AI models with Docker on Windows

I'll never forget the day I containerized my first LLaMA-based model on Windows. I'd wrestled with environment mismatches, tons of missing dependencies, and slow startup times until I realized: this isn't just a one-off container; it's part of a larger system. Getting it right meant thinking beyond "it works" and into "it works reliably, repeatably, and efficiently." That's the mindset we're bringing to this section. Let's learn how to package inference code into a clean, efficient Docker container on Windows.

When you're dealing with AI models, especially the larger or more complex ones, consistency becomes everything. Dependencies change, package versions shift, and small mismatches between environments can turn into hours of debugging you really do not want to be doing. This is where containerizing your inference code starts paying off immediately:

- **Reproducibility**: Every time you build and run your container, you know exactly what environment you're getting. No more "it worked fine on my laptop but breaks in production" conversations. Once it runs, it keeps running the same way everywhere.
- **Portability**: Whether you are running locally on Windows, pushing to a CI pipeline, or moving to a production server on Linux, your container behaves the same. You're not rewriting install scripts or hunting down platform quirks every time you deploy somewhere new.
- **Isolation**: Your model's dependencies stay fully self-contained. You don't have to worry about conflicting Python versions, system libraries, or some random package upgrade breaking half your toolchain. Each model container gets its own clean little sandbox.
- **Efficiency**: Once built, containers start up fast. That means you can spin up new instances easily, scale horizontally when you need more throughput, and tear them down when you don't. You're not loading up huge VMs or rebuilding environments every time.

Ultimately, containerizing your AI models takes what can often be a fragile, finicky deployment process and makes it something reliable, repeatable, and scalable. And once you've done it a few times, you won't want to run these things any other way.

In the following sections, we'll focus on choosing the right base image, structuring Dockerfiles for performance, exposing your model via HTTP APIs, and starting to tune for real-world usage.

By the end, you'll have a solid container you can build, run, and iterate with confidently. It's certainly not the easiest thing to do in the world, but oh my is it cool!

Choosing the right base image

One of the first decisions you will make when containerizing your models is which base image to build from. Honestly, getting this right up front makes your life much easier down the line.

For most Python-based models, you have a couple of really solid starting points:

- **python:3.11-slim**: This is usually my default for anything with a reasonable number of dependencies. It strips out a lot of unnecessary extras but still gives you enough to install most Python packages cleanly.
- **python:3.11-alpine**: This one is even smaller, but be careful. Alpine can be brilliant if your app and its dependencies fully support it, but you may run into compatibility issues with certain Python packages or anything that relies on native libraries. Test early if you go down this route.
- **Ubuntu or Debian variants**: If your model needs heavier native dependencies, such as `libtorch`, `onnxruntime-gpu`, or anything that compiles C extensions, these give you a more full-featured base to work with. Yes, the images are bigger, but sometimes the added compatibility saves you hours of fighting build errors.

As a rule of thumb: keep your base image as lean as you can get away with. Every megabyte you shave off here means faster image pulls, quicker startup, and less storage used across your environments. And trust me, once you are rebuilding containers multiple times a day, those savings add up quickly.

Writing the Dockerfile

Okay, once you've picked your base image, the next step is building out the Dockerfile properly. This is where a little bit of structure up front saves you loads of frustration later on, especially once you start tweaking dependencies or rebuilding your models frequently.

Here's a nice, clean example to take home for a FastAPI service wrapping an ONNX model:

```
FROM python:3.11-slim
WORKDIR /app
COPY requirements.txt .
RUN pip install --no-cache-dir -r requirements.txt
COPY . .
EXPOSE 8000
CMD ["uvicorn", "app:app", "--host", "0.0.0.0", "--port", "8000"]

```

Figure 7.3: Example Dockerfile for deploying a Python FastAPI app using Uvicorn on port 8000

So, what's going on here and why are we doing it like this?

- **Installation happens early**: By copying in your `requirements.txt` first and installing dependencies before copying the rest of your code, you're taking full advantage of Docker's layer caching. If you update your app code but your dependencies stay the same, Docker will skip re-installing the packages every time you rebuild. That speeds up your rebuilds massively once you get into your day-to-day dev loop.
- **We avoid package caches**: That `--no-cache-dir` flag tells `pip` not to keep around all the temporary download files after install. That keeps your image smaller and cleaner. Less clutter means faster pulls, which means quicker startups. Nice!
- **The command exposes a clean API endpoint**: Finally, `CMD` launches `uvicorn` directly inside the container, binding to `0.0.0.0` so it is accessible from outside. No Bash wrappers, no unnecessary shell layers: just straight to serving requests.

A Dockerfile like this gives you a solid, predictable foundation for your GenAI models. It keeps your containers light, rebuilds fast, and sets you up nicely for when you start layering in the other pieces of the stack later on.

> Note
>
> **Common errors to avoid**
>
> A few issues show up repeatedly when containerizing model servers. Forgetting to expose the port (`EXPOSE 8000`) means the service appears to "run" but nothing can reach it. Leaving out `--no-cache-dir` causes `pip` to stash large temporary artifacts that inflate your image size. Copying your entire project folder too early in the Dockerfile breaks layer caching, forcing full rebuilds on every change. And if you forget to bind to `0.0.0.0`, the API will only listen inside the container, not from your Windows host. These small details are the ones that catch most people on their first few builds.

Once the container is set up, you need something inside it to actually serve your model and respond to requests. And honestly, this is where FastAPI really shines: simple, clean, and incredibly quick to wire up.

Inside your `app.py`, you might have something like this:

```python
from fastapi import FastAPI
import onnxruntime as ort

model = ort.InferenceSession("model.onnx")
app = FastAPI()

@app.post("/predict")
async def predict(data: dict):
    inputs = data["inputs"]
    output = model.run(None, {"input": inputs})
    return {"output": output}

```

Figure 7.4: FastAPI application loading an ONNX model and exposing a /predict endpoint for inference

Let's break this down a bit:

1. You load your ONNX model directly when the container starts. That means the model's already sitting in memory, ready to respond the moment an API call comes in. No downloading models at startup, no waiting on external sources, and no nasty surprises if your internet connection goes flaky.
2. The `/predict` endpoint is kept nice and simple. It expects a JSON payload containing your input data, passes that into the model, runs inference, and sends back the output as JSON. You can easily expand this to include error handling, input validation, or more complex post-processing as your use case grows.
3. Because FastAPI is fully async out of the box, this structure also means you're already set up to scale nicely if you need to handle multiple requests at once. That becomes very handy once you start stacking more services into your pipeline later.

> **Note**
>
> One thing to think about as the load increases is how your model handles concurrency. FastAPI will happily serve multiple requests at once, but if the model is large or CPU-bound, you may want to batch inputs or queue requests so you don't overload the container. On Windows under WSL 2 especially, a small batching window can dramatically reduce contention and keep inference time predictable.

The key thing to take away here is that your inference server stays self-contained. The model lives inside the container alongside your code: no external dependencies at runtime, and nothing fragile about your deployment path. Once you've built this once, you can rebuild and redeploy it confidently anywhere, locally, in CI, or even onto a larger orchestrated setup.

Building and running on Windows

Alright, now that you've got your Dockerfile and your app code wired up, let's actually build and run this thing locally on Windows. This is where Docker makes the whole process feel almost too easy once you've done it a few times.

First, build your image from your project directory:

```
docker build -t genai-model:latest .
```

This tells Docker to take everything in your current directory, apply the Dockerfile we wrote earlier, and tag the resulting image as `genai-model:latest` so you can reference it easily going forward. The first build may take a minute or two as it pulls the base image and installs your dependencies, but after that, rebuilds are much faster thanks to Docker's caching.

Now let's actually run the container:

```
docker run --name genai-model -d -p 8000:8000 genai-model:latest
```

- `--name` gives your container an easy-to-reference name
- `-d` runs it in detached mode, so it doesn't tie up your terminal
- `-p 8000:8000` maps the container's internal port to your Windows `localhost`

At this point, your inference server should be live and listening. Let's test it by sending it a sample input via `curl`:

```
curl http://localhost:8000/predict -H "Content-Type: application/json" -d
"{\"inputs\": [[1.0, 2.0, 3.0]]}"
```

This simulates a real API call, and you should get a JSON response back with the model's output.

```
PS C:\Users\MikeSmith\GenAI> curl http://localhost:8000/predict -H

{"output": [[[0.823, 0.114, 0.063]]]}
```

Figure 7.5: Example curl request sending data to the FastAPI /predict endpoint and receiving model inference output

If you see that response come back successfully from both PowerShell and your browser, congratulations, you've got yourself a fully portable, self-contained model container running locally on Windows! You can shut it down, spin it back up, move it between machines, or plug it into your full pipeline later on without worrying about missing dependencies or broken environments. And that's exactly the kind of predictability you want when you're working with GenAI models that tend to get finicky if even one piece is off.

Now, while a lot of smaller models and simple pipelines will happily run inside your nice, slim Python images, sooner or later, you're going to hit a model that needs a bit more under the hood. Maybe it's a LLaMA variant, maybe it's a custom ONNX build, or maybe you are dealing with some specific framework that leans on native C libraries. This is where you start needing to think about native dependencies.

So, if your model needs GPU support or relies on libraries such as `libtorch`, `onnxruntime-gpu`, or anything compiled natively, your Dockerfile needs to account for that directly. This usually means building from a slightly heavier base image, such as Ubuntu or Debian, that includes support for these native packages.

Here's an example of what that might look like at the start of your Dockerfile:

```
FROM ubuntu:22.04

RUN apt-get update && apt-get install -y libprotobuf-dev libomp5 && \
    python3 -m pip install --no-cache-dir fastapi uvicorn onnxruntime
```

Figure 7.6: Example Dockerfile snippet installing native dependencies and Python packages

So, what's *actually* going on here?

- We're pulling in the `ubuntu:22.04` base image because it gives us full package manager access to install system libraries. That's often necessary when you need things such as `libprotobuf` or OpenMP to run your model correctly.

- We're using `apt-get` to install the native packages Docker can't pull in through `pip` alone. This way, when your app code tries to load the model, all the underlying system dependencies are already there inside the image.
- As usual, we're still keeping things as tidy as possible by installing Python packages with `--no-cache-dir` to avoid bloating the image unnecessarily.

This approach means that everything your model needs is fully self-contained inside the container: no surprises at runtime and no scrambling to rebuild your environment when something gets updated.

Yes, your image will be a bit larger than with the pure slim variants, but the trade-off is rock-solid compatibility, especially when you're dealing with more complex model stacks or running across different host machines.

Tuning for Windows performance

Now, because we're working on Windows with WSL 2 running under the hood, you do need to be a bit conscious of where your performance bottlenecks might sneak in. Most of the time, Docker on Windows behaves brilliantly, but file I/O is one of those areas where little decisions can have a big impact, especially when you start dealing with large model files or lots of read/write operations.

Here are a few things I've learned the hard way:

- **Use named volumes instead of mounting from C**: When you mount files directly from your Windows filesystem, such as `C:\Users\YourName\whatever`, Docker has to constantly bridge between Windows and Linux filesystems inside WSL. That translation layer works, but it's slower than you might expect, especially with larger model files or lots of small files. By using Docker volumes that live natively inside WSL's virtual filesystem, you avoid that overhead completely, and things run much more smoothly.
- **Keep model weights inside the container wherever possible**: If you can bake your model weights directly into your image as part of your Docker build, you eliminate the need for runtime filesystem access entirely. This means your container is self-contained and portable and avoids any reliance on external mounts or volumes to get started. It also removes one more thing that could break if you move between environments.
- **Where you do need volumes, stick to Linux-style paths**: Sometimes you still need shared volumes, for logs, temporary files, or intermediate results. In those cases, when you use the `-v` flag, make sure you're using Linux-style paths that map properly inside WSL, rather than trying to bridge directly into your Windows filesystem. Keeping

everything inside `/mnt/wsl/` or native Docker volumes helps avoid the quirks that can crop up with path resolution on Windows.

These might feel like small details, but they really do stack up when you're working with larger models or running lots of containers in parallel. A little bit of discipline here goes a long way to keeping your development workflow snappy and your containers behaving predictably as your stack grows.

Local monitoring

Alright, you've got your model container up and running. But before you declare victory and move on, you want to keep an eye on how it's actually behaving under the hood. While things may *appear* to be running fine, it's very easy for GenAI models to quietly chew through CPU, memory, or disk resources without you noticing, right up until everything slows to a crawl.

The simplest place to start is with `docker stats`. This gives you a live, real-time view of what your container is doing while it runs:

```
docker stats genai-model
```

CONTAINER ID	NAME	CPU %	MEM USAGE / LIMIT	MEM %	NET I/O
ab12cd34ef56	genai-model	27.35%	512MiB / 1GiB	50.00%	3.2MB / 2.1MB

Figure 7.7: Output from docker stats showing real-time CPU, memory, and network usage

This will stream live metrics showing you the following:

- **CPU usage**: If your model's inference loop is working the CPU harder than expected
- **Memory usage**: Models love RAM, and this is often where problems start first
- **Network I/O**: Useful if your model is fetching data or serving lots of requests
- **Disk I/O**: Particularly important if you're doing any caching or writing logs inside the container

The key here isn't to stare at this constantly but to build the habit of checking early and often, especially when you first introduce new models, add preprocessing steps, or change input data shapes. If you spot memory usage creeping close to your system limits or CPU sweating under load, that's usually your first hint that you either need to optimize the model, start batching requests differently, or bring some caching into play.

> **Note**
>
> **Remember**: Most GenAI models will happily accept as much RAM as you give them. The trick is knowing when they're using it unnecessarily.

Iterating and updating

Let's be honest, you're not going to get your model perfect the first time. You'll tweak it, fine-tune it, and retrain it, maybe change your preprocessing steps; this is completely normal in any GenAI workflow. So, you want your update process to be quick and reliable and not feel like you're rebuilding the entire world every time you make a change.

Here's how you handle updating your model inside your containerized workflow.

First, when you've got a new version of your model (say you retrained it or improved its accuracy), simply drop the updated `model.onnx` file into your project directory. Now, at this point, you've got a decision to make: do you want to rebuild your image using a proper versioned tag or just overwrite `latest` during dev work? My advice is to get into the habit of versioning your images properly. It'll save you confusion later.

```
docker build --no-cache -t genai-model:v2 .
```

That `--no-cache` flag makes sure you're fully rebuilding with the new model baked in, rather than Docker potentially trying to reuse old cached layers. It's a bit slower but guarantees you're not accidentally running stale layers when testing updates.

Now to redeploy:

```
docker stop genai-model
docker rm genai-model
docker run --name genai-model -d -p 8000:8000 genai-model:v2
```

Stop the old container, clean it up, and spin up the new one using your freshly built image. Clean, simple, predictable.

The nice part is, because of how we structured the Dockerfile earlier (installing dependencies first, copying the model afterward, you remember!), we're not rebuilding everything every single time. Docker only rebuilds the layers that have changed, which in most cases is just copying in our updated model file. That's what makes iteration fast, and once you get into this habit, you'll be updating and redeploying your models in minutes rather than hours.

Once you've got your model container built cleanly like this, you're in a great place. You can plug it straight into Swarm, Kubernetes, or even just a local Docker Compose stack when you start scaling things out.

So, that's one model down, but what happens when your business needs more than one? Most enterprise GenAI environments don't stop at a single model. You'll often find summarization, classification, and embedding models all running in parallel, each serving a different purpose but sharing the same data and orchestration layers.

Deploying a multi-model GenAI stack on Windows

Alright, let's get a little more real-world. In a typical enterprise setup, you're rarely running just one model; oh, we wish it were that simple sometimes! You might have a summarization model for reports, a sentiment classifier for feedback, and an embedding model powering search or recommendations (or something else) all working together, all isolated, and all running under Docker on Windows.

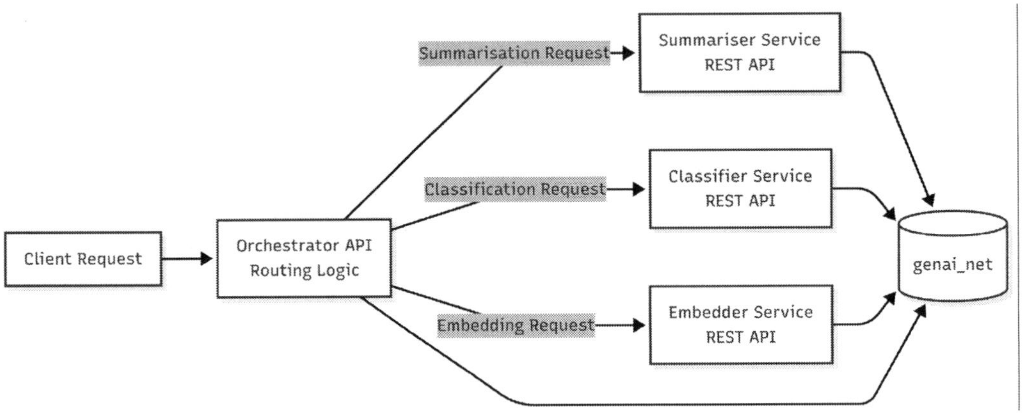

Figure 7.8: Orchestrator routing requests to model-specific containers inside the multi-model GenAI stack on Windows

Let's build a small but realistic example of that kind of setup so you can get your head around it.

First, here's a really simple Compose file to illustrate how you'd wire this all together locally under WSL 2:

```yaml
version: "3.9"
services:
  summariser:
    build: ./summariser
    ports:
      - "8001:8000"
    networks:
      - genai_net
    deploy:
      replicas: 2
    environment:
      - MODEL_PATH=/models/summariser.onnx

  classifier:
    build: ./classifier
    ports:
      - "8002:8000"
    networks:
      - genai_net
    environment:
      - MODEL_PATH=/models/classifier.onnx

  embedder:
    build: ./embedder
    ports:
      - "8003:8000"
    networks:
      - genai_net
    environment:
      - MODEL_PATH=/models/embedder.onnx

  orchestrator:
    build: ./orchestrator
    ports:
      - "8080:8080"
    depends_on:
      - summariser
      - classifier
      - embedder
    networks:
      - genai_net

networks:
  genai_net:
    driver: bridge
```

Figure 7.9: A multi-model GenAI stack running on Windows using Docker Compose

In this setup, note the following:

- Each model container exposes its own REST API.
- The orchestrator container acts as the central router. It decides which model to call based on the request type (text to summarize, sentiment to classify, etc.).
- All containers share a private Docker network (`genai_net`) so they can talk to each other cleanly without exposing internal ports to the host.

On Windows, you'd run this with a single command from PowerShell:

```
docker compose up -d
```

From there, you can test the orchestrator directly:

```
curl http://localhost:8080/api/analyse -H "Content-Type: application/json" -d
"{\"text\":\"This quarter's performance was strong.\"}"
```

The orchestrator calls the classifier first, then the summarizer, and finally enriches the response with embeddings from the embedder service, all via internal container-to-container traffic.

The real secret sauce of this design is that it scales. Each model container can be versioned, replaced, or horizontally scaled without touching the others. In enterprise pipelines, this architecture is what keeps AI systems reliable even as new models get introduced or replaced.

If you're deploying this inside a Windows enterprise environment, the only adjustments you'll typically make are the following:

- Defining Docker resource limits in `.wslconfig` (so each model doesn't eat all your RAM)
- Using Windows Active Directory credentials or Docker secrets for secure API access
- Pushing each image to your company's internal registry (for example, `registry.mycompany.com/genai/classifier:v1.2`)

Let's look at a quick example of how those adjustments might work in practice.

For example, imagine you're deploying the multi-model GenAI stack we built earlier, a summarizer, classifier, and embedder, inside your company's internal Windows environment. Each model runs smoothly in Docker, but now you need to prepare it for enterprise standards.

You start by defining resource limits in your `.wslconfig` file to make sure the stack doesn't overwhelm developer machines:

```
[wsl2]
memory=8GB
processors=4
```

Next, instead of hardcoding API keys for your models, you integrate Docker secrets with Windows Active Directory. The API container reads its credentials securely at runtime, as follows:

```
services:
            api:
            image: registry.mycompany.com/genai/orchestrator:v1.0
            secrets:
              - openai_api_key
secrets:
       openai_api_key:
       external: true
```

Finally, each image is tagged and pushed to your internal registry for traceability and version control:

```
docker tag classifier registry.mycompany.com/genai/classifier:v1.2
docker push registry.mycompany.com/genai/classifier:v1.2
```

This pattern keeps your deployment compliant with enterprise security and governance policies while maintaining the flexibility of your local Windows Docker setup.

We'll dig into orchestration properly a bit later on in this chapter, but the key thing here is that by keeping your container self-contained and well structured now, you're setting yourself up for much less hassle when it comes time to run multiple replicas or integrate it into a bigger pipeline.

Managing data for AI workflows

In a past role, I was fortunate enough to lead some data science students through their final year project at university. Their AI pipeline kept failing because latent data issues were hidden until the model output was already misbehaving. It was one of those jobs where I'd been there so long that I knew essentially *everything* about our architecture and infrastructure even if I didn't want to. We cleaned up the data ingestion stage and applied validation early, and suddenly, our model metrics stopped drifting for no reason. That moment taught me that data isn't just fuel; it's the fuel filter and pump, too. Getting data right at each stage sets the tone for everything that follows.

Let's explore how to build robust, containerized data workflows using Docker on Windows. We'll touch on ingestion, transformation, and storage using lightweight tools, as well as best practices for keeping everything organized, secure, and reliable.

Ingestion, caching, and vector storage

Let's be honest, your models are only ever going to be as good as the data you feed them. If the data going in is messy, broken, or incomplete, your GenAI stack will quietly start producing questionable results long before you even notice something's wrong. That's why getting your ingestion and cleansing process nailed early on is so important. The more you can catch upfront, the less you'll be debugging weird model behavior downstream.

This is your first defense against "garbage in, garbage out." Once bad data gets past this stage and hits your models, it can distort your outputs, ruin your training runs, or, worse, make you lose confidence in the whole system because you no longer trust what you are seeing. Often, these issues don't show up as big, dramatic failures. It might be a CSV missing a few fields, weird encodings sneaking in from external APIs, or data types drifting silently over time. If you do not catch it early, your models will happily work with junk, and you'll be left trying to figure out why your predictions suddenly feel off.

The cleanest approach is to isolate ingestion and cleansing into its own container. Let that container handle reading raw data from wherever it's coming in (API calls, file drops, message queues, or even direct database reads), validate the data against strict schemas, and only forward on clean, validated records. This keeps your model containers focused purely on inference and stops them from having to defend themselves against bad input.

The following diagram shows the flow of data through a typical GenAI pipeline running on Windows with Docker, from raw input to model inference and storage.

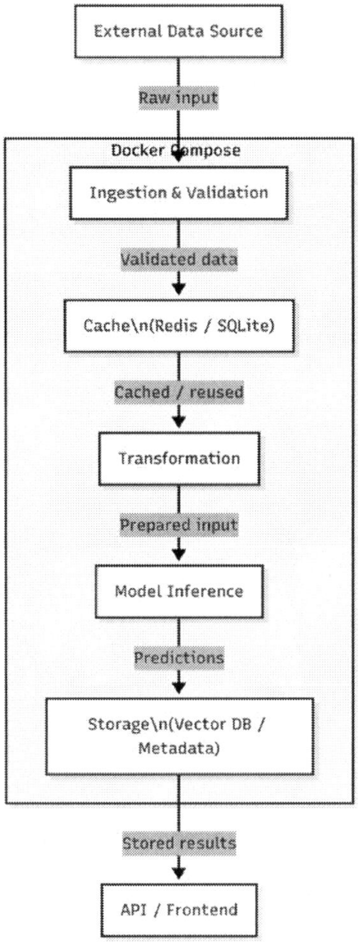

Figure 7.10: Compact data flow through a GenAI pipeline on Windows

For most people, a lightweight Python container running pandas or Pydantic is perfect for this job. If you're working at a higher scale or want to get fancy, you can also use Go or Rust for high-performance pipelines, but honestly, Python's readability and flexibility make it a solid first choice here.

Here's a nice starting point:

```
FROM python:3.11-slim
WORKDIR /app
COPY requirements.txt .
RUN pip install --no-cache-dir -r requirements.txt
COPY ingest.py .
CMD ["python", "ingest.py"]
```

Figure 7.11: Example Dockerfile for a lightweight Python ingestion service built on python:3.11-slim

It's simple and clean and gets the job done.

Inside `ingest.py`, your typical flow might look something like the following:

1. Read the raw data stream from your source.
2. Validate each record against your expected schema.
3. Log and discard any rows that fail validation (always log them; you'll want to know what you're dropping).
4. Output the clean, validated records to either `stdout` or a file, or pipe them directly into another container using a Docker socket or a message queue such as RabbitMQ or Kafka.

The key thing here is that we're not silently failing. If something's wrong, we catch it early, log it, and stop it from contaminating the rest of the pipeline.

Here's a really high-level example of what `inject.py` might look like to get you started.

```python
import pandas as pd

# simulate some  incoming data
data = [
    {"id": 1, "value": 42},
    {"id": 2, "value": None},  # Bad record
    {"id": 3, "value": 17}
]

valid_records = []

for record in data:
    try:
        if record["value"] is None:
            raise ValueError("Missing value")
        valid_records.append(record)
    except Exception as e:
        print(f"REJECTED record {record['id']}: {e}")

# lets output cleaned data
df = pd.DataFrame(valid_records)
df.to_csv("/data/cleaned.csv", index=False)
print(f"INGESTED {len(valid_records)} records successfully")

```

Figure 7.12: Example Python script simulating a simple data ingestion and validation process

This sets the basic pattern you'll see throughout your GenAI stack: ingest → validate → output. The model itself should never be responsible for untangling broken data. That work should already be done before the model even sees the request.

Note

Caching intermediate results

Once ingestion and validation are in place, the next part of the same data layer is a simple caching tier. When you are building GenAI pipelines, one of the easiest ways to quietly burn both time and CPU is to keep repeating the same processing steps for every request. If you are re-running tokenization, vectorization, or normalization every single time, even when the input has not changed, you are wasting cycles. Worse: you are making every inference slower than it needs to be. This is where caching starts to earn its keep.

> The pattern is pretty common: a lot of your data will follow similar shapes or even repeat across requests. Maybe you are chunking documents (breaking large texts into smaller, manageable pieces for processing), preprocessing large batches of text, or generating embeddings that rarely change. By caching those intermediate results, you skip all that repeated work on subsequent runs. The model still does what it needs to do, but only when it actually needs to. Less processing, faster responses, happier system.
>
> You do not need to get overly clever here either. This isn't enterprise-scale caching design; it's simply being smart about not doing redundant work. The faster you can feed preprocessed input into your model, the faster your pipeline responds overall.

For local development and small-to-medium pipelines, Redis and SQLite are both great options to drop into your Docker stack.

Here is a simple example of how you might wire Redis into your Compose file:

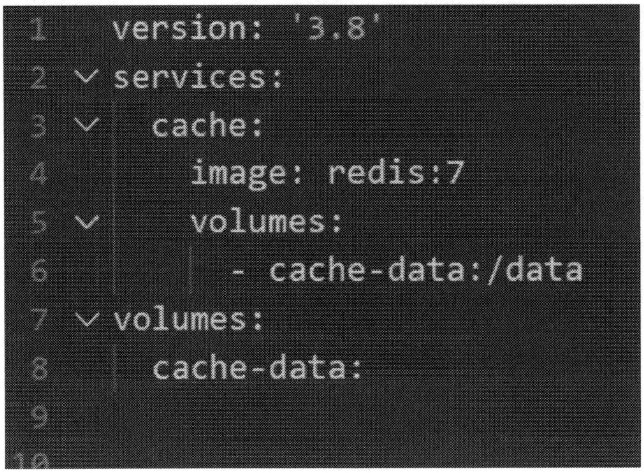

Figure 7.13: Example Docker Compose file defining a Redis cache service with a named volume

Now your ingestion container or your preprocessing service can hit the cache first, check whether a processed result already exists, and only run the heavier transforms if there's a cache miss.

However, there are a few key considerations:

- **Time to live (TTL)**: You want to automatically expire cache entries after a reasonable time period, so you are not clogging up storage with stale or unused results.

- **Isolation**: If you are running different versions of your pipeline for dev, staging, and prod, make sure your caches are isolated so you don't accidentally cross-contaminate results across environments.
- **Persistence**: Use volumes for Redis (or SQLite; your choice, I won't judge) so cached data sticks around even if the containers restart. That way, you don't lose your whole cache every time you stop and start Compose.

You're definitely not trying to build a bulletproof distributed caching layer here. You are simply putting some guardrails in place to avoid redoing work that's already been done once. When you're running models locally on limited resources, that extra efficiency starts to feel like a superpower.

Beyond caching, the data layer also needs somewhere durable to keep embeddings and metadata. Now, once you start generating embeddings or tracking metadata for your AI models, simple key-value caches such as Redis will only get you so far. At some point, you need something a bit more structured that can handle proper queries, searches, and storage without turning into a complete mess.

Your models rely heavily on *fast* lookups. Whether it is retrieving previous embeddings, doing similarity searches, or tracking model input history, you want that data available quickly and reliably in a flash! If you try to brute-force this with flat files or basic object storage, you'll quickly hit performance ceilings and start seeing your pipeline slow to a crawl and fall over. The more efficient you are here, the better your models scale without you needing to completely re-engineer your storage layer every few months.

You don't need to jump straight into heavyweight databases to get something effective. Here are a few very workable options for Docker-based GenAI stacks, especially for local dev and smaller deployments:

- **SQLite**: Dead simple, file-based, and very Docker-friendly. It is perfect for indexing embeddings, storing metadata, or just keeping track of which inputs have already been processed. For small to midsize datasets, SQLite is lightweight and fast enough to do the job. It's a really good entry point.
- **FAISS or Weaviate**: If you need to actually run similarity searches on your embeddings (such as nearest-neighbour lookups), these tools are specifically designed for vector search. They integrate easily with Docker and work great for local development or edge deployments where you want high performance without needing full external services.
- **DuckDB or in-memory options**: Coming a little out of left field here, for temporary analytics workloads, feature experimentation, or small pipelines that don't require persistence, DuckDB and in-memory structures can give you lightning-fast performance with minimal setup.

Let's take SQLite as a simple example you can easily build into your stack. Its name is not as cute as DuckDB but it's quickly becoming my personal go-to for databases for small workloads:

```
FROM python:3.11-slim
WORKDIR /app
RUN pip install fastapi sqlite-utils
COPY storage.py .
CMD ["python", "storage.py"]

```

Figure 7.14: Example Dockerfile for a lightweight FastAPI storage service built on python:3.11-slim

This gives you a nice, clean container that spins up your storage layer with FastAPI handling HTTP endpoints.

Inside `storage.py`, your workflow might be as follows:

1. On startup, open or create the database file on a Docker volume.
2. Check whether your tables exist; if not, create them.
3. Handle CRUD operations via FastAPI endpoints.
4. Keep all the storage logic fully encapsulated inside this one service.

This pattern gives you a proper standalone data service inside your Docker stack that you can scale, reuse, or replace later without needing to tear everything apart. You get predictable behavior, clear separation of concerns, and containers that are each doing one focused job, which is exactly where you want to be. Here is a really simple and pretty agnostic example of what `storage.py` might look like.

```python
from fastapi import FastAPI
import sqlite3
import os

# Path to the database file inside the Docker volume.
# This will sit inside our mounted volume so it survives restarts.
DB_PATH = "/data/storage.db"

# Make sure the directory exists (Docker volumes can sometimes start fresh)
os.makedirs(os.path.dirname(DB_PATH), exist_ok=True)

# Connect to the database - creates the file if it does not exist yet.
conn = sqlite3.connect(DB_PATH)
cursor = conn.cursor()

# Create the table if it is not already there.
# This keeps the service fully self-contained: no migrations, no manual steps.
cursor.execute("""
CREATE TABLE IF NOT EXISTS embeddings (
    id INTEGER PRIMARY KEY AUTOINCREMENT,
    text TEXT NOT NULL,
    vector BLOB NOT NULL
)
""")
conn.commit()

app = FastAPI()

# Basic endpoint to store a new embedding record.
# Simple and clean: we store both the text and its vector.
@app.post("/store")
def store_embedding(text: str, vector: bytes):
    cursor.execute("INSERT INTO embeddings (text, vector) VALUES (?, ?)", (text, vector))
    conn.commit()
    return {"status": "stored"}

# Simple lookup endpoint to retrieve an embedding by ID.
# If the ID is not found, we return a friendly error.
@app.get("/lookup/{id}")
def get_embedding(id: int):
    cursor.execute("SELECT text, vector FROM embeddings WHERE id = ?", (id,))
    result = cursor.fetchone()
    if result:
        return {"text": result[0], "vector": result[1]}
    else:
        return {"error": "Not found"}
```

Figure 7.15: Example FastAPI service defining a lightweight storage API that uses SQLite to save and retrieve text–vector pairs

Now that we've got our storage container behaving properly, let's pull the other services together and wire the full pipeline using Docker Compose.

Structuring Compose for a data workflow

This is where Compose really starts to shine and take some of the work off us. Once you have your ingestion, transformation, and model services containerized, you want to wire them all together into a proper pipeline that actually flows. Compose lets you do that cleanly, without having to hardcode hostnames, IPs, or startup scripts just to get things talking. If you prefer event-driven pipelines, you can also swap the volume handoff for a message queue such as RabbitMQ or Kafka, but for most Windows-based development flows, shared volumes keep things simpler and easier to debug.

Here's a nice example Compose file to pull the whole data flow together:

```yaml
version: '3.8'
services:
  ingester:
    build: ./ingester
    volumes:
      - cleaned-data:/data

  transformer:
    build: ./transformer
    volumes:
      - cleaned-data:/data:ro
      - transformed-data:/out

  model:
    image: genai-model:latest
    volumes:
      - transformed-data:/input:ro
    depends_on:
      - transformer

volumes:
  cleaned-data:
  transformed-data:
```

Figure 7.16: Example Docker Compose file wiring together ingester, transformer, and model services through shared Docker volumes

Okay, let's break down what is actually happening here:

- `ingester` reads raw input data from wherever you are sourcing it, cleans and validates it, and then writes the cleaned data into the shared `cleaned-data` volume.

- `transformer` picks up the cleaned data, applies any additional processing (feature extraction, embedding generation, normalization, etc), and then writes the transformed data into a second shared volume called `transformed-data`.
- `model` finally reads the fully prepped data from `transformed-data` and runs inference. At this stage, the model is getting clean, predictable input every time.

Notice how each step only touches the data it *needs*, and everything stays isolated via volumes. This makes debugging much easier because you can stop at any stage, inspect the files inside those volumes, and check exactly where things might have gone off the rails.

The `depends_on` flag helps Compose know which services need to be up before the next one starts. It does not wait for full readiness (you still want proper health checks for that), but it prevents obvious failures where one service tries to start before its upstream data even exists.

One of the nice side effects of structuring your pipeline like this is that it becomes extremely modular. You can swap out one service, rebuild one piece, or scale parts of the pipeline independently without needing to touch everything else. That flexibility starts to pay off very quickly as your stack grows and your experiments evolve.

Monitoring and securing data workflows

Even though we're often focused on monitoring the models themselves, the data pipeline deserves just as much love. If the ingestion breaks, if transformation silently starts failing, or if processing times start creeping up, your entire stack's output becomes questionable. This is where having some light but effective monitoring baked into your data pipeline pays off massively.

Metrics and logs

The first thing you want is simple, structured logging that gives you visibility into how your data pipeline is performing. This doesn't need to be complex telemetry straight away; even well-placed log lines can give you a surprisingly clear view of what's going on.

At a minimum, start by logging the following:

- **Record counts**: How many items you successfully ingested or transformed
- **Error counts**: How many records failed validation or were dropped
- **Processing durations**: How long each batch or run takes to process

For example, it could be something as simple as this inside your ingestion script:

```
print(f"INGESTED {count} records in {duration:.2f} seconds")
```

You can pipe these logs straight into `docker logs` for live monitoring while developing, and once your stack matures, you can expose these as HTTP endpoints to let something such as Prometheus scrape them automatically.

The key here is not to overthink it up front; you just want enough signal to spot when something starts behaving differently.

Health checks

Next, build lightweight health checks into your services. This helps Compose or Swarm orchestrate startup order and helps you catch failures faster.

For your ingestion and transformation containers, a simple `/health` endpoint that returns `HTTP 200` when the service is operational is usually enough:

```
@app.get("/health")
def healthcheck():
    return {"status": "ok"}
```

Then, inside your `docker-compose.yml`, you can wire in the `healthcheck:` option to track container readiness:

```
healthcheck:
  test: ["CMD", "curl", "-f", "http://localhost:8000/health"]
  interval: 30s
  retries: 3
```

This tells Compose not to move on until the service is properly responding. That becomes really helpful as your stack grows and downstream services start depending on earlier stages being ready before kicking off.

Think about it: when you build pipelines like this, you're no longer hoping everything is fine; you've got constant visibility. You know when ingestion slows down, when transformation is skipping records, or when something's quietly throwing exceptions. That means you can catch problems early, long before your model outputs start degrading and you end up wondering where it all went wrong.

So far, we've focused on visibility, making sure you can see when something goes wrong in your data flow. But monitoring is only half the story. The other half is keeping that data safe and properly isolated, even during local development. Even when you're working locally, and it feels like "just dev work," you're still handling real data that deserves proper care. It's easy to think security is something to worry about only once you hit production, but by that point, bad habits are already baked in. If you start isolating things correctly now, you'll save yourself a world of pain later.

Your GenAI stack might be running on your laptop, but it's still dealing with real user inputs, private embeddings, or training data that could be sensitive. These aren't the kinds of things you want leaking between containers or slipping into logs and backups where they don't belong. Keeping data separated from the start makes your environment cleaner, safer, and much easier to reason about as your stack grows.

Here are a few practical ways to protect your data as you build and monitor your stack:

- **Use separate volumes per data type**: Don't just dump everything into one shared Docker volume. Split your ingestion data, transformation outputs, embeddings, and logs into their own clearly named volumes. That way, if something fails or you need to clean up a piece of your pipeline, you're not accidentally wiping out everything else.
- **Limit service exposure**: Your model containers, ingestion workers, and data processors do not need to be directly exposed to the outside world. Keep them tucked away behind your API layer. This massively reduces your attack surface, even when running locally.
- **Store secrets properly**: Seriously, environment variables, `.env` files, or Docker secrets should hold your API keys, credentials, and tokens. *Never* hardcode these directly into your Dockerfiles or application code. This makes your stack portable, repeatable, and less risky if you share or version control your configs.
- **Set runtime permissions**: If a container only needs to read data, do not give it write access. For example, your model container might only need read access to the preprocessed data volume. Your ingestion container might be the only one allowed to write new files. This simple discipline goes a long way in preventing accidental overwrites, data loss, or even malicious activity if something were to break unexpectedly.

Remember, these are not heavyweight security mechanisms; they're just solid architectural guardrails. Think of them as handshake agreements between your containers. Each one knows its role, has access only to what it needs, and does not interfere with the rest of the stack. Later on, when we dive into full deployment best practices, we'll layer on stronger security controls, but if you nail these basics early, everything you build after this will sit on much stronger foundations.

Scaling considerations for data services

Okay, so it's one thing to build and test your data pipeline locally with a few hundred records. It is another thing entirely when you start feeding in real-world data at full scale. What feels instant when you are testing can suddenly become a bottleneck once you are processing thousands or millions of records, or when multiple users start hammering the system in parallel. This is where scaling your data services properly starts to matter. For example, a batch-heavy workload such as nightly document ingestion usually pressures the ingestion and transformation containers first, so scaling those horizontally gives the biggest improvement. In contrast, a streaming workflow such as real-time chat enrichment barely stresses ingestion but quickly pushes the model servers to their limit. Different workloads saturate different parts of the data layer, which is why scaling isn't one-size-fits-all.

- **Adding replicas where they count**: Ingestion and transformation stages are often the first places you will feel pressure when load increases. If you start to see processing queues building up or long ingestion delays, you can spin up additional replicas of these services to share the load.
  Because each container handles its slice of work independently, adding more replicas is often as simple as the following:

  ```
  docker-compose up --scale ingester=3
  ```

  You're still following the same processing logic, just spreading the load across more containers, so you're not bottlenecked by a single process trying to keep up.
- **Tune your caching layers**: Caching is lovely, but it isn't free. As you scale, your Redis container will need enough memory to handle whatever volume of intermediate data you're pushing into it. If you undersize it, you'll end up thrashing the cache and defeating the whole point. Make sure you tune Redis memory limits as your data grows and keep an eye on eviction policies so old cache entries get cleaned up safely.
- **Persistent data volumes matter**: In local dev, you can often get away with volatile storage and not worry too much about persistence between container restarts. But once you are running more permanent stacks, even on dev clusters, you want your data stored somewhere reliable. Docker volumes are great for this, but make sure those volumes are backed up, stored on resilient disks, or tied into proper cloud storage if you are deploying beyond your machine.
- **Orchestration makes life easier**: For early dev, Compose-local works brilliantly. But as your pipelines get heavier and you start to need resilience, failover, and proper service management, you're going to want to graduate into Swarm or Kubernetes. These tools

handle replication, restarts, node failovers, and scaling far more robustly than manual scripts.

This is where your earlier container design choices pay off, too! Because if you've kept your services clean, stateless, and well isolated, scaling out becomes a drop-in exercise instead of a rewrite.

PVC-like volumes on Windows

You buy one, you get one free!

That's a very British joke that not many of you will get, and I apologize for that, again!

No, I'm not trying to sell you new windows in this section. But since you are building this stack on Windows under WSL 2, we need to call out one very Windows-specific wrinkle: how volumes behave across the filesystem boundary.

> Note
>
> **Super-quick side note: what does PVC even mean?**
>
> In Kubernetes land, **PVC** stands for **Persistent Volume Claim**. It is basically the way Kubernetes handles persistent storage: you "claim" storage and Kubernetes matches that claim to physical or cloud storage behind the scenes. In the Docker world, we don't have PVCs per se, but named Docker volumes behave similarly. They give your containers persistent storage that survives restarts, rebuilds, and container crashes, without you needing to bind-mount folders directly from your Windows host.

That is why I'm cheekily calling them "PVC-like volumes" here, because conceptually, you are getting the same kind of safety, just with far less fuss.

The reason it matters is if you mount folders directly from your Windows filesystem (`C:\drives`), WSL 2 has to translate every file read and write across the Windows-Linux boundary. That translation adds latency, especially with lots of small files, and can quietly wreck your data pipeline performance once the volumes start filling up.

The smarter way to do it would be as follows:

- Use named Docker volumes wherever possible. These live fully on the Linux side of WSL 2 and avoid the overhead completely. Docker manages them directly, and performance is far smoother.
- If you absolutely must mount from Windows, use Linux-style paths, for example, `-v /mnt/c/data:/data`. This tells Docker exactly where the folder lives inside WSL's view

of your filesystem, and avoids some of the weird edge cases that can occur with path resolution on Windows.

- Avoid syncing large filesystems from Windows. Instead, try to copy the data you need directly into your containers or volumes inside WSL and let your containers operate entirely inside the Linux space. The less crossing back and forth between filesystems you do, the snappier and more reliable your stack will feel.

Following these simple practices keeps your data pipeline fast and predictable and avoids the dreaded "why does it run fine on Linux but crawl on my Windows box?" problem that bites a lot of people when they start building more ambitious GenAI stacks.

So, let's take a second. Containers give us consistency and composability, but data flow is where the rubber meets the road. Getting ingestion, caching, storage, and observability right means your GenAI pipeline isn't just functional; it's maintainable, secure, and performant. The data pieces we've containerized here form a scaffold for everything that follows, ensuring your models get what they need, when they need it, without surprises.

Performance is one thing, but predictability, security, and maintainability are what truly make containers production-ready. That's where best practices come in.

Best practices for AI deployments with Docker

Alright, let's start with a moment of truth: no one builds their perfect AI container stack on the first go. Ever. Zero exceptions.

Most of us stumble into a mess of half-built Dockerfiles, outdated Python dependencies, and weird permissions errors that show up only in production. You learn the hard way that what works on your laptop doesn't always scale, and what runs beautifully in a notebook cell might crash hard inside a container.

This section is here to help you avoid the worst of those traps. Trust me, I've fallen into them all before. It's not just about what you can do with Docker and AI on Windows 11, but how you should be doing it if you're trying to build something that lasts longer than a proof-of-concept stage. We're going to talk about structure, consistency, and some small habits that can save you hours of debugging down the line. These are the kind of deployment patterns that can quietly make the difference between a reliable GenAI setup and one that collapses under pressure.

Our focus here is simple: to walk through a set of best practices for deploying AI workloads with Docker on Windows 11. We'll look at how to think about container layouts, environment reproducibility, some security basics, and GPU visibility, as well as how to avoid pitfalls in multi-stage builds and dependency handling. So, let's dive in!

Start with smarter base images

Honestly, the easiest win, and one you have heard me push already, is choosing the right base image:

- **python:3.11-slim**: Your default, most of the time. It is small, well supported, and enough to install most packages.
- **python:3.11-alpine**: This is even smaller, but only if all your packages can handle `musl` rather than `glibc`. That's because Alpine uses `musl libc` instead of the more common `glibc`, and some AI packages (such as PyTorch, Transformers, or ONNX) either don't compile cleanly or behave strangely under `musl`.
- **Ubuntu or Debian**: When you genuinely need full native library support, compiled dependencies, or GPU integrations.

Remember: your base image size compounds. Every megabyte you start with gets multiplied as you build layers on top.

Multi-stage builds: Keep what you need, dump what you don't

This is one of my absolute favorite tools for trimming AI containers. I found this when we were looking to find ways to optimize one of our AI containers for a chatbot, of all things, and I've always been really proud of it since.

A multi-stage Dockerfile lets you separate your build-time work from your runtime container. You build all the heavy stuff in one stage, and copy only the final outputs into your slim runtime image. Here is an example:

```
# Stage 1: Build everything
FROM python:3.11-slim as builder
WORKDIR /app
COPY requirements.txt .
RUN pip install --no-cache-dir -r requirements.txt
COPY . .

# Stage 2: Minimal runtime
FROM python:3.11-slim
WORKDIR /app
COPY --from=builder /app .
CMD ["uvicorn", "app:app", "--host", "0.0.0.0", "--port", "8000"]
```

Figure 7.17: Example multi-stage Dockerfile that separates build and runtime stages

Now, any intermediate files, `pip` caches, or build dependencies are left behind in the builder stage. Your runtime container carries only the code, model weights, and runtime dependencies it actually needs.

Keep model weights out of the Docker build (when you can)

A weirdly sneaky source of bloat is bundling your model weights directly into your Docker image during build. It feels convenient, but every time you retrain, you rebuild the entire image.

Instead, separate your model weights into their own Docker volume or storage layer. Here is an example:

```
docker run -v model-storage:/models my-genai-container
```

Now, when you update model weights, you can simply update the volume contents without having to rebuild and push a new image every single time.

There are times where you *do* want model weights baked into your image for portability (edge deployments, air-gapped environments, that sort of thing), but for local development and frequent iteration, keep them separate. You will thank yourself when rebuilds go from 10 minutes to 10 seconds.

Avoid mounting from C:\ where possible...seriously!

This feels like a very Windows-specific problem, but worth restating: *do not bind-mount your Windows host filesystem directly into your containers for anything performance-critical.*

- Mounting `/mnt/c/...` works, functionally speaking, but incurs file translation overhead inside WSL 2.
- Named Docker volumes inside WSL 2 behave like true Linux filesystems: much faster for your model files, logs, and caches. You get the idea.

If you are loading 5 GB of embeddings from disk every time your model starts, that overhead becomes very noticeable. Keep as much as possible inside native Docker volumes.

Strip unnecessary packages and dev tools

A very common anti-pattern I see is leaving dev tools and libraries sitting inside production containers. Think about all the junk we leave behind without thinking about it:

- Compilers (`gcc`, `g++`)
- Build toolchains (`make`, `cmake`)
- Debugging tools (`vim`, `curl`, `git`)

None of these belong in your final runtime container unless you genuinely need them after startup. Install them only in your builder stage if you are compiling wheels or building extensions, and leave them behind when you copy into your runtime stage.

Watch out for pip cache

When you're using `pip` in your Dockerfiles, make sure you always include the following:

```
pip install --no-cache-dir
```

Why? Because by default, `pip` caches every downloaded package in a local cache directory, even if you're installing it straight into your environment and never plan to use the downloaded files again. This behavior is useful on your local machine (where you might reinstall the same packages regularly), but inside a Docker container? It's just dead weight.

That cached content gets baked into the image layer, quietly adding tens, or even hundreds, of megabytes to your image size. Worse, it's easy to overlook, because Docker will happily consider the build a success, leaving you with a bloated image and slower deployment times.

So, what does `--no-cache-dir` actually do? It tells `pip` not to save the downloaded package files to disk after installation. You still get the packages installed as normal, but without the lingering archive files taking up space.

> **Tip**
>
> If you're already struggling with large images and are not sure why, try rebuilding with this flag and checking the size difference. It's one of those sneaky optimizations that pays off with minimal effort.

If you're combining this with multi-stage builds, even better. Keep the layers tight and focused, install what you need, and don't keep the leftovers.

Build arguments for flexibility

When you're iterating quickly, especially in AI workflows where model versions and dataset snapshots change frequently, **Docker build arguments** (**ARG**) are a powerful tool for injecting flexibility into your image builds.

You can define an argument like so:

```
ARG MODEL_VERSION
ENV MODEL_VERSION=${MODEL_VERSION}
```

Then build your image with the following:

```
docker build --build-arg MODEL_VERSION=1.2.3 -t my-model:1.2.3
```

This pattern lets you easily swap out versions without rewriting your Dockerfile or hardcoding values into your environment. It's super useful when working in teams or automating builds via CI/CD pipelines. Different builds can then reference different model versions or configurations while using the same Dockerfile.

It's also a neat way to tag your images meaningfully (`my-model:1.2.3`), helping you track which build includes which version, especially when debugging or rolling back.

> **Note**
>
> ARG values are only available at build time, not runtime. If you need that value inside the container once it's running, you'll need to pass it into an `ENV` variable, as shown previously. This pattern gives you both build-time flexibility and runtime access, all from a single command.

In short: use build arguments to keep your Dockerfiles adaptable and your builds predictable even when everything else is changing.

Keep it predictable: Define your contracts early

The first thing you'll want to get into the habit of is defining clear, predictable contracts between your Docker images and the workloads they're expected to run. What I mean by contracts is that your container should make clear promises about what it expects, what it provides, and how it runs, so you're not relying on luck or squad knowledge every time it gets deployed. This means more than just pinning your dependencies in a `requirements.txt` file; it means taking an opinionated stance on the following:

- What data goes in
- What results come out
- What environment those processes expect to run in

This is actually pretty similar to contract testing in the API space, which I've spent a lot of time around in my software testing career. One of the most helpful evolutions there has been making those invisible assumptions explicit, so services fail fast, not silently. Docker images benefit from the same mindset. Set the boundaries early and define what "valid" looks like, and you'll save yourself a world of debugging later.

For example, if you're working with an inference container that expects a model file and an input image, make those inputs *explicit*. Don't assume they'll magically appear at `/models/latest.pt`. Use `ENV` variables or `--mount` bindings to formalize those entry points. This will massively help when someone else (or future you) picks up the image three months later.

Plus, for added clarity, you can also version your input and output formats using semantic naming or internal version markers. Your containers should be opinionated and descriptive, not vague and "it works if you know the magic incantation."

Prefer composition over complexity

It's tempting to cram everything into one container, but it turns into a monolith that's harder to scale, troubleshoot, and update.

Keep containers small and focused. Let each service do one job, then wire them together with Docker Compose. A typical split is a model server, a preprocessor, and optional logging or telemetry. On Windows 11 with WSL 2, Compose makes this easy to iterate on without rebuilding the entire stack for every change.

```
version: '3.8'

services:
model-server:
build:
context: ./model-server
ports:
- "8000:8000"
depends_on:
- preprocessor
networks:
- genai-net

preprocessor:
build:
context: ./preprocessor
ports:
- "8001:8001"
networks:
- genai-net

logger:
build:
context: ./logger
ports:
- "8002:8002"
networks:
- genai-net

networks:
genai-net:
```

Figure 7.18: Example Docker Compose file defining a multi-service GenAI stack with model-server, preprocessor, and logger containers

This kind of layout has other benefits too. Let's say your model server starts getting hammered with concurrent requests. You can scale just that service, maybe three replicas of the model server, but still only one instance of the logger. You're not locked into scaling the whole thing in lockstep. Also, because each piece is isolated, you can test or upgrade them independently without worrying about too many knock-on effects across the stack.

It feels a little cliché to say, but think of it as future-proofing. The decisions you make early on, such as separating out responsibilities and using Compose properly, will save you hours of debugging and awkward rebuilds later. It's not just about tidiness; it's about making change safer and experimentation cheaper. That really matters when you're working in fast-moving environments such as GenAI, where the next model, tool, or wrapper is always just around the corner.

Bake in default models and fallbacks

Let's be realistic: you won't always be deploying the freshest model checkpoint hot off the training server. Sometimes you're testing, sometimes you're debugging, and sometimes you just need something stable that won't move under your feet. I get it.

That's why it's smart to bake a known-good fallback model directly into your Docker image. You can override it at runtime if needed, but at least you've got something predictable to work with.

This really earns its keep in setups where models are pulled from external sources, such as a URL or an S3 bucket. If that download fails, or your auth token expires without warning, you don't want your whole container to curl up and die. Fallbacks give your container a soft landing. It might not be the newest model, but it still responds and behaves. That's a massive help in CI pipelines, resilience testing, or when you're onboarding someone who just wants to get the thing running without 10 environment variables and a VPN.

One pattern I like is setting an `ENV` variable that points to your stable checkpoint:

```
ENV DEFAULT_MODEL=/models/stable-checkpoint.pt
```

Figure 7.19: Example Dockerfile line setting an environment variable

Then, in your application logic, check for an override, maybe via another *env* var, a CLI flag, or a mounted file, and default back to the baked-in model if nothing is provided.

This way, the container runs clean whether or not the world around it is fully online and configured. You've built in a kind of safety net, and in real-world pipelines, that can make a big difference to how confident you feel with deploying and testing.

Make GPU access explicit, not assumed

Let's not beat around the bush: most of the serious AI workloads you're going to run will benefit hugely from GPU acceleration. But here's the catch: Docker doesn't hand over GPU access by default, and on Windows with WSL 2 and NVIDIA's tooling, it's very much an opt-in affair. Just because you have a GPU, and just because you're running inside a container, doesn't mean those two are talking.

So, you need to be intentional. When running your container, pass the `--gpus` flag explicitly:

```
docker run --gpus all my-inference-container
```

That line matters. Without it, your container may silently run on the CPU, slower, hotter, and potentially misleading in your test results. It's the kind of thing that can sneak by unnoticed until performance falls off a cliff.

I would always recommend surfacing GPU detection visibly in your logs too. Let the container tell you what it sees on startup. Again, I can't help it; I like transparency in my workflows and code. For PyTorch-based setups, this is a simple one-liner:

```
import torch
print("CUDA available:", torch.cuda.is_available())
```

> **Tip**
>
> **Compute Unified Device Architecture (CUDA)** is NVIDIA's parallel computing platform that lets software run tasks on the GPU instead of the CPU for faster processing. It's very cool and super useful for AI work.

That gives you a clear signal the moment the container boots. If you're using TensorFlow, ONNX, or anything else with a backend check, do the same. Wrap it in your start script or app entry point so it always runs.

More importantly, don't just fail silently if there's no GPU. Fall back to the CPU, log a warning, and move on if you can. Not every environment will be GPU-enabled, especially during development or when someone new is picking up your stack for the first time.

So basically, make it obvious and make it document itself. Always assume that someone, somewhere, will forget to pass the flag, so build your container to be forgiving, not fragile.

Deploying a secure, multi-service GenAI stack in production

So, we've talked a lot about what good practice looks like, but let's be honest, it's always more useful to see what that actually means in the wild.

Let's take everything we've covered so far (multi-stage builds, resource limits, non-root users, secrets management, and health checks) and roll it into a short but practical deployment you could genuinely run in an enterprise Windows environment.

This example is from one of my online courses and uses **Docker Compose v3.9**. It assumes you've already pushed your model image to a private registry.

```yaml
version: "3.9"

services:
  summariser:
    image: registry.mycorp.com/genai/summariser:1.0
    deploy:
      resources:
        limits:
          cpus: "1.0"
          memory: 2g
    environment:
      - MODEL_PATH=/models/summariser.onnx
    secrets:
      - openai_key
    healthcheck:
      test: ["CMD", "curl", "-f", "http://localhost:8080/health"]
      interval: 30s
      retries: 3
    restart: always
    user: appuser
    networks:
      - genai_net

  orchestrator:
    build:
      context: ./orchestrator
      target: runtime      # comes from a multi-stage Dockerfile
    ports:
      - "8080:8080"
    depends_on:
      summariser:
        condition: service_healthy
    secrets:
      - db_password
    user: appuser
    networks:
      - genai_net

secrets:
  openai_key:
    file: ./secrets/openai_key.txt
  db_password:
    file: ./secrets/db_password.txt

networks:
  genai_net:
    driver: bridge
```

Figure 7.20: Example docker-compose.yml showing a secure two-service GenAI stack

Now deploy it from PowerShell or your WSL 2 terminal:

```
docker stack deploy -c docker-compose.yml genai-prod
```

Within a few seconds, you'll have both services up, healthy, and wired together. Let's unpack what we've just done and why it matters:

- Resource limits stop any single container from stealing all your CPU or RAM

- Non-root users keep your containers honest; no more root-as-default builds
- Secrets are read from files at runtime, never baked into images or `.env` files
- Health checks give Docker a way to know whether a service is actually alive before letting others depend on it
- Multi-stage builds (see that `target: runtime line`) keep your production image lean, pulling only what it truly needs

Because the whole thing runs under `genai_net`, internal traffic stays private: no random ports hanging open to the outside world.

This pattern, while simple, scales beautifully. You can plug in a classifier or embedding model next week, add a caching layer, or roll it into a Swarm cluster or something similar without touching the core structure. The exact same principles hold whether you're running on a single developer laptop or across a GPU-enabled Windows enterprise node.

By grounding the best practices in an actual, working deployment, you can see that they're not abstract checklists; they're actually everyday patterns that make your AI stack secure, maintainable, and predictable.

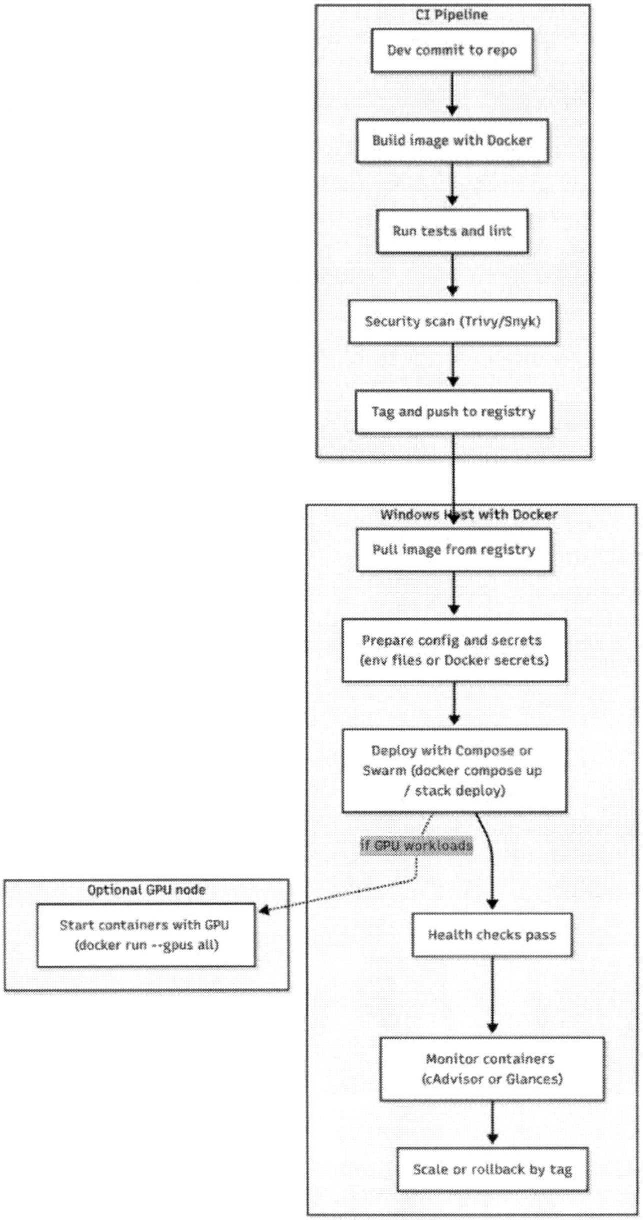

Figure 7.21: Sample deployment workflow on Windows

You can think of this deployment as the "reference build" for everything that follows. It shows what good looks like when all the right habits line up: lean containers, well-defined boundaries, and clean shutdowns. Once you've got this pattern working locally, the next logical step is learning how to keep those containers behaving politely when they're stopped, restarted, or scaled up. That's exactly what we'll cover next, making sure your AI containers know when and how to exit gracefully.

Don't forget the exit conditions

It sounds dead obvious, but you'd be surprised how often this one sneaks past: your AI containers need to know when they're done. If you're running a one-off batch job or processing a queue of requests, your container should wrap up and exit cleanly once the work is finished. No endless loops waiting for something that's never coming; no ghost processes keeping the container alive longer than it needs to be.

It's not just about tidiness either. If a container hangs around longer than expected, it can cause issues during CI runs, clog up orchestration tools such as Swarm or Kubernetes, or just make local dev more frustrating than it needs to be. I've personally sat watching a terminal wondering why my pipeline was stuck, only to realize the container had completed its task but forgot to exit, and no log line told me otherwise.

For services such as REST APIs or model servers, it's more about predictable shutdown. These don't exit on their own, obviously, but they do need to handle things such as `SIGINT` (interrupt signal such as pressing *Ctrl* + *C*) and `SIGTERM` (terminate signal through a shutdown request) gracefully. If someone hits *Ctrl* + *C*, or if the container is being stopped by Docker or your orchestrator, you want to make sure that things shut down nicely. Logs should be flushed and connections closed, and anything in memory should be handled before the process goes away.

Here's a really simple Python example of handling that cleanly:

```
import signal
import sys

def shutdown_handler(signum, frame):
    print("Gracefully shutting down...")
    # Here's where you'd close DB connections, save logs, etc.
    sys.exit(0)

signal.signal(signal.SIGTERM, shutdown_handler)
signal.signal(signal.SIGINT, shutdown_handler)
```

It doesn't look like much, but trust me, this kind of small addition makes a huge difference when your containers are running as part of something bigger. If you've ever had a Docker container killed mid-inference and lost output logs or partial state, you'll know exactly why this matters.

Back when I was neck-deep in performance testing, I spent a lot of time running Apache JMeter inside custom-built Docker containers. That's where I first hit some of these gotchas. The thing about building your own containers is, well, you tend to learn these lessons the hard way, usually when something breaks five minutes before a test run.

Good exit behavior makes your containers easier to test, debug, and deploy, and it's one of those things that nobody notices until it's missing. But once it's in place, everything downstream gets a bit smoother.

Secure by default

Even if you're only running locally or in a private dev cluster, build security habits early. "It's just internal" is exactly how bad defaults creep in and then get copied into wider use.

In practice, note the following:

- *Don't run as root* unless you have a clear reason. Create a non-root user in your Dockerfile and switch to it.
- *Pin base image versions.* Avoid `latest` so builds stay repeatable in CI.
- *Keep secrets out of images and code.* Use environment variables, `.env`, or Docker secrets so you can rotate credentials without rebuilds.
- *Scan images routinely.* Use Docker Desktop scanning (Snyk) or Trivy to catch known CVEs early.

On Windows 11 with WSL 2, you can run most of these tools as containers, so there's no excuse to skip them.

All these tips in this section all come back to a single mindset: building containers that are understandable, testable, and maintainable. You don't need to guess what they'll do; you should *know*. They should behave consistently on your machine, in CI, and in prod. You don't want to play detective every time something breaks.

Now, once you've applied these container optimizations, the difference isn't subtle; it's measurable. In practice, you can expect to do the following:

- *Cut container build times* from several minutes to just seconds, especially when leveraging targeted caching.
- *Shrink final image sizes* by hundreds of megabytes or even several gigabytes, depending on how aggressively you clean up dependencies and intermediate artifacts.

- *Speed up cold-start times* for container launches, which is crucial when scaling models or running short-lived workloads in dev/test environments.
- *Free up memory inside WSL 2*, giving more breathing room to other components of your GenAI stack (e.g., GPU drivers, orchestration tools, or local inference runtimes).

Most importantly: your stack becomes more predictable. Smaller, purpose-built images reduce the variability between builds. They spin up faster, they cache more reliably, and they reduce friction when deploying across environments, whether that's your Windows machine, a CI pipeline, or a remote cluster.

This isn't about squeezing performance for its own sake. It's about **discipline**. Make smart decisions early, strip out what you don't need, use build stages deliberately, cache sensibly, and avoid bloat, and you'll build infrastructure that scales with you, not against you.

As your models grow larger and pipelines get more complex, these small container choices will pay off exponentially.

The Big Lab: Scaling a GenAI feature in the Notes service

So, by now, the Notes service is behaving like a real application. It has a frontend, an API, persistent storage on Windows, sensible security, and enough monitoring that you're no longer flying blind. In this chapter, you've seen how GenAI stacks are really just collections of services: model containers, data layers, and small bits of routing glue.

In this Big Lab, you'll join those ideas up. All of this runs inside the same `notes-app` project you have been using since *Chapter 2*:

1. **Add a tiny GenAI summarizer service**: First, you're going to need a separate container that behaves like a GenAI model. To keep things predictable on Windows, this lab uses a tiny FastAPI service that pretends to be a summarizer. It works on a plain CPU and doesn't download any big models, but the container boundaries are virtually identical to a real GenAI stack.
   So, create a new folder inside `notes-app`:

```
notes-app/
  genai-summariser/
    Dockerfile
    app.py
    requirements.txt
```

Then, create `genai-summariser/requirements.txt`:

```
fastapi
uvicorn[standard]
Pydantic
```

Now, create `genai-summariser/app.py`:

```
from fastapi import FastAPI
from pydantic import BaseModel
import socket

app = FastAPI()
INSTANCE_NAME = socket.gethostname()

class Payload(BaseModel):
    text: str

@app.post("/summarise")
def summarise(payload: Payload):
    text = payload.text.strip()
    # Very simple "summary" to keep the lab light.
    if len(text) <= 160:
        summary = text
    else:
        summary = text[:157] + "..."
    return {
        "instance": INSTANCE_NAME,
        "summary": summary,
    }
```

Remember, this is a dumb model...the goal is to practice wiring and scaling the service, not to tune NLP.

Now, create `genai-summariser/Dockerfile`:

```
FROM python:3.11-slim

WORKDIR /app

COPY requirements.txt .
```

```
RUN pip install --no-cache-dir -r requirements.txt

COPY app.py .

EXPOSE 8000
CMD ["uvicorn", "app:app", "--host", "0.0.0.0", "--port", "8000"]
```

Build the image from the `notes-app` folder:

```
cd notes-app
docker build -t notes-genai-summariser ./genai-summariser
```

Amazing! You now have a standalone GenAI-style container that exposes `/summarise`.

2. **Wire the Notes API to call the GenAI service**: Next, you'll let the Notes API call the summarizer so the application can generate a summary of all saved notes.
   Open `api/app.py` and make sure you have `requests` installed in your API image. If your API uses a `requirements.txt`, add the following:

```
requests
```

Don't worry about changes right now; we'll rebuild the API image shortly.

At the top of `api/app.py`, import `socket`, `os`, and `requests`:

```
import os
import socket
import requests
```

Add a simple instance identifier for the API as well, so you can see which API container handled the call:

```
INSTANCE_NAME = socket.gethostname()
GENAI_URL = os.getenv("GENAI_URL", "http://genai-gateway/summarise")
```

Now add a new endpoint that collects all notes, concatenates them, and sends them to the GenAI service:

```
@app.get("/notes/summary")
def notes_summary():
    notes = load_notes_somehow()   # reuse your existing notes loading
```

```
logic
    combined = " ".join(notes)
    try:
        response = requests.post(
            GENAI_URL,
            json={"text": combined},
            timeout=5,
        )
        response.raise_for_status()
    except Exception as exc:
        return {
            "instance": INSTANCE_NAME,
            "status": "error",
            "error": str(exc),
        }

    data = response.json()
    return {
        "api_instance": INSTANCE_NAME,
        "genai_instance": data.get("instance"),
        "summary": data.get("summary"),
        "note_count": len(notes),
    }
```

Rebuild the API image:

```
docker build -t notes-api ./api
```

You'll not hit this endpoint yet. First, you need to bring the summarizer into Compose and put a gateway in front of it.

3. **Add the GenAI summarizer and gateway to Compose**: You're going to run two copies of the summarizer behind a small Nginx gateway. The Notes API will talk only to the gateway. The gateway will then decide which GenAI container handles each request. So, create a new folder for the Nginx config:

```
mkdir nginx-genai
```

Create nginx-genai/nginx.conf:

```
upstream genai_summariser {
    server genai-a:8000;
    server genai-b:8000;
}

server {
    listen 80;

    location / {
        proxy_pass http://genai_summariser;
        proxy_set_header Host $host;
        proxy_set_header X-Real-IP $remote_addr;
    }
}
```

Now, update compose.yaml. Inside services:, add three new services. The example assumes you still have the app-net and api-private networks from the earlier labs:

```
  genai-a:
    image: notes-genai-summariser
    networks:
      - api-private
      - app-net

  genai-b:
    image: notes-genai-summariser
    networks:
      - api-private
      - app-net

  genai-gateway:
    image: nginx:alpine
    container_name: notes-genai-gateway
    volumes:
      - ./nginx-genai/nginx.conf:/etc/nginx/conf.d/default.conf:ro
    ports:
      - "5002:80"
    depends_on:
      - genai-a
```

```
      - genai-b
    networks:
      - app-net
```

Finally, point the API at the gateway by adding an environment variable to the `api` service in `compose.yaml`:

```
  api:
    build: ./api
    environment:
      - GENAI_URL=http://genai-gateway/summarise
    # existing ports, volumes and networks here
```

The Notes API now knows to talk to the GenAI gateway rather than a hardcoded host.

4. **Bring up the stack and watch non-sticky load balancing**: Start everything from the `notes-app` folder:

```
docker compose up -d --build
```

Give the stack a few seconds to settle. Then, hit the new `summary` endpoint a few times:

```
curl http://localhost:5001/notes/summary
curl http://localhost:5001/notes/summary
curl http://localhost:5001/notes/summary
```

Look closely at the JSON. `api_instance` should stay the same if you only have one API container, but the `genai_instance` field should flip between two different values as Nginx sends traffic to `genai-a` and `genai-b` in a round-robin fashion.

Figure 7.22: GenAI traffic alternating between summarizer replicas

If you have the frontend wired up to call `/notes/summary`, refresh it a few times and watch the GenAI instance change there as well.

Well done! You've just added a small GenAI stack to the Notes service and load-balanced it across multiple model containers.

5. **Simulate failure and observe GenAI failover**: Contrary to popular belief, high availability isn't just for core APIs. If your GenAI feature disappears under load, users will still feel the outage. So, now you're going to kill one of the GenAI containers and prove that the Notes application carries on.
   List the running containers:

   ```
   docker compose ps
   ```

   You should see `genai-a`, `genai-b`, and `genai-gateway` alongside the rest of the stack.
   Stop one summarizer:

   ```
   docker compose stop genai-b
   ```

Now repeat the summary call:

```
curl http://localhost:5001/notes/summary
curl http://localhost:5001/notes/summary
curl http://localhost:5001/notes/summary
```

The `genai_instance` field should now stay constant. Nginx has one viable backend and sends every request there. From the client side, nothing has changed. The URL is the same, the contract is the same, and the feature is still working. That is the whole point.

Restart the second replica:

```
docker compose start genai-b
```

Call the endpoint again and you should see `genai_instance` alternating between two values once more.

6. **Try sticky versus non-sticky behavior**: Sometimes you want a client to keep talking to the same model instance. For example, a conversational GenAI feature may hold some context in memory that you do not want to jump around between containers. Nginx can do this with a single keyword. Open `nginx-genai/nginx.conf` and change the `upstream` block to the following:

```
upstream genai_summariser {
    ip_hash;
    server genai-a:8000;
    server genai-b:8000;
}
```

Save the file. Restart the gateway:

```
docker compose restart genai-gateway
```

Now, hit the `summary` endpoint several times from the same machine:

```
curl http://localhost:5001/notes/summary
curl http://localhost:5001/notes/summary
curl http://localhost:5001/notes/summary
```

You should see `genai_instance` stay fixed. Nginx uses the client IP to pick a backend and then sticks with that choice.

If you call the same endpoint from another device on your network, you may see it map to the other instance. That is sticky behavior in action.

Remove `ip_hash` and restart the gateway again if you want to return to pure round robin.

7. **Scale the GenAI service up and down**: Two replicas are nice for resilience. Scaling further is a one-line change now that the GenAI feature lives behind a gateway. Add a third summarizer service to `compose.yaml` by copying `genai-b` and renaming it `genai-c`:

```
  genai-c:
    image: notes-genai-summariser
    networks:
      - api-private
      - app-net
```

Update `nginx-genai/nginx.conf` so the `upstream` block knows about the third backend:

```
upstream genai_summariser {
    ip_hash;
    server genai-a:8000;
    server genai-b:8000;
    server genai-c:8000;
}
```

Bring the new replica online:

```
docker compose up -d --build
```

Hit the `summary` endpoint from different machines or browser profiles. Over time, you should see requests landing on three different `genai_instance` values.

To scale down again, stop and remove the extra replica:

```
docker compose stop genai-c
docker compose rm -f genai-c
```

Remove `genai-c` from `compose.yaml` and `nginx.conf`, then run the following:

```
docker compose up -d
```

You are back to two replicas without any changes to the Notes API or frontend code. Scaling the GenAI feature is purely a Compose and configuration concern.

8. **Tie GenAI scaling back into observability**: Before you move on, take advantage of the monitoring work you did in the previous Big Lab. With the stack running, open cAdvisor and `docker stats` while you hit `/notes/summary` repeatedly or let a small load script run. Watch for the following:
   - CPU and memory usage spread across `genai-a`, `genai-b`, and `genai-c`
   - Changes when you stop one of the containers
   - The gateway staying lightweight while the model containers do the work

   You've now got a clear picture of how a GenAI feature behaves under load, which containers carry the most weight, and how scaling affects resource usage on Windows.

You've taken the original Notes service and given it a GenAI-powered feature that runs as its own small stack. The summarizer lives in separate containers, sits behind a gateway, survives individual container failures, and can be scaled up or down without touching the application code. Monitoring shows you exactly how that feature behaves when users start to lean on it.

The stack is now highly available. In the next chapter, we will see how it behaves in more complex environments.

Summary

Building for AI will always be a bit messy. There's always going to be a newer model, a weirder dependency, or some sneaky little bug that shows up the night before you demo something. But if you approach your containers with a bit of discipline; version what you use, structure your builds properly, and favor smaller, focused images over one big "does-everything" container; you'll spend way less time putting out fires and more time doing the actual work that matters.

In short, keep your stack modular; each service, whether it's your model, data pipeline, API, or storage layer, should act as its own clean little box. They need to talk to each other, but never step on each other's toes. It's also far easier to build lean containers from the start than to trim bloated ones later, so optimize early using multi-stage builds, lightweight base images, and sensible resource caps. Finally, stay secure even when working locally. Handle secrets properly, separate your volumes, and treat your development stack with the same care you'd give to production.

Do those three things and Docker stops being just another developer tool; it becomes the foundation you build everything else on.

Next up, we'll take that foundation and move into the real world: enterprise environments. We'll look at what changes (and what stays the same) when you scale this up across multiple teams, environments, and workloads running side by side on Windows.

Get This Book's PDF Version and Exclusive Extras

Part 3

Docker in Real-World Use Cases

This is it, the home stretch. In this last part of the book, the focus shifts to how Docker is used in real organizations rather than just on a developer's laptop. You'll explore enterprise deployment patterns, hybrid cloud integration, and the realities of running Docker in production. This includes handling scale, integrating with cloud platforms, and diagnosing issues when things go wrong. By the end of this part, you'll understand how Docker fits into real-world Windows infrastructure and how to support, troubleshoot, and evolve containerized systems over time.

This part includes the following chapters:

8

Implementing Docker for Enterprise Workloads on Windows

When you've spent enough time working in or around enterprise organizations, especially those dealing with legacy systems, you start to realize that "getting it running" is only half the battle. The real challenge is getting it running predictably, repeatedly, and in a way that doesn't make your future self want to scream. That's where Docker really shines in the enterprise space. It's not about chasing the latest tool trend; it's about bringing repeatability, control, and confidence to how we ship and run software at scale.

This chapter's about taking Docker beyond the developer's sandbox, making it production-ready, supportable, and genuinely resilient in real-world enterprise environments. I'm talking about actual workloads, run by actual teams, with actual governance and risk concerns hanging over them. The sort of places where audit trails matter, uptime is sacred, and there's usually at least one mission-critical app built by someone who left the company 10 years ago.

By the end of this chapter, you'll know how to deploy, scale, and maintain Docker workloads in enterprise environments with confidence. You'll be able to containerize legacy Windows applications, implement high-availability strategies, balance workloads effectively, and build supportable, production-grade infrastructure on Windows.

We'll be covering the following main topics:

- Deploying Docker for enterprise applications
- Scaling Docker for high availability
- Load balancing Docker workloads

- Managing enterprise Docker infrastructure
- Troubleshooting and support for large workloads

Let's get started!

Technical requirements

The code files referenced in this chapter are available at `https://github.com/PacktPublishing/Mastering-Docker-on-Windows`.

Deploying Docker for enterprise applications

Our old server updates often involved crossed fingers and holding our collective breath. It wasn't exactly a scalable or sustainable model. Introducing Docker didn't just clean up our deployment processes; it completely reshaped how we thought about delivering software. It transformed our infrastructure from a house of cards into something robust, predictable, and maintainable.

Moving through this section, we're going to explore how you can effectively deploy Docker containers for enterprise applications on Windows environments. We're talking about the big projects here. We'll dive into practical strategies for preparing your enterprise apps, managing configurations securely, building robust Docker images, and ensuring predictable deployments at enterprise scale. We'll also tackle common enterprise-specific challenges such as legacy application support, managing Windows-based Docker containers, and handling secure environments.

Let's begin by looking at how to prepare your applications for the move into Docker.

> Note
>
> **Should your application be containerized?**
>
> Before you start writing Dockerfiles, stop and decide whether Docker is actually the right move for this workload. In enterprise environments, containerization is a choice, not an automatic upgrade.
>
> **Good candidates for Docker include the following**:
>
> - Stateless services, APIs, and background workers
> - Applications with externalized configuration
> - CI/CD-friendly builds and repeatable deployments
> - Legacy apps that are stable but painful to deploy consistently

> **Think twice before using these:**
>
> - Tight coupling to the host OS or hardware
> - Undocumented file paths, registry dependencies, or schedulers
> - GUI-heavy or desktop-style workloads
>
> **A VM may be the better option for these:**
>
> - The app changes rarely and is already stable
> - Compliance or vendor support requires a VM
> - You need a fast stabilization win, not a platform shift
>
> The goal isn't to containerize everything. It's to containerize the right things. If an application doesn't pass this gate, defer it and move on.

Preparing enterprise applications for Dockerization

Let's be honest, not every enterprise workload is ready, or even right, for Docker. One of the biggest fumbles I've seen is teams trying to containerize absolutely everything just because they can. Yeah, Docker's powerful, but it shines brightest when used with intention.

The real starting point with enterprise Dockerization is figuring out what should actually live in a container. Stateless services, REST APIs, batch jobs, microservices, anything that follows clean separation of concerns, these are all amazing candidates. Modern .NET Core apps, Spring Boot services, and most Node.js backends tend to slip into containers without much fuss. They're built with portability in mind and usually play nicely in a containerized world.

Legacy Windows applications... that's a whole other story. These are the ones that tend to be deeply tied to a specific OS version, expect certain registry keys, or depend on GUI components. That doesn't mean they can't be containerized, but it does mean you'll need to tread more carefully. You'll be dealing with Windows containers specifically, and they're heavier, more complex to build, and come with quirks that Linux containers just don't have.

If you're already working with a modern .NET Core application, you're in good shape. Dockerizing it might look as simple as this:

```
FROM mcr.microsoft.com/dotnet/aspnet:7.0-windowsservercore-ltsc2022
WORKDIR /app
COPY ./publish /app
EXPOSE 80
ENTRYPOINT ["dotnet", "YourApp.dll"]
```

Figure 8.1: Example Dockerfile for building and running a .NET 7 ASP.NET application in a Windows container

That's clean, repeatable, and easy to promote across environments.

> Note
>
> **Linux container equivalent (when applicable)**
>
> For teams running cross-platform workloads or targeting Linux hosts, the same application could use a Linux-based image:
>
> ```
> FROM mcr.microsoft.com/dotnet/aspnet:7.0
> WORKDIR /app
> COPY ./publish /app
> EXPOSE 80
> ENTRYPOINT ["dotnet", "YourApp.dll"]
> ```
>
> *Figure 8.2: Minimal Dockerfile for a .NET 7 ASP.NET application using a Linux-based runtime image, suitable for cross-platform or Linux-hosted environments.*
>
> Linux images are significantly smaller and faster to build, but they're only an option if the application and hosting environment support them. In enterprises with Windows-only dependencies or legacy .NET Framework workloads, Windows containers remain the practical choice. That's it. No more.

Now, contrast that with something built on the traditional .NET Framework. These are still really common in large enterprises, especially internal web apps and back-office tools, and they require Windows containers:

```
FROM mcr.microsoft.com/dotnet/framework/aspnet:4.8
COPY . /inetpub/wwwroot
```

Figure 8.3: Initial Dockerfile for a legacy .NET Framework 4.8 web application

This works, but here's the kicker: Windows-based images are significantly larger than their Linux counterparts. That has real consequences in the enterprise. Larger images mean longer build and deploy times, more disk space used in registries, and more pressure on CI/CD infrastructure.

So what do we do? We plan ahead. Think about how often you'll be building the image, how many environments it'll touch, and how you're going to distribute it. You might need to optimize your base image choice, strip out unnecessary files, and be deliberate about caching strategies. These are the kinds of decisions that turn a Docker experiment into a production-grade deployment.

It's also worth spending a bit of time on dependency discovery. I've worked with more than one team that moved a legacy app into a container only to realize halfway through testing that the thing was silently relying on a file path on the host machine that nobody had documented. It's surprisingly common. So, do the legwork. Audit the application's dependencies. Know what it needs from the host, what it reads and writes, and how it stores configuration. Docker is all about repeatability, and you can't repeat what you haven't accounted for.

So, before you rush to Dockerize your enterprise app, stop and ask: Is it a good fit? If yes, brilliant. Here's a quick checklist to help you decide what is typically a good fit for Docker in enterprise settings:

- **Stateless services**: APIs, microservices, or background workers that don't depend on persistent local state.
- **Portable apps**: Anything that already runs cleanly on multiple environments without manual tweaks.
- **Consistent dependencies**: Applications with well-defined, versioned dependencies that can be isolated easily.
- **Automatable builds**: Software that can be built, tested, and deployed through CI/CD without human intervention.
- **Legacy apps needing predictability**: Older .NET or Java applications that benefit from repeatable, isolated environments.

If your workload ticks most of these boxes, Docker's a strong fit. Docker's not a magic fix, but when used wisely, it absolutely earns its keep. The key here is being realistic.

Now, to make this real, let's use the Finance Dashboard I mentioned earlier, a web-based internal reporting tool built on the good old .NET, the kind of thing that still runs in countless finance departments today that don't use Cobol.

Before diving into Dockerfiles, it helps to understand the shape of the system we're working with.

At a high level, the Finance Dashboard consists of the following:

- An IIS-hosted legacy .NET Framework web application running in a Windows container

- A backend database (external to the container)
- A scheduled batch job that generates or refreshes reporting data
- Configuration and secrets injected at runtime, not baked into the image

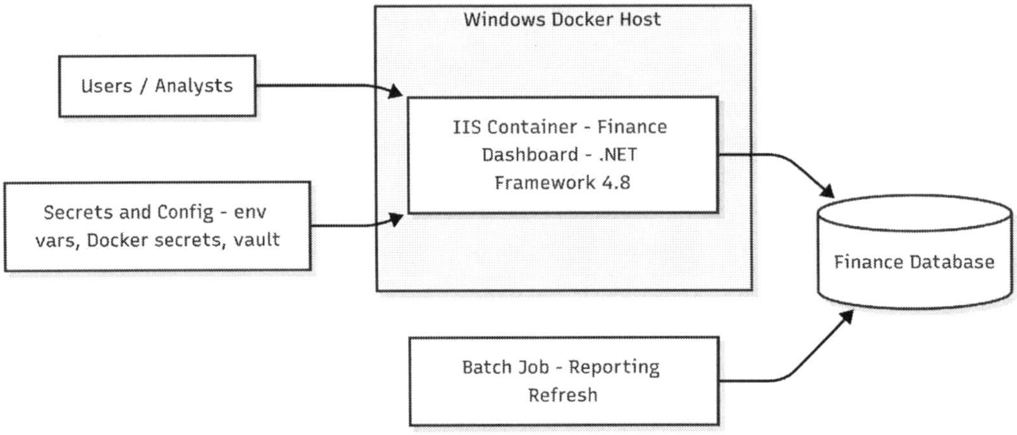

Figure 8.4: High-level Finance Dashboard architecture with an IIS Windows container

Here's what its initial Dockerfile might look like when containerized for the first time:

```
# Finance Dashboard - legacy .NET Framework 4.8 application
FROM mcr.microsoft.com/dotnet/framework/aspnet:4.8-windowsservercore-ltsc2019

# Set the working directory inside the container
WORKDIR /inetpub/wwwroot

# Copy the published web application from your build output
COPY ./publish/ .

# Expose port 80 for HTTP traffic
EXPOSE 80

# Define the default entry point
ENTRYPOINT ["C:\\ServiceMonitor.exe", "w3svc"]
```

Figure 8.5: Dockerfile for the Finance Dashboard containerizing a legacy .NET IIS application

This is what we'd call a "lift and shift" containerization; nothing fancy, just wrapping an existing IIS-hosted app so it can be deployed predictably.

The image runs on Windows Server Core LTSC 2019, which is perfect for older .NET Framework workloads. You'll notice that everything happens inside `/inetpub/wwwroot`, exactly like it would on a classic Windows Server, so migration is straightforward.

It's not the leanest or fastest image, but for a first step into containerizing enterprise web apps, this approach gives you stability and familiarity before you start optimizing.

With your application prepared and its dependencies understood, the next step is to build it on a dependable foundation, selecting and managing your base images.

Managing base images

In enterprise Docker work, consistency is everything. You're often working with regulated environments, change control boards, and security policies that don't like surprises, and rightly so. That's why one of the first rules I tend to push for is: no using the `latest` tags on base images.

Sure, it's tempting. Just slap `FROM python:3` or `FROM mcr.microsoft.com/dotnet/aspnet:latest` at the top of your Dockerfile and call it a day. But that tag can shift underneath you without warning, and suddenly your builds start failing or behaving differently. Even worse, the change might not break anything right away; it might just subtly alter behavior, which is the sort of thing that's almost impossible to debug in a production environment.

Instead, pin your base image versions deliberately. You want something like this:

```
FROM mcr.microsoft.com/dotnet/framework/aspnet:4.8-windowsservercore-ltsc2019
```

Or you want something even more specific, like this:

```
FROM mcr.microsoft.com/dotnet/framework/aspnet:4.8.0.12345-windowsservercore-
ltsc2019
```

That way, you're in total control. You know exactly what you're building on, and when it's time to upgrade, you can do so on your terms, with proper testing, documentation, and rollout plans. This is especially important in enterprise environments where change management and audit trails are non-negotiable. Rolling image changes into production by accident because "latest" got updated? Well, that's a fast way to lose confidence across the board.

There's another angle to this, too: network restrictions. Many large enterprises have outbound firewalls or proxy configurations that make it hard, almost impossible, to pull directly from public registries such as Docker Hub or Microsoft's MCR. And even if it's allowed, relying on that external link for every image pull isn't ideal when you're running at scale.

So, it's worth considering maintaining your own internal Docker registry. This could be something like Azure Container Registry, Amazon ECR, or a more flexible option such as JFrog Artifactory. You mirror the base images you need internally, pull from those instead of the public versions, and now you've got total control. You can even scan and sign those images to meet internal security standards before your developers or CI pipelines ever touch them.

It also helps with disaster recovery. If MCR or Docker Hub were ever to go offline, and yes, it's happened, your builds won't grind to a halt because you're not relying on a public service that's outside your control.

However, in enterprise setups, predictability isn't enough; compliance often demands proof that every image comes from a trusted source and hasn't been tampered with. That's where image signing comes in. The simplest option is **Docker Content Trust** (**DCT**), which uses Notary to sign and verify images automatically. You can enable it globally with one command:

```
setx DOCKER_CONTENT_TRUST 1
```

From that point on, every `docker pull` or `docker push` command will verify signatures and reject unsigned images. In regulated environments, this creates a clear trust chain; only verified, signed images make it into your environment. For teams with more advanced CI/CD pipelines, tools such as Cosign add another layer by signing images in your build pipeline itself, as in this example:

```
cosign sign --key cosign.key finacr.azurecr.io/finance-dashboard:1.0.0
```

Then, anyone downstream can verify that signature before deployment:

```
cosign verify --key cosign.pub finacr.azurecr.io/finance-dashboard:1.0.0
```

This small step satisfies most internal audit requirements around image provenance and software supply chain integrity, essential when your Docker workloads underpin regulated products or financial systems.

Signing images in CI

In practice, image signing usually happens automatically during the build pipeline. For example, in a GitHub Actions or Azure DevOps pipeline, the flow is typically the following:

1. Build the image.
2. Push it to the internal registry.
3. Sign it as part of the same job.

Now, a simplified pipeline step might look something like this:

```
docker build -t finacr.azurecr.io/finance-dashboard:1.0.0 .
docker push finacr.azurecr.io/finance-dashboard:1.0.0
```

```
cosign sign --key cosign.key finacr.azurecr.io/finance-dashboard:1.0.0
```

On deployment, the platform or release pipeline verifies the signature before running the image:

```
cosign verify --key cosign.pub finacr.azurecr.io/finance-dashboard:1.0.0
```

If verification fails, the deployment stops. Unsigned or tampered images never reach production. This keeps trust enforcement automated and consistent, without relying on manual checks or tribal knowledge.

So, let's recap: use pinned versions of your base images, mirror them internally where possible, and avoid pulling live from public sources during builds or deployments. It's a small bit of setup that pays off massively in predictability, security, and operational resilience. And if you're managing more than a handful of services, it's something you'll be very glad you locked down early.

For our Finance Dashboard, I pin the Windows base image to a specific LTSC build so it never drifts under our feet:

```
FROM mcr.microsoft.com/dotnet/framework/aspnet:4.8-windowsservercore-ltsc2019
```

If you want absolute reproducibility, lock by digest as well. Pull the image once, get its digest, then use the @sha256: form:

```
docker pull mcr.microsoft.com/dotnet/framework/aspnet:4.8-windowsservercore-
ltsc2019

docker inspect --format='{{index .RepoDigests 0}}' mcr.microsoft.com/dotnet/
framework/aspnet:4.8-windowsservercore-ltsc2019
```

> **Note**
>
> In regulated environments, I don't let build agents pull directly from MCR/Docker Hub. I mirror the exact base image into ACR, then build only from ACR.
>
> Create or use an existing ACR:
>
> ```
> az acr create -g rg-finance -n finacr --sku Standard
> ```
>
> Import (mirror) the Microsoft base image into ACR, and give it a clear, internal name and tag:
>
> ```
> az acr import
> -n finacr
> --source mcr.microsoft.com/dotnet/framework/aspnet:4.8-
> windowsservercore-ltsc2019
> --image base/aspnet:4.8-windowsservercore-ltsc2019
> ```

Securing and optimizing enterprise images

Every enterprise team has one of those horror stories. You know the kind: an API key committed to Git, a production password tucked neatly into a Dockerfile, or a credentials file accidentally included in a build artifact. We've seen them all, and honestly, most of them happen not out of carelessness, but because things weren't set up properly in the first place.

When you're working at enterprise scale, you can't afford to leave secrets floating around. That includes things such as database connection strings, loan portfolio API keys, and the SFTP credentials used for nightly report imports. The Finance Dashboard, for instance, connects to both a central loan database and a third-party credit-scoring feed, all of which need secure, audited handling.

The simplest way is with environment variables. For example, you can inject a secret at runtime like this:

```
docker run -d `
  -e DB_CONNECTION="Server=db.internal;Database=Loans;" `
  -e API_KEY="<<redacted>>" `
  -e SFTP_PASSWORD="<<redacted>>" `
  finacr.azurecr.io/finance-dashboard:1.0.5
```

That's fine for local or short-lived testing, but you'll want something more robust for real deployments. In Compose, you can define secrets and environment variables cleanly:

```yaml
services:
  finance-dashboard:
    image: finacr.azurecr.io/finance-dashboard:1.0.5
    secrets:
      - db_connection
      - sftp_password
    environment:
      - API_KEY_FILE=/run/secrets/db_connection
      - IMPORT_SFTP_USER=import_user

secrets:
  db_connection:
    external: true
  sftp_password:
    external: true
```

Figure 8.6: Example Docker Compose file defining external secrets and environment variables

Here, the credentials and keys live in Docker secrets, or in an external store such as Azure Key Vault, HashiCorp Vault, or AWS Secrets Manager. They're never baked into the image or checked into source control.

It also makes rotation easy: when the SFTP password changes or a new API key is issued, you just update the secret and redeploy, with no image rebuilds and no emergency commits.

This structure also makes it much easier to rotate secrets. Need to roll over an API key? Just update the value in your secret store, and redeploy: your containers stay untouched. No need to rebuild images or tweak config files directly. It's clean, traceable, and it works well in both development and production.

And for compliance-heavy environments, we know who we are. This pattern ticks a lot of boxes. You can show that secrets are encrypted, access is controlled, and nothing sensitive is being stored insecurely. It makes auditors happy, but more importantly, it protects your systems and your users.

One final tip. Treat all your environment variable values as potentially sensitive unless you're absolutely sure they're harmless. It's easy to forget that something such as `NODE_ENV=production` can safely live in plaintext, but that debug flag with a hardcoded test token? Not so much.

So, take the time to get your configuration and secret handling right upfront. It'll save you from awkward emails, rollback scrambles, and "*Who added that token to GitHub?*" moments later down the line. This is the kind of foundational stuff that makes the rest of your Docker-based workflows smoother, safer, and a lot more scalable. Once secrets and configurations are handled correctly, the next focus is efficiency: building lean, predictable images that perform well across enterprise environments.

One of the easiest wins is to get comfortable with multi-stage builds. If you've used these before with modern Linux-based apps, great, but it's just as relevant for traditional .NET Framework apps that still make up a huge part of the enterprise world. Here's a tidy example to illustrate the point:

```
FROM mcr.microsoft.com/dotnet/framework/sdk:4.8 AS build-env
WORKDIR /app
COPY . .
RUN msbuild /p:Configuration=Release

FROM mcr.microsoft.com/dotnet/framework/runtime:4.8
COPY --from=build-env /app/bin/Release /inetpub/wwwroot
```

Figure 8.7: Multi-stage Dockerfile for a .NET Framework 4.8 application

What we're doing here is separating the build phase from the runtime. The first stage uses the SDK image, which is big and full of tools, to compile the application. Then, we copy only the compiled artifacts into the final stage, which uses the much slimmer runtime image. This means all those extra build tools, caches, and temp files don't make it into production.

Why does that matter? Well, for one, your production image becomes dramatically smaller. That means faster image pulls when deploying, less disk usage on nodes, and lower risk of exposing unnecessary tools or dependencies. It also makes updates snappier; a 200 MB image will always move faster than a 2 GB one.

It also helps with compliance and security. Smaller images have a smaller attack surface. You're not shipping compilers, SDKs, or unused libraries into environments where they don't belong. And if your security team is running vulnerability scans on every image (and let's be honest, they should be), this setup keeps your scan results a lot cleaner.

Tip

A couple of bonus tips while we're here:

- Always `.dockerignore` files you don't need. Logs, build artifacts, config samples, `node_modules` folders, if you're containerizing frontends... they all sneak in if you're not careful.

- Pin your base image versions to avoid surprises during rebuilds, don't rely on latest unless you enjoy surprise regressions.
- If you're caching layers, do it properly. Install dependencies early, then copy the source. That way, small changes to your code base don't bust the whole build cache.

Efficient images aren't just nice to have; they're part of building a stack that performs well under load, scales without friction, and doesn't waste resources just getting out of bed. The more disciplined you are here, the smoother everything else gets later on.

Integrating with CI/CD pipelines

Let's be honest, if you're working in an enterprise environment, then you've almost certainly got a CI/CD pipeline humming away in the background, or at least, you should. Whether it's Jenkins, Azure DevOps, GitHub Actions, or something more bespoke, Docker integrates well with pretty much all of them.

But to really make it sing, especially at scale, there are a few best practices worth leaning into. By this point in the book, you already know how to tag, version, and promote Docker images, and if you need a refresher, there's a section near the end of this chapter, so I won't repeat it here. Instead, let's focus on how CI/CD behaves in a real enterprise environment: approvals, governance checks, image signing, automated rollbacks, and promoting a single tested artifact across environments.

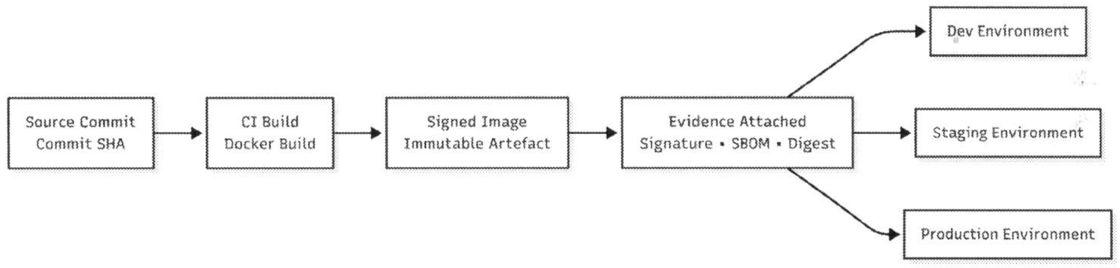

Figure 8.8: Single artifact CI/CD flow showing a signed image promoted from build through dev, staging, and production

A solid image build step might look like this:

Figure 8.9: Building and pushing a versioned enterprise image to an internal registry

In this example, we're building and pushing a tagged image for our enterprise app. The `docker build` command packages the application source code, installs its dependencies, and assigns it a clear semantic version (`1.4.2`). Once the build completes, the image is pushed to an internal registry (`myregistry`), ready to be promoted through environments such as staging and production.

Simple, clear, and repeatable. Everyone knows which version they're deploying. You can trace what's in production back to the exact commit that built it. And if something goes wrong, you've got a clear artifact to test or roll back to.

A common anti-pattern I've seen in enterprise pipelines is rebuilding the same app image separately for dev, test, and prod. It might feel like a clean separation at first, but you're essentially running unverified code in production, even if the builds came from the same branch. Don't do that. Nobody likes that.

Instead, build once, verify it in dev or staging, then promote the exact same image through your environments. That way, you know that what passed testing is exactly what's running in production, no surprises, no "*It worked on staging but not here*" issues.

You can do this by tagging and retagging:

```
docker tag myregistry/enterprise-app:1.4.2 myregistry/enterprise-app:staging

docker push myregistry/enterprise-app:staging
```

Later, when you're confident, you can do the following:

```
docker tag myregistry/enterprise-app:1.4.2 myregistry/enterprise-app:prod
docker push myregistry/enterprise-app:prod
```

It's a small habit, but one that pays off massively when you're managing dozens of services and deployment pipelines.

And finally, if you're in a regulated space (such as financial services, healthcare, or the public sector), consider signing your images. DCT (based on Notary) or tools such as Cosign let you cryptographically sign images and verify their origin and integrity. It's not mandatory for everyone, but if you need to meet compliance or audit requirements, having a verifiable signature chain for your containers makes those conversations much easier.

The overall takeaway here is that your CI/CD system shouldn't just automate builds and deployments. It should also provide clarity, traceability, and confidence. Clear tagging, consistent promotion, and a bit of forethought go a long way toward making your Docker workflows enterprise-grade.

Networking, storage, and Windows container considerations

Networking and storage might not be the most glamorous part of Docker deployment, but in enterprise setups, they can make or break your architecture. It's the sort of thing that works fine in a local dev environment, then suddenly collapses when scaled up across teams, environments, or regions, usually just before a deadline.

Storage

Let's start with storage. Wherever possible, use named volumes instead of bind mounts. Now, on Windows, bind mounts from the host filesystem (for example, `C:\ paths`) can introduce subtle issues in enterprise setups. Common pitfalls include path translation problems, CRLF line ending mismatches, file locking quirks, and noticeably slower I/O under WSL 2.

For anything beyond local development, prefer named volumes or managed storage rather than host bind mounts.

In production environments, named volumes are typically backed up using platform-level snapshot strategies, such as scheduled Azure Disk or Azure Files snapshots when running in

ACR-backed or cloud-hosted environments, especially on Windows with WSL 2, where bind-mounting from the Windows filesystem (such as `C:\ folders`) introduces latency and weird path quirks. Named volumes are managed by Docker itself, live entirely within the Linux VM on WSL 2, and give you much better performance and portability. Here's a tidy example:

```
version: '3.8'

services:
  enterprise-app:
    image: enterprise-app:1.0.0
    volumes:
      - enterprise-data:/data

volumes:
  enterprise-data:
```

Figure 8.10: Docker Compose example defining a named volume for persistent data storage

This approach also makes things easier to manage at scale. You can take a snapshot, back up, or migrate named volumes much more cleanly than juggling folder mounts across team machines or CI environments. And if you're using orchestration, this method carries forward nicely into Swarm or Kubernetes with minimal fuss.

Networking

Now, onto networking. I know, usually terrifying. Enterprise apps rarely run in isolation. They need to talk to other services, databases, authentication layers, or monitoring agents. It's tempting to rely on Docker's default bridge network, but for anything beyond local testing, that's not going to cut it.

Explicitly define your networks in Docker Compose or Swarm, so you know exactly who can talk to what. It helps enforce clear boundaries, supports security policies such as internal-only traffic, and makes service discovery more predictable. Here is an example:

```yaml
version: '3.8'

services:
  enterprise-app:
    image: enterprise-app:1.0.0
    volumes:
      - enterprise-data:/data

volumes:
  enterprise-data:
```

Figure 8.11: Docker Compose file defining a named volume for persistent storage in an enterprise container setup

This example defines a single-service, enterprise app, using a named volume called `enterprise-data`. That volume is mounted at `/data` inside the container. The named volume is declared under the top-level `volumes` section so Docker knows to manage it automatically. Using this structure keeps storage portable and avoids slow bind mounts from the host filesystem, especially important on Windows.

Windows considerations

Those same principles carry directly into Windows containers, which introduce their own quirks around size, performance, and resource management. So, if you're deploying Docker in an enterprise setting on Windows, there's no avoiding Windows containers eventually, as much as you might try, and they do come with their own quirks. These aren't showstoppers, far from it, but they do mean you need to be a little more deliberate with how you set things up compared to their leaner Linux cousins. In other words, don't treat them exactly the same, or they'll gently remind you who's boss:

- Let's start with **size**. Windows containers, particularly those based on full .NET Framework or legacy ASP.NET apps, tend to be a bit chunkier than Linux-based ones. We're not in Alpine anymore; base images can be multiple gigabytes before you even add your own code. That means longer build times, bigger pushes and pulls, and more pressure on your image storage, both locally and in registries. And if your organization has tight CI/CD time budgets or bandwidth-constrained environments, you'll definitely want to think ahead. This is where layering and efficient image management start to pay dividends. Even small gains at build time can add up across environments.

- Next, let's talk **resource management**. If you're running Docker Desktop on Windows using the WSL 2 backend, the container engine is actually living inside a lightweight Linux VM. It shares your host resources, but unless you step in, it'll happily take more than you'd like. A good move early on is to create a `.wslconfig` file in your user directory. This lets you set memory, CPU, and swap limits globally for all WSL environments. When you're running heavier enterprise-grade workloads, this makes Docker feel a lot less like a wildcard and a lot more like a controlled, testable platform.
- Then there's **IIS** (Microsoft's web server and application server). We all love a bit of IIS, and if your organization is still running traditional .NET Framework apps, you're likely dealing with it too. IIS inside containers needs a bit of care. Binding the site to the right port, ensuring the app pool starts up cleanly, and making sure everything lands in the right directory. Without these bits set correctly, IIS will quietly boot up but just not serve anything, which is the kind of bug that's a pain to spot under pressure.
  So, here's a practical starting point to avoid that:

```
FROM mcr.microsoft.com/dotnet/framework/aspnet:4.8

COPY . /inetpub/wwwroot

RUN powershell -Command `

    Import-Module WebAdministration; `

    New-Website -Name "EnterpriseApp" -PhysicalPath
    "C:\inetpub\wwwroot" -Port 80
```

Figure 8.12: Dockerfile example using PowerShell to configure and host an IIS website

  What this does is ensure that your application is registered with IIS and listening where you expect it. No more mysterious `404` errors when you know full well your code's in the container. It also gives you a repeatable, declarative way to set up your container environment the same way, every time.

- And finally, let's not forget the **wider implications**. Windows containers can be powerful tools for bridging legacy systems into more modern workflows. They let you containerize apps that can't quite be rebuilt yet, or services that are business-critical but architecturally stuck. And when paired with Docker Compose or Swarm, you still get many of the benefits of orchestration (scaling, health checks, and clean shutdowns) without needing to rewrite everything from scratch.

In short, Windows containers do ask a bit more of you upfront in terms of planning, image handling, and setup. But once you've got the hang of their rhythms, they're entirely workable and unlock a pathway to modernizing older services without the full cost of a rebuild. They're not your Linux-based dev buddy that just hums along out of the box, but given the right treatment, they're reliable, predictable, and surprisingly versatile.

Let them do their thing, and they'll quietly keep your legacy estate ticking while you build out the future.

Logging and monitoring

In enterprise applications, logging and monitoring aren't just a nice-to-have; they're a non-negotiable. If a container crashes or a service starts quietly misbehaving in production, the logs are often your first (and sometimes only) clue. And when the pressure's on, the difference between a smooth recovery and a prolonged outage is usually down to whether someone can read the logs and actually make sense of them.

So, with that in mind, we want to make sure that logs are clear, structured, and easy to feed into whatever central observability tooling your organization already leans on, whether that's ELK (my personal favourite), Splunk, Prometheus, Datadog, or something more bespoke.

Figure 8.13: Golden-path logging flow showing container logs emitted to stdout, shipped centrally, and surfaced via dashboards and alerts

The easiest win here is to keep your logs flowing to standard output. Docker's already set up to collect `stdout` and `stderr` from containers, and most log shippers and platforms are built with that expectation baked in. In .NET-based applications, a really handy way to structure those logs is with Serilog. With just a couple of configuration tweaks, you can have your app output structured JSON logs, which makes them far easier to parse and search once they land in a central logging system. No more grepping through plain text for that one error line that matters.

```
{
  "Serilog": {
    "Using": [ "Serilog.Sinks.Console" ],
    "MinimumLevel": "Information",
    "WriteTo": [
      {
        "Name": "Console",
        "Args": {
          "formatter": "Serilog.Formatting.Json.JsonFormatter, Serilog"
        }
      }
    ],
    "Enrich": [ "FromLogContext", "WithMachineName", "WithThreadId" ]
  }
}
```

Figure 8.14: Example Serilog configuration emitting structured JSON logs to standard output for centralized log ingestion

Structured JSON logs like this are far easier to index, filter, and correlate once they're ingested into central logging platforms.

And while it's tempting to just dump logs into a file somewhere in the container, don't. That approach might feel familiar, but it doesn't play well with containers. Files inside containers are ephemeral and hard to collect at scale. Stick with `stdout`, and you get portability, aggregation, and tooling support for free.

The next layer is health checks. These are often overlooked early on, but they're critical in enterprise setups. A container that's running isn't necessarily a healthy one, and orchestrators such as Compose or Swarm need a way to know the difference. That's where `healthcheck` definitions come in. Here's a quick Compose example:

```
services:
  enterprise-app:
    image: enterprise-app:1.0.0
    healthcheck:
      test: ["CMD", "curl", "-f", "http://localhost/healthcheck"]
      interval: 30s
      retries: 3
```

Figure 8.15: Docker Compose example defining a health check to monitor service availability

This setup runs a lightweight `curl` check against a health endpoint every 30 seconds. If the check fails three times in a row, Docker marks the container as unhealthy. That means Swarm or any orchestrator sitting on top can step in, restart the container, reroute traffic, or, at the very least, raise a flag for your support teams to jump in.

Naturally, this is just a starting point. You can go further by exposing custom metrics on a /`metrics` endpoint for Prometheus, or using readiness and liveness checks if you're operating in Kubernetes. And once you've got a reliable signal coming out of your services, you can wire alerts into Slack, Teams, PagerDuty, or whatever your support uses.

But even at this level, writing to `stdout` and including a basic health check, you're already ahead. You're making your containers easier to debug, safer to orchestrate, and much less mysterious when something starts to wobble.

Logging and health checks are two of those behind-the-scenes heroes. You won't hear much about them when everything's running smoothly, but the day you need them, you'll really need them, and you'll be really glad you took the time to get them right. It's the kind of thing that separates throwaway dev containers from something that's actually production-ready. And in enterprise settings, that makes all the difference.

So, one of the first large-scale Docker migrations I ever worked on was for a global finance organization. At the outset, the application landscape felt like a tangled mess: legacy apps, old servers, manual deployments, and teams who'd long forgotten how certain things actually worked. It reminded me a lot of one of the finance teams I used to work with years ago, a subprime loan reporting dashboard built on .NET with a tangle of Excel macros and nightly batch jobs. Let's use something like that as our running example through this chapter. We'll call it the *Finance Dashboard,* a simple internal web app that generates performance reports and exposes a few internal APIs for analysts. You can find the Dockerfile for it in the GitHub repository over at `https://github.com/PacktPublishing/Mastering-Docker-on-Windows`.

Deploying the Finance Dashboard

To make this real, let's walk through a simple end-to-end deployment of our Finance Dashboard app using Docker on Windows. We'll assume that you've already containerized the .NET Framework version of the Finance Dashboard using a working Dockerfile (you can find a reference Dockerfile for it in the book's GitHub repository under `Chapter 8`), so we can focus here on the deployment steps rather than image authoring:

> Note
>
> **Authenticate with Azure Container Registry**
>
> Before building or pushing images, make sure Docker is authenticated with your Azure Container Registry:
>
> ```
> az acr login -n finacr
> ```

> In CI pipelines, this is typically handled using a service principal or managed identity rather than an interactive login.

1. **Build the image**: This is simple enough and something we've done a few times now:

```
docker build -t finacr.azurecr.io/finance-dashboard:1.0.0 .
```

   In larger enterprise pipelines, ACR tasks are often used to prebuild and cache base layers, reducing cold-start build times and improving CI consistency across teams.

2. **Test it locally**: Let's run the container and expose port `8080`:

```
docker run -d -p 8080:80 finacr.azurecr.io/finance-dashboard:1.0.0
```

   Now, we can visit `http://localhost:8080` in our browser to verify that the app loads correctly.

3. **Push to your internal registry (ACR)**: We'll log in and push the tested images to our internal repo:

```
az acr login -n finacr
docker push finacr.azurecr.io/finance-dashboard:1.0.0
```

4. **Deploy via Docker Compose**: Okay, so now we can create a `docker-compose.yml` file to define the service, environment variables, and secrets:

```
version: "3.9"
services:
  finance-dashboard:
    image: finacr.azurecr.io/finance-dashboard:1.0.0
    ports:
      - "8080:80"
    secrets:
      - db_password
    environment:
      - DB_CONNECTION=Server=db.internal;Database=Loans;
secrets:
  db_password:
    external: true
healthcheck:
```

```
    test: ["CMD", "powershell", "-Command", "Invoke-WebRequest -
UseBasicParsing http://localhost/health"]
    interval: 30s
    timeout: 5s
    retries: 3
```

Note that in real deployments, this `/health` endpoint should return a lightweight `200 OK` response without touching downstream dependencies.

Then, we can deploy it with the following:

```
docker compose up -d
```

5. **Validate deployment**: Let's check the logs and container health:

```
docker ps
docker logs finance-dashboard
```

This workflow takes you from source code to a live, running container in a controlled, enterprise-friendly way, using reproducible builds, internal registry hosting, and clean configuration handling.

Deploying enterprise applications with Docker on Windows isn't simply about getting an app running in a container. It's about building robust, repeatable, and maintainable deployment strategies.

Remember the story I shared at the start? That legacy finance system went from fragile deployments to smooth, predictable container rollouts. That's the sort of real-world impact Docker can make in an enterprise setting. It wasn't quick or particularly easy, but it worked because of some of these steps we introduced along the way.

Scaling Docker for high availability

I was at one of the AWS conferences, and someone was telling me about a time they worked with a large logistics company that had just moved a chunk of its operations over to Docker. They were feeling pretty pleased with themselves, and rightly so. Containers were running, builds were automated, and everything felt modern. Then, one Monday morning, a single container stopped responding, and a critical internal service went down. It wasn't dramatic, but it was a wake-up call. "*So, we're just... hoping everything stays up?*" they asked. They said that was the moment they started talking about high availability, and the moment I started reading up on it myself.

Funny enough, I learned that same lesson during my time in subprime finance when our internal Finance Dashboard started creaking under end-of-month reporting spikes. Analysts would all hit the system at once to pull loan performance data, and suddenly, what ran fine all month would crawl or time out entirely. Scaling wasn't optional; it was survival.

So, I wanted to make a section in this book that goes beyond "it runs" and starts thinking in terms of resilience: specifically, how to scale Docker on Windows in a way that keeps your services up and running, even when something inevitably goes wrong.

To keep this section a smidge more grounded, let's stick with the Finance Dashboard example from earlier. At this point, with the app already containerized and running smoothly in a single instance, it's great for testing but not so great for an enterprise workload. Our goal now is to scale it so that if one instance goes down, another automatically takes over, and the system stays online without manual intervention.

In other words, we're taking the same Finance Dashboard container and preparing it for a high-availability setup using Docker Swarm. This will let us replicate the service, spread the load, and recover gracefully from node or container failures, all essential traits for enterprise reliability.

High availability with Docker Swarm

At a high level, **high availability** (**HA**) is just about making sure that your applications stay online no matter what. Whether that's a crashed container, a failed node, or a sudden spike in traffic, the system should either absorb the hit or recover quickly enough that no one really notices.

In practice, HA is about removing single points of failure. If one container stops, there should be another ready to take over. If one host dies, the workload shifts elsewhere. And importantly, it should all happen without you having to SSH into three servers at 2 a.m.

On Windows, though, this means thinking carefully about how containers are deployed, how services are replicated, and how orchestration is handled. Remember you're working with a layered setup (Windows, WSL 2, and Docker), so keeping things smooth and self-healing takes a bit of planning, but it's absolutely doable.

Now, the simplest way to add HA into your Docker setup on Windows is by using Docker Swarm. Unlike Kubernetes, which I love but we'll leave to another book, Swarm is built right into Docker and designed to be relatively easy to adopt.

First, you need to initialize your Swarm:

```
# Initialise Swarm on your main node
docker swarm init
```

```
# Deploy the Finance Dashboard with three replicas
docker service create --name finance-dashboard --replicas 3 -p 8080:80 `
finacr.azurecr.io/finance-dashboard:1.0.0
```

This sets your current machine as the manager node; think of it like the captain of the cluster. From here, you can add worker nodes and begin scaling services across them.

So, let's say you want to deploy a web service with three replicas:

```
docker service create --name webapp --replicas 3 -p 80:80 myregistry/webapp:latest
```

This spins up three instances of your container, distributed across available nodes. Swarm handles load balancing, restarts failed containers automatically, and ensures that the desired number of replicas stays consistent. You can inspect how it's going with the following:

```
$ docker service ls
ID             NAME      MODE         REPLICAS   IMAGE                        PORTS
x8gk1z5w9s5p   webapp    replicated   3/3        myregistry/webapp:latest     *:80->80/tcp

$ docker service ps webapp
ID             NAME       IMAGE                        NODE      DESIRED STATE   CURRENT ST
ocmlj1u3u7qe   webapp.1   myregistry/webapp:latest     node1     Running         Running 5
4v9enrqv8k3b   webapp.2   myregistry/webapp:latest     node2     Running         Running 4
c9kz0f7r3e6x   webapp.3   myregistry/webapp:latest     node3     Running         Running 4
```

Figure 8.16: Docker Swarm service listing showing replicated containers

Naturally, having one node is a single point of failure. So, the next bit is spreading the load.

If you've got access to additional Windows machines, or virtual machines running Windows with Docker, you can add them as worker nodes:

```
docker swarm join --token <worker-token> <manager-ip>:2377
```

Each new node joins the swarm and becomes available to host services. Swarm will automatically rebalance the workloads if needed.

But what if a node fails? Swarm should notice the failure, mark the node as unreachable, and spin up replacement containers on the remaining healthy nodes. It's not instant, but it's fast enough for most scenarios.

One of the main reasons I use the Finance Dashboard as an example in this book is that it's a project I was hands-on with in my past. When we first containerized the Finance Dashboard, the single-container setup worked fine for test users, but performance collapsed under any real load. The service relied on IIS inside Windows Server Core containers, and each instance could comfortably handle about 40–50 concurrent report requests before response times degraded really sharply.

So, to fix that, we introduced Docker Swarm. The goal was simple: distribute traffic across multiple replicas and let the cluster self-heal when one instance crashed during a heavy reporting run.

We started with three replicas and scaled up gradually while watching CPU and memory metrics:

```
#Deploy initial service
docker service create --name finance-dashboard --replicas 3 --publish
published=8080,target=80 finacr.azurecr.io/finance-dashboard:1.0.0
# Scale out during peak hours
docker service scale finance-dashboard=6
```

During end-of-month load testing – which was pretty huge if you've ever worked in finance – 6 replicas cut the average response time from about 12 seconds down to under 3 seconds, even while analysts were generating hundreds of reports simultaneously. Yes, containers failed, but when one container failed due to an IIS recycle limit, Swarm replaced it automatically within about 15 seconds, with no manual intervention and no outage.

We also accidentally discovered that Windows Server Core images consumed significant disk space and network bandwidth when scaled rapidly, so we optimized the base image using layer caching and pinned versions to reduce pull times by nearly half.

The result was a stable, enterprise-grade service that could absorb usage spikes gracefully and recover automatically, a far cry from the old manual IIS deployment model.

Don't forget that in this setup, you can also promote nodes to managers for redundancy:

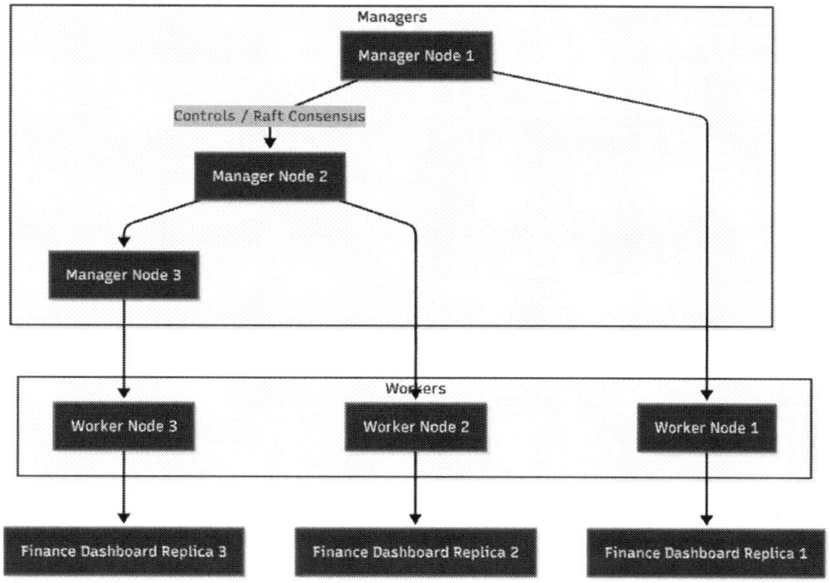

Figure 8.17: HA Swarm topology with multiple managers for consensus and workers

Docker Swarm managers use a Raft consensus model. In a three-manager cluster, a quorum of two managers is required for the cluster to make decisions. This means the platform can tolerate the loss of one manager node without impacting service availability:

```
# drain a node for planned maintenance
docker node update --availability drain manager-node-2
```

Draining a node ensures running tasks are rescheduled onto healthy nodes before maintenance begins, preserving availability.

Before we scale further, let's promote one of the worker nodes to a manager so the Swarm has proper redundancy. The following command shows how to elevate a node and then verify the updated manager set:

```
$ docker node promote node2
Node node2 promoted to a manager in the swarm.

$ docker node ls
ID                            HOSTNAME   STATUS    AVAILABILITY   MANAGER STATUS
v0dr0a3k7u5z77fwe1twlh95z *   node1      Ready     Active         Leader
nl8ktas3b6pu9nwn0k3k49skx     node2      Ready     Active         Reachable
zw7ifxt8qpjkbywe1fw1xwj28     node3      Ready     Active         Reachable
```

Figure 8.18: Promoting a worker node to a manager in Docker Swarm to enhance cluster redundancy

By default, Swarm uses a Raft consensus model, which needs a majority of manager nodes to make decisions. For most setups, having three managers gives you a good balance of resilience and complexity.

Spreading workloads with placement constraints

Okay, so let's say you've got a mix of services: a backend API, a frontend UI, and a background job processor. You might not want them all running on the same machine. Docker lets you apply placement constraints like this:

```
docker service create --name backend \
--replicas 2 \
--constraint 'node.labels.role == backend' \
myregistry/backend:latest
```

Figure 8.19: Docker service with node label constraints for controlled workload placement

This basically tells Docker Swarm, "Only run this service on nodes that have the label `role=backend`." It won't even attempt to place it anywhere else:

```
docker node update --label-add role=backend <node-name>
```

You can use any label keys and values that make sense to your architecture, things such as `role=frontend`, `zone=eu-west`, `type=highmem`, or even `owner=team-a`. It's entirely up to you and your conventions.

It's also brilliant for separating noisy neighbors. Maybe you've got a resource-intensive image classification service that spikes every time a request hits it, you can isolate that to a node that's built to handle the heat, without affecting your lightweight frontend services running elsewhere.

Scaling up and down

When traffic picks up, the last thing you want to be doing is scrambling to run `docker run` 10 times in a row while people are waiting on your app. It's not just tedious; it's error-prone, and in an enterprise environment, it's not scalable or sustainable.

This is exactly where Docker Swarm shines. Scaling becomes a single, simple instruction:

```
docker service scale webapp=10
```

That's it. No babysitting. No long scripts. Just one line, and Swarm takes care of spinning up the extra replicas, distributing them across your nodes, and ensuring they join the load-balanced service pool.

Want to bring it back down once the rush is over?

```
docker service scale webapp=3
```

Swarm handles all the grunt work behind the scenes: placement, scheduling, health checks, and routing. Your traffic still flows through as normal, and the system adapts to meet the load.

And if you want to get really fancy, you can even trigger this kind of scaling from an external tool. Maybe you've got a scheduled `cron` job that bumps your replicas at lunchtime, or a monitoring agent that kicks off a scale-up if CPU usage goes above 80 percent for 10 minutes straight. That kind of hands-off scaling is incredibly helpful once you're running production services that need to stay responsive regardless of what's going on behind the scenes.

Load balancing Docker workloads

I've worked on my fair share of "*Just hold your breath and deploy*" kind of apps, but one that always sticks with me is our Finance Dashboard, a chunky old internal web app that analysts hammered every Friday afternoon to generate their weekly loan performance reports. Everything was tightly coupled and fragile, and the build pipeline felt like it was held together with duct tape. Getting it into Docker was a step forward, but the real stability came once we sorted the load balancing. That's when the whole platform finally felt calm under pressure, when Docker stopped being just a packaging tool and started feeling like infrastructure we could trust.

We'll keep building on the *Finance Dashboard* example from earlier. By this point, we've deployed it as a Swarm service with multiple replicas. The next step is to make sure traffic is distributed evenly across those containers, so that no single instance gets overloaded during those Friday afternoon reporting rushes.

Docker Swarm makes this surprisingly straightforward. When we expose a port while creating a service, Swarm automatically sets up a routing mesh, a built-in layer that directs requests to any of the running replicas, no matter which node they're on. For our Finance Dashboard, that means each analyst's request for loan-performance data gets handled by whichever container is available, rather than hammering the same one repeatedly. You can see it in action with a single command:

```
# Deploy the Finance Dashboard frontend with built-in load balancing
docker service create `
  --name finance-dashboard `
  --replicas 3 `
  --publish published=8080,target=80 `
  finacr.azurecr.io/finance-dashboard:1.0.0
```

Now, requests to `http://localhost:8080` (or any node's IP in the Swarm) will automatically rotate between the running replicas.

To see how this works under the hood, let's unpack what Docker's routing mesh and internal load balancer are actually doing.

Understanding load balancing in Docker

So, first things first, what are we actually talking about when we say *load balancing* in Docker? Well, at its core, it's about spreading incoming traffic evenly across multiple running containers. Not just useful for high-traffic websites, but anything that handles concurrent users, background jobs, or API calls can benefit from having requests routed intelligently.

And it's not just about performance. Here's why it really matters:

- It stops any one container from getting completely hammered
- It means you can scale out or back in without fiddling with routing yourself
- It keeps things running smoothly during rolling updates or if something fails
- It helps you get more out of the resources you've already provisioned

If you're using Docker Swarm, this kind of balancing is built in. Any time you deploy a service with multiple replicas, Swarm gives you internal load balancing by default. It sets up what's called a *routing mesh,* a clever bit of networking that listens on the service's published port, then forwards requests to the active containers (Swarm calls them **tasks**) behind the scenes.

So, even without adding a reverse proxy or any extra tooling, you already get basic round-robin traffic distribution out of the box. Not bad for a few lines of YAML.

As we saw in the previous section, Swarm automatically load-balances across service replicas, so let's look at how that behaves under real traffic. You don't need to know where those containers are physically running. Swarm sorts that out for you. Requests come in, Swarm picks one of the replicas, and off they go.

Try opening up your browser or hitting `http://localhost:8080` with `curl` a few times. If you've got logging or container IDs exposed in the response, you'll see the traffic bouncing between the different replicas. That's your routing mesh in action, balancing requests without breaking a sweat.

To see exactly where those containers are running, use the following:

```
docker service ps frontend
```

```
$ docker service ps frontend

ID             NAME         IMAGE                        NODE     DESIRED STATE
ut5sy6g8d55h   frontend.1   myregistry/frontend:1.0.0    node-1   Running
ksh2f3z8shs9   frontend.2   myregistry/frontend:1.0.0    node-2   Running
q9jf73jw2zyx   frontend.3   myregistry/frontend:1.0.0    node-3   Running
```

Figure 8.20: Swarm service distribution showing frontend replicas running across multiple nodes

This kind of setup is ideal for stateless services, such as frontend UIs, APIs, or any workload where it doesn't matter which replica handles the request. Each one can take a request, process it, and return a response independently. You don't need sticky sessions, shared state, or anything clever to get good results here – just clean containers and a swarm that knows how to distribute traffic properly.

And the best part? You get this functionality by default, just by scaling your service. No extra config files, no third-party tools, and no magic proxies. It's all built into the platform.

The role of the routing mesh

One of the really clever bits about Swarm's built-in load balancing is the routing mesh. It's easy to miss just how much work it's doing behind the scenes. The short version? The routing mesh listens on all nodes for traffic to any published service port, regardless of whether that node is actually running one of the service's containers. What that means in practice is this:

- Traffic can hit any node in the swarm.
- It'll be routed internally to one of the service's containers.
- Docker will balance that request out for you, even if the container is running on a different host.

It's all handled through internal virtual networking, and it's round-robin by default. You don't need to mess around with setting up your own balancer for this to work; it's just baked in.

Now, it's elegant, no question, but there are a few things to be aware of. You don't get fancy balancing strategies or sticky sessions out of the box. And because traffic can be accepted on any node, you've got to make sure your firewall rules and network security groups allow it. In enterprise environments, that means checking that every node is reachable across the published ports; otherwise, requests can get silently dropped or blocked upstream.

Customizing service discovery and internal networking

Here's a bit that often goes unnoticed: how Docker services talk to each other inside the cluster. Swarm automatically creates an overlay network, and every service gets a DNS entry based on its name. No additional tooling or configuration needed. So, let's say you've got the following services running:

- Frontend
- Backend
- Database

Then, the frontend container can just hit `http://backend` to reach the backend. No hardcoded IPs, no environment-specific hostnames, no DNS fiddling. It's all wired up automatically.

That said, when your app grows beyond a few services, it's a good idea to get a bit more intentional with your networks. You can create your own overlay network like so:

```
docker network create --driver overlay my-net
```

Then, attach your services to that network explicitly:

```
docker service create --name frontend --network my-net myregistry/frontend
docker service create --name backend --network my-net myregistry/backend
```

Now those two services can discover each other by name, but they're also isolated from other unrelated services in the cluster. It's a small change that makes a big difference in larger systems, especially when you want to enforce cleaner service boundaries or tighten down inter-service access.

Working with external load balancers

Swarm's internal routing mesh will get you quite far on its own. But in enterprise environments, you're almost always going to be working with external load balancers too, whether that's a bit of physical server hardware, an NGINX reverse proxy, or cloud-native solutions such as Azure Application Gateway or AWS ALB. In these scenarios, the pattern is usually something like this:

- Publish your Docker service on a specific port (e.g., `--publish 443:443`)
- Point your external load balancer to the IP of one or more Swarm nodes
- Let the load balancer handle things such as SSL termination, sticky sessions, or path-based routing

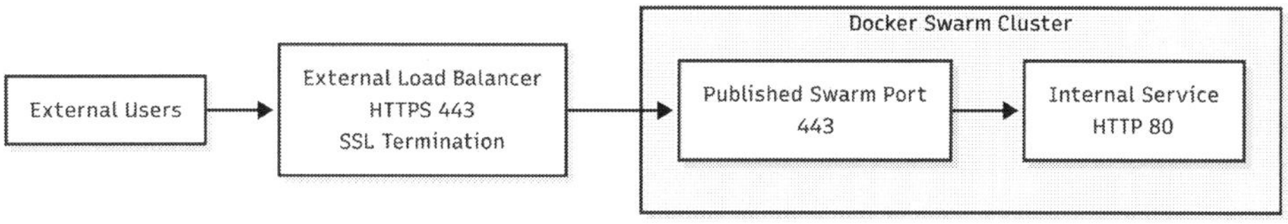

Figure 8.21: External load balancer terminating TLS on port 443 and forwarding traffic to a Docker Swarm service

In enterprise environments, TLS certificates are typically managed centrally at the external load balancer rather than inside containers. This simplifies certificate rotation, avoids duplicating secrets across services, and keeps container images free of long-lived credentials.

This gives you the best of both worlds: internal resilience from Swarm's routing mesh, and external flexibility from your existing traffic layer.

For example, here's a stripped-down NGINX configuration that load balances between two internal Docker containers:

```
upstream myapp {
  server app1.internal:8080;
  server app2.internal:8080;
}

server {
  listen 443 ssl;
  location / {
    proxy_pass http://myapp;
  }
}
```

Figure 8.22: NGINX configuration for SSL load balancing across internal Docker service replicas

You could tie this into Swarm's DNS-based discovery too so that your proxy is always talking to the right containers, even as they're scaled up, down, or rescheduled elsewhere.

In practice, this setup lets you manage your public-facing traffic using tools that your infrastructure team already knows, while Docker takes care of balancing and resilience behind the scenes. It's a clean divide between external control and internal automation.

Note

A note on sticky sessions

In some enterprise apps, particularly anything with user logins or in-session workflows, you'll find yourself needing sticky sessions. That is, keeping a user's traffic pinned to the same container across multiple requests. Maybe the app wasn't built with shared session storage, or maybe it's doing something session-sensitive in memory. Either way, it's a common requirement.

Now, Docker's built-in load balancing doesn't support stickiness natively. Out of the box, it just spreads requests around evenly using round-robin. But you do have options:

- Use an external load balancer that supports sticky sessions via IP affinity, cookies, or headers. NGINX, Traefik, or your cloud LB can usually handle this.

- Build some affinity logic into your application layer; this can be messy, but in tightly controlled systems, it's workable.
- Better still, move session state out of the container entirely. Something like Redis or a shared backend store means any replica can pick up where the last one left off.

So, sticky sessions aren't off the table; they just aren't Docker's concern. You'll need to decide who's going to own the "stickiness": the proxy, the app, or your session storage. But as long as someone's got it covered, it's not a blocker. Just another part of building enterprise-grade behavior on top of a containerized core.

Managing enterprise Docker infrastructure

Docker itself is pretty easy to get running. But keeping it reliable, scalable, and manageable across a large organization? That's where things get interesting.

Note

Enterprise governance baseline (a somewhat practical checklist)

Before running Docker at scale across teams and environments, you need to agree on a small set of non-negotiables between each other. This is governance:

Naming and labeling:

- Consistent service and image naming (no ad-hoc names)
- Mandatory labels on services and nodes: owner, environment (dev, staging, or prod), and data classification (public, internal, or restricted)

Change control:

- Explicit approval required for network changes, port exposure, and cross-service connectivity
- Changes recorded alongside the deployment pipeline, not handled manually

Resource ownership:

- Nodes labeled by capability (for example, `highmem`, `gpu`, or `batch`)
- Placement constraints used instead of "best effort" scheduling

Housekeeping:

- Automated weekly cleanup jobs for dangling images, unused volumes, and failed or abandoned builds
- Cleanup scoped by labels to avoid accidental deletion

This doesn't slow teams down. It prevents entropy. Once these rules are in place, Docker stops being a shared liability and starts behaving like a managed platform.

Let's keep the *Finance Dashboard* example rolling here. By this point, we've got the application deployed, scaled, and load-balanced across a few nodes in Swarm. It's stable under load, but now the focus shifts from "getting it working" to "keeping it organized." In enterprise environments, that means introducing structure, labeled nodes, managed networks, consistent volume usage, and automated cleanups, so that every deployment behaves predictably, no matter which team or environment it lands in.

```
# Label a high-memory node for Finance Dashboard workloads
docker node update --label-add role=finance-app type=highmem node-2

# Deploy the Finance Dashboard service to that labelled node
docker service create `
  --name finance-dashboard `
  --constraint 'node.labels.role==finance-app' `
  -p 8080:80 `
  finacr.azurecr.io/finance-dashboard:1.0.0
```

This small step prevents random container placement and keeps performance consistent, which is vital when you're running regulated, high-traffic apps across multiple teams.

Up to now, we've focused on how to build, deploy, and scale containers. This section covers something different: the day-to-day operational work that keeps a Docker estate healthy once it's already running. These aren't general best practices; they're the practical tasks teams rely on in real environments, such as managing nodes, structuring networks and volumes, and keeping behaviors consistent across dev, staging, and production.

By the end, I hope that these habits and patterns will help you and give you something to lean on, things that help keep your infrastructure tidy and maintainable, even when you're juggling multiple environments, teams, and internal constraints.

Nodes, labels, and tags

In any non-trivial Docker deployment, you're probably managing more than one machine. Even in a smaller Windows-based environment, you might have dedicated build servers, some high-memory nodes for AI workloads, and maybe a few lightweight VMs running peripheral services.

To avoid a mess later, start tagging and labeling your nodes early. For example, label your GPU-capable node:

```
docker node update --label-add capabilities=gpu machine-2
```

Or tag your memory-heavy build server:

```
docker node update --label-add type=builder-highmem build-1
```

These labels then become useful for filtering services during deployment, writing Compose files, or applying placement constraints within Swarm or other orchestrators. It also helps you (and others) remember which machine does what, without relying on hostnames or tribal knowledge. You can list nodes and labels like this:

```
$ docker node inspect node-1 --format '{{ json .Spec.Labels }}'

{
  "env": "production",
  "region": "eu-west",
  "type": "database"
}
```

Figure 8.23: Inspecting Docker node labels to identify environment, region, and workload type

Trust me, labeling is one of those things you don't appreciate until six months down the line when you're trying to figure out which of the machines can run that GPU-enabled Python model without blowing up.

Keeping Docker volumes under control

Volumes are brilliant when it comes to persistence; they're the go-to for keeping data safe between container runs. But once you scale out across environments or teams, they can turn into a bit of a mess if you're not careful. I've seen setups where no one really knew which volume was being used by what, or whether it was even still needed. That's where trouble starts. A few habits go a long way when it comes to volume hygiene:

- Stick to named volumes rather than host mounts. They're portable, cleaner, and behave the same across dev, staging, and production.
- Use read-only mounts wherever possible. If multiple services need access to something like reference data, this avoids accidental writes.
- Leverage volume drivers if you're using cloud storage or something distributed, such as Amazon EFS, Azure Files, or NFS, with a dedicated driver.

Oh, and to keep tabs on what's there, use the following:

```
docker volume ls
docker volume inspect <volume-name>
```

You can also label volumes at creation time:

```
docker volume create --label environment=prod --name prod-logs
```

Labeling makes clean-up jobs far less risky. Need to prune old volumes from a dev environment? Just filter by label. It's a lot better than scanning a long list of cryptic names and crossing your fingers you're not about to delete something important. The key here is being as proactive as you can. When you treat volumes as part of your infrastructure, not just as throwaway storage, you get much better predictability and fewer panicked rebuilds.

Keeping things predictable

Docker's networking model is pretty flexible, which is great until it gets out of hand. I've seen teams with half a dozen services all dumped onto the default bridge or host network, accidentally exposing ports, clashing with each other, and wondering why service discovery feels unreliable. If you want to avoid that kind of mess, a few small habits go a long way:

- Always create your own user-defined networks. The default ones are fine for quick tests, but they're not built for long-term clarity or control.

- Give your networks meaningful names such as `monitoring-net`, `internal-api-net`, or `shared-cache-net`. Trust me, you'll thank yourself later.
- Use aliases to simplify service discovery and keep container lookups readable.

Here's how that might look in Compose:

```
networks:
  app-net:
    driver: bridge
services:
  frontend:
    networks:
      - app-net
    depends_on:
      - backend
```

Figure 8.24: Docker Compose bridge network linking frontend and backend services with startup dependency control

This sort of setup makes service-to-service comms predictable, and when you need to tighten things down later, say, with firewall rules or network segmentation, then you're not ripping everything apart just to retrofit structure.

A bit of naming discipline and some upfront planning on your network layout can save a whole lot of rewiring down the line.

Managing resources and observability

We've already touched on resource limits back in *Chapter 6*: how to define them, what they control, and why they matter. But here, in the context of running Docker at enterprise scale on Windows, it's worth revisiting with a slightly different lens: fairness and stability across shared infrastructure.

On Windows 11, running Docker via WSL 2 means you're working inside a virtualized environment. And unless you've told it otherwise, that environment will happily consume every CPU cycle and chunk of memory it can. Not a problem when you're flying solo, but once you're running in a team setup, or sharing nodes between services, that kind of free-for-all can get messy fast.

The first thing you'll want to do is pin down some global limits for Docker Desktop using the `.wslconfig` file:

```
[wsl2]
memory=6GB
processors=4
swap=2GB
```

Figure 8.25: WSL 2 configuration file defining memory, processor, and swap limits

This sets the guardrails for WSL 2 itself, and by extension, Docker. It ensures that containers running locally don't crowd out the rest of your system or other containers trying to do their job. Then, inside your actual Compose definitions or Swarm services, it's best practice to set explicit caps at the container level:

```
deploy:
  resources:
    limits:
      cpus: '0.50'
      memory: 512M
```

Figure 8.26: Docker Compose resource limits defining CPU and memory caps

Even if you've done this earlier in development, now's the time to take it super seriously. In enterprise workloads on Windows, especially when you're running dozens of services or letting multiple teams deploy to the same infrastructure, limits aren't optional. They're part of how you prevent noisy neighbors, enforce basic fairness, and keep everything operating within its slice of the system.

So while this might look like something we've seen before, here it's pretty vital. Windows-based Docker setups need this kind of resource governance baked in from the start, because in production, it's not just about containers running smoothly, it's about everything running smoothly together.

Tracking in enterprise-scale Windows setups

Once resource boundaries are defined, the next step is visibility, tracking how those limits behave in production and catching early warning signs across your Windows environments.

We've already covered the basics of monitoring elsewhere in the book: `docker logs`, `docker stats`, all that good stuff. But this chapter isn't about individual containers. It's about running Docker at scale, across teams, on shared Windows infrastructure. That changes the game a bit.

Here, it's less about "Can I see what this container is doing" and more about "Can I trust what's happening across the system without babysitting it?" So, even though these commands aren't new, it's how you use them in enterprise environments that makes the difference.

Let's start with events. They're underused but seriously powerful:

```
docker events --filter 'event=stop' --filter 'container=enterprise-app'
```

Figure 8.27: Monitoring container life cycle events in real time using filtered docker events output

This gives you a live feed of what Docker is doing under the hood: containers starting, stopping, and failing health checks. Super useful when you're dealing with Swarm on Windows and things are being rescheduled across nodes. Then, there's our old friend:

```
docker stats
```

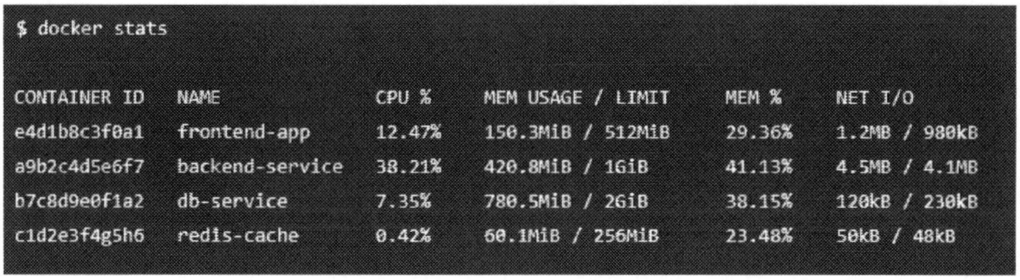

Figure 8.28: Using docker stats to monitor container CPU, memory, and network usage in real time

It shows you live resource usage per container. In a shared environment, it's a quick way to spot containers that are hogging CPU or memory before they cause issues for everyone else.

Yeah, it's a bit raw for long-term use, but as a first response when someone says "*The system's slow*," it gets the job done.

Now, because this is Windows and you're probably running everything inside WSL 2, you'll also want visibility into the underlying VM. That's where something such as WSL Exporter comes in; it gives you host-level metrics that Prometheus or Grafana can scrape.

Or, if you're not ready to roll out a full monitoring stack just yet, Docker Desktop's built-in dashboard is actually decent. It shows running containers, resource usage, and logs; it's enough to keep things moving while you build out something more serious.

The key takeaway here is don't wait until something breaks to think about observability. In a Windows-based enterprise setup, you want a feedback loop that helps you spot issues early, see what changed, and respond without guesswork. This stuff doesn't have to be complex; it just has to be consistent.

Switching between environments with Docker contexts

If you're juggling dev, test, and prod environments, as most enterprise setups eventually do, then constantly reconfiguring your Docker CLI gets old fast. You don't want to be messing around with manual SSH connections, changing environment variables, or wondering which server your next Docker push is heading to.

> **Note**
>
> When working across multiple environments, always confirm which Docker context is active before pushing images or updating services. It's very easy to deploy to the wrong environment by accident.
>
> Check the active context:
>
> ```
> docker context show
> ```
>
> List all available contexts:
>
> ```
> docker context ls
> ```
>
> Explicitly switch context before running destructive commands:
>
> ```
> docker context use staging
> ```
>
> Super hint: Make this a habit. Verifying context takes seconds and prevents accidental pushes or updates to the wrong cluster.

That's where Docker contexts come in. They let you switch between remote Docker daemons with a single command, without needing to leave your terminal or change machines. It's especially handy when you're supporting multiple teams or remote clusters from a single workstation. Here's how to create one:

```
docker context create staging --docker "host=ssh://user@staging-server"
```

And to switch over to it, use the following:

```
docker context use staging
```

From that point on, every Docker `build`, `run`, `ps`, `push`, and so on runs against the remote host you configured. No fiddling with SSH tunnels, no editing config files, no accidental deployments to the wrong environment.

It's properly useful on Windows 11 too, whether you're using WSL 2 or PowerShell. I've used it plenty of times to move between local development and remote staging servers during CI testing or patch rollout prep. If you're working in a multi-environment setup and still doing things manually, this is one of those quality-of-life improvements that pays off immediately. Think of it like having a context-aware CLI that just knows where you're pointing, without you having to double-check every command.

Maintaining security and hygiene

We've already talked about the dangers of baking secrets into your images, so I won't rehash the basics here (see what I did there?). But in an enterprise context, especially on shared Windows infrastructure, the stakes are higher. You're not just protecting access tokens, you're protecting production databases, customer data, and potentially, entire environments from exposure.

When working across environments and teams, you need to treat secrets as a first-class citizen. That means using Docker secrets wherever possible, even if you're just running Swarm locally for now:

```
docker secret create db_password secret.txt
```

In Compose, make sure that services reference secrets cleanly and consistently:

```yaml
secrets:
  db_password:
    external: true

services:
  backend:
    secrets:
      - db_password
```

Figure 8.29: Docker Compose example defining and attaching an external secret to a backend service

This approach keeps secrets off the image, out of logs, and isolated per container. And yes, it works fine on Windows 11 too; just remember that `.env`, `.secrets`, or any other sensitive files **must** be in your `.gitignore` file. It only takes one accidental push to GitHub to ruin your day.

At scale, it's also worth thinking about how secrets are rotated and expired. Stale tokens lying around for weeks is not a good look. Enterprise teams should integrate secret rotation into their CI pipelines or schedule it via a secrets management system, such as HashiCorp Vault, AWS Secrets Manager, or Azure Key Vault, depending on your stack.

Finally, ongoing security and cleanup go hand in hand, keeping secrets safe and removing outdated artifacts before they become liabilities.

And, while we're on the topic of keeping things secure and clean, remember that old images, dangling containers, and unused volumes can quietly pile up in the background. It's not just about disk space, either. Leaving old containers around can expose outdated dependencies or configurations you thought were gone.

You can start simple, and we're going back to our old friend, Prune!

```
docker system prune -f
docker volume prune -f
docker image prune -f
```

But for enterprise workloads, you'll want to be more surgical. Write scripts that remove only images older than *X* days, or untagged builds left over from failed CI runs. Run those as scheduled tasks or CI jobs during off-peak hours. It would look a little like this:

```
$cutoff = (Get-Date).AddDays(-7)
docker image ls --format "{{.Repository}} {{.ID}} {{.CreatedAt}}" | ForEach-Object {
    $parts = $_ -split " "
    $created = Get-Date "$($parts[2]) $($parts[3]) $($parts[4])"
    if ($created -lt $cutoff -and $parts[0] -eq "<none>") {
        docker image rm $parts[1] -f
    }
}
```

Figure 8.30: PowerShell script for automatically removing unused Docker images older than seven days

The goal is to keep your Docker environments tidy and predictable, without blowing away something important by accident. At this scale, good housekeeping will save you a lot of headaches in the future.

So, managing Docker infrastructure in an enterprise setting isn't just about running containers; it's about doing it in a way that's consistent, observable, and maintainable. From tagging nodes to keeping secrets safe, and setting resource limits to automating cleanups, every small improvement here adds up to smoother operations later.

It's the difference between "We've got Docker running somewhere" and "Our infrastructure is containerized and humming." These are the real-world practices that help you move fast without everything falling over as you scale.

Troubleshooting and support for large workloads

There's a very specific kind of panic that kicks in when production starts misbehaving under load. It might be tied to a new release, an unexpected spike in usage, or just bad timing, such as Friday afternoon, right before you were about to call it a week. The stack looked solid during testing, but now the logs have gone quiet, containers are restarting for no good reason, and your team's Slack is lighting up like a Christmas tree.

Let's circle back one last time to the *Finance Dashboard*. It's end-of-month again, analysts are hammering the system for loan performance reports, and suddenly, things start to creak. The app's Swarm replicas begin restarting, CPU usage spikes, and the logs show intermittent connection errors to the loan database.

This is exactly the kind of scenario that separates a smooth Docker setup from a truly enterprise-ready one. Everything we've built so far (versioned images, node labels, health checks, and resource limits) now proves its worth. Troubleshooting isn't about panic-fixing; it's about tracing what's changed, isolating the issue, and recovering without downtime.

This isn't the time for big architectural changes or clever optimizations. Right now, it's about stabilizing the system and keeping things online. And when you're running Docker at enterprise scale on Windows, knowing where to look and how to act without making things worse is half the battle.

In this part, I'm going to unpack some of the more common failure patterns that show up under heavy load: memory pressure taking down services, containers entering endless restart loops, and volumes not mounting when things get busy. We'll also walk through a few response strategies, what to check first, how to trace the root cause without guesswork, and how to triage without introducing even more risk.

By the time we get to the end, you should have a clear, repeatable approach for troubleshooting large workloads in production. Nothing fancy, just a reliable way to keep the platform steady while you figure out the real fix. Because sometimes, that's all you need.

Where to start when everything's on fire

In our Finance Dashboard example, the immediate symptom was container restarts under load, but the root cause turned out to be resource exhaustion. By following the same diagnostic steps, checking container status, logs, and resource metrics, we can trace problems like this quickly without disrupting production.

When production starts melting down, the most important thing you can do is not make it worse. And that starts by not panicking. Easier said than done when the alerts are going off, Slack's gone full red badge of doom, and people are asking if it's the network, the app, or just "Docker being Docker."

Your first job isn't to fix it, it's to understand what's changed. Ask yourself the following:

- Did we just ship something?
- Has there been a scaling event?
- Has a new customer just been onboarded?
- Is there a big batch job running unexpectedly?
- Has something been quietly degrading for a while, and no one noticed until now?

Nine times out of 10, something did change; your job is to identify what and where. Start with the basics:

```
docker ps --format "table {{.Names}}\t{{.Status}}\t{{.Image}}"
```

Figure 8.31: Formatted docker ps output showing container names, statuses, and image versions for quick health checks

This tells you what's running, what's restarting, and what image version each service is using. It's your quick sanity check. Did something suddenly start exiting or restarting in a loop? Is an old image still hanging around when it should have been updated?

Then, switch to resource usage:

```
docker stats
```

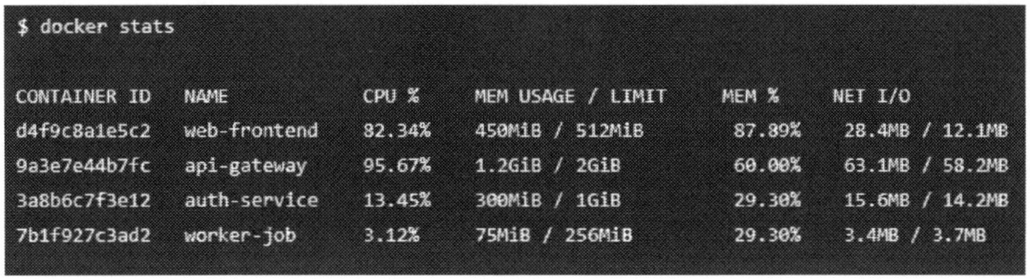

Figure 8.32: Using docker stats to monitor container resource utilization and detect performance bottlenecks

This gives you a live view of what's chewing up CPU or memory. Look for containers that are way above normal or ones that seem idle but are still getting traffic.

You're not trying to fix everything right away. You're building a picture of what's happening:

- Are services healthy but overloaded?
- Are containers crashing and restarting?
- Is one container hogging resources and starving the others?

Getting a feel for the shape of the problem helps you decide what comes next. Sometimes it's a runaway container. Sometimes it's an upstream API failing and causing a cascade. And sometimes, someone fat-fingered a deployment and didn't notice.

Whatever the case, slow down, get your bearings, and use the tools Docker gives you to read the environment. You'll move faster by starting slow.

Logs, events, and exit codes

Once you've got a handle on which containers are acting up, the next move is to dig into the signals they're giving off. Start with the logs, always. Docker makes this super straightforward:

```
docker logs my-api-service
```

```
Starting up API service...
Connecting to database at db.internal:5432...
[INFO] Loaded config from /etc/myapp/config.yml
[INFO] Listening on port 8080
Unhandled exception: timeout while contacting auth service
Retrying...
Unhandled exception: timeout while contacting auth service
Fatal error: auth service unavailable
Shutting down...
```

Figure 8.33: Application logs showing repeated timeouts while contacting the auth service, leading to a fatal shutdown

If a container's stuck in a restart loop or dying unexpectedly, this is usually where the clues live. Look for stack traces, out-of-memory errors, connection timeouts... anything that shows the container wasn't ready for prime time. And don't just read the last few lines. Scroll back and look at the full start and shutdown cycle. You're looking for patterns, not just surface noise.

For a more granular view of what the system is doing, `docker events` is your go-to. It gives you a live timeline of what's happening to that container – starts, stops, failures, health checks going sideways, the works:

```
docker events --filter container=my-api-service
```

```
2025-07-16T09:12:01.712443000Z container start  5d1f3a9b9c99 (image=my-api:1.2.3, name=my-api-s
2025-07-16T09:12:15.842117000Z container die    5d1f3a9b9c99 (exitCode=137, image=my-api:1.2.3,
2025-07-16T09:12:16.003944000Z container restart 5d1f3a9b9c99 (image=my-api:1.2.3, name=my-api-
2025-07-16T09:12:30.126487000Z container die    5d1f3a9b9c99 (exitCode=137, image=my-api:1.2.3,
2025-07-16T09:12:30.291027000Z container restart 5d1f3a9b9c99 (image=my-api:1.2.3, name=my-api-
```

Figure 8.34: The docker events output showing a restart loop caused by repeated container crashes (exit code 137)

This is really useful when you're trying to figure out whether something is crashing on its own or being killed off by the platform.

Now, pair that with exit codes. These can be surprisingly telling. For instance, if your container's dying with exit code 137, that's a SIGKILL, almost always memory exhaustion. Exit code 1? Usually, a failure in your entrypoint script or a runtime-level crash:

```
docker inspect my-api-service --format='{{.State.ExitCode}}'
```

Figure 8.35: Checking a container's exit code to identify why the service stopped or restarted

Getting comfortable reading these signals saves time and guesswork. You don't want to be rebooting things blindly in production. Know what your containers are trying to tell you. Here's a simple decision flow you can use when a container keeps restarting or failing, helping you narrow down the root cause quickly without jumping between tools:

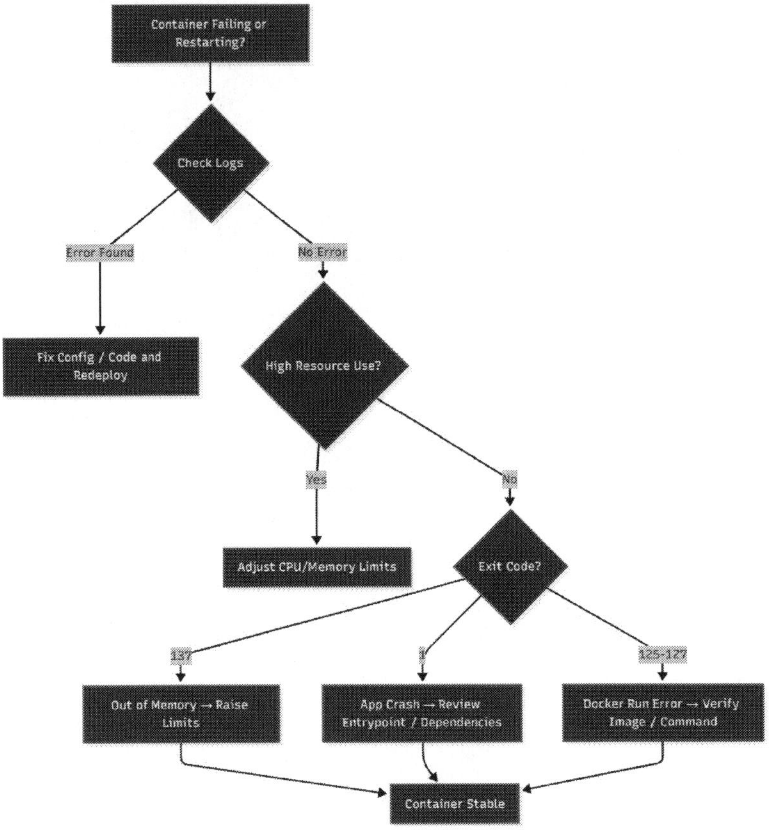

Figure 8.36: Quick troubleshooting decision flow for diagnosing container failures

In our Finance Dashboard, the first clue came from the logs. One replica showed repeated IIS restarts while others stayed healthy, a telltale sign of a configuration drift between nodes. This was exactly what happened to one of the Finance Dashboard services during a patch rollout, also why I kinda love this example. The health check misfired, Docker thought the container was failing, and a restart loop began. Understanding how to spot these early is what keeps a small issue from becoming a full outage.

One scenario worth calling out in a bit more detail is the restart loop, because it tends to escalate quickly and take other services down with it.

You'll spot the pattern in `docker ps`: the uptime never climbs past a few seconds, and the restart count starts ticking up like a broken metronome.

If you've got `restart: always` or a Swarm restart policy in play, Docker's going to keep doing what it's told, bringing the container back online over and over, no questions asked. This is great when it works, and an absolute nightmare when it doesn't.

The fix isn't to restart again and hope for the best. It's to work out why it's crashing in the first place. If the logs or exit codes point to memory pressure, then either reduce the workload or bump the container's memory limits. If it's a misconfigured environment variable, override it and redeploy clean. And if the app's just not ready to serve traffic on boot, you might need to build in a restart delay or bake in a proper health check so Docker knows to wait before routing requests.

Here are some common container exit codes and what they mean:

Exit code	Meaning	Typical cause	What to check next
`0`	Clean exit	Application shut down normally	Expected behavior
`1`	General error	App startup failure, bad config	Logs, entry point, environment variables
`125`	Docker error	Invalid run parameters	Docker command, flags
`126`	Command not executable	Permission or binary issue	`ENTRYPOINT` / `CMD`
`127`	Command not found	Missing binary or path	Image contents
`137`	Killed (SIGKILL)	Out of memory	Memory limits, `docker stats`, WSL configuration
`143`	Graceful stop (SIGTERM)	Container stopped or redeployed	Normal during updates

Table 8.1: Common container exit codes

Exit codes are often the fastest way to narrow the problem space during an incident. If you recognize the code, you can usually skip straight to the right subsystem.

During those heavy reporting runs, the Finance Dashboard's backend containers routinely hit memory ceilings. Adjusting per-service limits and monitoring with `docker stats` helped pinpoint the exact threshold before the system started swapping.

This is one of those scenarios where acting fast helps, but acting smart keeps it from happening again.

When resource pressure triggers failures

Another common failure pattern you'll see during troubleshooting is silent resource exhaustion. A container doesn't crash immediately; it just slows down the entire node until health checks fail or requests start timing out. When that happens, you're not dealing with best practice tuning; you're diagnosing a live incident caused by CPU or memory pressure.

That's why setting CPU and memory limits isn't just best practice, it's survival. In your Compose or Swarm service definitions, box things in properly:

```
services:
  heavy-worker:
    image: analytics-job:latest
    deploy:
      resources:
        limits:
          cpus: '2'
          memory: 2G
```

Figure 8.37: Resource-limited service configuration setting CPU and memory caps for a heavy processing container

That stops a runaway job from starving the rest of the system. It also makes behavior more predictable, which is what you want when you've got multiple teams deploying into shared infrastructure. On Windows, it's worth paying attention to WSL 2's memory and swap setup. If things get tight, WSL starts swapping to disk, and performance falls off a cliff. You're not just dealing with slow containers; you're in full-on I/O bottleneck territory.

You can spot memory pressure with `docker stats`, or by digging into `/proc/meminfo` inside your containers if you need the finer detail. Either way, it's better to catch it early than to find out during a 2 a.m. postmortem. Another common culprit in the Finance Dashboard environment was misconfigured internal networking between the web tier and the loan database API. When one overlay network desynced after a node restart, half the replicas went dark even though they appeared healthy.

When networking problems cause outages

Earlier in the chapter, we looked at how Docker networking is structured, but during an outage, the symptoms look very different. A service can appear healthy yet still fail to receive or route traffic correctly, leading to dropped requests, slow responses, or random `502` errors.

When that happens, you're not designing networks, you're diagnosing one that's misbehaving. You start seeing dropped requests, timeouts that stretch forever, or random `502` errors that make no sense on paper. First thing I always do is sanity-check the network setup:

```
docker network ls
docker network inspect <network-name>
```

Look out for services that aren't hooked into the right network, or ones that have accidentally ended up in isolation. It's easy to miss, especially when you're using Swarm overlays or Compose-based bridges. I've seen overlays get flaky after node failures, and I've seen Compose fall apart when someone restarts containers in the wrong order.

Network outage checklist (Swarm/Compose)

When a service looks healthy, but traffic is failing, work through this in order:

1. Inspect the network:

   ```
   docker network inspect <network-name>
   ```

   Confirm that services are attached to the expected network and not isolated.

2. Verify in-container DNS resolution:

   ```
   docker exec -it <container> nslookup api
   ```

   If DNS fails, suspect overlay or service discovery issues.

3. Check the Swarm endpoint mode:

   ```
   docker service inspect <service-name> --format
   '{{.Spec.EndpointSpec.Mode}}'
   ```

   Ensure services using the routing mesh are running in `vip` mode unless you explicitly require `dnsrr` (DNS round-robin).

4. Test service connectivity directly:

```
docker exec -it web curl http://api:8080/health
```

   This bypasses ingress and load balancing to isolate the problem.

5. Recreate overlays only after draining. If an overlay network is corrupted, run the following:

```
docker node update --availability drain <node-name>
```

   Drain traffic first, then safely remove and recreate the network.

If things still aren't talking, you can always drop into the container and try pinging or curling the other service directly:

```
docker exec -it web curl http://api:8080/health
```

If that fails, it's probably a DNS issue or a misconfigured overlay. In a pinch, restarting the Docker daemon or tearing down and rebuilding the network can clear things up, but don't do that in prod without draining traffic first. Been there. Not fun.

The trick is to assume nothing, double-check everything, and work step by step. Most Docker networking problems aren't subtle; they're just buried under a few layers of abstraction.

When to rebuild versus restart

It's a classic question: do I just bounce the container, or is this a deeper issue that needs a fresh image? Bit of a judgment call, but here's how I usually think about it:

- **Restart** when the container's acting up, but you're confident the image itself is solid. Maybe the app just needs a nudge.
- **Rebuild** if the image uses something such as `latest` or pulls in dynamic dependencies. Something upstream might've shifted without warning.
- **Restart the service** if you've changed environment variables, config values, or secrets and need the new settings to take effect cleanly.

Here's a quick rebuild versus restart decision guide:

Situation	Action	Why
Container is misbehaving but image is known good	Restart container	Fastest recovery, no artifact change

Situation	Action	Why
Environment variables or secrets changed	Restart service	New config is injected at runtime
Base image tag or digest changed	Rebuild image	SBOM and dependency chain have changed
SBOM differs from last known good build	Rebuild image	Dependency drift needs a clean artifact
Image built with `latest` or dynamic dependencies	Rebuild image	Upstream changes may have introduced breakage
Only application code changed	Rebuild image	New artifact required
Unsure what version is running	Inspect image labels, then decide	Verify before acting

Table 8.2: Rebuild versus restart decision guide

When in doubt, trust the artifact chain. If the base image or SBOM has changed, rebuild. If only the runtime configuration changed, restart.

A neat little habit is to bake a timestamp into each image build, such as a label or `ENV BUILD_TIME`, so you can confirm what version is running where. Trust, but verify.

Making failures easier to support

When you're dealing with a big Docker setup (multiple teams, environments, and moving parts), things will go wrong. That's just the nature of it. But what really matters is how quickly you can respond and recover when they do.

That's why I always recommend putting together some sort of lightweight playbook for the most common failure scenarios. Nothing fancy, just a few solid checklists for things such as the following:

- What to check first when memory starts spiking
- How to safely restart a service without disrupting everything
- Where logs live for each type of workload (especially if you've got a mix of Compose and Swarm)
- When to escalate to infrastructure, and when to just roll back and move on

This doesn't need to be a 30-page PDF locked in SharePoint. Even a Markdown file in your repo or a short page in the internal wiki can make a massive difference when someone's bleary-eyed at 3 a.m. trying to figure out why the API is flapping again.

Troubleshooting Docker at enterprise scale is really all about pattern recognition and practice. Read the logs early, know your exit codes, watch for flapping containers and memory pressure, and above all, get familiar with how your environment behaves when it's healthy.

The Big Lab: Running the Notes service across machines

Up to now, everything you've built has lived on one machine. That's perfect for learning, but it hides a real-world fact: stacks rarely stay on localhost.

In this part of the Big Lab, you'll move the Notes stack into a multi-host setup. You'll build and tag your images, push them to a registry, pull them from a second machine (or VM, I'm not precious), and deploy the same stack using a remote Docker context. The point isn't "production," it's proving your workflow works when the host changes.

By the end, you will be able to run the Notes stack locally, then point Docker at another machine and deploy the same stack there with a single command. Before we get started, let's go over what you'll need:

- Your existing Notes app/project from the earlier Big Labs.
- A Docker Hub account (or a private registry you can push to).
- A second host you can reach over the network. This can be a Linux VM, a spare PC, or a cloud VM, but honestly, Linux is easiest.
- SSH access to that second host (I'd recommend this one personally)

With everything in place, begin by following these steps to prepare your stack for multi-host deployment:

1. **Prepare your images for a registry**: Right now, your Compose file builds locally. For multi-host, you want images that can be pulled anywhere.
   From the `notes-app` folder, confirm that you can build cleanly:

   ```
   docker compose build
   ```

   Now, decide on your Docker Hub namespace. I'd use `DOCKERHUB_USER=yourname`.

   You'll tag images like this:

   - `yourname/notes-api:8.0`

  - `yourname/notes-frontend:8.0`
  - `yourname/notes-genai-summariser:8.0`

  Build and tag each image:

```
docker build -t yourname/notes-api:8.0 ./api
docker build -t yourname/notes-frontend:8.0 ./frontend
docker build -t yourname/notes-genai-summariser:8.0 ./genai-summariser
```

2. **Log in to Docker Hub and push**:

```
docker login
```

   Push the images:

```
docker push yourname/notes-api:8.0
docker push yourname/notes-frontend:8.0
docker push yourname/notes-genai-summariser:8.0
```

   If this is a private repo, that's fine. The remote host just needs permission to pull.

3. **Create a remote-ready Compose file**: You're going to make a "remote" Compose file that uses `image:` instead of `build:`. This avoids requiring the second machine to have your source code. Now, because you're using a Docker context, the Docker CLI on your machine is still the thing you type into, but every `docker` and `docker compose` command is executed against the remote Docker Engine on the other host, so the containers actually run over there, not on your laptop.
   Create a new file in `notes-app/`:

```
compose.remote.yaml
```

   Put this in it:

```
services:
  api:
    image: yourname/notes-api:8.0
    ports:
      - "5001:5000"
    env_file:
      - api.secrets
    environment:
```

```
      - GENAI_URL=http://genai-gateway/summarise
    volumes:
      - notes-data:/data
    networks:
      - app-net
      - api-private

  frontend:
    image: yourname/notes-frontend:8.0
    ports:
      - "8080:80"
    networks:
      - app-net
    read_only: true

  genai-a:
    image: yourname/notes-genai-summariser:8.0
    networks:
      - api-private
      - app-net

  genai-b:
    image: yourname/notes-genai-summariser:8.0
    networks:
      - api-private
      - app-net

  genai-gateway:
    image: nginx:alpine
    container_name: notes-genai-gateway
    volumes:
      - ./nginx-genai/nginx.conf:/etc/nginx/conf.d/default.conf:ro
    ports:
      - "5002:80"
    depends_on:
      - genai-a
      - genai-b
    networks:
      - app-net

volumes:
```

```
    notes-data:

  networks:
    app-net:
    api-private:
```

Key changes here are as follows:

- Everything uses `image:` not `build:`
- Data uses a named volume (`notes-data`) instead of `C:\notes-data`, so it works cross-platform

4. **Set up the second host**: On the second machine (or VM), you need Docker installed and running.
   Confirm it is reachable and Docker is working on that host by SSHing in and running:

```
docker version
docker ps
```

   Also, watch out for firewalls. Ensure that the firewall allows inbound access for the ports you want to test:

   - `8080` for the frontend
   - `5001` for the API
   - Optionally, `5002` for the GenAI gateway

   If this host is remote, open only what you need.

5. **Create a remote Docker context**: Back on your Windows machine, you're going to create a Docker context that points at the second host.
   If you can SSH to the host, this is the cleanest approach. Replace the following values:

   - `user` with your SSH username
   - `remote-host` with the hostname or IP

   Create the context:

```
docker context create notes-remote --docker "host=ssh://user@remote-host"
```

   Switch to it:

```
docker context use notes-remote
```

Confirm that Docker is now talking to the other machine:

```
docker ps
docker info
```

If `docker info` shows the remote host details, you're connected.

6. **Deploy the stack to the remote host**: Your Docker client is still on Windows, but the containers will run on the remote host.
   From your `notes-app` folder, deploy using the remote Compose file:

```
docker compose -f compose.remote.yaml up -d
```

   Now, check that the services are running on the remote machine:

```
docker compose -f compose.remote.yaml ps
```

7. **Validate end-to-end from your local machine**: From your Windows machine, hit the remote host over the network. Replace `remote-host` with the IP or hostname:
   Use this for the API:

```
curl http://remote-host:5001/notes
```

   Use this for the frontend (in a browser):

```
http://remote-host:8080
```

   Use this for the GenAI summary endpoint:

```
curl http://remote-host:5001/notes/summary
```

   If you already seeded notes earlier, you should see output immediately. If not, add one note with the API key header you created in the security Big Lab from *Chapter 5*.

8. **Prove portability by switching contexts**: This is the real lesson of this chapter; the workflow stays the same, but the target host changes.
   Switch back to your local Docker context:

```
docker context use default
```

Confirm that it is local again:

```
docker info
```

Now, you can run the local stack as before and deploy the remote stack when you need to, without changing the project, only the context and Compose file.

9. **Clean up the remote deployment**: When you're done, bring the remote stack down. Switch back to the remote context:

```
docker context use notes-remote
```

Then:

```
docker compose -f compose.remote.yaml down
```

If you want to remove the remote volume too, use the following:

```
docker compose -f compose.remote.yaml down -v
```

So, your stack now runs across machines. Next time, we'll bring it into enterprise territory.

Summary

Troubleshooting Docker at enterprise scale is really about pattern recognition and practice. Read the logs early, know your exit codes, watch for flapping containers and memory pressure, and get familiar with how your environment behaves when it's healthy. Most production incidents don't come out of nowhere; the signals are there long before anything actually breaks.

But none of this happens in isolation. Everything we've covered in this chapter, from containerizing legacy applications to scaling with Swarm, setting up clean load balancing, managing nodes and networks, and keeping your infrastructure organized, feeds directly into how recoverable your systems are when things go wrong. The point of building predictable, resilient foundations is that when production starts wobbling, you've already given yourself the space to respond intelligently rather than reactively.

That's the real mark of running Docker at enterprise scale on Windows: you're not just fixing issues, you're making sure they don't come back in the same shape twice. Solid patterns reinforce themselves over time, and every improvement you make to deployment, scaling, or observability strengthens your ability to support live systems under pressure.

In the next chapter, we will take these foundations into hybrid cloud environments. You'll see how Docker behaves when your workloads span on-premises and cloud platforms, how to integrate services across boundaries, and what new challenges appear when your infrastructure is no longer running in a single place.

Join us on Discord

For discussions around the book and to connect with your peers, join us on Discord at or scan the QR code below:

9

Docker and Hybrid Cloud Integration

I still remember my first hybrid cloud project. I thought it was going to be the worst of both worlds if I'm honest: on-prem headaches mixed with cloud unknowns. It felt like a recipe for late nights and early regrets. Then Docker showed up and changed the conversation completely. Once we wrapped the workload inside a container, it stopped caring whether it ran in a dusty server rack in the back of the office or on a shiny public cloud node. That was the moment hybrid went from terrifying to manageable.

This chapter is about why Docker can be the bridge that makes hybrid cloud work without feeling like a house of cards. We'll look at what hybrid cloud actually means in practice, where Docker fits in, patterns you can lean on, and the kind of lessons that usually come from someone else's pain.

By the end, you'll understand how Docker can smooth the rough edges of hybrid environments, and you'll have practical steps for integrating containers across on-prem and cloud platforms.

We'll be covering the following main topics:

- What do we mean by hybrid cloud?
- Managing multi-cloud deployments with Docker
- Securing data in hybrid cloud workflows
- Orchestrating hybrid cloud applications with Docker
- Best practices for Docker in hybrid clouds

Right, let's crack on then!

Technical requirements

The code files referenced in this chapter are available at `https://github.com/PacktPublishing/Mastering-Docker-on-Windows`.

What do we mean by hybrid cloud?

Stripped back, hybrid cloud just means you're running workloads across more than one environment. Usually, it's a mix of public cloud and private infrastructure. That private bit could be a big shiny data center or a few tired boxes humming away under someone's desk – we've all been there. Either way, the principle is the same: some workloads live on-prem, others in the cloud, and often the same application spans both.

Why would anyone do this, though? Well, sometimes you don't have a choice. Compliance might require sensitive data to stay on-site. Legacy systems might be welded to the hardware they came with. Mergers often leave companies with two or three different hosting setups, and nobody's ready for a full rebuild.

Other times it can be strategic. Maybe you want to keep core systems in-house but burst into the cloud for peak demand. Or, you're spreading risk across providers. Or, you just want to take a slow, low-risk path to modernization instead of a "big-bang" migration.

The big headache in all of this is consistency. You want your app to behave the same way whether it's on a rack in the basement or running in a managed service halfway across the globe. Containers can give you that. They package up your app, its dependencies, and runtime environment into one neat, portable unit. That means fewer surprises and much smoother movement between environments.

How Docker shapes hybrid cloud architecture

Hybrid environments only become manageable when you have a consistent way to package and run workloads, and Docker gives you exactly that. Containers flatten the differences between clouds, reduce the friction of moving workloads, and make the runtime predictable no matter where the application ends up. Once you understand this foundation, the rest of the hybrid story starts to fall into place.

Docker doesn't just help with packaging, though. It solves three of the nastiest problems in hybrid setups: portability, consistency, and isolation.

- **Portability**: Build once, run anywhere. Your app doesn't care if it's running on-prem, in Azure, or on AWS, because the container abstracts the messy bits of the host.

- **Consistency**: No more "works on my machine" moments. Hello, software testers! Whether you run locally, in a dev cluster, or in the cloud, the environment is predictable.
- **Isolation**: Containers keep things neat. Services live in their own boxes, which matters when you're mixing platforms and teams.

You'll still want to take advantage of native cloud services where they make sense. But Docker stops vendor lock-in from becoming a nightmare, and it gives you one format for everything.

Here are some of the most common scenarios where Docker can make life easier:

- **Cloud bursting for peak load**: You've got a workload that mostly lives on-prem, but every now and then, traffic spikes. End-of-month reporting, seasonal surges – you know the drill. With Docker, you package the workload once, then spin up containers in the cloud when you need extra capacity. No rewrites, no guesswork.
- **CI/CD across boundaries**: Your CI/CD pipeline might build and test in the cloud but deploy to an on-prem environment. Docker images are perfect for this. They're versioned, portable, and easy to push between registries. Tools such as Jenkins, GitHub Actions, and Azure DevOps all play nicely with Docker, so your pipeline doesn't care where the final deployment lands.
- **Local dev, remote deploy**: This is a personal favourite, gotta be honest. Developers build and test on their Windows machines using Docker Desktop and WSL 2, then deploy those exact same containers to a cloud-hosted cluster. You get speed and confidence without racking up cloud bills during development.
- **Gradual cloud migration**: Hybrid is often just a stage in the journey. You containerize apps now and keep them running on-prem while planning a move to a managed service such as **Azure Kubernetes Service** (**AKS**) later. Containers turn a painful, big-bang migration into a series of small, low-risk steps.

All of these patterns only work if you have reliable plumbing underneath them. Containers need a consistent place to live, a consistent way to move between environments, and a consistent method for talking to each other across cloud boundaries. That's where registries and networking come in, because they become the connective tissue that keeps a hybrid setup coherent rather than chaotic.

When your environments are split, a central registry becomes your absolute best friend. Push your images to **Azure Container Registry**, **Amazon ECR**, or a neutral hub such as **Docker Hub**, and you've got one source of truth for deployments. You can even mirror images internally for compliance or performance reasons.

Networking is trickier. Containers need to talk to each other, whether they're on-prem or in the cloud. For simple setups, a VPN or private link is enough. For more complex cases, you might need something such as Azure ExpressRoute or AWS Direct Connect to keep latency low and security tight.

Here are a few habits that might save you headaches later – think of this as a cheatsheet:

- **Pin your base images**: Don't rely on `latest`, ever! We've talked about this in the book already. You want predictable builds, not surprises.
- **Centralize secrets**: Never bake them into images. Use tools such as Docker secrets, Azure Key Vault, or AWS Secrets Manager.
- **Plan for latency**: Don't assume cloud-hosted services respond like local ones. Design with retries and timeouts in mind.
- **Monitor both sides**: Logging and metrics should flow into one place, so you see the whole picture, not half the story.

Here's where things get really interesting. Major cloud providers treat containers as first-class citizens, which makes hybrid integration smooth if you stick to a few principles.

Build your images locally or in CI. Push them to a registry, Azure Container Registry, Amazon ECR, or Docker Hub. From there, you can deploy the same image to an on-prem Docker Swarm, a cloud-based Kubernetes cluster, or a managed service such as Azure Container Instances or AWS ECS.

The workflow barely changes across environments. That's the real value here. You're not writing special scripts for each platform or dealing with vendor-specific quirks. Docker becomes the common language that everything speaks. Your CI/CD pipeline looks the same. Your build artifacts are the same. And when you decide to move a service from on-prem to the cloud, it's a redeploy, not a rebuild.

Hybrid cloud isn't going away. If anything, it's becoming the default for enterprise environments. The trick is making it feel less like juggling and more like orchestration. Docker gives you that layer of consistency that makes hybrid sane. Build once, run anywhere. Integrate with your cloud platform of choice. And keep your eyes open for those small details: registries, secrets, and networking that make or break a deployment. Before we expand the same concepts in *The Big Lab* later, we're going to anchor this chapter with a much smaller example. This lightweight service lets us show the hybrid flow clearly, without dragging in the full complexity of the Big Lab stack.

A practical hybrid lab scenario: One service, two clouds, one deployment workflow

Before we get any deeper into patterns and orchestration, it's probably worth grounding everything in a simple example that we can keep coming back to throughout the chapter. Hybrid cloud makes a lot more sense when you can picture something real running across two platforms rather than imagining a set of abstract diagrams. So, let's build a tiny .NET service, containerize it once, push it to both AWS and Azure, and then deploy it across a small Docker Swarm that stretches between the two.

It's a super light example but it covers the core workflow that almost every hybrid setup relies on. Build once. Push everywhere. Deploy consistently. Plus, I do love giving people working examples of code to demonstrate their learning.

1. We will keep the service deliberately small, so the focus stays on the hybrid flow rather than the application. It is a simple .NET 6 API in a folder called `HybridApi`. Once you have run `dotnet publish`, the Dockerfile looks like this:

```
FROM mcr.microsoft.com/dotnet/aspnet:6.0 AS base
WORKDIR /app
COPY ./publish .
ENTRYPOINT ["dotnet", "HybridApi.dll"]
```

2. Next, build the image:

```
dotnet publish -c Release -o publish
docker build -t hybrid-api:1.0.0 .
```

This gives you a single image that we will promote to multiple registries.

3. Hybrid environments almost always involve more than one registry. AWS has Elastic Container Registry; Azure has Azure Container Registry. The image does not change between them. All you do is add new tags.
    - Tag for AWS:

    ```
    docker tag hybrid-api:1.0.0 \
    123456789012.dkr.ecr.eu-west-1.amazonaws.com/hybrid-api:1.0.0
    ```

    - Tag for Azure:

    ```
    docker tag hybrid-api:1.0.0 \
    myregistry.azurecr.io/hybrid-api:1.0.0
    ```

4. Push both copies:

```
docker push 123456789012.dkr.ecr.eu-west-1.amazonaws.com/hybrid-api:1.0.0
docker push myregistry.azurecr.io/hybrid-api:1.0.0
```

One build. Two tags. Two pushes. You end up with a consistent artifact in both clouds, and we will rely on this pattern repeatedly as we move through the chapter.

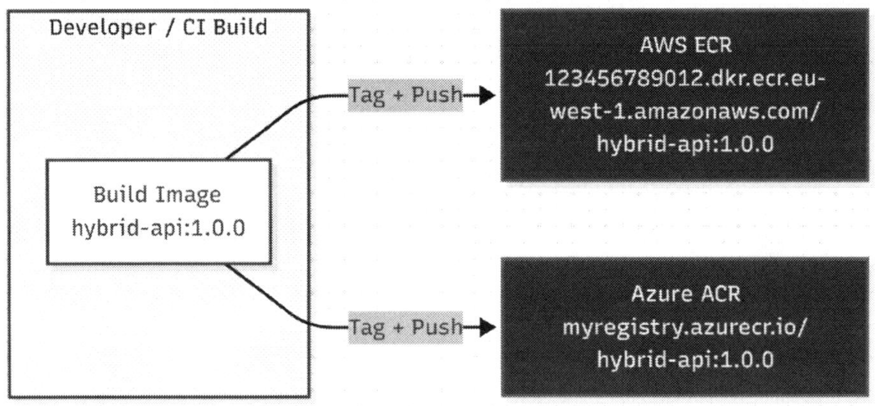

Figure 9.1: A single Docker image built once and pushed to both AWS ECR and Azure ACR for use across hybrid deployments

Now we need somewhere to run the service. The simplest orchestration setup for a hybrid demonstration is a two-node Docker Swarm cluster: one node in AWS acting as the manager and one node in Azure acting as a worker. As long as the nodes can communicate over the necessary ports, Swarm does not care where they live.

5. Initialize Swarm on the AWS node:

```
docker swarm init --advertise-addr <aws-private-ip>
```

6. This prints a `join` command. Run that on the Azure node:

```
docker swarm join --token <token> <aws-private-ip>:2377
```

   At this point, you've created a functional hybrid cluster. Both nodes share the same control plane even though they live in different cloud providers.

7. Services need a way to communicate securely between clouds. An encrypted overlay network is a clean way to handle this.

```
docker network create \
  --driver overlay \
  --opt encrypted \
  hybrid-net
```

   Swarm takes care of the encryption using IPsec under the hood. This is one of those small steps that saves a lot of pain later, especially when you start running workloads that need to talk across the cloud boundary.

8. Now we can deploy our container.

```
docker service create \
  --name hybrid-api \
  --replicas 2 \
  --network hybrid-net \
  -p 8080:80 \
  myregistry.azurecr.io/hybrid-api:1.0.0
```

   Swarm automatically places replicas across the available nodes. One might land on AWS, the other on Azure. Traffic coming into either cloud flows across the routing mesh to whichever replica is healthy.

If hybrid cloud is all about blending environments, multi-cloud is about juggling providers. The principles overlap, but the challenges shift, so let's look at what changes when you're dealing with more than one public cloud at the same time.

Managing multi-cloud deployments with Docker

I'll be honest, the first time someone said "we're going multi-cloud," my stomach sank a little. AWS was already enough to keep us busy, then Azure landed on the table, and somewhere along the line, a data science team quietly added Google Cloud into the mix. It felt like juggling three spinning plates while riding a unicycle. Technically possible, but definitely not my idea of a good time.

Then we leaned on Docker properly, and everything changed. Suddenly, "build once, run anywhere" wasn't a marketing line; it was the thing keeping us sane. Containers became the common thread between three very different platforms, and the whole mess started to feel manageable.

Now, the term "multi-cloud" gets thrown around a lot in strategy decks, like it's some magical end goal, but the reality is usually less glamorous. Stripped right back, it means running services across more than one public cloud. That might mean the following:

- AWS for production workloads
- Azure for dev and test environments
- GCP for data pipelines or AI models

Why would anyone do this to themselves, I hear you scream? A few reasons:

- **Compliance**: Some data needs to stay within specific regions or providers.
- **Vendor leverage**: Nobody likes being locked into a single supplier.
- **Mergers and acquisitions**: Suddenly, you've inherited someone else's stack.
- **Team choice**: Different teams picked their favourite clouds before the CIO started caring about standardization. It happens.

Whatever the reason, the headache is consistency. You want your apps to behave the same way everywhere, but each cloud has its own quirks, its own tooling, and its own learning curve. Docker gives you a way out of that mess. It packages your workload so that the runtime environment looks the same everywhere, whether it's Azure, AWS, or that Linux box under Gary's desk. Thanks, Gary.

Why Docker changes the game

Here's the big win: Docker lets you build once and run anywhere. Containers don't actually care if they're running on a VM in Azure or inside a Kubernetes Pod on AWS. If the host can run Docker (or containerd under the hood), your image just works. That gives you the following:

- **Portability**: The same image runs across all environments

- **Consistency**: You eliminate the "works on AWS but not on GCP" gremlins
- **Fewer surprises**: You debug and test one container image, not three separate builds

This is the reason multi-cloud stops feeling like a nightmare when you do it with Docker. You've flattened the differences between platforms, at least for the runtime layer.

To keep things concrete, this is exactly the pattern you saw earlier, in the *HybridApi* lab. We built the image once on a Windows workstation, then promoted that same artefact to both AWS ECR and Azure ACR without rebuilding anything. The only differences were the tags. Everything else stayed identical because that is the whole point of multi-cloud Docker workflows. A single build, a single digest, and two registries holding the same container.

When you are working across clouds, this consistency is what keeps your deployments predictable. The moment you start rebuilding images per cloud, you introduce drift. You end up chasing silly environment-specific bugs or trying to explain why the Azure version behaves differently from the AWS version. The *HybridApi* example avoids all of that by treating the image as the source of truth and keeping cloud differences outside the container.

I'm going to keep talking about this example as we go because the pattern never really changes. Build once. Promote everywhere. Configure at runtime. That is the backbone of multi-cloud Docker practice, whether you are juggling two clouds or five.

Handling config differences

Here's the bit Docker doesn't do for you: configuration. An app running in Azure might need different DNS endpoints or database credentials than the same app in AWS. Hardcoding those differences into the image? Really bad idea. The fix is to keep your containers generic and make the environments smart. Here are a few strategies that work for this:

- **Environment variables**: Fast and portable, but don't put secrets here in plain text.
- **Secrets managers**: Use AWS Secrets Manager, Azure Key Vault, or HashiCorp Vault.
- **Compose overrides**: Keep a base `docker-compose.yml` and layer on overrides for each environment.
- **Orchestration settings**: Kubernetes ConfigMaps and Secrets are your friends here.

Here's an example of Compose overrides using Compose:

```yaml
#docker-compose.yml
version: "3.9"
services:
  web:
    image: myapp:latest
    ports:
      - "80:80"
    environment:
      - ENVIRONMENT=production

```

Figure 9.2: Basic Docker Compose file deploying a web service

When you want to adjust settings for a specific environment without touching the base file, you add a Compose override like this one.

```yaml
#docker-compose.override.yml
version: "3.9"
services:
  web:
    environment:
      - ENVIRONMENT=development




```

Figure 9.3: Docker Compose override file replacing environment settings for local development

Essentially, the base file defines your default (production) configuration, while the override file injects development-specific settings without touching the original file. Docker Compose automatically applies both files when you run the following:

```
docker-compose up
```

The override replaces only the keys you specify, so the image and ports stay the same, but the `ENVIRONMENT` variable flips to development.

This approach works especially well in multi-cloud and multi-environment setups because it keeps the container image identical everywhere. You change behavior through configuration rather than rebuilding the whole image, which removes a whole category of drift and makes your deployments way more predictable. Once your image is stable, the next question becomes where that image should live, because registry choices have a direct impact on how easily you can move the same artifact across AWS, Azure, or GCP.

Should you pick one or use them all? My favourite answer is "it depends." Using each cloud's native registry reduces latency and avoids weird IAM issues. But for internal teams, mirroring everything in one central registry can simplify pipelines. Whichever you choose, automate the process in CI/CD so images get tagged and pushed everywhere in one go. Here's a simple visual showing how a single CI/CD pipeline can build once, sign the image, and promote it to multiple registries before deploying across different clouds.

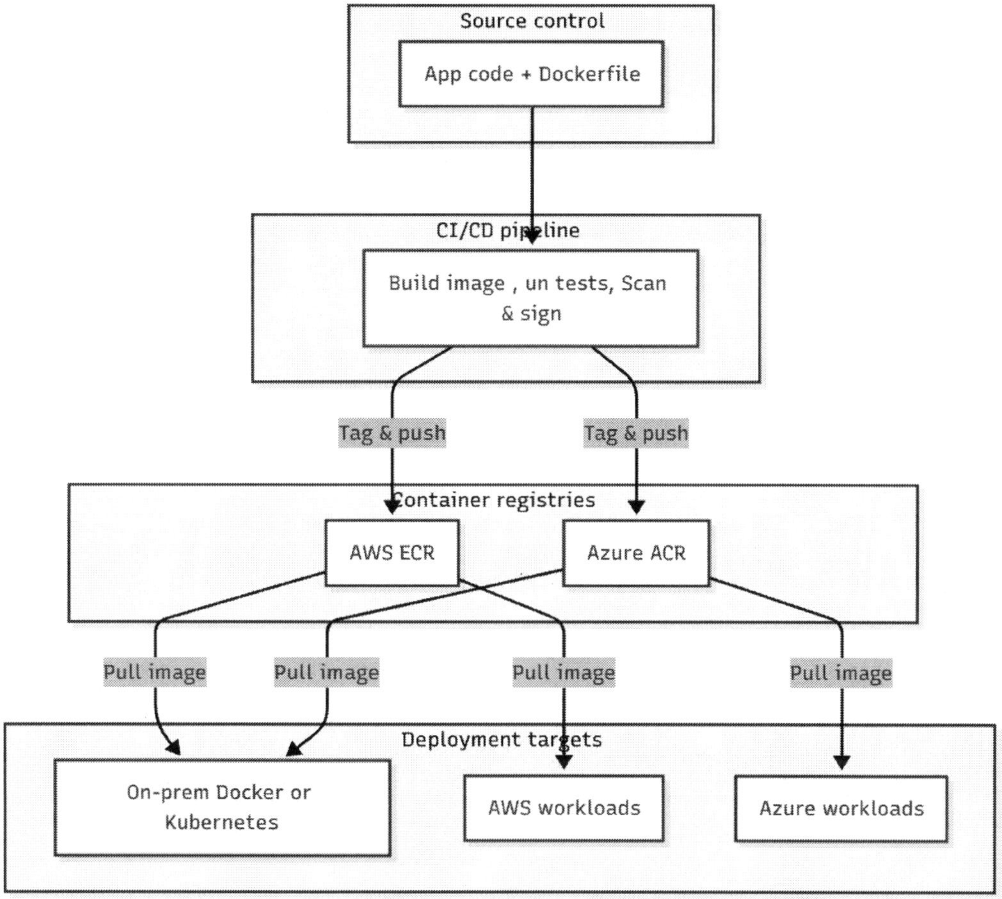

Figure 9.4: CI/CD pipeline that builds once, signs the image, and pushes to AWS and Azure in the same workflow

Avoiding common misconfigurations in multi-cloud deployments

Multi-cloud means more credentials to manage and more places for things to potentially go wrong. Now, I know we've gone over a lot of security stuff in this book already, but let's just go back over the super-basics:

- As I've mentioned, never bake secrets into images. Ever.
- Use Docker login with credential helpers for each cloud.
- Automate secret injection using your orchestrator or a vault service.
- Rotate keys regularly and scope them tightly.

For enterprise environments, consider signing your images with Docker Content Trust or Cosign. This lets you verify the integrity of images before they're deployed, which is a lifesaver for compliance-heavy industries. Hello GRC companies!

Here's an additional list of some super common pitfalls and how to dodge them:

- **Using latest tags everywhere**: I know, I keep going on about this, but it's so easy to get wrong as soon as you start getting confident with Docker. It's so tempting, I know. Slap `:latest` on your image and move on. The problem? That tag will shift under your feet without warning. One day, a new base image lands, and suddenly half your CI jobs start failing for reasons that make no sense. Always pin your versions. Be explicit, and when it's time to upgrade, do it deliberately with proper testing.
- **Rebuilding images for every environment**: This is a classic anti-pattern. If you're building a new image for dev, staging, and prod, you're asking for trouble. It's slow, inconsistent, and you lose traceability. Build the image once, verify it, then promote it through your environments by tagging it. That way, you know the thing you tested is the same thing you're shipping.
- **Hardcoding environment settings**: Nothing makes an image harder to maintain than baking config straight into it. The moment you need to tweak an API endpoint or rotate a secret, you're rebuilding and redeploying for no good reason. Keep your images clean and generic. Inject config at runtime with environment variables, overrides, or secrets managers. Your future self will thank you.
- **Forgetting IAM differences**: Every cloud has its own flavor of identity and access control. AWS IAM roles, Azure Managed Identities, GCP service accounts; they're all slightly different. If you leave this until the last minute, you'll be knee-deep in denied requests when you should be deploying. Plan your auth story early, script it where you

can, and keep credentials out of your containers. Seriously, never bake secrets into an image.

You see, multi-cloud sounds intimidating, but Docker gives you a way to make it manageable. You build one image, test it once, and deploy it anywhere. The trick is to keep your images generic, automate tagging and pushing, and manage config smartly at runtime. So, whether you're balancing AWS and Azure for compliance or using GCP for those fancy machine learning workloads, Docker helps you sidestep the worst of the complexity. You don't need to reinvent your process for every platform. Build once, configure cleanly, and deploy with confidence. That covers how to run the same workload across different clouds. Now we need to look at something far more fragile: what happens to your data when those environments start talking to each other.

Where hybrid cloud data workflows break and how Docker helps

If there's one thing that'll keep enterprise teams awake at night, it's the thought of sensitive data slipping through the cracks. Hybrid cloud setups, for all their flexibility, actually make this harder. You're juggling workloads across on-prem servers, public cloud clusters, and maybe a few rogue VMs someone spun up without telling you. The attack surface just multiplied, and so did the complexity.

To understand how Docker helps secure data in hybrid environments, it's more useful to start with how things usually break. Hybrid cloud failures are rarely exotic. They tend to come from the same small set of mistakes repeated across secrets, networking, and storage. The following sections walk through those failure modes and show how Docker reduces the risk of each one.

On a single cloud, security feels (relatively) tidy. You've got one IAM model, one set of networking controls, and one place to store secrets. Hybrid clouds blow that up. Now you're dealing with the following:

- Multiple IAM systems that don't talk to each other out of the box
- Different storage backends, some local, some cloud-based
- Data moving across networks you don't fully control
- Mixed compliance requirements for sensitive data

Docker sits right in the middle of all this. It abstracts the application layer, which is good, but it also means you need to be deliberate about how containers handle secrets, volumes, and traffic. If your security model is "we'll figure it out later," you're one leaked API key away from a very, very bad day.

Docker won't solve every security problem for you, but it does give you a strong foundation to build on.

To make this concrete, imagine a small notes service that stores user-generated text. Part of it runs on-prem because the data must stay inside the controlled network (a favourite of the finance world, let me tell you), while the API layer runs in Azure to handle public traffic. The two components need to talk to each other, but the data itself is sensitive enough that any misstep leaves you in hot water.

Hybrid data flows tend to fail in a few predictable ways, mainly around secrets, networking, and storage. Here are the most common failure modes, followed by the Docker mechanisms that are typically used to contain or mitigate them.

- **Failure mode: credentials baked into images. Mitigation: secrets stay out of the image**: In hybrid environments, this usually happens when teams hardcode database passwords or API keys into images so they can "just make it work" across clouds. The API needs credentials for the on-prem database, but those credentials are injected at runtime as Docker secrets rather than being hardcoded into the image. The container sees them only in-memory and never in the image layers, which prevents them from being leaked into registries or anywhere else.

```
echo "db-password-here" | docker secret create notes_db_password -
```

- **Failure mode: cross-cloud traffic sent unencrypted. Mitigation: encrypted overlay networks**: Without deliberate encryption, traffic between on-prem and cloud containers often traverses networks you don't fully control, exposing sensitive payloads in transit. The API container in Azure and the database connector on-prem run on an encrypted Docker overlay network. Everything crossing that boundary travels inside an AES-encrypted VXLAN tunnel managed by Docker, not by hand-rolled scripts or ad hoc VPN hacks.

```
docker network create \
  --driver overlay \
  --opt encrypted \
  notes-secure-net
```

- **Failure mode: sensitive data exposed via overly permissive mounts. Mitigation: scoped, named volumes with restricted access**: This typically shows up when host paths or shared mounts are reused across environments without tight access controls. The on-prem database uses a named volume with restricted permissions so only the database container can read or write to it. Nothing else on the host can touch it, and no accidental bind mounts leak sensitive data to the underlying OS.

```
volumes:
  notes_data:
    driver: local
```

- **Failure mode: sensitive data leaking through logs. Mitigation: deliberate log hygiene and centralized collection**: In hybrid setups, this risk is amplified because logs are often shipped across environments and retained long-term. The API logs only metadata. Full payloads are stripped before they even reach stdout, and logs are shipped over TLS to a central aggregator. This stops sensitive notes text from landing in plain text inside a cloud logging service.
- **Failure mode: long-lived credentials embedded in configs. Mitigation: platform-managed identities and scoped roles**: Hybrid deployments frequently fail here because each cloud has a different identity model, and teams fall back to static credentials. Azure uses a managed identity for outbound calls. On-prem uses a task role in Swarm. Neither environment stores long-lived tokens in the container or Compose files.

Taken together, this pattern shows a simple rule: the moment you split an application across clouds, your risks somewhat multiply. Docker won't remove those risks, but it gives you a clean, predictable structure so you can secure each link in the chain without improvising a hacky solution every time.

Best practices for securing data in hybrid clouds

Before you dive into Docker configs, sketch out how your data moves. Which services need access to customer PII? Which talk to databases on-prem versus in the cloud? Which workloads cross that boundary?

Why does this even matter? Because you can't protect what you don't understand. Data classification isn't glamorous, but it's the difference between locking down the crown jewels and wasting time encrypting the developer wiki, so get a digital whiteboard out or even some pens and pencils and start mapping out that flow.

Once you know the flow, you can apply Docker patterns with intent.

Use encrypted networks

Don't forget to use encrypted networks whenever you can. If your containers are talking across hybrid environments, don't simply trust the underlying network. Encrypt it.

Docker Swarm makes this a bit easier than most people realize. When you create an overlay network with the `--opt encrypted` flag, Docker automatically sets up AES encryption for traffic between containers on that network.

Why bother? Because that API request zipping between your Azure node and your on-prem node might pass through a network segment **you** don't control. Encrypted overlays mean even if someone sniffs packets, they won't see anything useful.

Don't let secrets leak into images

One of the most common mistakes I still see is teams hardcoding database credentials or API tokens straight into Dockerfiles. It's quick, it works, and it's an absolute nightmare for security. If that image ends up in a shared registry, congratulations, you've just published your secrets.

The fix? Keep secrets out of the image entirely. Docker has good built-in support for secrets when you're using Swarm, and it's really straightforward to set up:

```
echo "supersecurepassword" | docker secret create db_password -
```

This command creates a Docker secret called `db_password` with the value `supersecurepassword`. Then, this is the service definition:

```
services:
  db-client:
    image: myapp:latest
    secrets:
      - db_password
secrets:
  db_password:
    external: true

```

Figure 9.5: Using an external Docker secret to supply a database password to a client service

The container sees the secret as an in-memory file at runtime, never baked into the image. Rotate the secret, redeploy the service, and you're good.

If you're in Kubernetes, use ConfigMaps and Secrets instead. Same principle: inject at runtime, never hardcode.

Secure your volumes

Another good tip is securing your volumes. Hybrid workflows often involve shared storage, and that's a weak point if you don't lock it down. Whether you're mounting a cloud volume, using NFS, or sharing data through something such as Azure Files, make sure of the following:

- **At-rest encryption is enabled**: Most cloud providers offer this by default. But check it. Don't assume.
- **Access is scoped**: Only the containers that need the data should see the volume. Use `:ro` (read-only) mounts whenever possible.
- **Avoid host-path mounts**: Especially on Windows. They're tempting for quick setups, but they bypass a lot of isolation guarantees and can leak sensitive paths.

Here's an example using a named volume with read-only mode:

```
services:
  reports:
    image: reports-app:latest
    volumes:
      - secure-data:/data:ro
volumes:
  secure-data:
    driver: local
```

Figure 9.6: Mounting a read-only volume to protect sensitive data inside a container

Why does this matter? Because the fewer places your sensitive data touches, the smaller your blast radius when something goes wrong.

Watch your logs

Sadly, I've seen more than one breach traced back to logs. Developers love logging everything, including full payloads and environment variables. In hybrid setups, where logs often get shipped across networks, that's a massive risk. Here's what to do instead:

- Never log secrets or tokens. Strip them before they hit `stdout`.
- Use centralized logging over secure channels. TLS-enabled syslog, or a service such as ELK with HTTPS.
- Scrub or mask sensitive fields at the app layer. Docker can't fix this for you.

Remember, containers are ephemeral, but logs often stick around for years. Treat them like a liability.

Review CI/CD pipelines

Taking a moment to think about the weakest parts of a CI/CD pipeline, it's great to secure your runtime environment, but if your build pipeline leaks a secret or publishes an image to the wrong registry, you're toast. For hybrid setups, this is where things often go wrong because pipelines span multiple systems.

Here are a few non-negotiables from my time helping teams with these issues:

- Use ephemeral runners (tags in CI/CD tools) for sensitive builds, so no credentials linger.
- Never store plaintext secrets in CI config. Use vaults or secret managers.
- Sign your images. Tools such as Cosign and Docker Content Trust help prove an image came from you and hasn't been tampered with.

Here's a snippet from GitHub Actions that uses OIDC to fetch temporary credentials instead of storing keys:

```
permissions:
  id-token: write
  contents: read
```

Figure 9.7: Example permissions block granting write access to ID tokens and read access to repository contents

This lets your workflow request short-lived tokens from your cloud provider without hardcoding access keys.

Here's a CI/CD pipeline example pushing and signing Docker images for AWS ECR and Azure ACR using Cosign.

```yaml
name: Secure Docker Build

on:
  workflow_dispatch:

jobs:
  build-and-push:
    runs-on: [self-hosted, ephemeral]  # This ensures the runner is created for this job only
    steps:
      - name: Checkout code
        uses: actions/checkout@v3

      - name: Login to AWS ECR
        run: |
          aws ecr get-login-password --region eu-west-1 | \
          docker login --username AWS --password-stdin 123456789012.dkr.ecr.eu-west-1.amazonaws.com

      - name: Build Docker image
        run: docker build -t mysecureapp:latest .

      - name: Tag and Push
        run: |
          docker tag mysecureapp:latest 123456789012.dkr.ecr.eu-west-1.amazonaws.com/mysecureapp:latest
          docker push 123456789012.dkr.ecr.eu-west-1.amazonaws.com/mysecureapp:latest
```

Figure 9.8: Pushing and signing Docker images

Keep identity tight

You also want to keep identity tight. IAM is where hybrid gets messy, and let's be honest, nobody enjoys it. AWS wants IAM roles, Azure swears by Managed Identities, GCP loves service accounts, and none of them agree on anything. Fun times.

The simplest way to stay sane? Push identity management down to the orchestrator wherever possible. Let the platform do the heavy lifting:

- In AWS ECS, attach a task role so the container inherits permissions automatically.
- In Azure AKS, lean on Managed Identity for pods instead of hardcoding secrets.
- In Kubernetes, use workload identity mapping to keep Pod-to-cloud access clean and traceable.

What you don't want is credentials baked into Docker configs or Compose files. That's a recipe for pain and security reviews you don't want to attend. Rotate tokens on a schedule, lock down who can push or pull images, and keep audit logs tidy. That way, your identity setup isn't just secure, it's maintainable without giving you (more) gray hairs.

Okay, so hybrid clouds amplify risk because they multiply the moving parts. Docker gives you a common denominator in this, but it's not magic. You still need to encrypt data in transit, secure volumes at rest, keep secrets out of images, and lock down your build pipeline. The guiding principle? Assume compromise is possible and design so the blast radius stays small. If a container leaks, can it touch everything or just its own world? If a pipeline token escapes, does it expire in minutes or live forever? Ask those questions early.

So, that covers how to keep your data safe. Now we need to deal with the harder problem: how to run the whole application smoothly across multiple clouds without everything slipping out of sync.

Orchestrating hybrid cloud applications with Docker Swarm

Now, I'm not going to lie to you, this is one of those sections where I had to dig deep to make it as clear as possible. The truth is, the more moving parts you have, the harder it is to keep them playing nicely together. We've already looked at Docker running locally, we've covered app orchestration in isolation, and even dipped into multi-cloud deployments. But mix all of that together and you've basically signed up for an orchestration headache. Before we return to *The Big Lab* later in the chapter, it helps to anchor the hybrid concepts with a much smaller, self-contained example. *The Big Lab* spans multiple moving parts, which makes it harder to show the fundamentals cleanly, so this lightweight demonstration gives you a clear baseline. Once the core ideas are established, we'll fold the same principles back into the full Big Lab workflow.

Deploying a hybrid stack across AWS and Azure

To make this less abstract, imagine you've got a small two-service application: an API layer and a background worker. You want replicas running in both AWS and Azure for resilience and you want Swarm to decide where they land rather than hand-managing deployments. Here's what that looks like in practice.

1. First, form a swarm spanning both clouds – on the AWS node (the manager):

    ```
    docker swarm init --advertise-addr <aws-private-ip>
    ```

    And on the Azure node (the worker):

    ```
    docker swarm join --token <token> <aws-private-ip>:2377
    ```

Now you've got one logical cluster stretched across two clouds.

2. Now, create a shared, encrypted overlay network. This is the backbone that lets containers talk securely across clouds.

```
docker network create \
  --driver overlay \
  --opt encrypted \
  hybrid-net
```

3. Then deploy a simple stack using Swarm and Compose. A small `docker-compose.yml` might look like this:

```
version: "3.9"
services:
  api:
    image: myregistry.azurecr.io/hybrid-api:1.0.0
    networks:
      - hybrid-net
    deploy:
      replicas: 3

  worker:
    image: myregistry.azurecr.io/hybrid-worker:1.0.0
    networks:
      - hybrid-net
    deploy:
      replicas: 2

networks:
  hybrid-net:
    external: true
```

4. Then deploy it:

```
docker stack deploy -c docker-compose.yml hybrid-stack
```

Swarm places the replicas across AWS and Azure automatically. One cloud might run most of the API replicas during peak usage; the other might host extra workers overnight. You don't need custom scripts or per-cloud YAML. The orchestrator handles placement, networking, and failover.

Traffic routing should just work, no matter which cloud the client hits, Swarm's routing mesh forwards the request to a healthy API replica, whether it's in the same cloud or the other one. From your perspective, it's a single service. Under the hood, it's two clouds cooperating.

Why orchestration really matters in hybrid

Spinning up a single container is easy. Scaling that same service to run across three regions and two clouds, with load balancing, health checks, and secure networking? That's not a one-liner. Without orchestration, you'd be SSH-ing into boxes, running `docker run` like a lunatic, and hoping nothing breaks in the meantime.

Orchestration automates all that. It's about the following:

- Scheduling containers where they fit best
- Scaling up and down without manual intervention
- Healing when something crashes
- Networking containers across environments
- Rolling updates without nuking uptime

In short, orchestration lets you focus on services, not servers. And that becomes even more critical when your infrastructure spans multiple providers. Your options are Swarm, Kubernetes, and friends (Rancher, etc.).

For hybrid orchestration, the two names you'll hear the most are Docker Swarm and Kubernetes.

Docker Swarm is built straight into Docker, easy to set up, and great for smaller setups or teams that want a low-friction starting point. It supports overlay networks, service discovery, and scaling out with simple commands. Swarm can run across clouds, as long as nodes can talk securely over the network.

Kubernetes is the heavyweight champion. It's designed for complex, large-scale workloads and has native support across every major cloud. Kubernetes brings you advanced scheduling, auto-scaling, secrets management, and the whole CNCF toybox. But it's heavier to learn and manage.

Which should you use? If you're just dipping your toe into hybrid orchestration, start with Swarm. If you're aiming for serious multi-cloud Kubernetes clusters with AKS, EKS, or GKE, you'll need a bigger toolbox and a bit of patience.

Building a hybrid swarm

So, let's start with something practical. You've got two nodes, one on AWS and one on Azure. Both have Docker installed. We're going to create a Swarm cluster that spans them and deploy a service across both.

On the manager node (let's say AWS), initialize Swarm:

```
docker swarm init --advertise-addr
```

This spits out a `join` command. Run that on your Azure node:

```
docker swarm join --token :2377
```

Now both nodes are in the same swarm. Let's deploy something simple:

```
docker service create
--name hybrid-web
--replicas 4
--publish 80:80
nginx:alpine
```

Docker will spread those replicas across the available nodes. Traffic hitting either node on port `80` flows through Swarm's routing mesh to the right container. That's hybrid orchestration, the easy way.

Swarm abstracts the underlying nodes. It doesn't care whether the machine is in AWS, Azure, or your home lab. As long as there's network connectivity and TLS between them, it works.

```
$ docker swarm init
Swarm initialized: current node (abcd1234) is now a manager.

$ docker swarm join --token SWMTKN-1-abc123xyz <manager-ip>:2377
This node joined a swarm as a worker.

$ docker node ls
ID          HOSTNAME   STATUS  AVAILABILITY  MANAGER STATUS
abcd1234    node1      Ready   Active        Leader
efgh5678    node2      Ready   Active

$ docker service create --name webapp --replicas 3 -p 80:80 nginx:latest
vxyz8901qwe123 created

$ docker service ls
ID          NAME     MODE         REPLICAS  IMAGE
vxyz8901q   webapp   replicated   3/3       nginx:latest
```

Figure 9.9: Initializing a Swarm cluster, joining a worker node, and deploying a replicated NGINX service

The following diagram shows how the replicas are distributed across AWS and Azure, and how Swarm handles cross-cloud traffic through the encrypted overlay network:

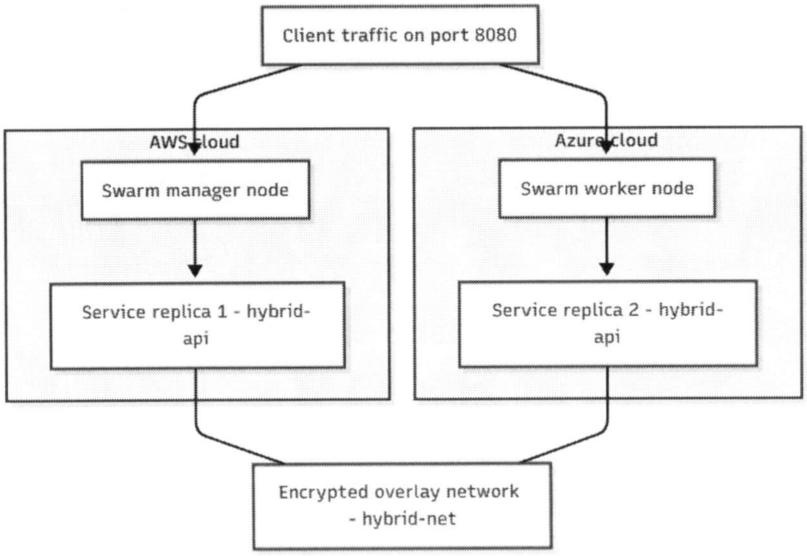

Figure 9.10: Hybrid Swarm topology with a manager in AWS, a worker in Azure, a shared encrypted overlay, and distributed service replicas

In this layout, you can see how Swarm treats both clouds as a single logical cluster. Client traffic can enter through either node, and the routing mesh forwards requests to whichever replica is healthy, even if that replica lives in the other cloud. The encrypted overlay underneath keeps cross-cloud communication secure without you having to manage any custom networking.

Networking is where most hybrid orchestration plans fall apart. Swarm uses overlay networks for cross-node communication, and these rely on each node being able to reach the others over specific ports (TCP 2377 for cluster management, TCP/UDP 7946 and 4789 for gossip and VXLAN). If you're crossing cloud boundaries, that means the following:

- Opening the right firewall rules in AWS Security Groups and Azure NSGs.
- Ensuring private IP ranges don't overlap (yes, it happens more often than you think).
- Using a VPN or Direct Connect for extra security, because raw public IP exposure is a nightmare waiting to happen.

A quick Swarm network creation looks like this:

```
docker network create
--driver overlay
--attachable
hybrid-net
```

Attach your services to this network and they can talk to each other across clouds.

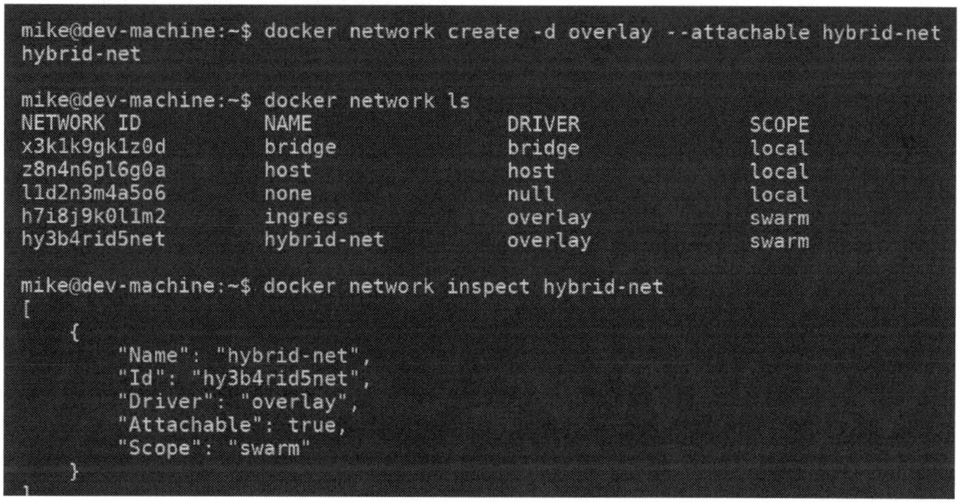

Figure 9.11: Creating and inspecting an attachable overlay network for hybrid Swarm deployments

If you think back to the *HybridApi* walk-through earlier in this chapter, this is exactly the orchestration behaviour we relied on. We created a small swarm with one manager in AWS and one worker in Azure, then deployed the same `hybrid-api` image to both nodes through a single service definition. Swarm handled the heavy lifting for us. We didn't need cloud-specific scripts, we didn't need separate deployment paths, and we didn't have to manually pin replicas to regions. The orchestrator simply took the image we pushed into Azure Container Registry and placed it wherever capacity was available.

This is the real value of using Swarm as your hybrid glue. A container running in AWS doesn't care that its neighbour happens to be in Azure because the networking, the service discovery, and the routing mesh abstract that away. The `HybridApi` example shows what this looks like in practice. You define the service once, attach it to the encrypted hybrid-net overlay, and Swarm handles the location and transport details. That consistency becomes even more important as you scale up and start mixing larger services, background workers, and stateful components across cloud boundaries.

The bit to keep in mind is that nothing about the image or the Compose file changes when you move from a single cloud to a hybrid cluster. All the complexity sits in the orchestrator and the network, not in the application. That is why we anchored the chapter around a single example. Once you see the pattern in the `HybridApi` deployment, everything else in hybrid orchestration becomes much easier to reason about.

Deploying with Compose across clouds

Docker Compose on its own isn't an orchestrator, but with Swarm mode, it becomes a handy way to manage multi-service apps across clouds.

Here's a basic `docker-compose.yml`:

```yaml
version: '3.8'
services:
  web:
    image: myapp:latest
    ports:
      - "80:80"
    networks:
      - hybrid-net
networks:
  hybrid-net:
    external: true
```

Figure 9.12: Docker Compose file attaching a web service to an external hybrid overlay network

Deploy it as a stack:

```
docker stack deploy -c docker-compose.yml hybrid-stack
```

Why does this matter? Compose gives you a familiar syntax, while Swarm handles the distribution. It's repeatable, declarative, and avoids hand-cranking service definitions.

```
Creating network hybrid-net
Creating service hybrid-stack_web
Stack hybrid-stack deployed
NAME            SERVICES        ORCHESTRATOR
hybrid-stack    1               Swarm
```

Figure 9.13: Deploying a Docker Stack using an external hybrid network

If your hybrid environment is getting serious, Kubernetes will almost certainly enter the picture. Every major cloud offers a managed flavor (EKS, AKS, GKE), and you can tie these together with tools such as Kubefed or service meshes (Istio, Linkerd).

The principle is the same: Docker still builds the images. Kubernetes then handles orchestration across clusters. You'll use YAML manifests, Helm charts, or GitOps workflows to keep everything consistent.

For example, a hybrid Kubernetes example might involve the following:

- An AKS cluster in Azure running your frontend
- An EKS cluster in AWS hosting your backend APIs
- Shared secrets managed via external secret stores such as HashiCorp Vault
- A service mesh routing traffic securely across both clusters

Admittedly, this is a bigger beast, but Docker remains central as the packaging format that makes hybrid possible in the first place.

Health checks and auto-healing

Whether you're on Swarm or Kubernetes, health checks are always going to be critical. They stop traffic from being sent to containers that are technically running but not ready.

In Swarm, you can add a health check to your service:

```
healthcheck: test: ["CMD", "curl", "-f", "http://localhost/health"] interval: 30s
retries: 3
```

If a container fails this, swarm replaces it. Kubernetes does something similar with `liveness` and `readiness` probes. These small checks keep hybrid setups from falling apart when a single node has a wobble.

> Note
>
> **A(nother) note on secrets and config**
>
> I know, you're probably sick of hearing about secrets and config by now, but in hybrid, they mean something slightly different. Hybrid orchestration means multiple environments and multiple sets of credentials. Naturally, as we discussed earlier in this chapter, never hardcode these into images. Use Swarm secrets, Kubernetes secrets, or external stores such as AWS Secrets Manager or Azure Key Vault to keep things secure.

Some orchestration tips for hybrid setups

There are a few habits that make hybrid orchestration far more reliable, especially when your services are spread across cloud boundaries.

- **Keep your configs dynamic**: Never bake environment settings into the image. It might seem easier in the moment – and it is! – but the second you move from AWS to Azure or into on-prem, it all falls apart. Inject config at runtime with `env vars`, secrets, or orchestrator tools such as ConfigMaps.

- **Pin your image versions**: I know I've said it before, a lot! But it matters even more here. Never trust `latest` in a multi-cloud world. It'll move underneath you, and you'll end up debugging why Azure is running one build while AWS is happily serving another. Pin your tags and promote the exact same image across environments.
- **Monitor connectivity like a hawk**: Hybrid networks are notoriously fragile. A flaky VPN or peering issue will ruin your day faster than a bad deployment. Build in alerts for node status and latency so you know the second things start wobbling, not when your users tell you.
- **Automate everything you can**: Your CI/CD pipeline should do the heavy lifting. Builds, tags, pushes to multiple registries, and triggering updates across clouds should all be automated. Manual steps in a hybrid environment are a recipe for drift and downtime.

So, as you can see, hybrid orchestration isn't magic, but it can feel like it once you've got the basics down. Yes, it's complex and requires you to have a good view of the orchestration topology, but Docker gives you the portable building blocks. Orchestration tools such as Swarm or Kubernetes turn those blocks into something resilient and predictable. Get your networking and secrets right early, lean on health checks, and automate deployments. Do that, and you'll find multi-cloud orchestration feels less like a circus act and more like a well-rehearsed performance.

With orchestration nailed down, the only thing left is the set of habits that keep hybrid workloads predictable over the long term. That's where these best practices come in.

Best practices for Docker in hybrid clouds

If you've made it this far in the chapter, firstly, thank you! You've already seen how to containerize workloads, deploy across multiple clouds, and glue everything together with orchestration. This section is going to feel a little different. Think of it as your hybrid cloud survival guide, a compact set of principles that will stop your setups from turning into spaghetti. Yes, there will be some overlap with things we've covered, but that's the point. These are the bits worth repeating, and if you only read one section of this chapter hoping to get something out of it, I hope it's this one.

You can flick back to this later when your brain's full of YAML and networking diagrams, and you just need a sense-check before hitting deploy. Let's not muck about, let's dive in...

Use private registries and mirror images

Hybrid deployments almost always hit network restrictions somewhere. Pulling from Docker Hub mid-deploy is a bad idea.

The why: Faster pulls, images live closer to workloads. Predictability, no surprises from public updates. Security, because you can scan and sign before production.

The how: Mirror your base images into ACR or ECR. Scan with Trivy or built-in registry tools.

Use this to push signed images:

```
DOCKER_CONTENT_TRUST=1 docker push myregistry.azurecr.io/myapp:1.3.0
```

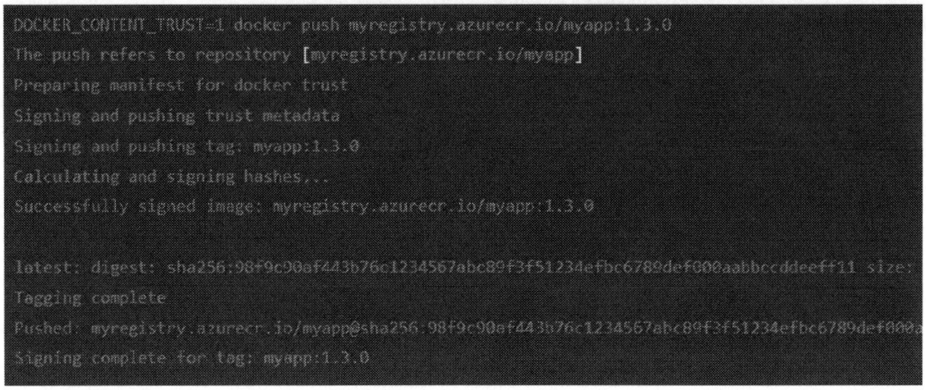

Figure 9.14: Pushing and signing a Docker image with Docker Content Trust enabled

Encrypt traffic

When containers talk across clouds, they're sending data over the internet. Encrypt that traffic, always.

The why: Plain-text traffic in hybrid setups is asking for trouble. Encryption isn't optional.

The how: For Swarm, use encrypted overlay networks:

```
docker network create
--driver overlay
--opt encrypted
hybrid-net
```

This uses IPsec under the hood, so traffic between containers is secure – perfect for multi-cloud services.

The following diagram shows how the encrypted overlay network links the AWS manager and Azure worker so that both hybrid API containers can communicate securely across clouds.

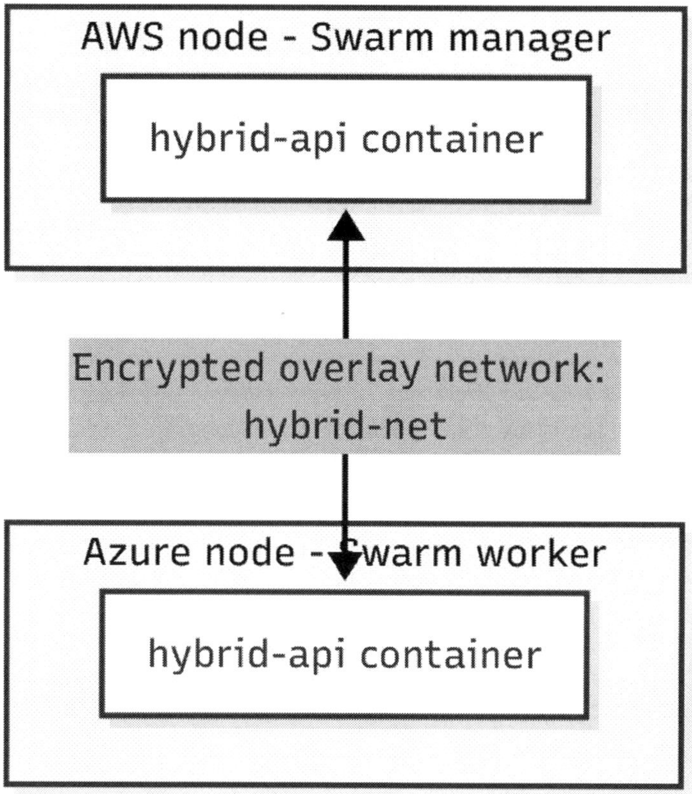

Figure 9.15: Encrypted overlay network spanning AWS and Azure

Automate the pipeline

Manual steps are fine for demos, not for production. Multi-cloud multiplies the chance of human error.

The why: If your process involves SSH-ing into nodes or running ad hoc `docker push` commands, you're one typo away from disaster.

The how: Let CI/CD do the heavy lifting: Build once, push to multiple registries, trigger orchestrator updates cleanly.

Here's an example from GitHub Actions:

```
jobs:
  build-and-push:
    runs-on: ubuntu-latest
    steps:
      - uses: actions/checkout@v3
      - name: Build image
        run: docker build -t myapp:${GITHUB_SHA} .
      - name: Push to AWS
        run: docker push 123456789012.dkr.ecr.eu-west-1.amazonaws.com/myapp:$
        {GITHUB_SHA}
      - name: Push to Azure
        run: docker push myregistry.azurecr.io/myapp:${GITHUB_SHA}
```

Figure 9.16: GitHub Actions workflow building a Docker image and pushing it to both AWS ECR and Azure Container Registry

Secrets stay out of Git

Sounds obvious, but it happens constantly.

The why: A leaked API key in a hybrid cloud isn't just embarrassing, it's a compliance nightmare.

The how: Use Docker secrets for Swarm:

```
echo "supersecurepassword" | docker secret create db_password -
```

This pipes the value straight into Docker's secret store, never touching an image or Git repo.

For Kubernetes, use Secrets or an external vault such as HashiCorp, AWS Secrets Manager, or Azure Key Vault. Oh, and rotate tokens regularly.

Monitor everything, everywhere

Hybrid adds layers, and every layer can fail quietly.

The why: If you're blind to what's happening, outages will blindside you.

The how: Centralize logs with stdout only, no container file logging. Add health checks so your orchestrator knows when to replace a container. Watch network latency across clouds, because hybrid links will break when you least expect it.

Here's an example health check in Compose:

```
healthcheck: test: ["CMD", "curl", "-f", "http://localhost/health"] interval: 30s
retries: 3
```

Plan for failure

Hybrid networks aren't stable, and they won't apologize when they drop.

The why: If you design for perfect conditions, you're designing for failure.

The how: Spread replicas across clouds. Use rolling updates and health checks for smooth deployments. Keep rollback logic baked into CI/CD.

These practices aren't exactly glamorous, but they're the difference between a hybrid setup that behaves predictably and one that slowly drifts out of control without you noticing it. Get the basics right, keep your images consistent, and let your tooling do the repetitive work. Do that, and the complexity of hybrid environments becomes something you can manage rather than something that manages you.

The Big Lab: Preparing the Notes service for enterprise CI/CD and hybrid infrastructure

Up to now, you've proven something really important: the notes service is portable. It runs on your machine, it runs on another host, and it behaves the same way each time. That already puts you ahead of a lot of "enterprise" stacks that are basically held together with tribal knowledge and sticky-back plastic.

In a large organization, though, portability is only half the story. The other half is reliability and traceability. People will come to you with questions such as the following:

- Where did this image come from?
- What commit produced it?
- What did we scan it with?
- What exactly got deployed?
- How do we promote the same artifact between environments without rebuilding it?
- How do we keep secrets and credentials out of Git?

So, that's what this Big Lab does. You'll take the notes stack and wrap it in the kind of CI/CD and infrastructure patterns that work in real organizations. Nothing over-engineered, just the minimum set of enterprise-grade habits that prevent those "but it worked yesterday" incidents.

By the end, your notes service will be the following:

- Built once in CI, tagged, and traceable
- Scanned before it is pushed

- Optionally signed for provenance
- Deployed using image references (not local builds)
- Structured for environment promotion (dev to staging to prod)

Here's what you'll need:

- Your existing `notes-app/` folder (from the earlier Big Labs).
- A container registry you can push to (a Docker Hub private repo is fine; ACR or ECR is also fine if you already have them).
- A remote host from *Chapter 8* (your "staging" box).
- GitHub (or Azure DevOps). This lab uses GitHub Actions because it's easy to follow.

Follow these steps:

1. **Create a proper "release" Compose file**: You already created `compose.remote.yaml` in *Chapter 8*. That's good. For enterprise use, we want the same idea but with explicit versioning and a cleaner separation between config and secrets.
   Create a new file in `notes-app/`:

   ```
   compose.release.yaml
   ```

   Use this as your base:

   ```
   services:
     api:
       image: ${IMAGE_API}
       ports:
         - "5001:5000"
       environment:
         - GENAI_URL=http://genai-gateway/summarise
       networks:
         - app-net
         - api-private
       healthcheck:
         test: ["CMD", "python", "-c", "import urllib.request;
   urllib.request.urlopen('http://localhost:5000/notes')"]
         interval: 30s
         timeout: 5s
         retries: 3

     frontend:
   ```

```
    image: ${IMAGE_FRONTEND}
    ports:
      - "8080:80"
    networks:
      - app-net
    read_only: true

  genai-a:
    image: ${IMAGE_GENAI}
    networks:
      - api-private
      - app-net

  genai-b:
    image: ${IMAGE_GENAI}
    networks:
      - api-private
      - app-net

  genai-gateway:
    image: nginx:alpine
    container_name: notes-genai-gateway
    volumes:
      - ./nginx-genai/nginx.conf:/etc/nginx/conf.d/default.conf:ro
    ports:
      - "5002:80"
    depends_on:
      - genai-a
      - genai-b
    networks:
      - app-net

networks:
  app-net:
  api-private:
```

Here are some key changes versus earlier labs:

- Everything is driven by environment variables such as `IMAGE_API`, so CI can inject the exact versions to deploy.

- We added a simple healthcheck on the API so deployments have a basic "is it alive" signal.
- No `build:` anywhere, because production-like environments should pull versioned artifacts, not compile source.

2. **Add basic image metadata for traceability**: Enterprise environments care about provenance. You want the image to answer: "What created you?"
   In each Dockerfile, add OCI labels. Start with `api/Dockerfile`. Near the top, add the following:

```
ARG VCS_REF=""
ARG BUILD_DATE=""

LABEL org.opencontainers.image.source="https://github.com/<your-org>/<your-repo>" \
      org.opencontainers.image.revision="${VCS_REF}" \
      org.opencontainers.image.created="${BUILD_DATE}"
```

   Do the same for the following:

   - `frontend/Dockerfile`
   - `genai-summariser/Dockerfile`

   You'll pass values for these in CI, so every built image carries its origin with it.

3. **Add a CI pipeline that builds once, tags, scans, and pushes**: In your repo, create the following:

```
.github/workflows/notes-release.yml
```

   Use this as your starting workflow. Replace placeholders such as `<lt;your-dockerhub-user>;` – you know the drill by now.

```
name: Notes Service Release

on:
  push:
    branches: ["main"]

jobs:
  build-scan-push:
    runs-on: ubuntu-latest
```

```
    env:
      REGISTRY: docker.io
      NAMESPACE: &lt;your-dockerhub-user>;
      VERSION: ${{ github.sha }}

    steps:
      - name: Checkout
        uses: actions/checkout@v4

      - name: Set build metadata
        id: meta
        run: |
          echo "BUILD_DATE=$(date -u +'%Y-%m-%dT%H:%M:%SZ')" &gt;&gt;
$GITHUB_ENV

      - name: Log in to registry
        uses: docker/login-action@v3
        with:
          username: ${{ secrets.DOCKERHUB_USER }}
          password: ${{ secrets.DOCKERHUB_TOKEN }}

      - name: Build API image
        run: |
          docker build \
            -t $NAMESPACE/notes-api:$VERSION \
            --build-arg VCS_REF=$VERSION \
            --build-arg BUILD_DATE=$BUILD_DATE \
            ./api

      - name: Build Frontend image
        run: |
          docker build \
            -t $NAMESPACE/notes-frontend:$VERSION \
            --build-arg VCS_REF=$VERSION \
            --build-arg BUILD_DATE=$BUILD_DATE \
            ./frontend

      - name: Build GenAI image
        run: |
          docker build \
```

```
            -t $NAMESPACE/notes-genai-summariser:$VERSION \
            --build-arg VCS_REF=$VERSION \
            --build-arg BUILD_DATE=$BUILD_DATE \
            ./genai-summariser

      - name: Scan images with Trivy
        uses: aquasecurity/trivy-action@0.24.0
        with:
          scan-type: image
          image-ref: ${{ env.NAMESPACE }}/notes-api:${{ env.VERSION }}
          format: table
          exit-code: "1"
          severity: "CRITICAL,HIGH"

      - name: Push images
        run: |
          docker push $NAMESPACE/notes-api:$VERSION
          docker push $NAMESPACE/notes-frontend:$VERSION
          docker push $NAMESPACE/notes-genai-summariser:$VERSION
```

Here's what this gives you:

- Every push to `main` creates images tagged with the commit SHA
- Trivy blocks the pipeline if it finds high/critical issues in the API image
- The images are published as immutable artifacts you can deploy anywhere

> **Note**
>
> Scanning only the API image is intentional here to keep the lab readable. In a real organization, you would scan all three images.

1. **Add optional signing for "prove this image came from us"**: Not every organization signs images yet, but the ones that do usually do it for compliance and supply chain assurance. This step is optional, but it is a very "enterprise" move, and it is easy to explain.

Add this after the push step *if* you want signing. You will need Cosign installed or use the official action. By this stage, I would imagine you've already gone through the chapter on security, so you might already have it installed...

```
    - name: Install Cosign
      uses: sigstore/cosign-installer@v3.6.0

    - name: Sign images (keyless)
      env:
        COSIGN_EXPERIMENTAL: "true"
      run: |
        cosign sign --yes $NAMESPACE/notes-api:$VERSION
        cosign sign --yes $NAMESPACE/notes-frontend:$VERSION
        cosign sign --yes $NAMESPACE/notes-genai-summariser:$VERSION
```

2. **Deploy the exact built artifact to your staging host**: This is the "enterprise" moment. No rebuilding on the server. No copying source code. Just pull and run the exact images CI produced.
   On your Windows machine, switch to your staging Docker context (from *Chapter 8*):

```
docker context use notes-remote
docker info
```

   Now set the image variables and deploy:

```
$env:IMAGE_API = "<your-dockerhub-user>/notes-api:<sha>"
$env:IMAGE_FRONTEND = "<your-dockerhub-user>/notes-frontend:<sha>"
$env:IMAGE_GENAI = "<your-dockerhub-user>/notes-genai-summariser:<sha>"

docker compose -f compose.release.yaml up -d
docker compose -f compose.release.yaml ps
```

   Now, validate from your local machine:

```
curl http://<remote-host>:5001/notes curl http://<remote-host>:5001/notes/
summary
```

3. **Add a clean promotion pattern**: "promote by tag, not rebuild": This is how mature pipelines avoid drift. When you decide a build is "good" (not just good enough), you do not rebuild it for production. You retag it.

In your CI, you can treat the following as follows:

- The commit SHA tag as immutable build output
- The staging tag as "currently in staging"
- The prod tag as "currently in production"

Manually, the idea looks like this:

```
docker pull <your-dockerhub-user>/notes-api:<sha>
docker tag <your-dockerhub-user>/notes-api:<sha> <your-dockerhub-user>/
notes-api:staging
docker push <your-dockerhub-user>/notes-api:staging
```

Do the same for the other images.

Now production deployments can target `:prod` while still knowing exactly what SHA it corresponds to via labels.

4. **Enterprise sanity checks you should do before calling it "ready"**: These are quick, but they are the sorts of checks that stop most painful post-release surprises.
   Confirm your containers are running the version you expect:

```
docker image inspect $env:IMAGE_API --format '{{json .Config.Labels}}'
```

   Confirm you are not relying on `latest` anywhere:

```
docker compose -f compose.release.yaml config | Select-String "latest"
```

   Confirm that "build does not exist" in the release file:

```
docker compose -f compose.release.yaml config | Select-String "build:"
```

   Dead easy – if any of those return something you did not expect, fix it now, not after someone else deploys it wrongly.

5. **Clean rollback: prove you can recover without drama**: Pick an older SHA and redeploy by swapping the environment variables.

```
$env:IMAGE_API = "<your-dockerhub-user>/notes-api:<older-sha>"
$env:IMAGE_FRONTEND = "<your-dockerhub-user>/notes-frontend:<older-sha>"
$env:IMAGE_GENAI = "<your-dockerhub-user>/notes-genai-summariser:<older-
sha>"
```

```
docker compose -f compose.release.yaml up -d
```

If rollback is "easy," people trust the pipeline. If rollback is "a war room," people start sneaking in manual fixes.

At this point, your notes service is no longer "a Compose demo." It's a stack with a release workflow:

- CI builds once
- Images are scanned, pushed, and optionally signed
- Staging deploys by digestible version, not rebuild
- Promotion is retagging, not recompiling
- Rollback is swapping a tag, not redoing a deployment

So, everything is ready for production reliability. In the next chapter, we will troubleshoot real-world failures.

Summary

If there's one theme running through this chapter, it's that hybrid and multi-cloud aren't just buzzwords; they're complexity generators. Different platforms, different rules, different moving parts. Left unchecked, that complexity will chew through your time and patience.

Docker gives you a bit of a fighting chance. By standardizing how you build and run workloads, it smooths the jagged edges of hybrid environments. We've seen how containers provide the portability that hybrid needs, why building once and running everywhere matters, and how to handle the messy bits such as configuration, identity, and secrets without introducing chaos.

We didn't stop at theory either. From securing data across networks to orchestrating services that span clouds, and finally pulling it all together with practical best practices, the idea has always been the same: keep things predictable, repeatable, and secure. Hybrid success isn't about perfection; it's about building resilience into your workflows so that when something fails, the system bends but doesn't break.

In the next chapter, we'll switch focus from building and running hybrid workloads to what happens when something goes wrong. Production issues look very different once containers, clouds, and orchestration are in the mix, so let's look at how to troubleshoot Docker when the stakes are highest.

Get This Book's PDF Version and Exclusive Extras

Scan the QR code (or go to `packtpub.com/unlock`). Search for this book by name, confirm the edition, and then follow the steps on the page.

UNLOCK NOW

Note: Keep your invoice handy. Purchases made directly from Packt don't require one.

10

Troubleshooting Docker in Production Environments

We've finally reached the last chapter, and this is where everything you've learned so far comes together. Up to this point, we've built images, composed multi-service stacks, secured them, scaled them, monitored them, and pushed them into increasingly complex environments. Well done! Now, though, we get to the part every real-world Docker user eventually faces: what happens when production stops behaving.

Not the neat, textbook failures. The weird ones. The ones that don't match the logs. The ones that only appear after a deployment you were absolutely certain wouldn't cause trouble. The ones that you and two other engineers reviewed and that kind that make you question whether staging and production are even running the same universe, never mind the same cloud.

This chapter is all about that horrible moment.

And I've had my share of them. When I first moved all our test environments over to Docker containers in a previous job, everything looked perfect on paper. Clean images, predictable dependencies, fully repeatable environments... the dream. And then the first one broke. Completely. It ran flawlessly on my machine, flawlessly in CI, flawlessly everywhere except the one environment where people actually needed it. I spent far too long chasing phantom bugs before discovering the container was missing a tiny `.env` variable that only existed in the old setup. It was my first real (and sadly not the last) lesson in container debugging: Docker removes a lot of chaos, but it absolutely punishes incorrect assumptions.

Originally, I thought of this chapter as a quick reference for previous *Best practice* sections, but in truth, we're going to work through a single real production failure from start to finish and use it to build a proper troubleshooting workflow you can apply pretty much anywhere. You'll see how to interrogate containers, validate images, check network paths, spot configuration drift, use debugging tools effectively, and recover a broken system without improvisation or professional guesswork.

By the end, you'll have a framework you can rely on when Docker doesn't do what you expect, along with some quick-reference diagrams, tables, and tooling guides you can return to long after this book is closed.

We'll be covering the following main topics:

- The production incident: A real production failure
- The Docker troubleshooting framework
- Applying the framework
- Troubleshooting references
- Recovery, automation, and prevention

Right then, we've put this off for far too long; let's start with what actually went wrong in production.

Technical requirements

The code files referenced in this chapter are available at `https://github.com/PacktPublishing/Mastering-Docker-on-Windows`.

The production incident: A real production failure

There's a moment every engineer secretly dreads. You push a small, harmless-looking update into production, watch the deployment logs scroll past, everything goes green, and you allow yourself to think, "*Phew, that was painless.*"

Five minutes later, reality taps you on the shoulder.

The first alert that fires is nothing too dramatic. A small latency bump on the API. Probably noise. Then another alert appears. Probably still noise. Then another. Probably not noise at this point. Suddenly, the API's 95th percentile looks like it's trying to scale a cliff face. Ten minutes later, support tickets start drifting in. The background worker begins restarting in that slow, miserable loop that tells you absolutely nothing useful. Redis is technically "healthy," but losing its mind with open connections. CPU usage is weirdly low across the board, which is always the most unnerving sign of all: things are breaking without actually breaking.

The stack in question is pretty simple.

A small web API. A Redis cache. A worker service. That's it. The backbone for most apps these days. You've deployed this exact combination hundreds of times. It passed integration. It passed staging. It behaved on your laptop. It behaved on everyone else's laptop. In other words, the usual suspects are ruled out pretty quickly.

No traffic spike. No overnight infrastructure patch. No firewall rules mysteriously toggled by someone who "didn't touch anything." No hidden feature flag accidentally flipped.

And because Docker likes to keep you humble, none of the failures align neatly:

- The API isn't completely down. It's just slow enough that users start refreshing their browsers in frustration.
- The worker isn't broken; it just never stays awake long enough to finish a task.
- Redis is responsive but drowning in connection churn.
- The logs contain absolutely nothing insightful. (Classic.)

I've been in situations like this more times than I'd admit publicly. It's never the dramatic, cinematic disaster where everything explodes at once. It's the quiet failures that get you, the quicksand ones, the weird ones where the system is "technically" up but behaving like it wants to retire early. Those are the ones that lead to three-hour rabbit holes because every container *looks* fine until you poke exactly the right part.

So that's the scenario we're going to work through here. Not a vague "containers can crash sometimes, check the logs" lecture. Not that there's anything wrong with that, but an actual production failure that mirrors the strange, frustrating, slightly embarrassing breakages we've all fought at some point. And again, I used to work in finance, so I've seen my fair share of them.

The point of this whole chapter is to stop troubleshooting from feeling like guesswork. We'll take this broken little stack and walk through it properly:

- What you check first (and what not to waste time on)
- How to interrogate the container itself, not just the logs
- How to validate the image layers, entrypoints, and build assumptions
- How to confirm the network path without falling into the "it's probably DNS" trap – though let's be honest, it is usually DNS... sorry, network people...
- How to spot environmental drift between staging and production
- How to recover safely without making things worse
- And finally, how to prevent this kind of problem from sneaking in again – that's the really important part

We'll also bring in tools we haven't really touched before – Dive, Dockle, ctop, Trivy, and the VS Code Docker extension – so you can see what they look like in a real debugging session rather than a theoretical note.

Think of this as the moment in the book where we stop talking about Docker and start *using* it the way you do when the fire alarm goes off. This is the scenario that hopefully ties all the previous chapters together without rehashing them. Everything from this point forward is about applying what you know, filling in the gaps, and building a repeatable workflow for those times when Docker decides to do something mega unhelpful in production.

Right then. Something in production just went sideways. Let's go and find out why.

The Docker troubleshooting framework

When something breaks in production, the worst thing you can do is start guessing. I've done that more times than I'd like to admit, usually at stupid o'clock in the morning, and it always leads to the same outcome: wasted time, wrong assumptions, and a fix that works by accident rather than understanding. The trick is to have a structure that forces you to slow down (which is hard if every senior manager wants an update at the same time), check the right things in the right order, and avoid diving straight into rabbit holes.

This is the framework I personally fall back on whenever a containerized system stops behaving. It's simple enough to remember under pressure but detailed enough to stop you chasing the wrong problem. Think of it like a mental flowchart you run through automatically whenever something looks weird. And don't worry, we'll go over how to actually execute all of this soon. Let's just understand it first.

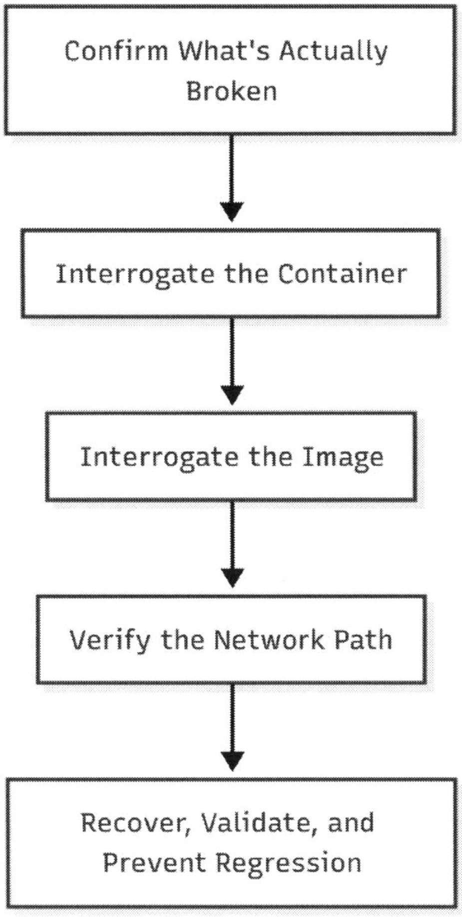

Figure 10.1: My high-level troubleshooting flow showing the five core steps

Let's briefly discuss each.

Confirm what's actually broken

It sounds painfully obvious, but this is the step teams skip the most. Especially in a panic. You need to separate *symptoms* from *failures*.

Users see 500 errors; that doesn't tell you *which* service failed. A worker is restarting; that doesn't tell you *why*. Redis connections spike; this could be the cause or the effect.

Start by checking some of the basics:

- Which containers are running, paused, or stuck in restart loops?

- Are requests even reaching the service?
- Is the problem global or isolated to a subset of users?
- Do logs and metrics show a consistent pattern or a scattershot mess?

You're not fixing anything here. You're just establishing the boundaries of the blast radius.

Interrogate the container

Once you know which service is misbehaving, get inside it. This is where most troubleshooting actually happens. Not in dashboards. Not in abstract theory. Inside the container with your hands in the guts of the thing. When you drop into a shell, check the following:

- Environment variables
- Mounted directories
- Config files you *think* should exist
- Processes actually running
- Network access, DNS resolution, and connection attempts
- Whether health checks are passing internally

Half of all "mystery failures" come down to something such as the following:

- A missing environment variable,
- A wrong hostname,
- A config file that was present in staging but not in production

Containers are predictable, but the environment around them rarely is.

Interrogate the image

If the container looks fine on the inside, the next suspect is the image itself. Images are one of the easiest places for subtle breakages to hide. Some of the reasons could be the following:

- Stale build layers
- Wrong build stage copied
- Outdated dependencies
- Missing binaries
- Baked-in dev configs you forgot existed (we all do it)
- Stray scripts or paths that don't line up anymore

You can also use some additional tools that give you visibility you can't get from logs alone. Don't worry, we'll go over these shortly in this chapter:

- **Dive** shows you exactly what's inside each layer and what changed

- **Dockle/Trivy** catches misconfigurations and vulnerabilities
- `docker history` shows you the build commands responsible for each layer

Your goal here is to confirm that the image deployed to production is *actually* the image you meant to ship, not some cached relic Docker has clung onto since last year.

Verify the network path

Networking issues are the great equalizer. They make experienced engineers stare at the wall, questioning their entire career choices sometimes. The problem is rarely "the network" in the abstract. It's one of a handful of practical breakpoints:

- DNS resolution inside the container (the obvious one)
- Wrong internal hostname
- Wrong network attached
- Port mismatches (host vs. container)
- Accidental exposure to the wrong subnet (this one will trip you up when you least expect it)
- Firewall rules quietly dropping traffic
- WSL 2 *oddities* on Windows hosts (sometimes explainable, sometimes not)

At this point, you're not running `ping` for fun. You're proving or disproving assumptions:

"*Does the API container actually know how to talk to Redis, or have we all just been pretending it does?*"

If the container can't resolve the service hostname or if you discover it's on the default bridge network all by itself, you're done – you've found the fault line.

Recover, validate, and prevent regressions

Once you know *what* broke, the last step is to recover without making the situation worse. Harder than it sounds sometimes. That means the following:

- Choosing whether to restart, roll back, or redeploy
- Validating the fix in a controlled way
- Confirming that logs/metrics behave normally
- Adding or adjusting health checks
- Closing any gaps that allowed the issue to slip through (CI config, env drift, or missing tests)

This is also the point where you automate the lesson. If the failure was predictable, the fix should be too.

This step turns "*We solved the outage*" into "*This outage won't repeat itself quietly next month.*" This is something that I use pretty much daily in my software testing career – if something breaks, the most important thing we want to do is to make sure it doesn't happen again.

Here's why this framework matters: Docker-based systems fail in ways that are annoyingly subtle. You can't always rely on instinct, and you definitely can't rely on one-off commands you saw in a blog post two years ago. Even if that blog post was mine!

This structured approach does a few things, especially for my brain (remember this is *my* framework), which may or may not suffer from ADHD, which is worse during a crisis. It speeds up troubleshooting, reduces panic, stops blame-chasing, reveals problems you would otherwise miss, and gives you a mental model to fall back on every time

Everything in the rest of this chapter uses this framework. First, we're going to apply it step by step to *the production incident*. Then, we'll build out diagrams, quick-reference tables, and tooling guides you can use as shortcuts when you're knee-deep in a real outage.

So, how about we actually put it to work, eh?

Applying the framework

Now that we've got a framework, let's actually use it. We'll take the production failure from earlier – the production incident (the slow API, the miserable restart-looping worker, and Redis melting down under connection churn) and run through the exact steps you'd take to isolate the root cause. No shortcuts. Nothing. Just the practical debugging flow you'd follow on a real system (and I have several times) when time is tight, and people are watching.

I'm keeping everything focused on what you *actually do*, not necessarily the theory behind it. This is the bit you'll mentally replay the next time something breaks in production. So, first off...

Confirm what's actually broken

When production is wobbling, your first instinct is often "*I know what it is.*" You don't. Truth is, no one does. You start by proving what the system is actually doing:

1. The first step would be to see the real container state using the following:

   ```
   docker ps --format "table {{.Names}}\t{{.Status}}\t{{.Image}}"
   ```

   This gives you a truthful snapshot of reality. Who's up, who's down, who's restarting, who's sipping in limbo. The `STATUS` column instantly exposes crash loops or containers exiting quietly between restarts:

```
NAMES     STATUS                          IMAGE
api       Up 7 minutes                    myapp/api:prod
worker    Restarting (1) 17 seconds ago   myapp/worker:prod
redis     Up 7 minutes                    redis:7.2
```

Figure 10.2: A quick snapshot showing the API and Redis running normally while the worker repeatedly restarts

This tells you which containers deserve your attention first. If `worker` is restarting every 20 seconds, focus shifts there immediately.

2. Next, let's look at API logs for surface symptoms:

```
docker logs api --tail 20
```

The API is where user-facing issues show up first. You're checking whether it's failing on its own or reacting to another service dying behind it. Are there timeouts? Connection errors? Request pile-ups? If the API is reporting Redis timeouts, that tells you "the API is downstream of the real problem."

```
2025-11-14T09:32:11Z  INFO  Request GET /reports/summary started
2025-11-14T09:32:11Z  ERROR Redis connection timeout after 2000ms
2025-11-14T09:32:11Z  WARN  Falling back to stale cache data
2025-11-14T09:32:11Z  INFO  Request GET /reports/summary completed in 2412ms (status: 500)

2025-11-14T09:32:12Z  INFO  Request POST /tasks/queue started
2025-11-14T09:32:12Z  ERROR Failed to enqueue task: Redis not reachable
2025-11-14T09:32:12Z  ERROR Upstream error: redis:6379 connection refused
2025-11-14T09:32:12Z  INFO  Request POST /tasks/queue completed in 918ms (status: 503)

2025-11-14T09:32:13Z  INFO  Health check: starting
2025-11-14T09:32:15Z  ERROR Health check failed: unable to ping Redis
2025-11-14T09:32:15Z  WARN  API degraded — retrying in 5s

2025-11-14T09:32:16Z  INFO  Request GET /status started
2025-11-14T09:32:16Z  INFO  Request GET /status completed in 3ms (status: 200)

2025-11-14T09:32:17Z  INFO  Request GET /reports/summary started
2025-11-14T09:32:17Z  ERROR Redis connection timeout after 2000ms
2025-11-14T09:32:17Z  INFO  Request GET /reports/summary completed in 2311ms (status: 500)
```

Figure 10.3: Recent API logs showing repeated Redis timeouts and connection failures

3. Now, inspect the `worker` logs:

```
docker logs worker --tail 20
```

A restarting container often emits critical clues just before it dies, including missing configs, import failures, startup exceptions, and whether the worker ever gets fully online or dies during its initialization phase. This narrows down whether your issue is runtime, configuration, or image-related. This is important.

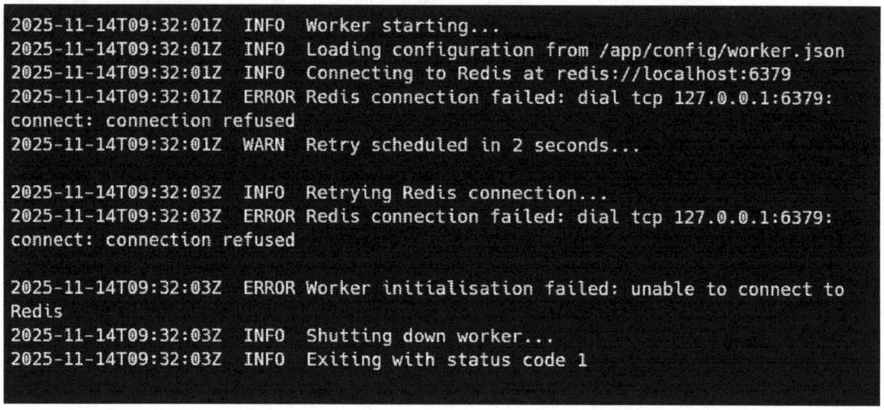

Figure 10.4: Worker logs showing repeated connection failures to the wrong Redis hostname (localhost)

With the worker's failure pattern now confirmed in the logs, the next step is to look inside the container itself to verify whether its runtime environment matches what you think you deployed.

Next up, interrogate the container!

1. Once you know *which* service is failing, you need to validate its real environment. Staging and production aren't identical, no matter what anyone claims:

   ```
   docker exec -it worker sh
   ```

   Logs can lie by omission. The inside of the container does not. Dropping into a shell gives you the ground truth. It tells you exactly what the container sees: its filesystem, its environment variables, and its runtime context, with zero assumptions.

2. Okay, now let's check the critical environment variables:

   ```
   env | grep REDIS
   ```

   Most "mysterious" production failures come from misconfigured environment variables. A wrong hostname or missing password can break everything without producing a helpful error, whether staging and production have drifted. If Redis is set to `redis.internal` in staging but `localhost` in production, you've found your smoking gun.

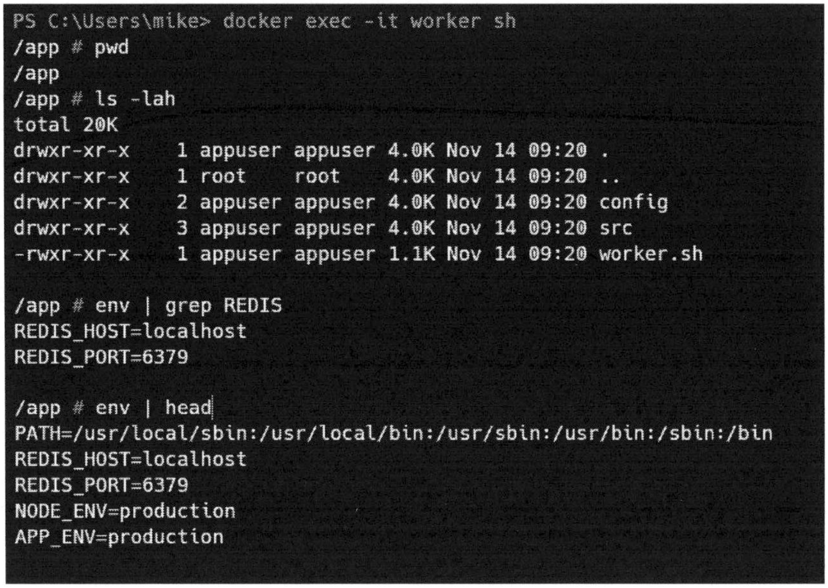

Figure 10.5: Accessing the worker container from a host PowerShell session

3. Don't forget to test DNS and connection reachability:

```
ping redis
curl http://redis:6379
```

Knowing whether the container *can actually find and talk to Redis* is a massive part of isolating failures. This will tell you that if DNS is broken, the hostname doesn't resolve. If the connection hangs, the port isn't reachable. If the connection is refused, then it's the wrong port or Redis isn't listening, and if it's a slow response, there is some latent network issue. This separates network issues from application issues immediately.

```
/app # ping redis
PING redis (10.0.3.12): 56 data bytes
64 bytes from 10.0.3.12: seq=0 ttl=64 time=185.7 ms
64 bytes from 10.0.3.12: seq=1 ttl=64 time=243.1 ms
Request timeout for icmp_seq 2
64 bytes from 10.0.3.12: seq=3 ttl=64 time=392.6 ms
Request timeout for icmp_seq 4
64 bytes from 10.0.3.12: seq=5 ttl=64 time=267.4 ms
^C
--- redis ping statistics ---
6 packets transmitted, 4 packets received, 33% packet loss
round-trip min/avg/max = 185.7/272.2/392.6 ms
```

Figure 10.6: Mixed ping results showing intermittent timeouts and high latency

4. Okay, now let's inspect the `config` files:

```
ls -lah /app/config
```

The image might contain a `config` file your container never receives at runtime, especially if you rely on mounted volumes; whether key runtime configs exist, are readable, or differ from what you think you deployed.

```
/app # ls -lah /app/config
total 12K
drwxr-xr-x    2 appuser appuser 4.0K Nov 14 09:20 .
drwxr-xr-x    1 appuser appuser 4.0K Nov 14 09:20 ..
-rw-r--r--    1 appuser appuser 1.2K Nov 14 09:20 workerr.json
-rw-r--r--    1 appuser appuser  612 Nov 14 09:20 redis.json
```

Figure 10.7: Inspecting the /app/config directory to confirm which config files the container actually has at runtime

By now, you've ruled out the obvious runtime issues. The container's environment isn't wrong, incomplete, or behaving inconsistently. But if everything *looks* correct on the inside and the failures don't add up, the next logical suspect isn't the container at all. It's the thing that created it. Containers only run what the image gives them.

So, if the runtime view doesn't explain the behavior, it's time to turn your attention to the image itself.

Interrogate the image

There are a few standard steps I'd follow when investigating an image from a failing container:

1. First, check the image that the container is actually using:

   ```
   docker inspect --format='{{.Config.Image}}' worker
   ```

   You may think production is running `myapp:prod`. Docker may disagree. Cached tags, stale images, and registry pull failures can silently deploy the wrong version. This will tell you whether production is actually running the image you expect, not a ghost from a previous release.

   ```
   PS C:\Users\mike> docker inspect --format='{{.Config.Image}}' worker
   myapp:latest
   ```

   Figure 10.8: The worker container is running myapp:latest instead of the expected myapp:prod

2. Next, inspect the image history:

   ```
   docker history myapp:prod
   ```

   This exposes the exact commands used to build each layer. If something was accidentally rebuilt or left uncached, it'll stand out immediately. It will tell you if there are any unexpected layers, `COPY` stages pulling the wrong content, dependencies that ballooned unexpectedly, and outdated cache.

   ```
   PS C:\Users\mike> docker history myapp:prod
   IMAGE          CREATED       CREATED BY                         SIZE
   a92f1dbf0b33   2 days ago    COPY ./dev-config/ /app/config/    12MB
   9b77e23bbbd0   2 days ago    RUN npm install                    145MB
   1c22bbde4411   2 days ago    COPY ./src /app/src                3MB
   574e12cc9aa0   2 days ago    COPY ./package.json /app/          1KB
   c42a1a0c7ad3   4 weeks ago   FROM node:18-alpine                5MB
   ```

   Figure 10.9: The image history reveals an unexpected layer and an abnormally large dependency install

   So, what's wrong here?

   A `COPY` command is pulling from `./dev-config/` instead of the correct production config directory. The `npm install` layer has ballooned to 145 MB, way above a typical production build, suggesting that dev dependencies were included or caching broke, and the build is only *2 days old*, so this isn't a legacy-image issue; it's a faulty build.

3. Let's mix things up a bit; let's analyze contents with Dive:

```
dive myapp:prod
```

Dive (you can install this using the Chocolatey command we used in *Chapter 5* on Windows: `choco install dive`) gives you a visual diff of what actually ended up in each layer. This is where you discover missing build outputs, wrong files copied, dev config accidentally baked into prod, and dependency drift. This will tell you whether the image *itself* is broken before it even reaches a container.

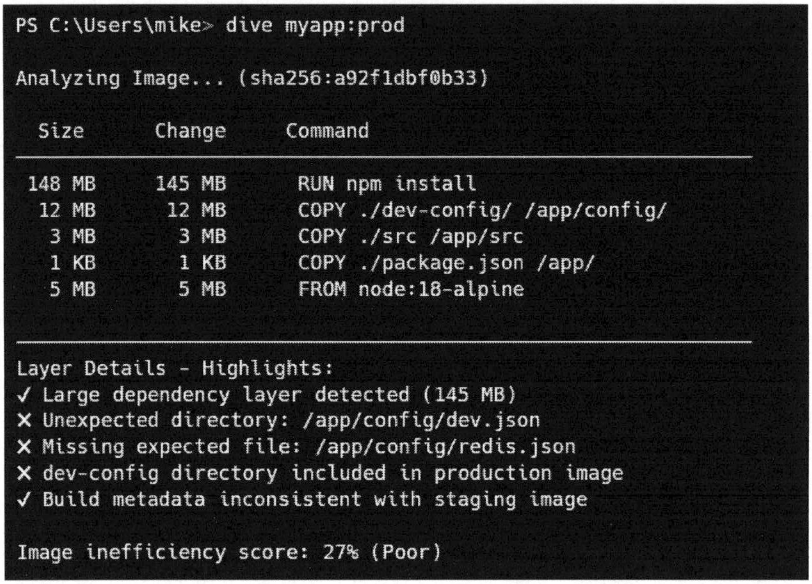

Figure 10.10: Dive exposes a bloated dependency layer and an incorrect dev-config directory inside the image

4. Lastly, run an isolated debug shell:

```
docker run -it --rm myapp:prod sh
```

This lets you inspect the image independent of Compose volumes, overrides, and environment variables. It'll tell you whether the image is valid on its own, without environmental influence. If it fails here, you know the problem is in your Dockerfile or build pipeline.

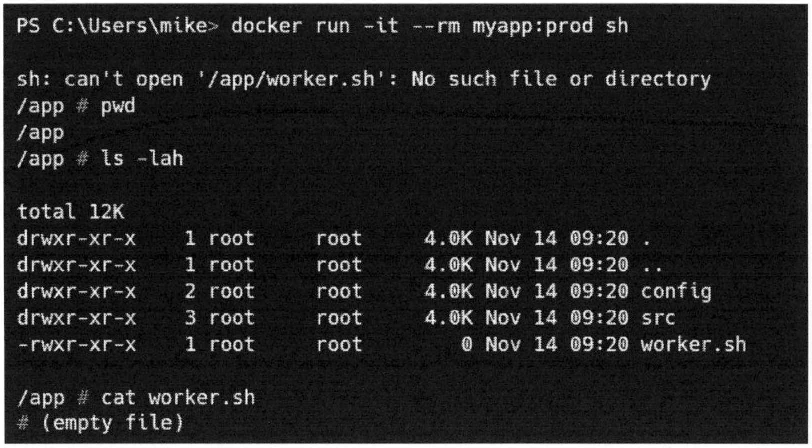

Figure 10.11: Launching the image in isolation reveals a broken worker.sh entrypoint script – it's empty

At this point, you've ruled out both the container's environment and the image itself. The filesystem looks sane, the build pipeline isn't the culprit, and nothing inside the image explains the behavior we're seeing. That leaves one of the most common and most painful suspects.

Verify the network path

If the app can't consistently talk to what it depends on, none of the internal checks matter. It's time to verify the network path:

1. First up, let's inspect container networking:

```
docker inspect api | grep -A5 Networks
```

   If services aren't on the same network, Docker's DNS won't work. This is one of the most common causes of "mystery" connection failures. It'll tell you whether the API and worker can even see each other.

```
"Networks": {
    "frontend": {
        "IPAMConfig": {},
        "Links": null,
        "Aliases": [
            "api",
            "api_1"
        ],
        "NetworkID": "8f3c9d1c2a4a",
--
    "bridge": {
        "IPAMConfig": null,
        "Links": null,
        "Aliases": [
            "api"
        ],
        "NetworkID": "3b19a8d0f6b1"
    }
```

Figure 10.12: The API container is attached only to the frontend and the default bridge network, not the shared backend

2. Next up, let's inspect the actual Docker network:

```
docker network inspect backend
```

Networks can have stale endpoints, duplicate names, or missing containers, especially after partial deployments or crashes. This will tell you whether the network routing is correct and whether the membership list looks sane.

```
[
    {
        "Name": "backend",
        "Id": "7c1f98d1f2bc3e3c5d8d2484c41e50a4c9e4afba7e20fb89a3f2e2e12af17df3",
        "Created": "2025-11-14T09:10:22.123456789Z",
        "Scope": "local",
        "Driver": "bridge",
        "IPAM": {
            "Driver": "default",
            "Config": [
                {
                    "Subnet": "10.0.3.0/24",
                    "Gateway": "10.0.3.1"
                }
            ]
        },
        "Containers": {
            "c82afba13d9fdd12e41b1487af2911c327c2e3a55b7ee3cf4f6d2b8e1b33216c": {
                "Name": "worker",
                "EndpointID": "4de82d939fcb85a1277c9f2e57a8b4620c9d80ec5b0e238cbaf18ac3b108e2e2",
                "MacAddress": "02:42:0a:00:03:05",
                "IPv4Address": "10.0.3.5/24",
                "IPv6Address": ""
            },
            "f3e9ac1d77d5c1a819bf2fbc11c572bd450f06f3b491fe8ce1e8932a0c9d34ab": {
                "Name": "redis",
                "EndpointID": "59cfe7397c2a83c9a44c572cc3d2a511064d4716b69226638a85c0384bc4b9ef",
                "MacAddress": "02:42:0a:00:03:06",
                "IPv4Address": "10.0.3.6/24",
                "IPv6Address": ""
            },
            "stale-endpoint-12cf": {
                "Name": "api_old_1",
                "EndpointID": "",
                "MacAddress": "",
                "IPv4Address": "",
                "IPv6Address": ""
            }
        }
    }
]
```

Figure 10.13: Output of the docker network inspect backend command

Inspecting the backend network shows the worker and Redis attached correctly, but the API container is missing entirely, and a `stale api_old_1` endpoint is still present.

3. So, now let's test DNS inside the containers:

```
docker exec -it api sh -c "nslookup redis"
```

The host-level DNS working means nothing if Docker's internal resolver isn't. This should tell you whether the API can even resolve Redis via internal service discovery.

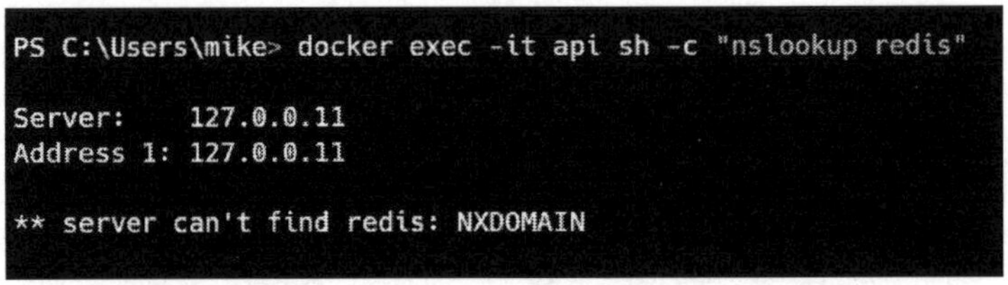

Figure 10.14: Running nslookup inside the API container

The output shows Docker's internal DNS can't resolve Redis at all.

4. Finally, let's test connection latency and port access:

```
docker exec -it api sh -c "curl -v redis:6379"
```

Even if DNS resolves, the service may not actually be reachable over the network.

This should tell you whether the connection is a success, and then we can move on. If it times out, then it's most likely a routing or firewall issue. If there is a handshake issue, then it's most likely the wrong port, and if there is an immediate refusal, then the service is most likely not listening.

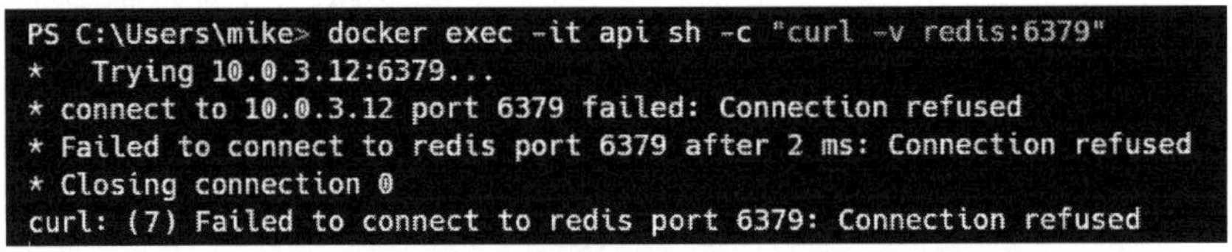

Figure 10.15: API container attempting to connect to Redis

Here, we can see that the API container can resolve the Redis hostname, but the connection is immediately refused, indicating that Redis isn't reachable on that port or the API is pointing at the wrong instance.

Here is a quick-reference table to help you understand the curl outcomes and what they mean:

curl behavior	What it means	Likely cause
Connection succeeds	Network path is healthy	Move on to app-level debugging
Connection refused (instant)	Port reachable, but nothing is listening	Wrong port, wrong service, or service crashed

curl behavior	What it means	Likely cause
Operation timed out	Packet never reached target, or no return traffic	Firewall rule, routing issue, or wrong network
Couldn't resolve host	DNS lookup failed	Containers not on the same network; DNS misconfiguration
TLS handshake errors	Service reachable, but wrong protocol	Hitting an HTTPS service with HTTP; wrong port

Table 10.1: Common curl outcomes

So, by now, the picture is clear: the containers aren't discovering each other properly, the network path is unreliable, and the application is failing for reasons that have nothing to do with code. But now that you've isolated the root cause, the only thing left is to put the system back together safely.

Recover, validate, and prevent regressions

Troubleshooting gets you to the answer. Recovery is where you make it stick:

1. Let's recover, validate, and prevent regressions! Once you've found the root cause, you can recover carefully by recreating the affected containers:

   ```
   docker compose up -d --force-recreate api worker
   ```

   You want a clean recreation based on the corrected config/image, not whatever state Docker cached earlier. This will tell you whether the containers now stabilize and stop restarting, confirming your fix.

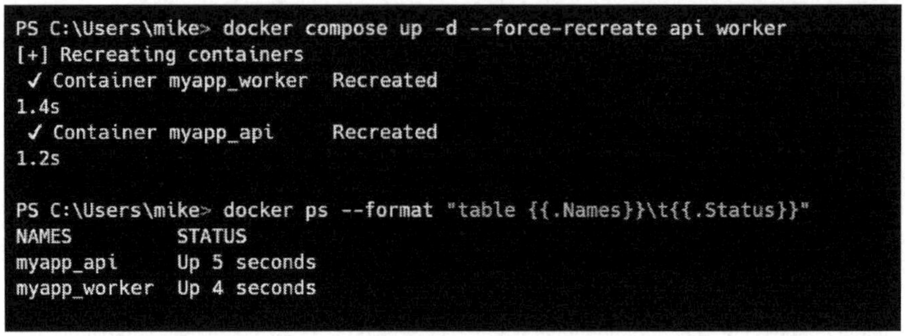

Figure 10.16: Recreating the API and worker containers forces Docker to start them with the corrected configuration and a clean state

2. Don't forget, watch logs during recovery:

```
docker logs -f worker
```

Live logs reveal whether the service starts smoothly or fails during initialization again. This will show you whether you genuinely fixed the issue or only kicked the problem down the road.

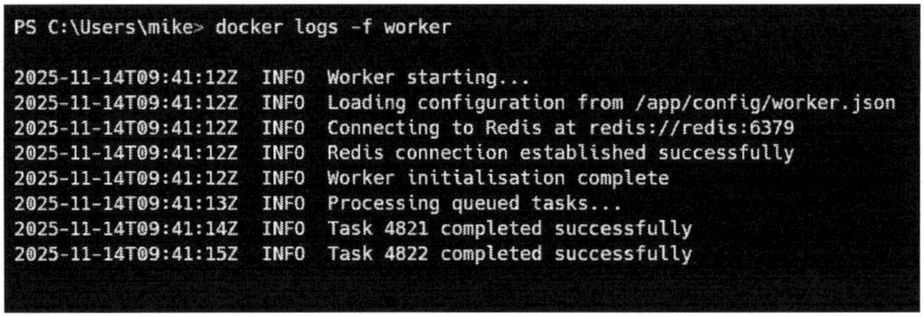

Figure 10.17: Live worker logs after the fix show successful initialization

3. Also, monitor stabilization:

```
docker stats
```

A fix that looks good initially can still be unhealthy under load. It can reveal whether CPU/memory/network I/O are normalizing or if something else is brewing.

```
PS C:\Users\mike> docker stats
CONTAINER        CPU %     MEM USAGE / LIMIT     MEM %     NET I/O             BLOCK I/O     PIDS
myapp_api        1.23%     82.4MiB / 512MiB      16.0%     8.1kB / 7.9kB       0B / 0B       12
myapp_worker     0.67%     54.2MiB / 512MiB      10.5%     12.7kB / 10.3kB     0B / 0B       9
redis            0.15%     10.3MiB / 100MiB      10.3%     5.1kB / 4.4kB       0B / 0B       4
```

Figure 10.18: docker stats confirms that the API, worker, and Redis containers have returned to stable resource usage after the fix

Now, don't just stop at "it's fixed." That's how the same bug comes back six months later, wearing a slightly different hat. Here's how you actually lock this one down:

- **Add or tighten health checks**: Make sure the worker and API have health endpoints that *actually* validate connectivity to Redis, not just "process is running." If Redis is unreachable, the container should go unhealthy and get restarted or taken out of rotation before users even notice.
- **Add CI checks for required environment variables**: Your pipeline should fail fast if core variables such as `REDIS_HOST` or `REDIS_PORT` are missing or set to obviously bogus defaults. A simple validation script or smoke test in CI is enough to stop bad configs ever reaching production.
- **Validate Dockerfile `COPY` stages**: Double-check that you're copying the right config directories and build artifacts for production. If you've got `dev-config` and `prod-config`, make it impossible to mix them up by naming, structure, or explicit build arguments. The goal is to stop "oops, wrong folder" from being a deployable state.
- **Add alerts for this specific failure pattern**: You've just seen how this breaks. Redis connection errors, worker restart loops, API 5xx spikes. Turn that pattern into an alert. If the same symptoms start to emerge again, you want a notification long before users start raising tickets with support.
- **Document the root cause and the fix**: Write it down. Future-you and the rest of the team will actually see it: what happened, how you diagnosed it, what the fix was, and what safeguards were added. Next time something smells similar, you've got a shortcut.

That's the difference between "*We survived an outage*" and "*We hardened the system*." One is a bad evening. The other is a permanent upgrade.

By the time you've worked through the containers, the image, and the network path, the pattern becomes impossible to ignore. Nothing exotic failed. Nothing fancy. Docker didn't glitch. Redis didn't collapse. The network wasn't having an identity crisis.

The problem was drift.

Staging had the correct Redis hostname, `redis.internal`, but production had `localhost`.

That single difference meant the worker was trying to connect to Redis inside its own container. Every attempt hit `127.0.0.1` and died immediately. The worker restarted because it couldn't initialize. The API kept timing out because it was depending on a worker that never came online. Meanwhile, Redis looked unhealthy purely because the API was repeatedly hammering the wrong target.

It wasn't the image.

It wasn't the build.

It wasn't networking magic.

It was one environment variable set incorrectly in one environment that caused a cascade effect.

Correct the hostname, redeploy, and everything snaps back into place: the worker stays up, Redis stabilizes, latency drops, and the API behaves like nothing ever happened. Bob's your uncle!

And that's the point. Problems like this hide in plain sight. You can stare at metrics, logs, and dashboards all day and never see the real culprit unless you follow a structured process: interrogate the container, interrogate the image, verify the network path, and only then make a conclusion. Without that order, you end up chasing symptoms instead of causes. Trust me, I've done it far too many times in my job and personal containerization.

Now that the production incident is fully traced from failure to fix, the next step is to build the practical tools that let you shortcut this entire process when it's 2 a.m. and something important is on fire.

Let's put together the diagrams, tables, and quick-reference material that make this workflow super fast.

Troubleshooting references

This section is the "Grab it when something breaks" part of the chapter. No narrative, no hand-holding; just the diagrams, tools, and tables you'll use when you need answers quickly. Everything here condenses the workflow you followed in the walkthrough into fast, repeatable actions.

With the high-level flow in place, as discussed at the start of the chapter (*Figure 10.1*), the next step is to translate that structure into practical shortcuts you can use under pressure. These tables boil the entire troubleshooting process down into quick decisions: what you're seeing, what it probably means, and what to run next.

The first step is to identify the cause by examining the symptoms, what to run, and what to fix:

Symptom	Likely cause	Commands to run	Fix

Container keeps restarting	Bad config
	Missing env vars
	Failing entrypoint
		`docker logs`
		`docker inspect`
		`docker exec`
			Fix config
			Correct env vars
			Patch entrypoint

API returns `500/503` intermittently	Downstream service unreachable	`curl`
		`ping`
		`nslookup`
			Fix network
			Correct service hostname
			Reconnect container

DNS resolution fails	Containers not on same network	`docker inspect <container>` `docker network inspect`	Attach containers to same user-defined network
Image behaves differently in prod	Stale layers Wrong `COPY` stage	`docker history`, `dive`, `docker run -it <image> sh`	Fix Dockerfile Rebuild Correct staging/prod build steps
Latency spikes only in prod	Hidden network issue Routing problems	`ping`, `curl -v`, `docker stats`	Fix network Review service mesh/overlay config
Worker crashes on startup	Missing config file Wrong permissions	`docker exec`, `ls -lah`, `cat`	Replace config Fix permissions Rebuild image

Table 10.2: Quick reference for common symptoms

Once you've identified the likely cause, you need the right tools to confirm it. The following reference tables summarize the most common mechanisms you'll adjust during recovery, restart behavior, logging drivers, and resource flags, so you can zero in on the operational fix rather than rereading our earlier chapters:

- Restart policies (when to use which):

Policy	Behavior	Use when
`no`	Never restart	Debugging locally
`on-failure`	Restart only on non-zero exit	App fails occasionally, but shouldn't self-loop
`always`	Restart unconditionally	Production services that must stay up
`unless-stopped`	Restart unless manually stopped	Long-running background workers

Table 10.3: Restart policy options

- Logging drivers (strengths and weaknesses):

Driver	Strengths	Weaknesses
`json-file`	Default, simple	Not centralized, logs vanish on removal
`syslog`	Integrates with host/ syslog infra	Needs external collector
`fluentd`	Great for large distributed setups	Requires Fluentd/Fluent Bit env
`awslogs` / `cloud drivers`	Centralized cloud logging	Ties you to cloud vendor
`gelf`	Structured logging	Needs GELF endpoint (Graylog, etc.)

Table 10.4: Comparison of Docker logging drivers

- Resource flags (what they mean):

Flag	Meaning	Why it matters
`--memory`	Max RAM allowed	Prevents OOM crashes taking down host
`--memory-reservation`	Soft memory target	Helps scheduler avoid noisy neighbors
`--cpus`	CPU time available	Keeps heavy services from starving others
`--cpuset-cpus`	Pin to specific cores	Useful for latency-sensitive workloads

Table 10.5: Key Docker resource flags

Troubleshooting becomes dramatically easier when you have the right tools at hand. The following utilities (Dive, Dockle, ctop, Trivy, and the VS Code Docker extension) help you validate images, scan for drift, inspect resource usage in real time, and visualize what's actually happening inside your containers. We haven't gone through all of them in this book, but that leaves you some opportunity for experimentation in the future:

- **Dive**: Used for inspecting image layers, spotting accidental dev files, and checking bloat.
  Use it when the container looks fine, but the image behaves wrong.
- **Dockle**: Used for security and configuration linting.
  Use it when you want to catch misconfigurations early in CI.
- **ctop**: Tool for understanding real-time resource usage per container.
  Use it when you suspect memory leaks or CPU spikes.
- **Trivy**: Used for vulnerability and config scanning.
  Use it when you want to validate images or base layers before shipping.
- **VS Code Docker extension**: Used for visualizing containers, logs, images, and volumes.
  Use it when you need a quick overview or want to browse the filesystem visually.

Networking failures can look random until you've seen enough of them to spot the patterns. Here's a quick reference for the most common symptoms you'll hit in Docker environments and what each one really means.

Outcome	Meaning
`NXDOMAIN on nslookup`	Wrong network/DNS resolver can't find service
`curl: Connection refused`	Port reachable but nothing listening (wrong port or service down)
`curl: Operation timed out`	Routing/overlay issue or firewall dropping packets
`Latency > 150ms inside same host`	Network congestion, a misconfigured bridge, or overlay instability
`API → Redis failing but Redis healthy`	Wrong hostname or container not attached to correct network

Table 10.6: Common networking failure patterns

Once you've found the fault, the goal is to recover cleanly and prevent the problem from ever slipping back into production. This final checklist wraps up the essential steps that turn a one-off fix into a lasting improvement:

- Recreate container with `--force-recreate`
- Validate logs in real time (`docker logs -f`)
- Check `docker stats` for stabilizing resource usage
- Patch the Dockerfile/Compose file
- Add missing health checks
- Add alert rules for this failure pattern
- Document the root cause

All of these diagrams, tools, and quick-reference tables give you fast answers when the pressure is on, but they only solve half the problem. Troubleshooting gets the system back on its feet; the real value comes from making sure the same issue never sneaks back in again.

That's where recovery, automation, and prevention come in.

Recovery, automation, and prevention

We touched on these ideas earlier when discussing fixes, but this section shifts from the theory to the operational reality of how you make a recovery durable, repeatable, and hands-off.

Fixing the problem is great, but let's be honest: if all we do is fix it, we'll be right back here again in a few months... probably at 11 p.m., probably after someone just "pushed a tiny config update." Recovery isn't about getting the lights back on; it's about making sure the lights stay on without you babysitting them. So now that everything's stabilized again, let's talk about the part that really matters: making the fix durable, predictable, and frankly, a bit boring. Because boring infrastructure is the dream.

A lot of teams stop the moment the logs go quiet, and honestly, that's how half of the "weird intermittent issues" in production get born. You need to prove, properly, that the fix holds under real conditions. Get your receipts and get ready to show them. Ask yourself three questions:

- **Do the containers stay healthy?**
  "Running" doesn't count. If the health checks are flipping between healthy and unhealthy like a Windows 98 progress bar, you've still got work to do.
- **Does the system behave correctly under traffic?**
  Metrics should settle cleanly. Spikes, drops, and flapping endpoints all mean the problem is still lurking somewhere, waiting for the right moment to reappear.
- **Does the system survive a restart?**
  If a reboot throws the whole stack back into panic mode, you haven't fixed the root cause; you've just bribed it to act normal for a bit.

Clean recovery is about consistency. "*It works on my machine*" means nothing; "*It works every time*" is what you're aiming for.

If you ever catch yourself thinking, "*We should probably restart that container if it dies,*" the answer is *yes*, and Docker can already do it for you. There's no trophy for manually restarting services, sadly. Most people treat health checks as "*Is the container up?*" Don't do that. A meaningful health check tests behavior: can it reach Redis? Can it respond to a basic request? Does it initialize correctly every single time? If the answer to any of that is "*No,*" the container isn't healthy. Once health checks are in place, your orchestrator can finally behave like an adult: restarting sick containers, killing stuck ones, shifting traffic away from broken instances, and automatically recovering from the weird stuff. You **shouldn't** be in the loop for any of this.

Every time you find something broken inside a container, trace it back to the image. Nine times out of ten, the mistake started there. After an incident, ask the obvious but easy-to-forget questions: Did we copy the right files? Did we accidentally ship dev configs? Did a cached build step silently reuse something old? Could CI have caught this earlier? Tools such as Dive, Dockle, and Trivy aren't "nice-to-have" debugging extras; they can be safety rails for your pipeline. If a broken image never gets built, it never gets deployed. Problems solved before they exist are the best kind.

And, of course, the entire production incident happened because staging and production drifted apart. Not dramatically, but just enough to cause chaos. This is where you tighten the screws. Configuration needs to live in code, not as tribal knowledge tied to whichever engineer last touched it. Required environment variables should have templates or examples, so nobody invents their own "special" production-only values. CI should outright refuse to build anything if a critical variable is missing or obviously wrong. A deployment should never succeed with something like `REDIS_HOST=localhost` hiding in the config. If your environments can't drift, an entire category of bugs simply disappears.

Don't forget about monitoring. Good monitoring isn't about building 400 dashboards nobody ever reads; it's about catching the moment something starts drifting toward downtime. This incident gives you a perfect set of early-warning signals to turn into alerts. If a container starts falling into restart loops, you want to know. If Redis timeouts start creeping in, that should ping you long before the API begins throwing `500` errors. DNS failures between containers are another early symptom worth watching, as is any sudden rise in latency between internal services. Even resolving the wrong hostname is a red flag that service discovery is slipping out of sync. The system should warn you the moment trouble starts forming, not when users start noticing.

And finally, please document it. Not for bureaucracy; for future you. A tiny amount of written context can save hours the next time something wobbles. Capture what broke, why it broke, how you found it, what fixed it, and what guardrails you added. That turns a messy outage into institutional memory. So when someone spots logs that even vaguely resemble this incident a few months from now, they're not guessing in the dark; they know exactly where to start.

Troubleshooting is never about heroics; it's about having a repeatable way to bring order to chaos. With the right workflow, the right guardrails, and a bit of discipline, Docker stops feeling unpredictable and starts feeling like something you can genuinely rely on.

You've now got everything you need to keep your containers healthy, your environments consistent, and your production outages as rare and uninteresting as possible. Go build something solid and let Docker get out of your way.

The Big Lab: The final incident

This is the last lap of the Notes service. You're going to break the stack in ways that feel annoyingly, depressingly real, then bring it back using the same troubleshooting flow you just learned: detection → diagnosis → fix → prevention.

Everything here assumes that you're in your existing `notes-app/` folder with your usual Compose stack.

1. Before you start, bring the stack up clean:

```
docker compose up -d --build
docker compose ps
```

2. Before anything else, set your "known good" baseline. You need a quick baseline so you know what "healthy" looks like:

```
curl http://localhost:5001/notes
curl http://localhost:8080
```

3. Now, take a backup of your `notes` file so you can restore it later. In earlier labs, you used `C:\notes-data` as the host path, so we'll keep that:

```
mkdir C:\notes-data\backup -ErrorAction SilentlyContinue
copy C:\notes-data\notes.json C:\notes-data\backup\notes.json.bak -Force
```

Deep breath...here we go...

Incident 1: Break the API on purpose

1. Make the API crash loop by killing it and starting it with a bad command. This simulates a bad entrypoint or a broken startup script:

```
docker compose stop api
docker compose rm -f api
docker compose run -d --name notes-app-api --service-ports api powershell -
c "exit 1"
```

2. If that last line looks odd on a Linux-based container, good. It is. That's the point. You've just forced a "starts then dies" scenario. Now, check reality:

```
docker compose ps
docker logs api --tail 50
```

3. **Diagnosis**: Use the core triage commands:

```
docker events --since 5m
docker inspect api
docker top api
```

   Stop `docker events` with *Ctrl* + *C* once you've seen the restart behavior.

4. **Fix**: Bring the API back the normal way:

```
docker compose up -d --force-recreate api
docker compose ps
curl http://localhost:5001/notes
```

5. **Prevention**: If a service must not silently flap, add a health check and treat "healthy" as the standard, not "running."

Incident 2: Introduce a bad environment variable

This is the classic "staging worked, prod didn't" failure. Love these ones...

1. **Break it**: Edit your `api.secrets` file (or whichever file you use) and deliberately set a wrong value. For example, set an API key that your frontend or curl calls won't match anymore. Then, recreate the API so the change takes effect:

```
docker compose up -d --force-recreate api
```

2. **Detect and diagnose**: Confirm that it's actually using what you think:

```
docker logs api --tail 50
docker exec -it api sh -c "env | sort"
docker inspect api --format='{{json .Config.Env}}'
```

3. **Fix**: Put the correct value back, then recreate again:

```
docker compose up -d --force-recreate api
curl http://localhost:5001/notes
```

4. **Prevention**: Don't rely on "*Someone remembers the right value.*" Keep a template file checked in (example only, not the actual key!). Validate the required variables in CI, and fail fast if something critical is missing or obviously wrong.

Incident 3: Corrupt notes.json

This simulates real-life data damage. Your API will often fail when it tries to parse JSON:

1. **Break it**: Overwrite the file with invalid JSON:

```
Set-Content -Path C:\notes-data\notes.json -Value "{ this is not valid
json"
```

Now, hit the API:

```
curl http://localhost:5001/notes
docker logs api --tail 50
```

2. **Diagnose**: Prove that the container sees the same file and contents:

```
docker compose exec api sh
ls -lah /data
cat /data/notes.json
exit
```

3. **Fix**: Restore the backup you created at the start:

```
copy C:\notes-data\backup\notes.json.bak C:\notes-data\notes.json -Force
docker compose restart api
curl http://localhost:5001/notes
```

4. **Prevention**: Two simple guardrails that pay off are as follows:
    - Write to a `temp` file, then atomically replace the real file
    - Keep a rolling backup before every write, even if it's just `notes.json.bak`

Incident 4: Make the frontend unable to reach the API

There are a few ways to do this. The most realistic is a network or name resolution issue:

1. **Break it**: Break it by removing network connectivity for the API:

    1. Find the network name first:

    ```
    docker network ls
    ```

    2. Now, inspect the API container's network attachments:

    ```
    docker inspect api --format='{{json .NetworkSettings.Networks}}'
    ```

    3. Disconnect the API from the network your frontend uses (often `app-net` in your labs). Replace `<network-name>` with the real one you see:

    ```
    docker network disconnect <network-name> notes-app-api
    ```

2. **Detect**: Refresh the frontend in the browser:

    ```
    http://localhost:8080
    ```

    Then, confirm from the CLI:

    ```
    docker logs frontend --tail 50
    docker logs api --tail 50
    docker compose ps
    ```

3. **Diagnose**: From inside the frontend container, prove what the frontend can or can't see:

    ```
    docker compose exec frontend sh -c "wget -qO- http://api:5000/notes"
    ```

4. **Fix**: Reconnect the container to the correct network:

    ```
    docker network connect <network-name> notes-app-api
    docker compose restart api
    ```

Retest it:

```
curl http://localhost:5001/notes
```

5. **Prevention**: User-defined networks are not at all optional in multi-container apps. If you're relying on defaults, you're relying on luck. Sorry...

Incident 5: Drop a container or remove it entirely

This is a blunt one, but it happens, especially during messy deployments. I used to call this the sledgehammer test...

1. **Break it**: Remove the API container completely:

```
docker rm -f notes-app-api
docker compose ps
```

2. **Detect and diagnose**: Your frontend should fail again. Confirm that the daemon agrees:

```
docker compose ps
docker events --since 5m
```

3. **Fix**: Bring the API back:

```
docker compose up -d api
docker compose ps
curl http://localhost:5001/notes
```

4. **Prevention**: If you need resilience, you need the following:
   - Health checks that actually test dependencies
   - Restart policies that match reality
   - Monitoring that alerts on restart loops and missing containers, not just CPU graphs

Close out: Prove the incident life cycle

At this point, you should be able to do this without thinking:

```
docker compose ps
docker compose logs -f --tail 25
docker stats
```

Stop following logs with *Ctrl + C*.

Take a breath! You've just closed the entire *Big Lab* arc. Well done!

Across these 10 chapters, you built a real application, grew it, secured it, scaled it, broke it (realistically), fixed it, and prepared it for production. That's exactly what mastering Docker on Windows looks like.

Summary

If you're looking for the *Troubleshooting Docker tips* section, you've gone a tiny bit too far. Otherwise, this is the bit where the book ends.

When we kicked this off, we started with the very first building blocks: the system requirements, getting Docker Desktop running on Windows, and those essential commands that make containers feel less like magic and more like a tool you can control. We worked our way up through Dockerfiles, image optimization, custom networks, secure communication, and keeping data safe and persistent with volumes.

We didn't just stay in "Hello World" territory. We built multi-service setups with Docker Compose, locked them down with security best practices, tuned them to run efficiently, and explored what it really means to scale, whether that's for AI workflows, enterprise deployments, or entire hybrid cloud environments.

And we dealt with reality. We looked at what happens when things break, from subtle network quirks to containers that just won't start, and we explored how to monitor, log, and even automate recovery so you spend less time firefighting and more time building.

If there's a thread running through it all, it's this: *Docker isn't just a way to run software, it's a way to think about building, shipping, and running applications in a world that never truly sits still.* You've learned how to design with intent, secure from the start, scale without fear, and automate the repetitive so you can focus on the meaningful.

So many of the tips, patterns, and lessons in this book came from my own experience, and if I'm honest, from my own mistakes. Sometimes the best insights come from those "*Why on earth did that happen?*" moments. And that's okay. That's how we learn in this field, by trying, by breaking things, by failing, by figuring them out again, and by carrying those lessons forward.

Writing this book has been a personal journey for me, too. It's my first and hopefully not my last technical book, and it's taught me as much about discipline and clarity as it has about Docker. My hope is that you walk away from these pages not just knowing how to use Docker but feeling confident enough to push it further, to experiment, to break things, and to make them better.

Technology will keep moving. Docker will change. New tools will come along. But the mindset you've built here, of curiosity, structure, and problem-solving, will serve you well, whatever comes next.

So, thank you for coming along for the ride. Now, go build something great, and may your containers always be healthy.

Join us on Discord

For discussions around the book and to connect with your peers, join us on Discord at or scan the QR code below:

11

Unlock Your Exclusive Benefits

Your copy of this book includes the following exclusive benefits:

- Next-gen Packt Reader
- DRM-free PDF/ePub downloads

Follow the guide below to unlock them. The process takes only a few minutes and needs to be completed once.

Unlock this Book's Free Benefits in 3 Easy Steps

Step 1

Keep your purchase invoice ready for *Step 3*. If you have a physical copy, scan it using your phone and save it as a PDF, JPG, or PNG.

For more help on finding your invoice, visit `https://www.packtpub.com/unlock-benefits/help`.

> Note
>
> **Note**: If you bought this book directly from Packt, no invoice is required. After *Step 2*, you can access your exclusive content right away.

Step 2

Scan the QR code or go to `packtpub.com/unlock`.

On the page that opens (similar to *Figure 11.1* on desktop), search for this book by name and select the correct edition.

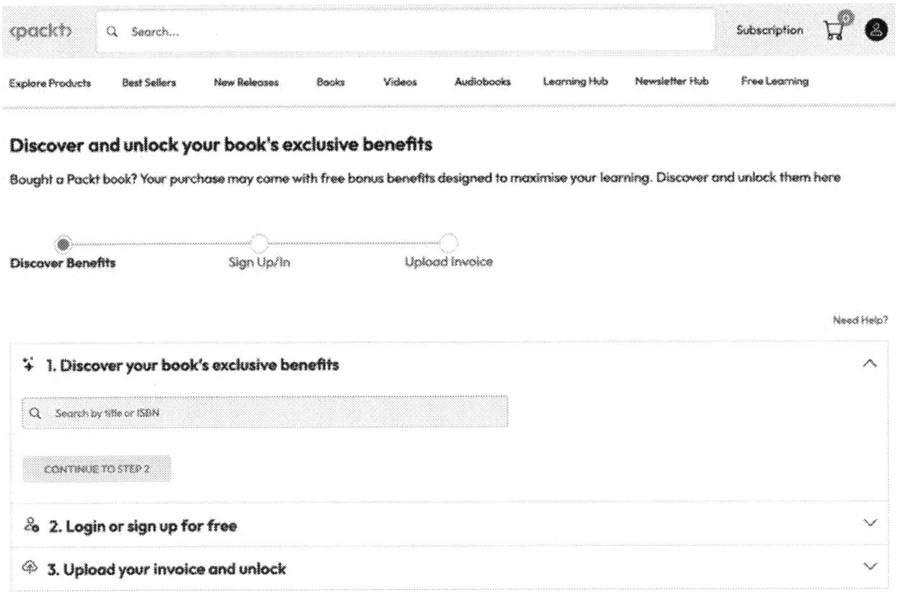

Figure 11.1: Packt unlock landing page on desktop

Step 3

After selecting your book, sign in to your Packt account or create one for free. Then upload your invoice (PDF, PNG, or JPG, up to 10 MB). Follow the on-screen instructions to finish the process.

Need help?

If you get stuck and need help, visit `https://www.packtpub.com/unlock-benefits/help` for a detailed FAQ on how to find your invoices and more. This QR code will take you to the help page.

Note

Note: If you are still facing issues, reach out to `customercare@packt.com`

Stay Sharp in Cloud and DevOps – Join 44,000+ Subscribers of CloudPro

CloudPro is a weekly newsletter for cloud professionals who want to stay current on the fast-evolving world of cloud computing, DevOps, and infrastructure engineering.

Every issue delivers focused, high-signal content on topics like:

- AWS, GCP & multi-cloud architecture
- Containers, Kubernetes & orchestration
- **Infrastructure as Code** (**IaC**) with Terraform, Pulumi, etc.
- Platform engineering & automation workflows
- Observability, performance tuning, and reliability best practices

Whether you're a cloud engineer, SRE, DevOps practitioner, or platform lead, CloudPro helps you stay on top of what matters, without the noise.

Scan the QR code to join for free and get weekly insights straight to your inbox:

`https://packt.link/cloudpro`

Other Books You May Enjoy

If you enjoyed this book, you may be interested in these other books by Packt:

The Ultimate Docker Container Book – Third Edition

Dr. Gabriel N. Schenker

ISBN: 9781804613986

- Understand the benefits of using containers
- Manage Docker containers effectively
- Create and manage Docker images
- Explore data volumes and environment variables
- Master distributed application architecture
- Deep dive into Docker networking
- Use Docker Compose for multi-service apps
- Deploy apps on major cloud platforms

Kubernetes for Generative AI Solutions

Ashok Srirama, Sukirti Gupta

ISBN: 9781836209935

- Explore GenAI deployment stack, agents, RAG, and model fine-tuning
- Implement HPA, VPA, and Karpenter for efficient autoscaling
- Optimize GPU usage with fractional allocation, MIG, and MPS setups
- Reduce cloud costs and monitor spending with Kubecost tools
- Secure GenAI workloads with RBAC, encryption, and service meshes
- Monitor system health and performance using Prometheus and Grafana
- Ensure high availability and disaster recovery for GenAI systems
- Automate GenAI pipelines for continuous integration and delivery

The Kubernetes Bible – Second Edition

Gineesh Madapparambath, Russ McKendrick

ISBN: 9781835464717

- Secure your Kubernetes clusters with advanced techniques
- Implement scalable deployments and autoscaling strategies
- Design and learn to build production-grade containerized applications
- Manage Kubernetes effectively on major cloud platforms (GKE, EKS, AKS)
- Utilize advanced networking and service management practices
- Use Helm charts and Kubernetes Operators for robust security measures
- Optimize in-cluster traffic routing with advanced configurations
- Enhance security with techniques like Immutable ConfigMaps and RBAC

Packt is searching for authors like you

If you're interested in becoming an author for Packt, please visit `http://authors.packt.com` and apply today. We have worked with thousands of developers and tech professionals, just like you, to help them share their insight with the global tech community. You can make a general application, apply for a specific hot topic that we are recruiting an author for, or submit your own idea.

Share your thoughts

Now you've finished *Mastering Docker on Windows*, we'd love to hear your thoughts! Scan the QR code below to go straight to the Amazon review page for this book and share your feedback or leave a review on the site that you purchased it from.

`https://packt.link/r/183664051X`

Your review is important to us and the tech community and will help us make sure we're delivering excellent quality content.

Index

Made in United States
Orlando, FL
04 November 2026

90201657R00269